Two Lenses on
the Korean Ethos

CW01497717

Two Lenses on the Korean Ethos

*Key Cultural Concepts and
Their Appearance in Cinema*

KEUMSIL KIM YOON AND
BRUCE WILLIAMS

McFarland & Company, Inc., Publishers
Jefferson, North Carolina

ISBN 978-0-7864-9682-2 (softcover : acid free paper) ∞
ISBN 978-1-4766-1787-9 (ebook)

LIBRARY OF CONGRESS CATALOGUING DATA ARE AVAILABLE

BRITISH LIBRARY CATALOGUING DATA ARE AVAILABLE

On the front cover: map and film strip © 2014 iStock/Thinkstock

Manufactured in the United States of America

*McFarland & Company, Inc., Publishers
Box 611, Jefferson, North Carolina 28640
www.mcfarlandpub.com*

Contents

Preface

Two Lenses on the Korean Ethos presents a cutting-edge approach to cultural studies, employing a combination of key cultural words and the cinema. Juxtaposing Maslow's basic human needs with culture-specific variations, the book elucidates these concepts through historical, literary and artistic contexts. This constitutes a radical departure from other studies on key cultural words that examine the topic from a lexical-semantic or an anthropological-linguistic perspective. The book then proceeds to consider how these concepts are visualized in the cinema and presents close readings of 13 films. These include three films from North Korea that demonstrate how the concepts are still present in different forms, despite 60 years of separation. These visualizations bring viewers closer to a national ethos. This book demonstrates that, even within transnational discourse, the cultural-specific is still omnipresent, and an in-depth understanding of key cultural concepts invites rich expanded readings.

The first author, a linguist, became interested in this specific avenue of research while preparing and teaching new courses in Asian studies, and specifically in East Asian/American cross-cultural communication. She discovered a dearth of quality academic materials on Korean key cultural concepts as well as difficulties in explaining such concepts and to what they apply without recourse to linguistics terms and methodology that would be problematical to students in other disciplines.

The second author, a cinema studies specialist who teaches courses in such national film traditions as those of Spain and Argentina, approached the issue from the opposite direction, realizing the difficulties students have in understanding a national ethos through film alone. Together, the authors conceived of the cinema as a vehicle for visualizing cultural concepts and, in turn, of cultural concepts as a key to unlocking the cinema's potential for revealing a national ethos.

Our research began with an extensive review of existing scholarship on key cultural words and a subsequent juxtaposition of key Korean cultural concepts with Maslow's notion of basic human needs. We then proceeded to uncover how these concepts appear in Korean history, literature and other art forms. From a cinema perspective, we conducted an investigation into theoretical perspectives that focused primarily on language and cinema and on film and cultural theory. We then posited how key cultural words can serve as anchors in the viewing of films. Our research subsequently turned to the close readings of film narratives mediated by key cultural concepts that constitute the main portion of our work. Finally, we explored how such concepts invite multiple yet not contradictory readings of the films discussed.

Two Lenses on the Korean Ethos investigates at length the concept of key cultural words and those cultural concepts that define Korean ethos. We have spent considerably more time discussing how these concepts are transmitted in traditional Korean society than how they are perpetuated in the case of the younger generation, marginalized groups or the diaspora. These perspectives will prove to be the subject of a subsequent study. Although there exist a number of such words, we have focused on the most salient. This book looks at issues from the domain of film theory that bear directly upon our project. In both cases, we have purposefully avoided highly theoretical discussions so as to render our arguments comprehensible to a wider range of readers. We have intentionally left out of our discussions a number of interesting debates in cinematic transnationalisms in favor of pursuing those issues that allow us to uncover cultural specificity. The South Korean films analyzed all stem from recent decades and are elucidative examples of the New Korean Cinema. Though with due regard for the high quality of films of the Golden Age, we have not included them in our discussions since films of recent years would more probably appeal to readers. Likewise, all three films from North Korea that we have chosen to include in our close readings were made after 2000. In all cases, we have focused our analyses specifically on how key cultural concepts that define a Korean ethos are visualized by our selected films and have avoided other more sociopolitical approaches, even were they of equal value.

This book fills significant gaps in discussions of both key cultural words and areas in cinema studies related to cross-cultural analyses. To date, major texts on key cultural words have either failed to mention Korea at all or restricted themselves to a single concept. Moreover, a limited number of studies on Korean cultural words are available only in Korean. In a like manner, although the New Korean Cinema has invited a number of excellent analyses, several of these focus on how these works travel across borders and lead to transnational readings. Only one study incorporates an exploration of a key cultural word. These works will be discussed in the chapters that follow.

The present work is distinct from the previously mentioned works in that its focus is on the discovery of a Korean *ethos*. Moreover, it is the only work that has deployed a combination of key cultural words and the cinema as a vehicle for exploring any given ethos. It thus provides a model for future studies on other cultures.

Two Lenses on the Korean Ethos is appropriate for a wide range of readers, including scholars and researchers wishing to explore a unique approach to understanding cultures. For them, it can serve as model for examining other cultural contexts. It is also designed for professors and students of East Asian cultures who wish to explore Korean *ethos* in a new and dynamic way. Given that the work is written by and large in nontechnical terms, it will also appeal to non-academic readers interested in Korean culture and cinema. Finally, it provides an invaluable tool for ethnic Koreans desiring to obtain a greater understanding of their cultural heritage.

Introduction

The Korean peninsula is becoming an international flashpoint in diverse areas ranging from North Korea's weapons program to copious South Korean victories on the international golf scene. South Korea, a war-torn country only 60 years ago, has achieved an unbelievable record of growth and global integration, rapidly becoming a high-tech, industrialized economy. According to the *Factbook of the Central Intelligence Agency* (2013), South Korea's GDP per capita was comparable to that of poorer countries in Africa and Asia only four decades ago, but today the country is the world's 12th largest economy. Furthermore, contemporary South Korean culture (a phenomenon known as the "Korean Wave," 한류 in Korean, transliterated as *Hallyu* or *Hanryu*) has become popular in many parts of the world.[1] Consequently, Korea-related studies and publications (e.g., dealing with language and linguistics, sociology, political science, ethnic studies, and cultural studies) are increasing in number.

Despite this proliferation of studies, there is still much investigation necessary into Korean society, its people, and their lifestyles. Such an investigation is very challenging and complex due largely to the rapid transformations in socioeconomic, political, and cultural arenas. For instance, new patterns of demographics have been seen in South Korea, in that families often limit themselves to one child and, at the same time, one notes an increased number of elderly people, who now are less likely to be taken care of by their children. Migration also comes to play in the new Korea, with countries of origin remaining in flux. Although to date numbers remain relatively small, Korean males, particularly in rural areas, have married foreign women, while migrant men have provided a necessary work force. Other transformations in labor have been witnessed as well. In the recent past, South Korea saw an upswing in labor movements and union activism, which called into question traditional hierarchical culture. Today, we encounter yet another societal issue—namely, the high unemployment rate of young people due to increased automation in the industrial sector and stagnant economic growth. Changes have been found in education as well. South Korea has been internationalizing instruction with a growing interaction at the university level between Koreans and non–Koreans and with English becoming, to an increasing degree, a language of instruction. In a like manner, due to South Korea's strong participation in the global economy, Koreans both at home and abroad have developed a keen sense of international consumer trends.

Despite our due acknowledgment of such changes, we posit that traces of cultural concepts that have been constructed over the centuries have not been erased. Rather, they appear in transmuted, yet equally vibrant forms. For the same reason, despite the political division of the Korean peninsula, we argue that these cultural concepts are still very much present in North Korea. After all, the partitioning of Korea dates back only 60 years. The situation is not unlike that of communist Albania, which, despite its almost total isolation for over 45 years from surrounding Albanophone territories, maintained a good number of cultural traits with its neighbors. We will refer to the amalgam of such pervasive cultural concepts as "ethos," using the term in a way that implies a thread weaving its way through divergent social, economic and political contexts rather than a static and essentialist norm.

For a Westerner, approaching Korean ethos requires an unmitigated undoing of known interactional strategies. Totally new skills and thought processes are required. At first glance, one can liken the approach to Korean ethos to the unnerving experience of Americans driving for the first time in Britain or Ireland. Reversing the sense of direction to which they are accustomed, these neophytes must cope with driving on the left while steering on the right. This challenge implies an urgent retooling of cognitive-motor processes. A good deal of the difficulty Westerners have in confronting Korean ethos plays out in day-to-day encounters and specifically deals with the fact that long-established Korean morals and ethics are situational rather than unfluctuating, as in individualistic cultures. As one confronts the Korean way of being, similar paradigmatic shifts are required. The intuitive path one is used to following, from a Western perspective, can lead to naught. Often, one must "do the opposite" of what comes naturally, shift one's position in the encounter, cut across lanes of cultural prescriptions, and find the proper path. But here is where the analogy with the driving experience ends. Whereas negotiating a round-about simply consists of learning a new set of skills and choices that, once learned, prove themselves to be invariable, such invariability does not transfer to Korean culture. Westerners have learned to view ethics and behavior from absolute and stable perspectives. Their notion of good and bad is like the world presented in a John Ford western, where a secure system of values is in place and we feel comforted by its universality. It is often hard for them to understand Korean ethos, which is situational, yet which, once the parameters of a situation are in place, is governed by morals just as unwavering as Western values.

This book provides a roadmap to Korean ethos, and specifically, to how this ethos is represented in the cinema. It can be useful to Anglophones, heritage Koreans, or even native Koreans who wish to explore their own culture at greater depth. It uses as its search engine a unique combination of key cultural words and the cinema. The former provide a vehicle through which complex cultural concepts can be conveyed in a highly condensed form. Key cultural words can constitute an *a priori* approach to Korean culture, as one can intellectually ascertain background and meaning even before having authentic exposure to cultural contexts. And, especially when such concepts are framed in terms of the merging of the universal with the cultural-specific, as we will demonstrate, they offer gateways to understanding. Nonetheless, when used in isolation, they may seem abstract and distant to the cultural learner. Something is needed to make them come alive. The cinema provides an excellent vehicle through which such concepts can be visualized and intuited. The cinema, in this case, refers not only to the specific structure and themes of a given film, but also to the overall viewing experience as defined from a socio-interactional perspective. This ensures a more complete cultural experience by providing an *a posteriori* reinforcement, inasmuch as concepts already grasped intellectually can be rendered more real and meaningful. The process, however, is symbiotic. An understanding of key cultural concepts can also draw a foreign viewer closer to a Korean experience of the cinema.

The approach employed in this book is unique. Although a number of studies have used either key cultural words or film to approach a new culture, the two paths have never met. The meeting of key cultural words and film can permit prior knowledge to be sensed on a deeper level, allowing the cultural learner a more holistic experience of Korean ethos. In the discussion that follows, we will briefly explain the importance of the study of key cultural words and subsequently of the illustrative role of the cinema in rendering such concepts intelligible.

Culture through Keywords and Film

Steven Tadelis opens a discussion in *The American Economic Review* with a question and answer:

What is a name? It is exactly the label that summarizes the physical attributes, past behavior, and other characteristics of the carrier of that name. In our language-based society this is our way of representing a large amount of information in a word or two. We label anything we can perceive or recognize with a unique name in order to distinguish it from everything else in our world. This is also true for firms: once a firm is established, it is recognized by its name, which is uniquely associated with its characteristics and past performance [1999, 548].

Although Tadelis's theoretical model, investigation, argument, and discussion are related to the field of economics, his concept concerning a name is applicable to other disciplines and areas, including cultural studies. That is, the way this book views culture through key words is similar to how Tadelis views the name of a firm.

Key cultural words recapitulate cultural attributes, traditional ways of being, and characteristics of people who use these terms, thus presenting a great deal of information about society and history as well. Roy Harris deems words to be "collective products of social interaction, essential instruments through which human beings constitute and articulate their world" (1988, ix). Likewise, this book approaches key cultural words as a distinctive tool for examining and recognizing abridging how people of a particular culture have constituted and articulated the society in which they have lived.

A field that has addressed more directly the issue of the relationship between culture and language/words is cultural/linguistic anthropology (or anthropological linguistics). This field presents the view that language is a product of words, and the premise that there are culture-specific words in every language is one of its classical arguments. Edward Sapir (1949) asserts that culture and language should be explained not by reference to a universal standard, but rather by reference to the particular environment in which the culture and language occur. Furthermore, Benjamin Lee Whorf (1956), a student and later colleague of Sapir, puts forward a principle of linguistic relativity, often called the *Whorfian hypothesis*. Demonstrating that culture is largely determined by language, he argues that different cultures perceive the world in distinct ways, and that language plays a central role in creation of a worldview. Culturally essential objects, conditions, and processes usually are defined by a plethora of words, while things that cultures perceive as unimportant are usually assigned one or two words. A classic example of this view involves "snow-related terms." While mainstream Americans use only a handful of terms to describe snow (e.g., "snow," "sleet," "freezing rain," and a few others), Inuits have a great number of lexical terms and expressions that describe snow: snow that is falling, snow on the ground, snow in blocks, snow that makes wavy patterns, and so forth. Thus, it is essential that sufficient vocabulary exist for description of the snow-related daily life of Inuits.

The idea of culture-specificity reflected in words has been discussed in various ways. For instance, Ronald Wardhaugh (2002) notes, "If language A has a word for a particular concept, then that word makes it easier for speakers of language A to refer to that concept than speakers of language B, who lack such a word and are forced to use a circumlocution" (223). Lyle Campbell (1996) points out that speakers of the Native American Zuni language do not have words to distinguish between yellow and orange, and that the reidentification of some objects is more difficult for those who speak Zuni than for English-speaking people.

Considering Sapir's view that "vocabulary is a very sensitive index of the culture of people" (1949, 162), one can raise simple, yet crucial questions. Are all the words listed in dictionaries directly connected to culture? Which sorts of words are deemed culture-bound words? Which words help us understand the broad range of human thought and the communication practices of a particular culture? Which kinds of words represent characteristics of a way of life? Which words can be significant and revealing about a respective culture? To reiterate, what are the key words that represent the core cultural charges of a culture?

Anna Wierzbicka (1997), who views each language as having key conceptual words that are culture-bound, distills skillfully a number of possible answers related to these questions. She argues that *key words* are "words which are particularly important and revealing in a given culture" and that "offer invaluable insight into the culture" (15–16). Drawing upon examples from English, Russian, Polish, German, and Japanese, she demonstrates that cultural analysis can gain important insights from linguistic semantics. Wierzbicka provides "natural semantic metalanguage" to explain the chosen key words. She further considers that entire cultural domains are organized around focal points, and aims to uncover, by investigating these focal points in depth, the general organizing principles that contribute to a cultural domain as a whole, or that cross a number of domains through explanatory power. Wierzbicka deftly links "lexicon as a key" to ethno-sociology, cultural psychology, ethno-philosophy, history, and politics.

Other books have addressed key culture-based words by providing situations, contexts, and stories in which those words are used and/or implied, and/or by underlining key concepts by illustrating some main characteristics of behavior that have been observed in daily life. For instance, Takeo Doi's *The Anatomy of Dependence* (1973) describes at length the Japanese term *amae,* which explains a uniquely Japanese need to be in favor with others and which involves a trustful dependence, as evidenced in the relationship of infants with their mothers. Doi claims that the ideal relationship is that of the parent–child dyad in terms of the degree of closeness, and points out that Japanese are consciously aware of those upon whom they depend. Similarly, Ge Gao and Stella Ting-Toomey's *Communicating Effectively with the Chinese* (1998) is centered on a number of key words (e.g., *gang qing, mian zi,* and *ke qi,* roughly translated as "feeling," "face," and "politeness"). It examines Chinese-specific ways of communication, addresses problematic areas of Chinese and North American encounters, and explains the main causes for cross-cultural miscommunication. William Gudykunst and Tsukasa Nishida's *Bridging Japanese/North American Differences* (1994) uses key words (e.g., *enryo, on,* and *giri,* roughly translated as "reserve," "indebtedness," and "duty") not only to describe Japanese ways of interaction, but also to explain similarities and differences in communication patterns between Japan and the United States. Also, while speaking of East Asian (i.e., Chinese, Japanese, and Korean) and North American cross-cultural communication, we must mention Susan Oak and Virginia Martin's *American/Korean Contrasts.* Although not depending heavily upon key conceptual words, as do the two aforementioned books on Chinese and Japanese communication, it discusses basic concepts (e.g., *chemyeon, nunchi, gibun, jeong, bunwigi,* and *han,* loosely translated as "face," "situational reading," "mood," "feeling," "atmosphere," and "regret") that are associated with expectations of one's own behavior and the behavior of others (2000, 28–37).

More recently, Boyé Lafayette De Mente's *Japan's Cultural Code Words* (2004) introduces 233 key terms that explain the attitudes and behavior of the Japanese, providing current and historical nuances of the terms that the author has selected. It may be worthwhile to mention that, unlike the aforementioned three books, this text is written by a non-native speaker who suggests, "Westerners have traditionally been intrigued by Asian attitudes and behavior that have been perceived as ranging from cute, quaint, and seductive to strange and sometimes savage" (12). De Mente continues to advocate for the importance of cultural code words: "The best and fastest way to an understanding of the emotional and traditional side of Japanese attitudes and behavior is through their 'business and cultural code words'—terms that reveal their psychology and philosophy in far most depth and precision than any Rorschach test" (13).

There are also a number of articles devoted to key cultural words. Martin Cortazzi and Wei Wei Shen (2001) examine six Chinese terms that have played a key role in Confucian heritage cultures. Wei Li, Hua Zhu, and Yue Li (2001) study the key Chinese concept of "harmony" and investigate how Chinese seek to achieve interpersonal harmony in face-to-face interactions. Similarly, Hui-Ching Chang (2001) explores how "social harmony" as cultural performance is conducted by Chinese in their conversation at the surface level. From a cross-cultural perspective, Akio Yabuuchi (2004) uncovers the notion of "face" in Chinese, Japanese, and U.S. American cultures. Furthermore, Xiao-Pin Chen and Chao Chen (2004) discuss the notion of the Chinese term *guanxi* ("personal connection"), which has been viewed as a necessary condition for having a successful business in China.

Despite difference in research focus, approach, and language, there is a common message that the aforementioned books and articles convey: culture can be well studied through key words. As Anna Wierzbicka (1997) has demonstrated with regard to five languages, the concept of culture through key words holds across languages and cultures. Yet, one should note that the approach researchers take to describe and elucidate key words unique to given cultures is discipline-specific and/or depends upon their ultimate academic goals. The question remains, however, whether a cultural learner can truly gain a "feeling" and "intuition" for cultural processes exclusively through the vehicle of key cultural words.

Whereas these words are cognitively, intellectually, and linguistically great tools that can be used to explore, discuss, and explain culture, they lack what is needed to properly integrate what is being processed. One needs another means to match up with or set against prior knowledge regarding a culture, or, more specifically, the backdrop of the existing internalized cultural rules. One requires a separate activity to further process what has been perceived and comprehended through key cultural words, from which one may have formed a hypothesis regarding the culture in question. That hypothesis needs to be tested, modified, and/or confirmed through interactional feedback that serves as a catalyst for meaning, negotiation, and recasts. Without further processing of this kind, cultural fossilization may occur, through which incorrect knowledge of a given ethos may be permanently incorporated into a person's cultural competence.

In this book, we will use the terms "key cultural words" and "key cultural concepts" interchangeably, depending upon our immediate focus. We do this to avoid the implication that the words are actually spoken in the films.

Film is an ideal vehicle for preventing such cultural fossilization. It is an engaging tool for rendering key cultural words transparent. To understand its role, we must refer for a moment to semiotics and psychoanalysis. Although many of these discussions may be familiar to virtually all scholars and students of the cinema, and may even have become quite hackneyed, they assume a refreshed meaning when bounced off the notion of key cultural words. Much of this engagement has to do with the ways in which classical Hollywood feature films and their international counterparts manipulate their own codes so that the viewer is drawn into a fictional world. Such theoreticians as Jean-Louis Baudry (1974–1975) and Stephen Heath (1981) have explored the notion of *suture,* which consists of a complex series of conventions regarding screen and off-screen space, and how these serve, at least in classical cinema, to connect or *suture* the viewer seamlessly into the narrative. Partially involving the processes of shot/counter-shot, suture masks the discursive construction of the film and absorbs viewers without their knowledge. Viewers participate in an uninterrupted and cohesive narrative. They unconsciously co-opt the ideology presented by the film. We need only cite the example of James Cameron's *Aliens* (1986), which, while drawing viewers into an engaging sci-fi experience, positions them in ideological identification with Reaganomics. Such a process is closely related to the notion of the cinematic "gaze," with regard to both the on-screen and the spectatorial process. Viewers of a classical film gaze seamlessly at the unfolding events on the screen in a way reflecting the look of one on-screen character to another. This process, like suture, is rendered invisible by the classical cinema.

From the perspective of cognitive psychology, Torben Grodal (1999) explores the subjectivity of the viewing process and provides another argument for the way in which we become engaged with films. He stresses that a viewer will try to construct a film character's perceptions:

> He will try, for example, to construct the field of vision of the actant by generalizing his/her own perceptual experience into an objective and transformational model: what would I have seen if I had been in the same place as the actant.... The viewer will further construct the actant's body-surface sensations in so far as these are indicated by the context (for instance, if the actant is being hit or tickled) [89].

Grodal sees the film viewing experience not only as engaging, but also as subjective and emotional. In response to David Bordwell's argument that a spectator's comprehension of film narrative can be separated from her or his emotional responses (Bordwell 1989, 30), he questions whether a viewer can "understand" the narrative of Hitchcock's *Psycho* (1960) without an emotional reaction. Grodal argues, "The emotional response is just as much a part of the narrative as are the 'cognitive' inferences for our understanding of the intradiegetic relations" (1–2).

Approaching such questions from a phenomenological point of view, Vivian Sobchack (1992) has examined the directness of film viewing and considered how one comes to see with one's own eyes another's experience. For Sobchack:

> Cinema thus transposes, without completely transforming, those modes of being alive and consciously embodied in the world that count for each of us. As *direct* experience, as experience centered in that particular, situated, and solely occupied existence sensed first as "Here, where the world touches" and then as "Here, where the world is sensible, here where I am" [4].

In her discussion, Sobchack recoups the importance of the subjective mode of experience and the need to address the "life-world in which we live as sensible and significant beings" (308). Sobchack quotes Ridley Scott's *Blade Runner* (1982) by asserting, "If you could only see what I've seen with your eyes." Summing up the cinema experience, Sobchack stresses, "The perception and expressive medium through which we engage the articulation of this seemingly-impossible desire for intersubjectivity is the very medium through which this desire is visibly and objectively fulfilled" (309).

Yet, from a cross-cultural perspective, one can wonder to what extent the intersubjectivity Sobchack suggests is truly possible from the viewing of a film alone. Is this intersubjectivity really visibly and objectively fulfilled by the medium when strong cultural differences separate the film's autochthonous context and the viewer's own experience? The multilayered quote from *Blade Runner,* originally uttered by a technologically produced "replicant," throws into question the "who" and "what" of the viewing experience. In other words, just *whose* eyes are viewing *what* and *through what lens?* In our case in point, the "who" refers to the viewer desiring closer approximation to a given culture. The "what" ideally refers to the culture itself.

In recent decades, in contrast, considerably more emphasis has been placed on film as a truly transnational phenomenon, and theoreticians very rarely, if ever, question that the viewer assumes multiple positions of identification while watching a film. Such recent criticism suggests that viewers can escape from their own cultural frame and assume diverse spectatorial positions. It is further understood that viewers bring to the experience their own cultural, political, and socioeconomic baggage. Three individuals enjoying a movie together may essentially be watching three different films. These theories parallel learner-oriented notions of pedagogy. As is the case with Freire's dialogic learning experience, viewers are free to understand a film in their own way. If one's concern is film as a transnational phenomenon, such an issue may be just fine. Divergent viewings help us understanding shared and distinct heritages.

But if one is seeking to explore film as a gateway toward a given culture, and thereby to enhance the very viewing of the film, such multiple readings of films may well muddy the work's autochthonous context. Different readings tend to reveal commonalities; we relate to what we see from our *own* perspective. Conversely, a viewer may miss altogether elements that are specific to the film's original culture. One of the strengths of the cinema—the subjectivity implicit in the viewing process—is, in this sense, the medium's greatest weakness.

And here we have it. Key cultural words are concise and multifaceted; they are nuanced and penetrate a culture at a given level. Alone, however, they can be emotionless and theoretical to the neophyte. In contrast, films can lend themselves to impassioned and emotional viewings—but these can be scattered and unfocused. Nonetheless, key cultural words and the cinema can work symbiotically. Knowledge of key cultural words can help orient the viewing experience, leading the spectator toward greater cultural knowledge. Conversely, film can serve as a vehicle through which cultural words can take their first breath.

Methodology and Organization

In this book, the use of the words *Korean* and *Koreans* does not imply a static core culture. Rather, in due recognition of the previously mentioned social transformations, it seeks to unearth continuities still present in divergent and transmuting forms. In a like manner, our use of key cultural words and cinema should not be construed as suggesting that the book explores issues of culture and cinema *per se.* Instead, it serves to elucidate Korean ethos as an aggregate of fluid cultural traits. In all cases, we eschew highly theoretical approaches in favor of allowing the two lenses to inform each other and meld.

This book consists of two parts: Contextual Framework and Key Cultural Words through Film Narratives. Part I is divided into three chapters and is devoted to contextual and historical aspects of key cultural words and cinema. Chapter 1 describes the approach that this book adopts for a better understanding of key cultural words. Chapter 2 explains and analyzes in depth *han* and *jeong,* the two most representative cultural concepts of Korean culture, and *deok,* the most challenging concept for Koreans to explain to non–Koreans and thus the most difficult for foreigners to grasp its full meaning. Five other cultural words (*chung* and *hyo, chemyeon* and *ye,* and *cheol*) are embedded under the discussion of *deok.* While Chapter 2 draws primarily upon more historical and traditional inscriptions of the cultural concepts, Chapter 3 highlights the importance of employing the cinema in conjunction with an indepth knowledge of key cultural words to better understand a culture at large; it also provides a brief panorama of the cinemas of South and North Korea.

The five chapters of Part II, drawing upon the aforementioned key cultural concepts, present an analysis of film narratives. Chapter 4 explores cinematic visualizations of *han,* arguably the most defining concept of Korean ethos. Chapter 5 fleshes out distinct manifestations of diverse types of *jeong* in film. Chapter 6 addresses *deok* in more open filmic texts. Other concepts, such as *chung/hyo, chemyeon/ye, and cheol,* are briefly embedded into the discussion as needed. Chapter 7 offers an overview of cinema in North Korea from the perspective of national ideology, and presents readings of films mediated by the key cultural concepts. Chapter 8 offers expanded viewings that, all the while rooted in the key cultural concepts examined earlier, press beyond the narrative-based analyses of the previous four chapters. Finally, the Conclusion reframes cultural and cinematic approaches to Korean ethos and underscores the uniqueness of our two-lensed approach.

Introductory Remarks

In Part I, we introduce the two lenses that compose our approach to a Korean ethos, key cultural words and cinema. In Chapter 1, we assess the notion of key cultural words and their multilayered meaning. We further draw a parallel between Maslow's notion of basic human needs and Korean key cultural concepts. In Chapter 2, we examine in depth the cultural words introduced. Through history, literature and art, we explore their origins, complexities, diverse manifestations and related phenomena. Chapter 3 integrates the cinema into the discussion of key cultural words. It looks at language and the cinema, the anchoring role of key cultural words in film viewing, and the viewing experience and cultural understanding. Finally, it provides a brief overview of the cinemas of South and North Korea, which constitute our objects of study.

Chapter 1

Understanding Key (Cultural) Words

The Power of Keywords: Connectivity

The term "keywords" has been widely and extensively employed. At the time of the writing of this chapter, when "keyword" was entered as a search term in Google, 1,150,000,000 hits appeared, with "key" alone yielding 1,360,000,000 results. The term "love" saw 4,330,000,000 hits, four times more than for "keyword," which is understandable inasmuch as "love" is one of the words human beings are likely to use most frequently. Interestingly, however, when "freedom" was entered, the result was 315,000 hits, four times fewer than for the term "keyword." Similarly, "mother" produced 786,000,000 hits, approximately 40 percent fewer than for "keyword," while "father," resulted in 379,000,000 hits, roughly 60 percent fewer.

What does the high frequency of the term "keyword" indicate? What is our initial understanding of this word? There may be no single answer to this question given that there are so many meanings attached to the term. The first dictionary and literal meaning of "key" denotes a small metal instrument for fastening or unfastening the lock of a door or anything shaped and used in a similar manner. Subsequently, other secondary meanings convey a scale, a system of tones in music, and a set of levers that can be depressed, just to mention a few. Figuratively, "key" also carries an extensive range of meaning, including an answer to puzzles or problems, an important thing or person, a tone of voice, and so forth.

There is an obvious penchant among academic researchers for the term "keyword," which foregrounds its importance in the research process. Nonetheless, academicians employ it differently across disciplines and individual studies to meet their own research objectives. *Linguistics and Language Behavior Abstracts,* which indexes international literature in linguistics and related disciplines in the language sciences, lists (as of April 2011) 376 published works that use the term "keyword" as a keyword of the work; 49 of these even have the term in their titles.

A review of these 49 abstracts reveals that a most powerful aspect of "keyword" lies in the *connectivity* that the term serves. For example, Jean-Jacques Weber and Kristine Horner (2010) address how language-in-education policies in European Union member-states have been influenced by EU policies at large; they examine how an identical cluster of keywords (which includes, in particular, "diversity," "social cohesion," and "integration," as well as "exclusion" as their negative counterpart) emerges from and informs such policies, both in Luxembourg and other European countries. Anna Wierzbicka (2010) deals with the role of cultural keywords. By focusing on the Russian key cultural concept of *sud'ba* and on Nabokov's continued reliance on this concept in his English-language books, she aims to illuminate the immigrant condition and the miscommunication inherent in cross-cultural communication. Shirley Leitch and Sally Davenport (2007) examine the ways in which strategic ambiguity in the use of keywords serves an enabling function within a discourse marked by conflict and ideological divisions. Martin Jay (1998) presents an anthology of essays unified by the common theme of cultural keywords serving as focal concepts for the organization of experience, thought, and lives. Mark Olsen (1989) discusses French interest and participation in the American Revolution and the role of pro–American sentiment in the formation of French revolutionary ideology and language by examining political keywords that are cognates in French and English. Henry Kahane and Renee Kahane (1984) espouse the view that social and political movements crystallize in sets of terms that shape their image and that are the key to their interpretation.

The connectivity aspect of keywords is also strongly shown in the areas of corpus linguistics. For instance, Mike Conway (2010) uses statistically derived keywords to characterize texts; such an approach has become an important research method for digital humanists and corpus linguists in areas such as literary analysis and the exploration of genre difference. Peter Garrett, Angie Williams, and Betsy Evans (2005) outline a method of data collection which they term "keywords," considering the approach in relation to information processing theory and the elicitation of stereotypes. Jon Dale Erickson (2001) explores the assessment of text using the occurrence of keywords, and demonstrates that that the keyword-computer–based system shows statistical promise as a method of grading content-specific essays in college courses.

Some researchers argue that the connectivity aspect of keywords is better observed in the work of Bruce Burgett and Glenn Hendler (2007), whose *Keywords for American Cultural Studies,* contains 64 essays from scholars of various fields. Each essay is devoted to a single term, such as "ethnicity" or "religion." The book provides a survey of widespread academic buzzwords, which serve as stepping stones for exploring new areas of inquiry in interdisciplinary cultural studies. In this work, a keyword opens up or closes an argument by allowing discussants to generate critical and creative thinking. That is, the goal of discussion is not to arrive at a consensus, but rather to encourage constructive contestation. In other words, the purpose of using "keywords" in this book is to expand the existing fields of knowledge for further research and reflection.

A related work on the term "keywords" is Raymond Williams's (1983) *Keywords: A Vocabulary of Culture and Society,* which has been revised and edited by Tony Bennett, Lawrence Grossberg, and Meaghan Morris (2005). Both editions show the rich and violent impact of cultures on words and demonstrate how constant change in culture is reflected in words. Their approach is culturally rather than etymologically oriented, and encapsulates practices and debates from a variety of disciplines and interdisciplinary fields. What is more interesting about Williams's book is that it includes blank pages at the end to signal both a continuation of previous and an invitation for new inquiries. The revised and edited version of Williams's book calls into question crucial subjectivities located within a culture.

There is no doubt that "keywords" invite and encourage people to think, reflect, and continue to search all what circulates around words. They constitute a linguistic device that at once enriches our way of thinking of issues and reveals the interconnectedness of various cultural studies.

Words: Multilayered Meaning

We think and talk in words. While recognizing the connectivity aspect of key words, we cannot but raise a fundamental question: is the meaning of a word revealed in the way its user employs it? We often say or ask, "No, that's not what I meant," "What do you mean by xxx?" "What does xxx mean to you?" and so forth. Two books by Deborah Tannen, *That's Not What I Meant* (1986) and *You Just Don't Understand* (1990), deal with issues centered on these questions. Tannen writes, "Whereas words convey information, how we speak those words ... communicates what we think we are doing when we speak.... In other words, how we say what we say communicates social meanings" (1986, 16).

Although Tannen's work focuses on differences in conversational styles among individuals as well as specifically between women and men, it clearly shows that a word's meaning is multilayered. In other words, the meaning of a word carries several features that are not always readily understandable or easily discernible. Moreover, given that linguists, including lexicologists, semanticians, pragmaticians,

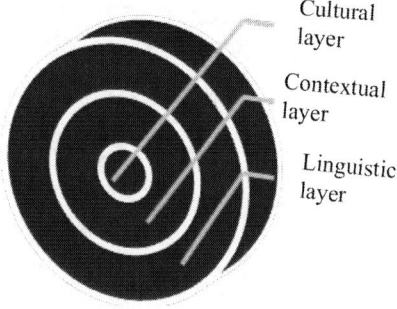

Figure 1.
Word: Multilayered Meaning.

and sociolinguists, have different ways of dealing with word meaning, one cannot devise a single way of encompassing all the various modes of word-meaning. Nevertheless, a discussion on how we look at the aspect of multilayered meaning (namely, linguistic, contextual, and cultural layers) is in order. Our discussion here will lead to an understanding of how this book arrives at taking "basic human needs" as the starting point for understanding culture through key words.

Linguistic Layer

The (formal) linguistic layer refers to a notion of meaning defined as having two components/aspects: *reference* and *sense.* "Reference" denotes *information content,* anything real or imagined that a person may talk about. The aspect of reference draws upon behaviorism in that words are viewed as linguistic units that name or refer to things or actions; the labels attached to objects (e.g., room, bed) or action words (e.g., go, sleep) are examples of this direct approach to meaning. This direct approach has its roots in the stimulus–response theories of John Watson (1930), which are directly associated with the school of radical behaviorism. The initial idea is to identify the response that a given word induces in the hearer or reader. These behaviorist roots require that whatever concerns speakers and hearers with regard to meaning should be accessible to observation.

The behaviorist approach to meaning has been criticized inasmuch as there are a large number of words that cannot be associated with things or actions in a clear way. This criticism alludes to another aspect/component of meaning, referred to as "sense." Sense is the system of the paradigmatic and syntagmatic relationships between a lexical unit (i.e., a form–function composite that represents a lexical form and single meaning of a lexeme) and other lexical units in a language. Sense implies *mental representation* in that the relationship can be made through the use of our minds. For example, while the reference of "mother" is what the term indicates, the sense of "mother" evokes personal meaning and affect. Generally speaking, meanings are things that are grasped, stored, and assembled in the minds of language users.

Moving from a general discussion of meanings to a definition of a "word," linguists would describe a word as "the smallest free form of meaning in a language." This definition sounds impeccable in that a word carries meaning. Yet, it simply refers to the surface of meaning, which we name the "linguistic layer," or what people usually call the "dictionary meaning." This layer is isolated from the actual context in which the word is used. This is the kind of meaning that most foreign-language learners have traditionally learned in a formal classroom setting and that people get through a dictionary. One may note that some dictionaries list different meanings of a particular word and also provide examples of how it is used in a phrase or sentence. Yet, what is given in the dictionary is still an isolated meaning in that it lacks the context in which the word used.

Contextual Layer

The second layer of meaning is contextual. The meaning of a word in use is attached to a given situation; it cannot be elucidated without consideration of the interactions between the speaker and the hearer in a particular context, since the psychological states of the speaker and hearer are not static. Consider Humpty Dumpty's frequently cited position in Lewis Caroll's *Through the Looking Glass* (1872):

> "When I use a word," Humpty Dumpty said in a rather scornful way, "it means just what I choose it to mean—neither more nor less." "The question is," asks Alice, "whether you *can* make words mean so many different things." "The question is," said Humpty Dumpty, "which is to be master—that's all" [72].

Such a position regarding words recalls that of Mikhail Bakhtin (1986), who asserts:

> The words of a language belong to nobody, but still we hear those words only in particular individual utterances, we read them in particular individual works, and in such cases the words already have not a typical but also (depending on the genre) a more or less clearly reflected individual expression, which is determined by the unrepeatable individual context of the utterance [88].

Here, Bakhtin stresses the importance of the contact between the linguistic meaning and the concrete reality that takes place in the utterance; according to him, it is the contact that creates "the spark of expression."

With regard to the non-immediacy of meaning, the contextual layer appears to be challenging in comparison to the linguistic layer, which can be easily solved by a dictionary. While the linguistic meaning exists inside the mind that processes language, the contextual meaning involves the mind that is on the alert in a given social environment. That is, it takes pragmatic competence to understand meaning composed of what Herbert Paul Grice (1989) calls "natural and non-natural meaning." According to Grice, natural meaning involves cause and effect, and non-natural meaning lies in the intentions of the speaker in communicating something to the listener. In simple terms, natural meaning can be associated with the conventional sign attached to the kind of meaning—namely literal/linguistic meaning; in contrast, non-natural meaning is associated with the speaker's nonconventional meaning.

Anita Avramides (1989, 40–41) illustrates Grice's distinction between these two meaning as follows. In the case of a sentence such as "The occurrence of thunder means that there will be a storm," we cannot argue about what was meant by that thunder; that is, a natural meaning arises. In contrast, an utterance such as "Your face is red" allows us to argue over what was meant by these words; a non-natural meaning is thus present. In other words, there occurs what Grice also calls "implicature," an inference based not only on an utterance, but also on assumptions about what the speaker is trying to achieve. For example, "Your face is red" could mean "Please stop drinking" if spoken while dining; it could also be the question "Are you embarrassed?" if said to a shy person when discussing an uncomfortable topic.

Here, the hearer may not catch the meaning that the speaker wants to convey. However, as the conversation/interaction goes on, the word's non-natural meaning will be understood. That is, the non-immediacy of understanding can be solved without much delay and, therefore, the contextual layer can be considered less problematic than the cultural layers that will be discussed next.

Cultural Layer

The cultural layer of meaning of certain words—especially culture-bound words that involve intangible, culture-specific features—is extremely hard to explain to those who are not exposed to the culture. This difficulty is well illustrated in the area of translation. Although it is quite possible to translate anything from one language into any other language, it has been commonly observed that the translation of culture-embedded words is highly problematic. Let us consider further problems in translation.

No one would argue against a view that language cannot exist unless it is immersed in the context of culture (Juri Lotman and Boris Uspensky, 1978) or that language is the heart of the body of culture (Susan Bassnett, 1991). Yet, the question as to how to render culture-bound words has been addressed in many studies (Mona Baker, 1992; Peter Newmark, 1988; Douglas Robinson, 1997; Cristina Schaffner and Uwe Wiesemann, 2001), and the difficulty in translating culture-bound words that denote concepts associated with way of life, culture, and social and historical development has been experienced by most translators.

Translators have tried to use a number of strategies to convey the exact meaning of a source-language word. For instance, a source-language word is transferred into a target-language text in its original form, which is referred as *transference, cultural borrowing,* or *naturalization.* A great number of English words of French origin (e.g., *cuisine, cul-de-sac, francophone*) are examples of this type. Sometimes they are translated into target-language words, a process referred to as *calque* or *loan translation.* For example, the English word "email" is translated as "*courier électronique*" in French. Furthermore, a loan word may be used with explanation in the culture-free words of a target language. For example, the French word *cul-de-sac* is explained as "a road closed at one end'" in English; similarly, *déjà vu* in French is explained as "the feeling that something happening has occurred before."

Yet, the translation endeavor has not always been successful. Even concrete and tangible words are hard to translate if there are differences in lifestyle between the two countries or regions in question. A French–English bilingual individual reports, "The reason why I use so many words in English when I speak with French-speaking people is because I find it very hard to convey certain ideas or information about my daily life in the country [the United States]." Notions such as "daycare center," "finger food," "window shopping," and "pot-luck dinners" need a few sentences to be explained in French (Grojean, 1982, 150).

With regard to nontangible words, explaining the concepts encapsulated in culture-specific words is an even more challenging endeavor; some words are deeply ingrained in the culture, and speakers acquire meanings attached to these cultural words as they grow up and use them instinctively and intuitively. For instance, the Chinese concept of *he,* commonly translated as "harmony" in English, may seem very easy to understand. Nevertheless, people who have not lived in Chinese culture may not be able to feel its meaning since it involves so many semantic features and its semantic property is multifarious. Cortazzi and Shen write, "*He* refers to 'harmony,' 'peace,' or 'equilibrium' in human relationships; to the cosmic order of the universe, and the relationship between the former and the latter" (2001, 130). They further note that *he* reflects, in some ways, one aspect of *li* (roughly translated as "propriety" in English), for which the written character "symbolizes one's relationship with God" (129).

Another noteworthy remark on translation involves differences in the use of lexical pattern. Hannu Kemppainen (2004) introduces a corpus-based method for the study of ideology realization in translated and nontranslated texts, specifically Russian–Finnish translations and original (nontranslated) Finnish texts on Finnish political history. He focuses on one of the translation-specific key words—the word *ystavyys,* meaning "friendship." The analysis of the key word in a broader context shows a clear difference between translations and nontranslations in the use of this word. The differences are manifested in the use of lexical patterns. For example, the word *ystavyys* is frequently collocated with "and" in translations, but not in nontranslations. This kind of difference implies a possibly misleading interpretation of a text in terms of what Kemppanen calls "semantic prosody."

The delicate difficulty of wording is well illustrated in many books pertinent to the lives of bilingual speakers. In his commentary to Pushkin's *Eugene Onegin*, Vladimir Nabokov (1991) discusses the untranslatability of the Russian word *toska.*

Amy Tan (1990), in an essay titled "The Language of Discretion," addresses an issue similar to the Whorfian hypothesis, which was described in the Introduction to this book; she questions whether our perception of the world and our interaction with it are defined by the language we speak:

> To this day, I wonder which parts of my behavior were shaped by Chinese, which by English. I am tempted to think, for example, that if I am of two minds on some matter it is due to the richness of my linguistic experiences, not to any personal tendencies toward wishy-washiness. But which mind says what? [267].

More recently, Michele Koven (2007) provides an empirically based theoretical account of how the same speakers enact, experience, and are perceived by others to have different identities in their two languages. He writes, "When I speak Portuguese, automatically, I'm in a different world.... It's a different color" (1). Similarly, the problematical cultural interactions and difficult multicultural conflicts shown in the personal stories compiled by Mary Besemeres and Anna Wierzbicka (2007) confirm that different cultures have different implicit norms that carry significant weight in some people's lives.

The difficulty of the translation of culture-bound words and the language experiences of bilingual individuals indicate that the cultural layer of meaning is not readily discernible and requires an understanding that is connected to and/or parallel with one's own experience. More importantly, it suggests the need for the development of a new approach to understanding culture through culture-bound words, which are deeply rooted in one's way of being.

A Starting Point: Basic Human Needs

Clifford Geertz, a highly influential specialist in symbolic anthropology, pays prime attention to the role of symbols constructing public meaning. He argues:

> The concept of culture I espouse ... is essentially a semiotic one. Believing, with Max Weber, that man is an animal suspended in webs of significance he himself has spun, I take culture to be those webs, and the analysis of it to be therefore not an experimental science in search of law but an interpretive one in search of meaning [1973, 5].

According to Geertz, a culture has a repertoire of forms. He further writes, "One can move between forms in search of broader unities or informing contrasts. One can even compare forms from different cultures to define their character in reciprocal relief" (453). This view implies that there are universals in human experience, yet these are principles that are defined through variables and parameters.

It is virtually undeniable that there is a certain degree of similarity and difference in basic human needs and motivations across cultures. In other words, while basic needs are relevant to all individuals, there should also be culture-specific aspects thereof. Furthermore, considering Sapir's aforementioned view that "vocabulary is a very sensitive index of the culture of people" (1949, 162), we assume that there are some key words that are closely associated with these basic needs.

In 1943, Maslow set up a hierarchic theory of basic human needs consisting of five levels: (1) *physiological needs,* such as food, clothing, shelter, and other bodily needs; (2) *safety needs,* which can be interpreted to imply the desire for a predictable, orderly world in which injustice and inconsistency are under control, and in which there are grievance procedures for individual protection; (3) *love and belongingness needs,* which comprise emotionally based relationships such as friendship, intimacy, supportive family, and community; (4) *esteem needs,* which denote both self-esteem and respect by others, and for which individuals engage themselves to gain recognition and undertake activ-

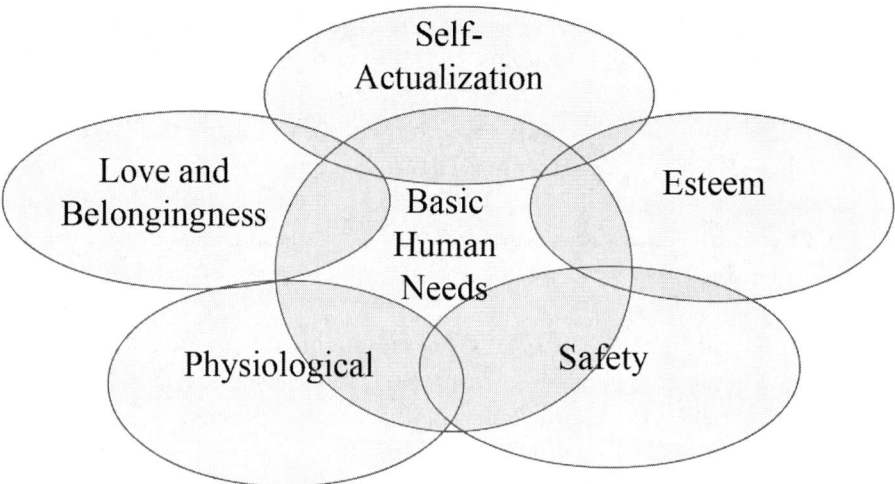

Figure 2. Basic Human Needs (Theories of Maslow and Others).

ities that give them a sense of contribution; and (5) *self-actualization needs,* which entail one's need to be and do what one was "born to do." In Maslow's view the person does not feel the need for a higher level until the demands of the lower level(s) have been satisfied.

Maslow's theory has not gone without criticism, especially at the level of its hierarchical order, due to insufficient evidence for the ranking of needs. However, regardless of the argument regarding the hierarchical order, Maslow's theory has become one of the most popular and often-cited theories of human motivation, and some researchers have proposed similar types of needs. For instance, Clayton Alderfer (1972) developed a comparable hierarchy with his ERG theory: *existence* (various forms of material desires), *relatedness* (involving relationships with significant others), and *growth* (that which impels a person to make creative or productive effects on himself and his environment). Eugene Mathes (1981) proposed only three levels—*physiological, belongingness,* and *self-actualization*—considering *security* and *self-esteem* to be unwarranted. While some researchers such as Alderfer and Mathes have reduced/condensed the number of need-level/category, others have expanded its category. For instance, Manfred Max-Neef (1991), who views fundamental human needs as nonhierarchical and even ontological in that they stem from the very condition of being human, classifies fundamental needs in nine categories: substance, protection, affection, understanding, participation, leisure, creation, identity, and freedom. Moreover, he further categorizes these needs in terms of being (qualities), having (things), doing (actions), and interacting (settings).

Whether basic needs are organized into five, three, nine, or more categories, they all recognize the simple truth that humans are social beings whose lives involve others. That is, "man is by nature a social animal." This hackneyed phrase may have its roots in the writings of Aristotle who, in the fourth century B.C., argued, "It is evident that the state is a creation of nature, and man is by nature a political animal" (Tripp, 1970, 485). Considering that to be *political* (translated from the Greek word *politikos,* which in turn was derived from *polis,* meaning "city-state") is to be a member of a *polis* or a citizen, being a citizen implies being a part of the society and contributing to the good of the whole. From this perspective, all types of basic human needs are interconnected, and all needs cannot be met without involvement of others; it is impossible to meet bodily needs all by oneself. Similarly, it is infeasible to realize one's full potential without interaction with others.

At the same time, one cannot ignore the fact that human beings come into the world alone and die alone; this basic truth implies that human beings are independent. Thus, one could state, "A human is by nature a private animal," and offer a sound argument against Aristotle. It is worthwhile to note here that these two sides of human beings (social and private) are addressed in the field of communication. Tannen writes, "There are the universal human needs that motivate communication: the needs to be connected to others and to be left alone. Trying to honor these conflicting needs puts us in a double bind" (1986, 17).

Having two sides as human beings and conflicting needs is universal; the concept of duality exists in all cultures. Yet, what is culture-specific is the degree of emphasis on one side/need with respect to the other, and the purposes and expectations thereof. Thus, this book, while adopting the concept of Maslow's five types of basic needs, explores how these needs are relevant to Koreans and which cultural words reflect their particular ways of thinking, behaving, and interacting with others.

Cultural Variation of Basic Human Needs

It seems natural that, when dealing with variation, it is usually the dichotomous aspect that is first brought to attention. One could argue that this is due to the fact that our mind is accustomed to two opposite body parts (i.e., left and right eyes, ears, hands, and feet). That is, it appears to be a natural tendency of human beings to perceive and think in two opposite ways. In fact, this tendency is reflected in many areas of research. For example, Isabel Briggs

Myers (1962) makes a distinction between extroversion and introversion, sensing and intuition, thinking and feeling, and judging and perceiving, to account for variation in personality. For learning style variation, Ellis Paul Torrance (1980) notes the difference between left-brain dominance and right-brain dominance. Similarly, Madeline Elizabeth Ehrman and Betty Lou Leaver (2003) present a dichotomous aspect of nine styles (e.g., field independence versus dependence, inductive versus deductive, and impulsive versus reflective) associated with second-language acquisition. By the same token, the concepts of "individualistic and collectivistic cultures" (Geert Hofstede and Michael Harris Bond, 1984) and "low- and high-context" (Edward Hall, 1976) are frequently used to explain differences and similarities across cultures.

The notion of such dichotomous aspects of human beings and their culture is applied here to describe the cultural variation in basic human needs through the use of the term "transcultural cues." This term denotes cultural prompts that connect basic concepts to culture-specific ones. It is used to show that (1) basic human needs are both universal and culture-specific; (2) conceptual cues denote the similarities and differences between two cultures; and (3) a culture-based cue is a leading indicator of a key cultural word.

Each type of need presented in Maslow's theory is paralleled with a concept(s) that is deeply rooted in a particular culture (i.e., Korean culture in this book). That is, while observing each type of need in Korean culture, one also notes that there are certain differences in the degree of emphasis placed on that need and in its ways of conceptualization. We aim to capture the particular means of conceiving each need by introducing culture-bound words. The introduction of these words is not to constrain our view of culture, as might be implied by Wittgenstein's 1922 claim, "The limit of my language means the limits of my world" (1988, 149). On the contrary, the introduction of sociohistorically reflected words will enhance our spectrum of perception of a culture, considering that the semantic properties of a cultural word are far-reaching, yet can be framed in various ways.

Physiological Needs: Physical Strength versus Inner Strength

The physiological-bodily need (e.g., food, clothing, shelter, air, water) is the very first in terms of Maslow's hierarchy of needs. The bodily need is obvious; no one would dispute its inevitability for the survival of human beings. However, what should be noted here is that continued existence requires not only the bodily needs for *physical strength,* but also the *inner strength* to withstand hardship and suffer patiently when lacking materials for survival as well as when confronting adversity and misfortune. While physical strength is applied in day-to-day tangible activities, inner strength sets out "hope" for those who are in insurmountable pain or difficulty.

It is evident that humans need both physical strength and inner strength, and that both are interrelated. However, a high degree of emphasis on inner strength appears to be culture-specific, as shown in Korean culture. From a historical point of view, one could argue that survival in Korean culture is characterized by inner strength as opposed to physical strength. Although one must satisfy physiological-bodily needs to survive, Koreans have a tendency to perceive inner strength as being that which makes one endure sufferings for survival. This view has its roots in the unfortunate internal strife, external threats, and foreign invasions to which Korea was repeatedly subjected throughout history.

A marked example that illustrates the inner strength of Koreans is the economic prosperity of South Korea following the Korean War (1950–1953). The war left the country in an unimaginably deplorable state: one encountered homelessness, hunger, and the loss of or separation from family members, to name but a few consequences. Nevertheless, South Korea was able to lay the groundwork for economic development, which propelled its emergence as one of the 10 major trading countries in the world. The slogan "We, too, can do it," with which the country managed to modernize the rural areas and build national confidence, illustrates how Koreans are resilient in overcoming the hardships they are facing, and demonstrates just how strong and self-reliant they can be under the most adverse of conditions. Such a trait reminds us of the Korean proverb, "A misfortune turns into a blessing."

However, this proverb might be considered overly optimistic, for misfortune does not always turn into a blessing, even when people strive extremely hard at the risk of their lives. To this effect, one must note that there is a constructive dimension implicit in the unfruitful endeavor of Koreans. At the end of each trial, a kind of *yearning* is generated in the person's mind; this feeling can be described as a negative emotional burden. Such an unresolved feeling is expressed through a Korean cultural term called *han*/ 한.

Han is commonly translated as "grudge," "heartburning," "rancor," "spite," "hatred," or something similar in English dictionaries, yet no translation can accurately capture this term. It is a most deeply seated Korean cultural trait that one can feel rather than understand. Nevertheless, *han* has been deemed a driving force, impelling Koreans to continue to hope and strive until whatever in question is resolved. In other words, it generates "inner strength," and, from the perspective of others, it can be very positive or negative. We will study *han* in depth in Chapter 2.

Safety Needs: Equal Rights versus Moral Goodness

The second type of needs that Maslow discusses comprises *safety needs*. Human beings need to feel safe from all kinds of threats, including wild animals, extreme temperature, criminals, and tyranny, and further require insurance in various areas (e.g., health, job, old age). We all need to be protected from diverse forms of maltreatment, hostility, and exploitation, and we all want the world to be predictable, amenable, orderly, and well organized. That is, a good society is expected to make its members feel safe, and a "social order" should be maintained. A question arises here: what makes the society orderly? In other words, what is the basis of social order? Is this basis universal or culture-specific?

What this question calls for immediately in U.S. culture is "equality." The concept of safety needs associated with "social order" is inseparable from the idea of equality. *Equality-based safety* is predicated upon the view that all human beings are equal and should be treated equally, and that protection should be granted to all individuals. From an equality standpoint, safety is exercised through law, legally binding contracts, consistency in grievance procedures, and so on. In other words, the "well-being of individuals" is (or is supposed to be) protected "legally" and "uniformly," regardless of such social parameters as age, race, gender, and ethnicity.

However, equality is not a universal trait across societies. Traditionally, in some cases (China, Korea), human beings have been classified in terms of the social parameters (e.g., social class, age, gender) by which individuals are ranked. A type of ranked relationship is well captured in the *samgang-oryun/*삼강오륜 (translated as three bonds and five cardinal relationships), a set of principles taught by Confucianism. The three bonds are (1) sovereign to subject, (2) parent to child, and (3) husband to wife. The five cardinal relationships define these three bonds and two additional bonds (i.e., senior to junior and friend to friend).

In a hierarchical society of this type, the safety-associated social order involves *moral goodness*. A person at the lower rank (i.e., subject, son, wife, junior) is expected to obey and show respect. By the same token, the party/person with a higher rank is expected to display goodness and virtue and to take good care of the person with a lower rank. This sequential order is not intended to rank people who gain dominance over or subjugation of others, but rather to make the people of a higher rank/elderly conscious of the example they set and cautious of their words and deeds. It places the elderly/high-ranked people in the position to advise the younger/low-ranked people in matters of behavior. That is, obedience, deference and benevolence are "moral obligations" that are practiced to meet safety needs, and this "hierarchical harmony" is valued.

Two cultural terms capturing moral goodness in Korean culture are *chung*/ 충 (roughly translated as "loyalty") and *hyo*/ 효 (meaning "filial piety"). Loyalty in the traditional Korean sense is quite different from what the word means to mainstream Americans. In Korean ethos, loyalty includes the concept of *uiri*/ 의리, which can be described as "situational ethics" in that it highlights absolute integrity to the maintenance of perfect harmony between two parties (or persons) *in a given situation*. This harmony could appear unreliable to mainstream Americans, who value equal rights more than relational/social harmony. Similarly, while filial piety is essentially an attempt to repay indebtedness to parents, it covers the Korean sense of loyalty in that it has been viewed as the source of all virtues.

Love/Belongingness Needs: Privacy versus Interference

According to Maslow, if both physiological and safety needs are met fairly, then another type of need will emerge—namely, *love and belongingness*. This third type of need deals with the *affective*, social-psychological aspect of human needs, which encompasses the emotionally based bonds of friendship, intimate relationships, supportive family, and community. All humans are individuals who are also members of a group. They belong to various groups (e.g., family, school, community) and engage in diverse activities that generate a *sense of love and belongingness*.

This need of love/belongingness can be associated with the *object relation theory*, which describes the process of developing a mind as one grows in relation to another in the environment. Object relations theorists, such as W.R.D. Fairbairn (1951) and Kenneth Newman and Howard Bacal (1989), place less emphasis on the drives of aggression and sexuality as a motivational force and devote more attention to human relationships as the primary motivational force in life. They suggest that humans have an innate drive to develop and maintain relationships. Although we have little sense of ourselves early in life, we develop the ego-self/self-structure (personality) through relationships with people around us inasmuch as we internalize part of ourselves. We see that young children, as they grow, become more aware both of themselves as individuals and of their place among others. They are cognizant of their feelings and needs; they discover that they are part of a unit of other people; and they learn and understand that they belong to many different types of groups.

Here, again, arises a debate as to the culture-specificity of this need. While the fact that the self exists in relation to others is universally understood, the way in which the self is viewed may be different across cultures. A basic question to be raised regarding the culture-specificity of self-concept is, who is the primary controller of the self? That is, who typically controls one's life and self, or those of others?

It has been widely viewed that people are in control of their own lives in individualistic cultures (e.g., the United States); that is, the self is a *self-geared person*. It is the self (before anyone else) who assesses feelings and group membership. Moreover, while searching for and enjoying love and belongingness, individuals maintain a certain level of "privacy." They respect each other's privacy and maintain a certain level of social distance.

However, in collectivist cultures (e.g., Korea), people are not often in control of their lives. The self is viewed as being incomplete if it is separated from others; the self is an *other-oriented person*. The sense of love and belongingness in Korean ethos lies in a total involvement at the social and psychological level. That is, interference is commonly expected among close people, while privacy is respected only when it is requested. Interference is seen as a way of generating good and trusting mutual feelings, which lead to the building up of what in Korean is called *jeong*/ 정, a term roughly translated as "emotional attachment and bond." *Jeong* manifests itself in all types of social interactions, including those between parents and children, and between siblings, friends, and lovers. We will analyze *jeong* in depth in Chapter 2.

Esteem Needs: Individual Strategy versus Social Prescription

The fourth category of human needs is the *need for esteem*. This category addresses both self-esteem and respect by others. People engage themselves to gain recognition and pursue activities that give them a sense of contribution. This category appears to be quite similar to the third category (i.e., love and belongingness) in that it highlights the *relatedness of humans* at the social-psychological level.

However, what distinguishes this category from the need for love/belongingness lies in an individual's particular motivation—namely an "instrumental-extrinsic motivation" that comes from outside of the individual, and that drives him or her to do things for tangible incentives or rewards. Moreover, this "instrumental-extrinsic motivation" coexists and cooperates with what Erving Goffman (1967) calls "face." Goffman discusses face in reference to how people present themselves in social situations, asserting:

> Much of the activity occurring during an encounter can be understood as an effort on everyone's part to get through the occasion and all the unanticipated and unintentional events that can cast participants in an undesirable light, without disrupting the relationships of the participants [41].

According to Goffman, if better face is established, we feel good; if expectations are not fulfilled, we feel bad or hurt.

Penelope Brown and Stephen Levinson have further developed Goffman's concept of face and suggest politeness strategies that are associated with self-esteem and respect. They view face as being composed of "two specific kinds of desires (face-wants) attributed by interactants to one another: the desire to be unimpeded in one's actions (negative face), and the desire (in some respects) to be approved of (positive face)" (1987, 13). They argue that a face-threatening act (FTA) often requires a mitigating statement or polite statement to avoid breaking the line of communication, and outline four main types of strategies: bold on record (not attempting to minimize the threat), negative politeness (attempting to minimize the threat to the hearer's positive face), positive politeness (attempting to show respect for the hearer's ability to maintain autonomy), and off-record or indirect strategy (attempting to remove the speaker from the potential for being imposing). Here, it should be noted that these politeness strategies are optional; individuals "choose" an appropriate strategy depending on the goal they intend to achieve. In other words, the way of establishing better face to meet the need for esteem is an individually based strategy.

As addressed in the aforementioned types of needs, one is led to raise a question regarding the culture-specific aspect of the need. More precisely, the question remains as to whether the term "face" (or an equivalent term) is conceptualized in the same way across cultures. Ako Yabuuchi (2004) looks into the nature of face as a socio-psycho-linguistic concept through examination of its varying conceptualizations and components in Chinese, Japanese and American cultures; "face" is *mien-tzu* in Chinese, and *menboku* (or *taimen*) in Japanese. She explains:

> Chinese *mien-tzu* covers not only the qualification for receiving a certain amount of social resources, but also the amount of social resources itself and the relationships that bring in social resources. On the other hand, Japanese *menboku* and *taimen* signify only the qualification and English face not only signifies the qualification but also is inclined to self-projected qualification which is situationally defined [288].

In Korean culture, a somewhat equivalent concept of face is *chemyeon/* 체면 (translated roughly as "face" in many Korean–English dictionaries).

However, there is a fundamental difference between face as conceptualized in U.S./individualistic cultures and that in Korean culture. While the former refers to a person's self-claim resulting from a particular contact, the latter is a socially prescribed concept. In other words, while *esteem needs* exist in Korean culture, it is the society (or community) that ascribes esteem for the individual.

Consequently, face-work in Korean culture is stipulated by somewhat absolute social standards, and thus is applied consistently to different situations and relationships. A higher *chemyeon* is given to a person of a higher social position. That is, it is not individually negotiable, and the process of enacting *chemyeon* is often viewed as a pass–fail dichotomy. Furthermore, it is appraised by not only interactional partners but also by others. From the perspective of Korean *chemyeon*, politeness for the esteem need is manifested on the basis of *socially prescribed rules,* similar to what Koreans call *ye/* 예, a term translated roughly as "polite manners/proprieties." We will study two interrelated terms in depth in Chapter 3.

Self-Actualization Needs: Aptitude versus Whole-Person

The fifth category that Maslow discusses is the *need for self-actualization* (growth needs); this has to do with a person's need to be and do what the person is *born to do.* In Maslow's view, one feels this need after all the other needs have been satisfied. That is, self-actualization is the final level of psychological development that can be achieved when actualization of the full personal potential takes place.

Whether or not we agree with Maslow's view of hierarchical order, numerous social psychologists (e.g., Robert Gardener and Wallace Lambert, 1972; Edward Deci, 1975; Robert Gardner and Peter MacIntyre, 1991) would concur that this need underlines both *intrinsic motivation,* which comes from within the individual, and *extrinsic motivation,* which stems from outside of the individual and drives the individual to do things for tangible incentives or rewards. From the perspective of intrinsic motivation, the growth dimension is often seen as intangible, as it represents an intrinsic aspect of a self who is in process of becoming or realizing his or her potential. By the same token, from the perspective of extrinsic motivation, one needs to find self-fulfillment and realize one's potential, which leads to "self-transcendence" (i.e., connecting to something beyond the ego or helping others find self-fulfillment and realize their potential). As Maslow and Lowery (1998) note, these two types of motivations needed for self-actualization are observed in Maslow's later differentiation of the growth needs of self-actualization in that two levels are allowed: the lower/sublevel and the general/overall level. The lower level includes cognitive needs (e.g., knowing, understanding, and exploring) and aesthetic needs (e.g., symmetry, order, and beauty). The general level consists of self-actualization and self-transcendence.

It is by and large indisputable that reaching self-actualization and finding self-fulfillment are highly desirable and respected across cultures. However, two interrelated issues have been often overlooked when discussing this growth need: (1) who sets the content of self-actualization and (2) whether there is an end-product of actualization.

In Korean culture, which emphasizes the aspect of "other-oriented/interdependent self," the content of self-actualization is what the general public perceives as *socially prestigious*, rather than what each individual is capable of achieving (or "born to do" in Maslow's terms). Furthermore, the concept of self-actualization in Korean culture underlines a "process" (keep wanting to achieve a higher level of social prestige) rather than an "outcome." One has always to move to the next level, which leads in turn to another level. There is actually no ending point for a person who wants to achieve; the end-product of self-actualization is not static, as the content of the socially perceived prestige changes.

To further link to the point of this section (i.e., cross-cultural variation in basic human needs), it is worth mentioning what Kurt Goldstein (1934) has noted about self-actualization. According to Goldstein, this concept is "the tendency to actualize, as much as possible, [the organism's] individual capacities" (1995, 140) in the world. He considers self-actualization as a "driving life force" for making the most of "one's abilities," which will lead to determining the path of one's life. That is, Goldstein appears to view self-actualization as a "process" (as Korean ethos does) rather than an "outcome." Yet, it should be noted that the content of self-actualization has to do with what one is born to do, a concept that many Koreans have had a tendency to overlook.

Goldstein's view of self-actualization as a driving life force can be paralleled with what Korean would consider "becoming the whole person through *cheol*/철," a cultural term roughly translated as "discretion," "wisdom," "good sense," "prudence," "appropriate behavior," "timely deeds/behavior," and so forth. The difference between "self-actualization" and *cheol* is very delicate, in that it lies in the degree of tangibility. Maslow's self-actualization, especially its general level, is "aptitude oriented"; one is to search for and cultivate what he or she is born with and realize one's full potential. In contrast, *cheol* is "whole-person oriented," in that it requires mindfulness for the difficulties that lie ahead, which could be beyond and/or irrelevant to one's aptitude, and thus hard to measure. Another term closely related to *cheol* is *deok/*덕 (marginally translated as "virtue," "moral goodness," or "moral excellence"), which human beings want to cultivate while living. It is an important normative value in that one's social status should be the result of the amount of virtue that one can demonstrate rather than by one's birth. We will discuss these terms thoroughly in Chapter 2.

Table 1 summarizes the cultural variations of the basic human needs and associated culture-bound words in Korean that will be described in depth in the following chapter.

Table 1. Cultural Variation of the Basic Human Needs

Basic Human Needs (Maslow)	Cultural Variation		Associated-Key Cultural Words
	U.S. Perspectives	Korea Perspectives	Korean
Physiological needs	Physical strength	Inner strength	*Han*
Safety needs	Equal rights (individual right)	Moral goodness (hierarchical harmony)	*Chung* and *hyo*
Love and belongingness needs	Privacy respected (self-oriented other)	Interference expected (other-oriented self)	*Jeong*
Esteem needs	Individual strategic politeness (individual face)	Socially prescribed manners (public face)	*Chemyeon*
Self-actualization needs	Aptitude-oriented outcomes	Whole person-oriented process	*Cheol* and *deok*

To recapitulate, this chapter has provided a first step toward understanding key cultural words. The chapter began by setting a tone for key words, of which a primary function is "connectivity"; that is, key words invite and encourage people to think, reflect, and continue to search for the interconnectedness among various elements. Next, the chapter presented three layers of word meaning, since an understanding of words is not always unproblematic, especially when two languages are involved (e.g., translation and the discourse of bilingual speakers.) A recognition of the difficulty of dealing with the cultural meaning of words then directed us to posit Maslow's basic human needs as a point of departure for a better grasp of key cultural words. The exploration was subsequently funneled through cultural cues of such needs and their variations from a traditional Korean perspective. Finally, the specific key Korean cultural words were drawn into the discussion; these will be explained and analyzed in depth in Chapter 2.

Chapter 2

Korean Key Cultural Words

There are indeed many traditional keywords that can serve to elucidate Korean culture. In the previous chapter, we identified eight key Korean cultural words—namely, *han*/한; *chung*/충; *hyo*/효 and *jeong*/정; *chemyeon*/체면 and *ye*/예; and *cheol*/철 and *deok*/덕, which were introduced in conjunction with Abraham Maslow's five categorical human needs (physiological, safety, belongingness, esteem, and self-actualization.). We must note that this is not the only possible list of Korean key cultural words; other researchers may come up with different lists of key words depending on their focus of study. Nevertheless, they would concur that these constitute a number of the important tenets that have influenced Korean ethos and traditional social and interpersonal behavior. The present chapter will explore how these key cultural words are rooted in Korean history and culture, and illustrate their importance for an understanding of behavioral and communicational norms.

Unlike the five categories of basic human needs identified by Maslow's theory, this chapter will be divided into three major sections (i.e., *han*, *jeong*, and *deok*), with an understanding that the others are equally important and thus discussed in the chapter. This division is attributed to the following factors. *Han* and *jeong* are widely considered to be the most representative of Korean cultural traits. We will note that they account for the most frequently presented themes in traditional literature, arts, music, and theater. Such a perspective has also been recognized in scholarly research. For instance, Sang-Chin Choi (1993) views these two cultural words as playing important psychological and phenomenological roles in the experiential mind of Koreans.

Deok is the most challenging concept for Koreans to explain to non–Koreans, and, as mentioned before, it is hard for foreigners to grasp its full meaning. Even Koreans may not be able to define it inasmuch as it includes so many minor virtues, the list of which will differ from individual to individual. Furthermore, while the concepts of *han* and *jeong* are uniquely Korean per se, one can view that *deok* is very similar to the concept of *de,* a Chinese concept; one can even argue that its lexical and semantic origin is Chinese. As for the complexity of its meaning, it is worthwhile to note that there are over 50 minor virtues included in *de* in the Confucian Analects (Chichung Huang, 1997, 16). Given this broad scope of meaning, the other key cultural words that we mentioned earlier (i.e., *chung, hyo, chemyeon, ye,* and *cheol*) will be embedded in the discussion of *deok.*

The following sections examine how these words have been historically and culturally ingrained in Korean ways of thinking, behaving, and living.

Han/한

A folk song titled "Arirang"/아리랑, known to most Koreans, is often considered to be the unofficial national anthem of South Korea.[1] It has the following lyrics:

> *Arirang arirang arariyo (Arirang arirang arariyo)*
> *Arirang gogaereul neomeoganda* (You are going over Arirang hill)
> *Nareul beorigo gasineun nimeun* (My love, you are leaving me)
> *Sibrido mot gaseo balbyeong nanda* (Your feet will be sore
> before you go ten li [four kilometers])
> (Underwood and Underwood, 2002, 363)

"Arirang" is not a static song, and it has many versions that vary from region to region (e.g., Kyeonggi, Jeongseon, Jindo, Miryang), and divergent speculations as to its origin. Yet they have one thing in common: the lyrics and melody of "Arirang" convey lonely despondency, a confession of love, as well as regret at parting.[2] The message is deeply rooted in the hearts of Koreans, who have, throughout history, been very adept at swallowing their anger and sorrow. "Arirang" expresses "the pain and grief of separation, as if the sad melody embodied the emotion of yearning and Korean *han* (deep frustrated and pent-up sorrow)" (Underwood and Underwood, 363). That is, the popularity of the song suggests that Koreans have *han*; hence, they can relate this concept to the sentiments of "Arirang."

What, then, is *han* that is so profoundly inscribed as a Korean cultural trait and is evidenced in all types of unfortunate situations? It is a highly complex notion, difficult to describe in words, and has deep affective roots. Its physical manifestations, either individual or collective, may eventually become visible and obvious. Nonetheless, *han,* by and large, is something that is felt, experienced, and kept within. In what follows, we will delineate it by examining five areas: (1) historical aspects of *han* and its two sides, (2) its manifestation in art forms, (3) its characteristics, (4) modes of *han*-venting, and (5) *han* in modern society.

Historical Aspects of Han and Its Two Sides

The term *han* is commonly used in titles of traditional songs, books, and proverbs, as well as in daily life. Thus it appears to have been understood throughout the country's long history. Researchers who do not speak Korean, however, will note that resources related to *han* written in other languages are scarce, so they may have difficulty in conceptualizing this ethnically core emotion.

In response to this dearth of studies, Chang-Hee Son (2000) has been instrumental in exploring *han* in English. His *Haan of Minjung Theology and Han of Han Philosophy* separates the concept into two distinct categories: the first, spelled *haan,* emerges from the theological perspective of *minjung* (meaning "people, the masses, populace"), while the other, written as *han,* is philosophical in nature. Providing a phenomenological description of the historical development of *minjung,* Son discusses *haan* from a theological perspective, revealing that the premises or tenets of this concept can be discretely applied to many different social and national contexts. Another noteworthy point lies in the fact that *hanism* is viewed as a metaphysical system of thought closely related to process and relation thought in the West. Son argues, "*Hanism* ... is responsive to and harmonious with modern concepts such as Whiteheadian process philosophy and Oliver's metaphysic of relation" (120). Nevertheless, he does not imply that *hanism* competes with modern concepts. In the culmination of his analysis, he discusses *han* in relation to *haan.*

Two Sides of Han: Won-Han and Jeong-Han. While the aforementioned work by Chang-Hee Son brings us closer to the ethno-semantic property of the word *han,* its focus is theological in nature. Nevertheless, traditional Koreans, whether theologically oriented or not, would just feel its meaning. Thus, there arise two closely related questions: what is *han* to Koreans and what is *han* on Korean turf?

A paper titled "*I ttangeso haneun mueosinga*/이 땅에서 한(恨)은 무엇인가," (translated as "What is *han* in this land?") by Ko Un (1990), a most well-known poet in Korea, is enlightening to those who would search for the meaning of *han.* Ko Un traces the origin of *han* back to the life of the ancient northern nomadic people, who formed a community on the basis of their combative sprit and strong hostile feelings toward their adversaries. When they became conquerors for a certain period of time, they expressed their joy through shamanistic ritual festivals and ceremonies. However, if they failed to conquer, they were eager to get revenge with extreme hatred. Thus a militant sprit was engendered to overcome their setbacks. This type of *han* is often called *won-han/* 원 한; it is revenge or justice-transformation oriented. It is interesting to note here that Luke Kim (1996) stresses Ko Un's view from a perspective of Korean ethos in a medical journal; he writes, "Koreans are born from the womb of *han,* grow up in the bosom of *han,* live out *han,* and die leaving *han* behind" (16).

Historically speaking, another type of *han* emerged when the nomadic tribes in Manchuria or Siberia moved to the plains of the southern peninsula. The indigenous people experienced painfully sad sentiments resulting from their ignominious defeat and loss of land. As a result of the overthrow of the agrarian culture of the southern peninsula in the seventh century by the Silla dynasty in alliance with the Tang forces, the nomadic people became scattered and, in the process, lost their military spirit and the concurrent ability to overcome defeat. At the same time, they experienced a sentiment of sorrow and grief. That is, they acquiesced to their vulnerable situation and limitations. This passive acceptance led to a breed of *han* called *jeong-han/* 정 한, which describes sorrow, distress, and unresolved sentiment, and is self-compliance oriented. It is a state of emotional mind that acknowledges unfortunate, heartbreaking circumstances. Simply put, it is a *han* of passive acceptance and resignation.

During the period of the Goryeo dynasty (9th–14th centuries) and the Yi dynasty (15th–early 20th century), both types of *won-han* and *jeong-han* were observed. *Jeong-han,* the self-compliant *han,* was strengthened throughout the dynasties, and such reinforcement can be attributed to the longstanding inflexibility of political parties, economic inequality and the Confucian-oriented feudalistic social system that fostered class and gender discrimination.[3] Perhaps the idea that men are superior to women heightens the preference for a son over a daughter, and aggravates the degree of *han* among women. While *jeong-han* was present in life of the common people and powerless women, *won-han*—revenge or justice-transformation-oriented *han*—was also commonly observed in this period of time; there were constant conflicts and strife, and numerous changes in leading figures, which implied the existence of a form of revenge among ruling classes. That is to say, the two sides of *han* have existed either side by side or one after the other.[4]

Han is not simply the private emotion of a person who has suffered a lot;

it is a pervasive "collective" emotional state among Koreans, who have historically experienced an abundance of tragedies and pain. As Korea is geographically situated as a bridge among China, Japan and Russia, it has been invaded and occupied frequently by surrounding military forces. Korea has even become a tributary nation of China and Japan. Under foreign military occupation, "the Land of the Morning Calm" has been repeatedly crushed, burned, and destroyed. It is very ironic that one hears, "The Korean people are a peace-loving nation. They never tried any invasion of other countries" (Institute for Education of Overseas Koreans 1986, 59). This statement may sound complimentary, but it is also cynical and unpleasant inasmuch as it reminds Koreans of the unfortunate invasions and interventions of other nations, leading to Korea's political, economic, and diplomatic exploitation. It underscores the powerlessness of a country.

The first part of the 20th century constituted another notable period of forging *han* in the political realm. Following its liberation from Japan, Korea was divided into two parts, a tragic victim of superpower Cold War strategy. Millions of people migrated from North Korea to South Korea, leaving behind family members, relatives and friends. The Korean War (1950–1953) destroyed not only the country, but also individual families, who suffered the loss of husbands and sons. Each war, and each political and social turmoil, brought suffering and unbearable distress to Korea.

The historical aspects of the development of *han* and its two-sidedness may be likened to a photo montage, in that the phenomenon is similar to a composite image produced by blending multiple images to create a fully realized whole. One advantage of a photo montage is that it can be used to juxtapose or overlay images that can never be seen together in real life, adding a note of surreality to the finished image. Likewise, while individual Koreans could have their own mental image of *han,* which may vary from person to person, they would agree that, collectively, those perceptions represent a sort of photo montage of the concept.

The three levels of *han* that Sang-Chin Choi (1993) describes fit the notion of a photo montage: a *han* stemming from one's own emotional state (i.e., grief, regret, sorrow, self-pity resulting from maltreatment, and failure to meet one's needs in comparison with others), a *han* of aesthetic sentiment transformed from self-emotional involvement, and a *han* of personality characteristic of the bearers of this trait. Similarly, the four stages of *han* he identifies reflect *won-han* and *jeong-han*. The first stage is similar to *won-han* as described earlier. The second stage is one of the mitigation of one's feelings by attributing the unfortunate situation partially to oneself, and the third stage is one of reflection on a given unfortunate situation and various feelings and questions. The second and third stages conform to what we call *jeong-han*. The last stage is a state free from one's own pain and uncertainty of life, achieved by positioning oneself as a third person/observer; one appears peaceful, quiet, or somewhat embittered.

Han *Manifested in Art Forms*

Han has been manifested in a number of art forms, including novels, autobiographies, poems, songs, dances, and artwork. The following discussion presents a few examples.

Hanjungnok/ 한중록 (恨中錄), a collection of memoirs of Hyegyeong-gung Hong Ssi written in 1795, 1801, 1802, and 1805, has the word han as the first word of its title. The second word is jung, meaning "middle," and the third is nok, denoting "record." From the title, one can immediately guess that the collection is centered on *han*. It is figuratively translated as "Records Written in Silence" or "Memoires of Lady Hyegyeong." These memoires are collected in The Memoirs of Lady Hyegyeong: The Autobiographical Writings of a Crown Princess of Eighteenth-Century Korea (Jahyun Kim Habouch, 1996). This work constitutes a unique document of a historical incident and the ensuing political turmoil, as seen through eyes of an ill-fated crown princess. The crown princess is, on the one hand, caught in the conundrum of human drama at a deeply private level and, on the other hand, enmeshed in the vortex of court intrigue as a public figure. She narrates her life as a royal wife and daughter-in-law from a female perspective.

Toji/ 토지 (Land) by Park Kyung-Ni (2003), an epic novel consisting of 21 volumes published in serial form over the course of a quarter century (1969–1994), is an enticing saga and panorama of Korean village life during the early 20th century, a period in which Japan held strong sway over Korea. The novel opens in 1897, a turbulent time during which the Korean people were struggling against ever-deepening threats of Japanese aggression. At the heart of novel is a series of grave internal clashes and conflicts between Korean conservatives, who seek to preserve the ancient culture of a basically agrarian society, and modernizers, who envision Korea's imminent ruin unless it develops the industrial power requisite for self-defense in an ever more hardhearted world.

Many traditional folk songs are cited when discussing *han*. For example, "*Cheongsanbyeolgok*"/ 청산별곡 (Green Mountain Special Tune), a verse of eight stanzas, depicts the spirit and sentiment of the *Goryeo* people, who lost their homes to a Mongolian invasion during the 13th century, and their unstable society of internal conflicts (Dong Uk Sin, 1982).[5] Another well-cited traditional folk song, likely to have had its origin in the Dong Hak peasant revolution of 1893–1895 is "*Saeya Saeya Parang Saeya*" /새야새야 파랑새야(Bird, Bird, Blue Bird). The song is roughly translated as "*Oh, bird, bird, blue bird/Do not sit in the field of green beans/If the green bean flowers fall/ The merchant of green-lentil jelly will leave in tears*" (authors' translation). In the song, "Blue bird" refers to Japanese soldiers, while "green bean" is a nickname given to General Jeon, Bongjun, the leader of the revolution, who was short in stature. "Green bean field" denotes the group of revolutionary peasants, and "merchant of green-lentil jelly" indicates the people of the Joseon dynasty. Such folk songs are almost spontaneously or impulsively generated among ordinary people, without a composer or a particular lyricist, and handed down from mouth to mouth.

Another elucidative example of *han* can be seen in the mental processes of the narrator of "*Nalgae*"/ 날개 (Wings), a short story by Yi Sang (1910–1937), one of the most innovative writers in modern Korean literature. "Wings" focuses on an alienated man and his semi-schizophrenic life. The story can be read as an allegorical indictment against colonial oppression, as an existential withdrawal from the absurdities and insanities of contemporary life, or, more prosaically, as the schizophrenic decline of a kept man. What the story shows here is his will to fight, to be free from his incapacity, as implied in the last lines of the story: "Oh, Wings, sprout once more! Let's fly. Let's fly again. Oh, let's fly just once more!" (Chung Chong-wha, 1995, 123). The story is in part autobiographical. Yi Sang died of tuberculosis at the age of only 27, while imprisoned in Tokyo on charges of "thought offense." He characterizes himself as split between 19th-century solemn morality and 20th-century modernity, labeling himself a vagrant who slipped into a crack between the centuries with the sole intent of collapsing there. Sang-Chin Choi and Gyuseong Han (2008) would argue that the psychological complexity of Yi Sang's inquiry into life, the indeterminate nature of self, self-preservation, self-repression, and the emancipation of self, illustrate the "*simjeong* psychology" of *han*. (Note that these authors' article transliterates 심정 as *shimcheong* while we transliterate it as *simjeong*.) They describe *simjeong* (literally translated as "mind" or "sentiment") as "a complex cultural emotional state operating in Korean society" (219).

Characteristics of Han: *Paradoxical Conundrum*

What is most intriguing and fascinating about *han* is its *paradoxical conundrum*. While *han* conveys a negative meaning in that it denotes a feeling that no one wants to have, it also suggests a positive aspect. It is a driving force for reaching what one wants to achieve. In other words, it sets free a spirit of "hope" that allows its bearer to generate the inner strength necessary to continue striving and overcoming obstacles. As mentioned earlier, Park Kyung-Ni (1994), the author of *Land,* reveals how Koreans struggle to overcome the contradictions of life. When they are poor, they think of *han* and, therefore, work hard to buy lots of land. When they are ignorant, they are mindful of *han* and, therefore, educate their children to deliver themselves from *han.* We cannot, however, completely release ourselves from *han* in this world, because the concept also implies hope for the future.

Interested Koreans would observe how the contradiction of *han* (sadness and hope) functions in three well-known classic stories: "*Simcheong-Jeon*" (The Tale of Simcheong), "*Heungbu-Jeon*" (The Tale of Heungbu), and "*Chunhyang-Jeon*" (The Tale of Chunhyang). These tales display a common duality and paradox, despite their distinct thematics. "*Simcheong-Jeon*" tells of a daughter who dies at sea to restore her blind father's vision and is subsequently reborn, surrounded by flowers. The theme of "*Heungbu-Jeon*" is poverty; Heungbu, poor, yet diligent and caring, becomes rich through a seed brought by a swallow whose leg had been broken and who was later cured by the protagonist. In "*Chunhyang-Jeon,*" the foreground is oppression; Chunhyang is imprisoned for the sake of her loyalty to her lover and is, in the end, freed by him once he has gained empowerment. These stories display comic elements alongside the tragic situations in which the protagonists find themselves. The essence of *han* in these stories stems from the duality and the contradiction between tragedy and comedy. We note that there are many other Korean stories in which sobs and unrestrained laughter, gravity and jest, pessimism and optimism, are juxtaposed.

From a religious perspective, this paradoxical conundrum is also identified by Paul Tchang Ryeol Kim, Bishop of Jeju Catholic Diocese, who views *han* as a very unique ethnic trait that functions beneficially:

> At one level *han* appears to be the legacy of a curse, but in reality, it has been a kind of blessing, because it has been the catalyst to cause us to search for God.... God uses *han* to shake us up, to wake us from our sleep, and thus He makes us realize the vanity of life, the ultimate emptiness of the things of this world. Through *han* He prevents us from finding satisfaction in earthly things and stimulates us to search for the absolute and everlasting.... I used to ardently wish that *han* would disappear from our land but today, as I have come to realize that *han* is a precious gifts bestowed on the Korean race by God, my attitude has changed.... *Han* was the inspiration of our Catholic martyrs, and as long as *han* exists the Korean people will remain a religious people, even if our

economic strength increases tenfold. *Han* has truly been a messenger of God, and through it the Korean people are blessed race! [Kim Paul Tchang Ryeol, 1986].

The view of *han* as a great asset for faith in Korea appears to be very convincing inasmuch as numerous religions, including Catholicism, diverse Protestant denominations, Buddhism, and even superstitious and occult sects, have prospered in Korea. That is, the core aspect of religion that underlines "sorrow and hope" coincides with the concept of *han.*

Modes of Han-*Venting*

The dual aspect and paradoxical conundrum that *han* represents implies that it is not something that can be uprooted, but rather something that needs to be vented. That is, *han*-venting is as significant as *han*-bearing in Korean culture and leads us to think of ways of releasing it. Earlier, we discussed two sides of *han: won-han,* which we named "the revenge-oriented *han,*" and *jeong-han,* "the self-compliance *han.*" Whether the former or the latter prevails, its venting has been considered highly important, and this is reflected in the aforementioned aspect of the paradoxical conundrum of *han.* While *han*-venting is situation-specific, three modes of this release have been commonly discussed: (1) *han*-venting through the reliance upon super-nature; (2) *han*-venting through others, especially children, grandchildren, and/or siblings; and (3) *han*-venting through the building up of inner strength and self-discipline.

The first mode of *han*-venting is related to the shamanistic practices dating back to the Neolithic period. When those with *han* are in a vulnerable position where nothing can be done, they consequently turn to super-nature. Inasmuch as human beings are limited, it is common for them to put faith in a supernatural being, who might be able to resolve the issue over which they have no control. Although shamanism does not have a systematic structure, it encompasses traditional beliefs and practices that involve a variety of abilities: diagnosis and cure; control over weather; and divination, the interpretation of dreams, the resolution of possible conflicts between the living and the dead, and sometimes the provocation of human suffering. It draws upon spirits and demons that are believed to dwell in objects in the natural world, including rocks, trees, mountains, streams, and celestial bodies.[6] Korean shamanism uses complex forms of a ritual called *gut/*굿, which involves the invocation of ancestral souls, dance, chant, and the narration of the life story of a *han*-ridden person, all of which are intended to release *han.*[7]

From the aforementioned *minjung* theological perspective (Chang-Hee

Son, 2000), shamanism has played an important role in deepening the roots of *han* through *han*-venting. Moreover, given that in Korea, unlike in many other countries, the Christian Gospel has been remarkably well received and Buddhism is enjoying a revival, one can argue that, as long as Korean culture is not separated from the experience of *han, han*-venting will permit all forms of religion to thrive in Korea.

The second mode of *han*-venting involves reliance on others, especially children (and even grandchildren). Traditional Koreans have a strong tendency to honor the wishes of their parents when planning for the future. Children are expected to vent the *han* of their parents out of filial piety—one of the most common ethical norms, which will be discussed later. Children, who have observed the *han* of their parents or grandparents and have heard about it while growing up, receive suggestions as to what they could or should do from their parents, relatives, or other in-group members. However, it should be noted that whether *han*-venting is spurred by a suggestion or not, it is a manifestation of deep love for the *han*-bearer. Filial piety–related *han*-venting continues in various forms, even when parents have died, and consists of a serious pursuit of what the parents had wanted during their life. It is believed that ancestors will continue to take care of living descendants and, therefore, their life achievements and wishes should continue to be respected just as they were while the ancestors were living.

The third mode of *han*-venting is the building up of inner strength and self-discipline associated with one's performance, particularly the manner in which one functions effectively to carry out a task meaningful to oneself. From the perspective of performance, this may seem to be similar to Maslow's concept of self-actualization. However, this approach to *han*-venting has to do with what is laid down deep under the heart or soul, while self-actualization involves a person's need to be and do what he or she is born to do. In other words, the driving force for performance in the context of *han*-venting is the self-will to release *han* by doing something, which can involve literature, music, arts, games, or special tasks. Prime examples of this are the previously mentioned *Hanjungnok* (Records Written in Silence) by Hyegyeonggung Hong Ssi and "*Nalgae*" (Wings) by Yi Sang.

Han-*Venting in Modern Society*

The Korean War resulted in the extensive exposure of South Koreans to Western cultures, especially American materialism. A large number of American liberators arrived in South Korea, bringing with them their own cultural values. Moreover, in recent years, hundreds of thousands of people have traveled to and from Korea each year. Consequently, changes in values began to appear in the 1960s. In turn, we now find a wide gap between older Koreans, who want to hold on to traditional values, and younger generations, who have become more comfortable with Westernized values. In this climate of change, one would wonder how the *han* that had been developed and fostered in older societies has been conceptualized today.

As society transforms itself, people change as well. Yet, long, historically based cultural traits do not disappear so easily. As in the older, traditional society, rank, status, and hierarchy are very important to today's mainstream Koreans. What is different from the older culture is that contemporary society encourages people to take control over their environment; this tendency stands in sharp contrast to core values such as "the acceptance of fate" and "birthright inheritance" that had been commonly observed in the past. The change in attitude toward their fate leads traditional Koreans to pursue arduously a better life by overcoming all of the hardships they confront. Here again, we should be reminded of the importance of "inner strength" for survival, which was discussed in Chapter 1.

One can further remark that the scope of content for today's *han* in individuals has been considerably broadened. While *han* in older societies is mostly related to poverty, hierarchical social class, and gender discrimination, the concept in modern society goes further. It is associated with a wide range of unfortunate matters and situations, including the loss of a person, land, and other treasures; the lack of a child/son; the absence of educational opportunities and advancement (admission to a top university or employment with a prestigious company); the privation of professional advancement; deficiency in physical appearance; and other concerns.

To recap this discussion, the third approach to *han*-venting in modern society is immediate and tangible, and includes the hope for children's future through the hard work of the war survivors, the hope for pleasing parents/family by means of high achievement in academic work, and the hope for a better living condition that results from the endless opportunities for making money in a capitalist environment. Journalist and author of over 30 books, Boyé De Mente, who has lived in East Asia for an extensive period, writes, "Koreans say the extraordinary energy, dedication, and sacrifices that were responsible for much of the economic miracle they achieved during the 1960s–1979s flowed from the release of the pent-up psychic force of *han*" (1988, 129). In a similar vein, Robert Kohls, who has lived and traveled in more than 90 countries, is bewildered by Koreans who never take "no" for an answer and who demonstrate astounding persistence. He writes, "One of the surest keys to functioning successfully in Korea is understanding the complex procedures by which Koreans pursue what they want.... You will hear it over and over again: 'Yes, I know it cannot be done, but please do it anyway'" (149). These were the words Kohls systematically heard after he had explained carefully and thoroughly why it was impossible for him to do whatever incredible thing had just been requested of him.

To close the discussion of *han,* let us recall that in Chapter 1, the cultural word *han* was associated with inner strength in terms of survival needs when discussing cultural variations in the basic human needs. Unlike many other cultures, Korean culture stresses the importance of inner strength in the process of survival. Its importance is well denoted in an expression that is frequently used when confronting a highly difficult situation or when dealing with a highly important matter: *jukgi (animyeon) salgi*/ 죽기 (아니면)살기) (literally translated as "if not dying, living," which means "risking one's life for something"). What should be observed here is the word order between "dying and living." In Korean, when the two words "live/life" and "die/death" are used together, the word "die/death" comes before "live/life." For instance, one says "a matter of death and life" in Korean, as opposed to "a matter of life and death" in English. This Korean expression indicates one's determination to "do," even at the risk of one's life, and, in the process, to endure. It applies to all kinds of difficulties pertinent to any type of want, be it physical, psychological, social, financial, or educational.

Jeong/ 정

Rodney Tyson (1997) decided to explore the meaning of *jeong* after his visit to the National Museum of Modern Art in Seoul. He noticed that several of the sculptures that were on display had the title "*Jeong*" and that several other titles included the word *jeong.* Several examples of these and their literal translations (in parentheses) include *Oneun Jeong Ganeun Jeong*/오는 정 가는 정 (Coming *Jeong,* Going *Jeong*), *Jeong ttaemune*/ 정 때문에 (Because of *Jeong*), and *Jeong eopneun saram*/ 정 없는 사람 (A Person without *Jeong*). Tyson subsequently sent out a questionnaire with nine open questions concerning the definition and use of the word *jeong,* which was completed by nine Koreans. The results revealed that the nine native subjects themselves failed to agree on a simple definition. Based upon the data from the survey, interviews, and other materials considered in his study, Tyson states, "A true definition for this word, if one is possible at all, may lie in a deeper understanding of its usage within its cultural context" (16). In the following section, we investigate *jeong* by streamlining its characteristics and by examining its various types.

Characteristics of Jeong

Sang Chin Choi and Soo Hyang Choi (2001) open their paper on *cheong* (they use the letters "ch" instead of "j") as follows: "The Korean culture is often called a culture of *Cheong* and *Cheong* discourse is one of the most commonly felt psychological dimensions that Koreans encounter in their daily life" (69). Choi and Choi analyze the structural properties that underpin the concept of *jeong* on the basis of the replies of 36 Korean university students, underscoring that *jeong* both embodies the emotional links among individuals tied to each other by a feeling of we-ness and constitutes a display of their human side.

The analysis of Choi and Choi's study concludes that Western models of the nature of persons and of social interrelationships are inadequate to explain the socioemotional characteristics of Koreans. This conclusion could imply that one may not be able to associate the concept of *jeong* with "love/belongingness," the third category of Maslow's basic human needs. Yet, its association is evident in terms of the relationship between self and other. What is distinctive, though, is how the self is viewed. The self in Korean culture is viewed as being incomplete if it is separated from others. The self is an *other-oriented person,* as opposed to a *self-oriented person.* These contrasts underscore that the English word "man" or "person" places stress on separateness, free will, and individuality, positing the self as an independent entity. In contrast, "self" from the perspective of *jeong* is a "relational-oriented person" whose interpersonal relationships revolve around "*jeong.*" That is, *jeong* is what makes us say "we/our," rather than "I/my."[8]

The following characteristics of *jeong* further describe the "we-ness" of in-group membership. The general definition of *jeong* is sometimes expressed by *in-jeong*/인정 (the humanness that applies to all people, including relatives, neighbors, and community members), which resembles a big family in that its members rejoice, fight, and sometimes stop talking to each other for a while, but then empathize with each other, laugh, and continue onward. We can note the following:

1. Jeong *consists of two facets (as a coin has two sides), internal and external.* The internal facet is what is *within* an individual's heart, an aspect

that is understood universally. The external facet is located *between* individuals. It is this external facet, around which interpersonal relationships revolve, that is distinctive from other cultures.

2. Jeong *functions as an interpersonal resource* that serves as an important mechanism in controlling personal relationships. It bridges the gap of emotional isolation and separateness from each other, establishing an emotional connectedness that encompasses all feelings, including joy, anger, affection, sadness, and fear. (Bonded by *jeong,* collective efforts toward a common goal, overcoming crises, and survival are common practices of in-groups.)

3. Jeong *involves a loving heart in nature as well as loving deeds.* However, unlike an erotic love that can be described as hot, fiery, dynamic, intense, mercurial, pleasurable, unpredictable and powerful, *jeong* is quiet, gentle, giving, nurturing, connected, attached, steady, loyal, dependable, considerate, devoted and sacrificial.

4. Jeong *often overrules logic.* It is manifested through loyalty and commitment without validation, or reason. Interactions, whether formal or private, often carry the assumption of noncontractual commitment, as greater value and significance are placed on maintaining *jeong* and loyalty in relationships. This is opposed to the aspect of relationships without *jeong* that are characterized by rationality, objective social norms, individual interests, social justice and equity.

5. Jeong *often neglects out-group members.* The phenomenon of "in-group versus out-group" is ubiquitous in Korea. Warm, rich interpersonal relationships and caring shown among in-group members are not frequently encountered among people not bound by the "we-ness" category. Private circumstances, including special and personal connections, can lead to actions that are unfair, injust, or rude in the eyes of outsiders. Furthermore, *jeong* has the potential to lead people to protect their fellow in-group members and discriminate against outsiders.

6. Jeong *pushes away privacy*, in that connectedness in life is more important and meaningful than the preservation of privacy. *Jeong* grows on a person bit by bit, so it takes time to build and give it. It is something to be nurtured through a sustained period of rooting and bonding, which means privacy cannot help people build *jeong.* That is, privacy is an obstacle in that one should allow "interference" to build and maintain *jeong.* Westerners may fear that their personal and private lives can be easily encroached upon or interfered with by *jeong-*

bonded people; this could be a source of conflict and tension for them.

7. Jeong *is intended to be unbreakable even if one wants to break it.* Once it is built into the relationship and forms a bond, it is sticky and persistent, as reflected in the expression *"kkeunkkeunhada"* / 끈끈하다 ("sticky, gluey"), which Koreans often use to describe an aspect of their "we-ness." *Jeong* can be described as chewing gum in that it keeps stretching out when one tries to break it or bite it off. The expression *"goun jeong, miun jeong"* / 고운 정, 미운 정 (literally translated as "beautiful *jeong,* hateful *jeong*") implies that *jeong* is unbreakable even if the relationship goes through hateful and turbulent periods.

8. Jeong *is an important factor in the etiology of hwa-byeong*/ 화병 (literally translated as the "illness of anger"), a culture-bound syndrome characterized by multiple somatic and psychological symptoms, which is believed to be caused by repressed anger. If the bond that has been formed through *jeong*-building is betrayed, tremendous hurt and anger can ensue; it can become as hateful and destructive as it was previously positive and nurturing.

In sum, in spite of some negative aspects and side effects of *jeong,* Koreans would claim that *jeong*-bonded relations are highly nurturing and enhance and refine one's life. In other words, *jeong* is as important an ingredient in Korean life as kimchi is in Korean meals.

Types of Jeong

The image of *jeong* is like a pattern or picture created with small pieces of diverse, intangible materials with different colors representing various forms of interpersonal relationships. Just as a mosaic reveals an aspect of interior decoration, or of cultural and spiritual significance (in the case of a cathedral), so *jeong* represents the aesthetic pieces that reside in the Korean affect. These aesthetic pieces can be divided into the five categories described in Jong Un Hyun's *Jeong-iran mueosinga?*/ 정이란 무엇인가? (What is *Jeong?*) (2011). Jong explores *jeong* in four different interpersonal relationships: *jeong* between spouses, *jeong* between brothers, *jeong* between lovers, and *jeong* between friends. He also discusses *jeong* given to objects and places. His exploration of each type of *jeong* is well illustrated by means of classic examples, some of which will be used in this book as well, though our illustration will be different in style and language. In this book, we categorize five categories of *jeong*: (1) motherly/fatherly *jeong,* (2) *jeong* between siblings, (3) *jeong* between spouses, (4) *jeong* between friends, and (5) *jeong* between lovers.

MO-JEONG (MOTHERLY JEONG)

It is interesting that Jong (2011) does not deal with the *mo-jeong*/모정 (*jeong* given by a mother) that individuals experience from their earliest moments in the arms of their caretaker, usually a mother. As the mother's tenderness fills the heart of the baby, the latter feels good. An affectionate trust is being built without logic or reason, which exists for the rest of one's life. Babies will be exposed to a similar *jeong* as they enter into contact with their father; this feeling is termed *bu-jeong*/부정 (fatherly *jeong*). The reason why Jong does not include such paternal *jeong* in his discussions seems to lie in the assumption that parental love and affection are universal and exist in all cultures. Nevertheless, this type of *jeong* is an essential part of the mosaic of *jeong* in Korean culture; it represents a culture-specific trait in that it is often closely tied to *han* and the concept of *hyo* (filial piety). With lyrics written by Yang, Judang (1903–1977) and music by Lee, Heungryeol (1909–1980), *Eomeoni Maeum*/어머니 마음 (Mother's Heart), a 1930s song that is frequently sung on Mother's Day as well as on other special occasions, conveys a special sentiment toward the mother. Stressing that there is nothing greater under the sky than a mother's love, the first stanza tells of how a mother forgets the agony of birth, struggles to raise her children, keeps them warm and dry, and undergoes great hardship.

In Korean folklore and literature, a number of celebrated stories depict *mo-jeong,* and each illustrates a particular aspect of this concept. A frequently told story is the tale of "Han Seokbong's Mother." Han Seokbong (1543–1605) was a most respected calligrapher in the Joseon dynasty, whose success was largely due to the way in which he was raised by his mother. A well-known anecdote from this story proceeds as follows: One day, Seokbong, very homesick and feeling that he has received enough training, returns home. His mother suggests a competition between him and herself. In the dark she will slice long rice cakes, an extremely dangerous act. At the same time, Seokbong will perform calligraphy. If his written characters look better than his mother's slices of the rice cakes in terms of neatness and form, he can stay at home. If not, he must return to the training site. In the light of day, Seokbong sees that his mother's sliced rice cakes are very neatly and uniformly sliced while the characters he wrote are crooked and sloppy. He goes back to continue his studies, only to become one of the greatest calligraphers in Korean history after years of training.[9]

Jeong between Siblings

Siblings grow up together and spend a good deal of their childhood socializing with one another. This genetic and physical closeness may be marked by the development of strong emotional bonds such as love. Yet the emotional bond between siblings is often complicated and is influenced by such factors as parental treatment, birth order, personality, and personal experiences outside the family. Generally speaking, in early childhood, siblings are constant companions and playmates. During adolescence and in adulthood, ties between once-close siblings may temporarily weaken as they exert their individuality and independence. However, in traditional Korean culture, siblings have been expected to continue to share their struggles and triumphs with each other. There are a number of stories depicting this solid bonding.

A folk tale titled *"Hyeongje tugeum"* / 형제 투금 (Brothers' Thrown Gold) tells of two brothers who throw away gold to maintain their fraternal love (Choi Sangsoo, 1957; Jong Un Hyun, 2011). In this story, the brothers find two pieces of gold on a road. While they are crossing a river, the younger brother throws his gold piece into the water. When his brother asks why, he replies that he has always loved his brother, yet he had begun to have an antagonistic feeling toward him upon finding the gold piece. Therefore, he thought that the gold was not a good omen and felt it best to throw it away so as to keep loving his brother. Having heard his young brother's explanation, the older brother also throws his gold piece away.

A painting titled *"Hyeongje geubnando"* / 형제 급난도 (Painting of Brothers Facing Danger), set in the year following the Japanese invasion of Korea in 1592, depicts an elder brother who has saved his own life and that of his younger brother, who had been badly wounded by a Japanese (Jong Un Hyun, 2011). The painting features four tableaus: the older brother carrying the younger on his back as the enemy approaches; the shooting of an arrow at the enemy; the brothers running to the mountains after repulsing the enemy; and the older brother consoling the younger brother atop the mountain. The painting is accompanied by the words of famous writers of the period. Owned by Lee Mancheol, it is registered as a cultural artifact (#217) of the State of Gyeongbuk in South Korea (*Wolgan changseok hyeongje geubnando*).

Jeong between Spouses

Westerners may wonder to what extent traditional Korean couples love each other, given that they do not seem to express their affection verbally. This absence of verbal expression, in fact, was even encouraged centuries ago when couples lived with their parents. Nevertheless, their love for each other is not any less than that of couples of other cultures, as is illustrated in numerous proverbs. In traditional society, women had many constraints and difficulties imposed upon them by men, yet they appreciated their husbands, as indicated in such sayings as "Just as (I) like pickle juice even if it is old, so (I) like my husband even if he is old." Furthermore, they feel that support from their husband is better than that of their children, as expressed in the saying "Eat meals provided by a husband comfortably lying down; eat meals provided by a son sitting down; eat meals provided by a daughter standing." Interestingly enough, similar appreciative feelings toward a wife are implied in husband-oriented sayings: "A bad wife is better than 10 devoted sons," "Wives and shoes are better when old," and "A man can forget the enemy who killed his father, but cannot forget the enemy who killed his wife." That is, husbands perceive wives as comforting and easy to get along with once one has had them for some time. Thus, one would state, "One who abandons his good old wife will fail in everything."[10]

As it was a traditional norm for women to serve their husbands well, the appreciation on the part of husbands for the loving care proffered by their wives has been expressed after the latter have died or while the former were in political exile. For instance, Kim Jeong Hee (1786–1856), who was widely known for his calligraphy and painting, wrote poems in honor of his wife, who had to take care of all family-related affairs in his place when he was in exile. A number of poets, such as Lee Dal (1561–1618) and Lee Seo-U (1633–1709), composed *"Domangsi"* / 도망시 (poem mourning for a wife) to describe their great appreciation, regret, and love beyond death; this poem evokes the beauty of serene testimony.

In 1998, a letter written in 1586 by the wife of Lee Eung-Tae (1555–1586) in memory of the love of her husband, was found while his remains were being exhumed to be reburied at a new site (Jong Un Hyun, 2011). She had put the letter in his tomb together with sandals that she had corded herself with hemp and her own hair so that her husband could wear them while transiting to the next world. The letter and other related materials have been placed in the museum of Andong University (Guinam An, 1998).

JEONG BETWEEN FRIENDS (*U-jeong* / 우정)

In the course of the emotional development of the individual, friendship comes after parental bonding and occurs simultaneously with bonding with siblings. While blood-related bonding occurs naturally, a close relationship with non-blood-related individuals is not developed effortlessly. Given that this type of friendship, which is grounded in a concern on the part of each friend for the welfare of the other and involves some degree of intimacy, seems central to our lives, it is nevertheless interesting to note that, according to a *USA Today Report,* 25 percent of Americans have no one in whom to confide (Janet Kornblum, 2006). This figure means that Americans have one-third fewer close friends and confidants than just two decades ago. According to a study by Miller McPherson, Lynn Smith-Lovin, and Matthew Brashears (2006), in 1985, the average American had three people in whom they could confide important matters. The decrease implies that people may be relying more upon immediate family. This trend seems to be indicative of the awareness that our emphasis on individual independence and freedom may have gone too far. In other words, one can argue that individualism has been overemphasized, such that each individual may exist for himself or herself without a sense of belonging and community.

In Korean culture, friendship, termed as *u-jeong* (special feelings between friends), has been highly valued. This type of *jeong* refers to a sense of fidelity and solidarity, the willingness to take care of each other under all situations. It is similar to the mutual bond of camaraderie or brotherhood developed between two soldiers who have fought together in frontline trenches and shared life and death experiences. It can also develop among classmates in high school or college, among friends who share a faith or interest, and among professional colleagues who work very closely with each other. What Westerners may find interesting here is that many Koreans would go to a *jeong*-bonded person instead of going to see a professional counselor when they have a problem. It is hard for them to open up to a mental health professional who is a stranger, without developing some degree of *jeong*-bonding trust, which will take time. In *jeong*-trust relations, they are able to talk and really open up to each other for intense sharing and understanding, as well as for mutual advice.

A large number of poems about friends and *u-jeong* describe a friendship that is deeper and longer-lasting than one between ordinary friends. In the first part of the poem "*Beos*"/ 벗 (another Korean term for "friend"), Cho, Byung-hwa (1921– 2003), a very prolific, and popular poet, describes a friend as a lamplight, a shelter for existence, an invisible journey into tomorrow, and warm tears touching the heart.

Similarly, Kim, So-wol (1902–1943), who is more popular and widely read than any other modern poet, compares in the poem "*Nim gwa Beos*"/ 님 과 벗 (Lover and Friend) a friend to a lover in a concise, yet profound way. He describes a friend as a comfort in sorrow, an obvious metaphor of the role of alcohol in the poet's life, and as a pure delight in love.

Lee, Hae-in, (1945–), a catholic nun and poet, who is well-read and well-known for her choice of simple and plain words, yet whose style is nonetheless touching, describes the kind of friend she wants to be in a poem titled "*Beos-ege*" / 벗에게 (To a Friend). For Lee, a friend is not unlike a white bellflower that one can cultivate every day with care; friends ultimately become as one in the well of the soul.

Another key example that illustrates the greatness of *u-jeong* is a poem titled "*Geu sarameul gajyeossneunga*" / 그사람을 가졌는가 (Do You Have This Person?), by Ham, Sok Hon. The poem questions whether we have a person to whom we can entrust our spouse and children, and the thought of whom will allows us to leave the world with a smile, as well as whether we can be such a person to others.

JEONG BETWEEN LOVERS (*AE-JEONG* / 애정)

When two persons are attracted to each other, they want to share their thoughts so that their minds grow and become complete. Furthermore, they aspire to come together in such a way as to balance each other like magnets of opposite poles. Their emotional bonding is often so powerful that they sacrifice their own lives. While the physical, cognitive, and emotional bonding appears to be universal, *jeong* between lovers in Korean traditional culture is characterized by its unique aspect of yearning, a persistent and strong desire often tinged with sadness because the object of desire is not within immediate reach. It is associated with various melancholic feelings: loneliness in the wake of a lover's departure, a lover's grudge, a lover's dissipated life, the desire and imagination of a lover, and a long-cherished wish for everlasting love.

The emotional bonding of this kind is well reflected in *sijo* (verses), a Korean poetic form. For example, Hwang Jini (1522–1565), a *gisaeng* (official female entertainer) who was well known for her exceptional beauty, charming quick wit, and extraordinary intellect, depicts the yearning, exquisite longing for someone, and the torment of being alone. One of her most famous verses is "*Dongjisdal ginagin bameul*" / 동짓달 기나긴 밤을 (Longest Night of Winter), which we have translated as follows: "*Were I only to grasp the core of this longest of winter nights/And gently crease it into the breath of a spring quilt/And lovingly unravel it the night my lover returns*" (Yeo, Sang-deok, 2013).

Another interesting aspect of *ae-jeong* is that even the wrench of parting becomes sublimated as a work of art, as reflected in a poem "*Zindallae*" / 진달 래 (Azalea Flowers) by Kim So-wol (1902–1934), whose work was published posthumously. The opening stanzas of the poem describe how, once love has ended, a woman makes a path of azaleas for her lover to follow as he leaves (Ko, Chang-soo, 1984, 23).

In addition to this *jeong* between adult lovers, *jeong* may exist between teenagers, being characterized by the simplicity of a pure love that defies hardship. For example, "*Sonagi*"/소나기 (Rain Shower), written by Hwang Sun-Won in 1959, is a well-known short story in which rain causes and symbolizes the short-lived but heart-rending, tragic love between boy and girl. The story begins with a boy encountering a girl playing by the stream on his way back home. The themes touched upon include nostalgia for lost innocence, the fragility of human life, the contrast between ancient rural ways and the difficulties of the modern city life, and the simplicity of true joy. What is extraordinary in this story is not only the love evinced by the boy, but also the sentiment of the girl, who has been sick. Just before she dies, she requests, "When I die, please bury me in the clothes I'm wearing now" (Chung, 1995, 19). The clothes reflect her treasured memory of the boy: a pink sweater that has a dark-brown stain from when the boy had carried her on his back when a ditch proved to be too wide for her to jump across. One may argue that this tale should be considered as an example of *u-jeong* (*jeong* between friends), as described earlier. However, we have opted to consider it from the perspective of *ae-jeong,* in light of the girl's final request.

To close the discussion of *jeong,* we can make an analogy similar to what we did with *han,* that of a photo montage. In the case of *jeong,* we use two images: *air* and *mosaic. Jeong* is like air; we cannot see it, but we perceive, feel, and sense it, and we cannot live without it. Furthermore, no one would argue that air is not a common denominator of the existence of human beings in that it is a prerequisite for life. Likewise, *jeong* is not visible or tangible, yet in Korean culture one can hardly live without it. No Korean would contest the statement that *jeong* is a common denominator of Korean life. In this analogy, a question arises inasmuch as air is made of various gases such as nitrogen, oxygen, argon, and carbon dioxide: what is *jeong* made of?

To answer this question, we borrow once again the image of a mosaic, the art of creating images through the assemblage of small pieces of colored glass, stone, or other materials. This mosaic image can be repictured in terms of a tree, which has many branches. Each branch shares most of semantic features that we mentioned previously, yet each is distinct in terms of persons involved in it.

Deok/덕 and Other Associated Cultural Words

As stated earlier, the concept of *deok* may be the most challenging and elusive for non–Koreans, especially Westerners, to understand because it is closely associated with many other cultural concepts such as *chung, hyo, che-myeon, ye,* and *cheol* that Chapter 1 briefly introduced. Given that these concepts are critical for understanding Korean culture, and that they are associated with *deok,* we will first discuss *chung* and *hyo,* then subsequently turn to *chemyeon* and *ye,* and finally explore *deok* along with *cheol.*

Chung/충 *and* Hyo/효 *(Loyalty and Filial Piety)*

Moral Goodness and Obligation for Social Order. We associated the "safety needs" of Maslow's model with moral goodness in Korean culture.[11] Traditionally, the two Korean cultural terms that have been crucial for understanding the importance of moral goodness are *chung,* roughly translated as loyalty to sovereign/country, and *hyo,* translated as filial piety to parents.[12] Both terms have been considered highly important moral values that have guided the minds and spirits of the Korean people. Both could be compared to the faces of a coin: they cannot be thought of separately, in that societal filial piety embraces individual filial piety, and individual filial piety in turn leads to societal/national filial piety.

The nature of goodness is based on the love, bonding and affection that begins at the earliest stages of a person's development, in the form of parental love. In traditional Korean culture, the moral values of *hyo* are such that they must never be sacrificed for any other value; they are incomparably higher and should absolutely be the first to be sought after. *Hyo* is not just something good to strive toward; rather, it touches a person's very being.

Furthermore, the moral values of *hyo* imply a new type of "must," a feeling of the obligation to do right for or be good to others. Parents give their children the ultimate gift of life, which in turn offers people the opportunity to live in the world. In a more general sense, the elders of society and all those who have come and gone before us provide us with the history, culture, and tradition that define the world in which we live. Therefore, *hyo* is an expansive concept with a matching range of obligations; subsequently, *chung* arises not from blind obedience to the dictates of decorum, but rather as a profound and heartfelt sense of gratitude, honor, and respect for the society or group to which one belongs. In other words, given that the virtue of *hyo* is respect and gratitude toward our parents who brought us into the world and raised us, it is believed that devotion to one's county is, in fact, a way of fulfilling one's true filial duty. *Hyo* is the basis on which people love their family, society, and the person who leads the nation. From this view, *hyo* is a generator of *chung,* and *chung* is viewed as a broad expression of *hyo* in traditional culture.

From the perspective of Maslow's safety needs, we can argue that *chung* and *hyo* meet these needs by bringing good social order. During the Korean dynasties, chung was not a concept that was imposed upon the lower classes by the aristocracy as means of coercing them into obedience, but rather a practice that out of necessity began with the leaders of society. *Chung* was a belief that was held to be as important for the upper classes as for the lower classes. This spirit of compassion can eradicate the sufferings of the nation and allow the people to enjoy a life of peace and happiness. Similarly, *hyo* is not imposed by parents; it is the act of repaying the love and grace of another person. This implies that the love for parents is so precious that one lives one's own life repaying that love with gratitude and devotion. Filial devotion to parents is learned by children and, in turn, is handed down by them to their own children. Thus, we can consider that the moral goodness and obligations for social order that are exhibited in *chung* and *hyo* meet the safety need that Maslow discusses.

However, one can put forth a counter-argument in terms of safety needs. The concepts of *chung* and *hyo* are rooted in moral principles that exist irrespective of laws or agreements. These principles simply emerge as the result of an intuitive moral sense, yet they are at the very core of ethics. When the principles of *chung* and *hyo* are in conflict with duties imposed by laws, ethical persons are expected to honor the moral principles, even if it means being prosecuted. Thus, the safety need implied in *chung* and *hyo* should be understood as "inner peace," especially when individuals strive to be loyal despite difficulties present in their environment. Inner peace is connected to the belief that one's *chung* and *hyo* will lead one to focus on what one is blessed with to handle the bumps along the way as much as humanly possible. Let's examine each concept further in historical contexts.

CHUNG (LOYALTY)

Chung in Traditional Society. *Chung* implies power distance in that the less powerful members in the society, the organization, or the group accept that power is distributed unequally. Although this hierarchical relationship seems undesirable, it provides the basis for group cohesion; in a vertical relationship, the more powerful person does a favor for the less powerful person, with the result that the person for whom the favor is done owes a debt to the generous superior. In the vertical relationship, the favor is expected to be accepted with gratitude, since it is evidence of the giver's benevolence or generosity.

Traditional Korean ethics had its genesis in Confucianism; hence, such concepts as *chung* and *hyo* have counterparts in Chinese culture. To make *chung* acceptable to the Koreans, the Confucians who dominated the Joseon Court equated group consciousness with morality and made it the law of the land. Between 1400 and 1900, the concept of group consciousness became so deeply embedded in the psyche of Korean ethos that it is still visible today— over 100 years after it was discarded as the "official morality" during the last years of the Joseon dynasty. One of the outgrowths of this Confucian influence was the emotional and intellectual homogenization of Korean culture to the point that *chung,* or "group consciousness," virtually replaced individual awareness.

Loyalty in the traditional Korean sense was (and often still is) quite different from what the word means to Westerners. Broadly speaking, loyalty in the Western sense is an ethical position based on an unchanging principle, whereas loyalty in the traditional Korean sense can be described as "situational ethics." In other words, what is ethical today may not be ethical tomorrow if the situation changes. Yet, *chung* causes people expected to remain loyal to the person, the party, or the society in which they are initially engaged.

A most exemplary person who incarnated "loyalty" was Jeong Mong-ju (1337–1392), whose scholarly work earned him great respect in the Goryeo dynasty (918–1392), and who held an important government position engaging various national projects. His death symbolized his faithful allegiance to the king and the Goryeo dynasty, the predecessor of the Joseon dynasty (Lee, 1987). Late in the 14th century, the family of Yi Seong-gye, who became the first ruler of the Joseon dynasty, and his followers were maneuvering for their takeover of the Korean state. However, they were frustrated by Jeong Mong-ju's refusal to modify his allegiance to the Goryeo state. One evening at a gathering, Yi Bang-won, one of the sons of Yi Seong-gye, approached Jeong Mong-ju with a poem that suggested his adoption of a more flexible way of responding to the changes then taking place in the state. Jeong Mong-ju replied with his own poem, which we have translated as follows: "*Although I may die one-hundred fold/ Although my body will turn to ashes, and whether or not my spirit exits become dust/ if my soul endures/ Can anything alter the steadfast devotion/ that radiates to the one I serve most dearly.*" This poem, in which Jeong emphasizes that his loyalty to the Goryeo dynasty would never change, is frequently cited. As Koo and Nahm (1997) note, it is very famous in the history of Korean literature, "perhaps more for the nature of the event which it captures than its actual literary merit" (437).

Another famous story focusing on *chung* focuses on Admiral Yi Sun-sin (1545–1598), who was famous for his victories against the Japanese navy in the Imjin War during the Joseon dynasty (Chang, *Hak-Geun*, 2002). He was well respected for his exemplary conduct on and off the battlefield. Despite never having received naval training or having participated in naval combat prior to the war, and despite being constantly outnumbered and under-supplied, he became one of the few admirals in world history who remained undefeated after many battles. However, his brilliance and accomplishments so soon in his career made his superiors jealous, and they falsely accused him of desertion during battle. Yi was stripped of his official rank, imprisoned, and tortured. After his release, he was allowed to fight as an unlisted soldier, an *baekui jonggun* / 백의종군 (literally meaning "soldier serving in a white robe," denoting a soldier serving in a war as a commoner). After a short period of time, Yi was reappointed as the commander of the navy of three provinces. He died, mortally wounded by a single bullet during the Battle of Noryang in 1598, when the Japanese army was on the verge of being completely expelled from the Korean peninsula. The royal court bestowed various honors upon him, including a posthumous title of "*chung-mu-gong*" / 충무공 (Duke of Loy-alty and Warfare).

Another historical period during which *chung* was particularly distinctive was during Japanese colonial rule (1910–1945), a time of numerous uprisings. A large number of edification movement leaders (e.g., An Chang-ho), military leaders (e.g., An Jung-geun), and poets (e.g., Yoon Dong-ju) provided great examples of *chung* to the nation (Nahm, 1973). In addition, some religious and student leaders showed their *chung* to the nation in an extraordinary man-ner. For example, Yu Gwan-sun (1904–1920), a high school student who was a key organizer of the March 1 demonstration in 1919, has been considered a great heroine; on that day, hundreds of thousands of Koreans joined in demon-strations to declare Korea's natural right for independence, and tens of thou-sands people were arrested.[13] This nonviolent peaceful movement is a highly significant marker in modern Korean history. As Michael Edson Robinson (1988) writes, "Korean nationalism had become a mass phenomenon, no longer the monopoly of Westernized intellectual elites" (3).

Chung in Modern Society. Traditionally, the concept of *chung* was applied to a country, a military, a political group, and its designated leader. In modern and contemporary society, it has been extended to the company for which people work. A variation on the term would be "conformity." Today, joining a large and traditional company is like being initiated into a flock of prestigious people, where conformity in both attitude and behavior are the guiding principles. It is a moral imperative to conform, follow principles, and perform one's duties toward other members of the organization. Conformity is extrapolated to include the concept of absolute integrity, loyalty and the highest standard of Confucian morality, with the goal being to maintain perfect social harmony. A person who violates the moral obligations will be labeled as lacking integrity or honor. Traditionally, Korean employees have rarely changed the company where they began their career; this lifetime devotion to a company, however, has begun to change in the 21st century.

Hyo (Filial Piety to Parent)

***Hyo* in Traditional Society.** *Hyo* has been an inseparable part of traditional Korean society. One can deem it more important than *chung,* considering that it continues to be strongly encouraged and exercised, although its forms have been changed since the era of Korean modernization. Two interrelated Korean proverbs illustrate the high degree of importance of *hyo:* "There are numerous kinds of virtuous deeds; the root of all is filial piety" and "There are numerous kinds of sinful deeds; the root of all is filial impiety." Since parents bring us into this world and raise us, being grateful to them and serving them well is the most basic of all human virtues. Generally speaking, *hyo* suggests five rules for life: show the utmost respect to one's parents; always take care of one's body, which is their heritance to oneself; contribute well to society so as to make your parents' name proud; offer sacrifices to parents; and maintain your devotion through ceremonies and rituals when parents die.

Many would argue that, given that morality originates from one's family and that order within the family is directly connected to that of the nation, filial piety is recognized as the foremost principle for maintaining the Korean nation. This idea has been taught to children and youth as part of moral education. It has been emphasized as the single most important virtue for an individual, given that the nation can be peaceful only when families are well managed through cultivation of their morals.

Non-Koreans believe that the concept of filial piety lies at the heart of Confucianism and neo–Confucianism; in this sense, it was especially salient in traditional Chinese culture. Nonetheless, Clark Sorensen (1990, 4) observes that Koreans do not see filial piety "as a foreign import but rather as a part of a vital, pan–Asian tradition which ancient Koreans had a role in forming."[14] In fact, filial piety was stressed from one dynasty to the other, from the Silla kingdom all the way to the Joseon dynasty. Even today, it is the most repeatedly taught ethical concept during childhood (and even adulthood).

A striking example of viewing *hyo* as a native Korean concept can be found in *Sesokogye*/세속오계 (Five Commandments for Laymen), the precepts that Wongan, a Buddhist monk of the Silla dynasty (57 B.C.–A.D. 935) taught to the Hwarang (meaning "the flower of youth"), a unique social group active at the time. Through communal life and rite, the Hwarang learned the traditional values of society; through military arts, poetry, and music, they attained mutual understanding and friendship, and appreciated the beauty of order and harmony (Lee and de Bary, 1997, 54–56). The five secular injunctions/ principles that the Hwarang were obliged to follow were loyalty to the sovereign, filial piety to parents, loyalty to one's friends, fighting in battle without retreating, and killing only when necessary. They were groomed to show a single-minded filial piety to their parents and loyalty to the country.

The high degree of importance ascribed to filial piety continued to be deeply rooted in Korean culture in that this virtue was deemed imperative for the centralization of power. For instance, King Seongjong, the sixth emperor of the Goryeo dynasty (918–1392), showed how politically significant filial piety was. Jae-Eun Kang (2006, 99) writes, "The intention of the king was to make royal vassals by commending the filial among common people." The principle of national unity thus implies both a harmonious home and service to the state, and the key relationship was between vassal and king, in accordance with Confucian virtue.

The Joseon dynasty was also marked by filial piety. Scholars and politicians accepted one of the basic assumptions of Confucian political theory— that a good state automatically results if individuals scrupulously cultivate the garden of their own family duties, and that filial piety will be the foundation for building stable families. Books on filial piety were ordered and were widely spread throughout the country, making it the essential basis for the maintenance of order. Examples of the best filial sons and daughters were praised, and villages made a point of commemorating those who showed exemplary filial piety by building monuments. Many filial sons, daughters and daughter-in-laws whose names and filial acts were recorded in *Joseon Wangjo Sillok* (True Records of the Joseon Dynasty).[15]

In addition to the institutionalization of filial piety throughout Korean history, many touching stories about filial piety quickly spread out throughout the country. Though its origin remains unknown, "The Tale of Simcheong" is the most popular story of filial piety in Korea; it focuses on a girl named Simcheong, who serves her blind father Sim with utmost devotion.[16] It is told as a story (Chung Chong-hwa, 1989, 114–115) as well as sung as a *pansori* (oral narratives performed by professional singers, woven to fit the emotions, sentiments and sensibility of Korean people) (Daeseok Seo and Peter Lee, 2005, 299–320).

***Hyo* in Modern Society.** In the traditional view of *hyo*, children owe a debt to their parents inasmuch as the latter have conceived and raised them. Paying back the parents' benevolence—what the parents have done for their children—is commonly expected. That is, children have the obligation to support their parents, especially when they are old; by the same token, parents have the right to ask their children for support of various kinds. Even if parents are fine financially and do not request much assistance, they commonly expect that their children will offer some allowance and/or buy things for them.

However, as society changes, the ways of doing *hyo* differ from family to family. *Hyo* can simply imply being good to parents by showing love and respect and by not being rebellious; engaging in good conduct not just toward parents but also outside of the home so as to bring a good name to the parents and ancestors; getting good grades and going to a prestigious university; getting employed by a prestigious company or organization; performing one's job well so as to obtain the material means to support one's parents; ensuring male heirs; celebrating and commemorating significant days; paying for special sightseeing trips arranged by travel agencies, called *hyodo gwangwang*/효도 관광 (sightseeing based on filial piety), a popular gift to aging parents; showing sorrow for their sickness and taking good care of them; and displaying profound grief upon their death.

While ways of performing *hyo* may have changed as society changes, *jesa*/ 제사 (ancestral rites of homage paid to parents and grandparents on the eve of the anniversary of their death) remains an important Korean custom.[17] Given the Korean ethos that the relationship between the dead and the living is not cut off and that the ancestors will continue to take care of their living children and grandchildren, descendants perform filial duties by means of *jesa* as well as in their own respective ways. *Hyo* is thereby frequently linked to *han* (all kinds of emotional burdens), in that *han* can be released by one's descendants if it was not released in one's lifetime. This idea endorses the importance of the ritual ceremony of the *jesa* even in this rapidly changing society.

Chemyeon/체면 *and* Ye/예 *(Face and Social Appropriateness)*

All human beings want to feel good about themselves and strive to find "esteem" (Maslow's fourth category of need) both "internally," by judging themselves and deeming themselves worthy by their own criteria and "externally," by engaging themselves so as to gain recognition through activities that provide a sense of contribution, thereby judging themselves by what others think of them. In Chapter 1, we linked this notion of esteem to the concept of "face" (Brown and Levinson, 1987; Goffman, 1967), and to the very characteristically Korean brand of face called *chemyeon*. That is, whereas "face" is known to be a universal social–psychological concept, the ways it is conceptualized vary considerably across cultures. For instance, "face" as manifested in U.S./individualist culture refers to the positive social value that a person claims for himself or herself during a particular contact. In contrast, in Korean culture, *chemyeon* (face) is a socially prescribed concept; it is oriented toward class, society, and position. It often entails opinions, views, and perceptions of others, rather than just those of conversational partners. That is, face is not individually negotiable; it is mostly considered as a pass–fail binary. Therefore, its loss often makes it hard for the person involved to function properly within the group/community. This social-prestige image of "esteem" carries with it much emotional attachment. A further investigation of the concept of *chemyeon* reveals that it has two contrasting sides: a prestigious aspect and a valueless aspect.

Two Contrasting Aspects of *Chemyeon*

The Prestigious Aspect of *Chemyeon*. The concept of *chemyeon* reflects social stratification. It is especially associated with the upper class, called *yangban*/양반, and less so with the two other classes, *seomin*/서민 (middle class) and *cheonmin*/천민 (lower class). Although many traditional societies demonstrate such a three-tiered class system, the characteristics of each class, especially the *yangban*, are culturally very distinctive.

During the Silla dynasty, the social system had followed the *aristocracy of blue blood* (Bok Jin Han et al., 2002, 241). The term *yangban*, referring to the upper/ruling class composed of scholar-bureaucrats (called *munban*/문반) and high-ranking military officers (called *muban*/무반), took root in the bureaucratic hierarchy of the Goryeo dynasty, which allowed more flexibility in the employment of bureaucrats, so as to take in influential regional families. The *yangban* system entered into full swing in the late Joseon dynasty, a time in which *yangbans* who passed the civil service examination dominated the society (Koo and Nahm, 1997, 277) by powerfully exerting their weight in all important areas including politics and the economy.

The concept of the *yangban* was extended not only to bureaucrats, but also to their families and relatives, due to the special importance placed on blood ties. One cultural trait of the *yanban* class was the establishment of *gahun*/가훈 (house rules) to reinforce the cultivation of the moral potential of the individual as well as of his family and relatives. House rules were aimed at making the relationships within a kin group smooth and spreading an educational influence even into the domestic sphere of the house in a humanizing way. They represent an idealized code of conduct based on the assumption that people have to be constantly encouraged to seek moral perfection. It was rationalized and hoped that, if the principal members of the family were to observe and follow the rules of proper conduct, even the domestic servants could be persuaded to lead moral lives. An illustrative example of the house rules was prepared by Sin Sukchu (1417–1475), a scholar and politician of the Joseon dynasty; it contains the essence of moral capabilities. These rules include "Making the Mind Discerning," "Being Circumspect in Behavior," "Being Studious," "Managing a Household," "Holding Office," and "Instructing Women" (Lee and de Bary 1997, 323–326).

Rules of this kind were an impeccable means to protect the great social prestige and image associated with *chemyeon*. Furthermore, the concept of *yangban*-related *chemyeon* became associated with hierarchical rank. A higher form of *chemyeon* is given to a person of a higher rank; it is additionally expected that a higher form of *chemyeon* is shown in a public situation than in a private situation. A loss of *chemyeon* in a lower-ranked person is not critical for the *chemyeon* of a person of a higher rank, but the reverse is never true. This is in stark contrast with the notion of "esteem" in individualistic cultures, which one is expected to give/show regardless of one's social position.

The Valueless Aspect of *Chemyeon*. While *yangban* were expected to care a great deal about their behavior and follow strict rules in consideration of their responsibilities, they exploited many privileges, including the confiscation of a portion of the harvest from their land tenants, their exemption from labor for the government, their exercising of relatively light duties, and the receipt of minimal punishment for any criminal acts. This dishonorable aspect of a *yanban*'s life was severely criticized by scholars of *silhak* (practical learning) from the early 17th century. Shocked at the living conditions of their poor fellow men and women, which stood in sharp contrast to the empty ideas and talk of the authorities, these scholars indicted the theoretical arguments of Confucian scholars and advocated political, economic, and social reform. A noted scholar of *silhak* was Yi Ik (1681–1763), who combined the depth of Chinese scholarship and Western science and religion at a very high level of research in a treatise titled "Discourse and Concerns for the Underprivileged" (Yi Ik, *Jangseokgak Royal Digital Archives*).

Some great writers also decried the societal ills of the time and promoted urgent reform. For instance, Park Ji-won (1737–1805), a prominent scholar, thinker, and novelist, drew upon the satirical genre, replete with humor and irony, to awaken the public. One of his famous stories is "*Yangban Jeon*" (The Tale of *Yangban*) (Chung, 1989, 38–42; Kim and Park, 2011). It tells the story of a local rich man who buys the title *yangban* from a much-admired *yangban,* after the latter becomes indebted to the government. The town magistrate accepts the transaction with regret. The magistrate, however, insists on drawing up a deed that will clearly state the specified privileges and obligations of a *yangban.* Upon hearing all the restrictions and inconveniences, the rich man comes to the conclusion that he has bought a useless title, refuses the deed, and never again utters the word *yangban.*

Another story by of Park Ji-won that illustrates the empty aspect of *chemyon* is "*Heosaeng Jeon*" (The Tale of Heosaeng) (Chung, 1989, 27–37; Kim and Park, 2011). It tells of a devoted scholar and *yangban* whose name is Heosaeng. After seven years of poverty, and following his wife's accusation that he has studied impractical, old classics that have no impact in the real world, Heosaeng breaks with his studies and decides to do something useful. He borrows money from a local rich man with his good name and *yangban* status as collateral. He then moves to a town, a trading center for agricultural goods. After five years of prosperity, Heosaeng decides to return home, and divides the bulk of his money among the people whom he had moved to an uninhabited island to cultivate it. One day, a high official hears of Heosaeng's exploits and pays a visit to hear his views on how to make the country strong and prosperous. Heosaeng makes several audacious suggestions. However, the official finds all his ideas hard to implement in the Korea of that time. Upon hearing the response, Heosaeng perceives that the country is not ready for true scholars with grand ideas, and he disappears.

CHEMYEON-ASSOCIATED BEHAVIOR: *YE* (SOCIAL APPROPRIATENESS)

Chemyeon is stipulated by social standard and applied consistently to relationships and different situations. That is, people are expected to treat each other in accordance with the distinctions set out in this hierarchy/stratification by displaying the "appropriate social behavior," which Koreans call *ye,* marginally translated as "courtesy, good manners, proprieties, etiquette, decorum." Notably, Korea has been known as "the country of courteous people in the East" (Luke Kim, 2010, 23; Nung Jai Park, 2008, 133). Although this sobriquet refers to the fact that Korea has not invaded any countries, it is also used to indicate the importance of *ye* (social appropriateness) during interactions. That is, it is critical to show *ye* to maintain good relationships. Most bad feelings come directly from ignoring *chemyeon*-associated *ye.*

Chemyeon can be given and maintained by saying the right things at the right time in a right manner on a special day and in daily life. An example of

such special-day behavior is *sebae*/ 세배 or "the beginning of the year bow"—
courtesy calls on those whom people deem important, during which they bow
and ask for their continued support during the new year. In daily verbal interaction, interlocutors are expected to use appropriate honorific forms of address
and appropriate honorific particles, which reflect the relationship of the persons involved. They are expected to avoid comments or behavior that would
hurt the other person's feelings or harm their "social face." They can show
appreciation and give compliments, but must deny compliments when received
so as to display modesty; that is, one simultaneously raises others and lowers
oneself. Nonverbal *ye* includes bowing at the right time and in the right manner, offering the best seat, starting eating at the right time, and so on. It also
involves giving/receiving the right objects or suitable amounts of money at
the appropriate time and place for special occasions, such as birthdays, anniver-
saries, weddings, and funerals.

CHEMYEON IN MODERN SOCIETY

One might argue that in modern society, the class of *yangban*-nobility
cannot function properly and that its identification criteria become very subjective and variable. It has been observed that a large range of professionals
(e.g., bureaucrats, professors, lawyers, medical doctors, movie stars, TV per-
sonalities, business executives) and people of wealth consider themselves the
so-called upper class and enjoy the precious cultural vestiges left by the *yangban,* who were the erstwhile leaders of society. From this perspective, as some
scholars note, *yangban* has become a cultural rather than a legal concept.

Furthermore, although many liberal Koreans may want to reject the concept of *yangban* given that it is hierarchical in nature, the term *yangban* is used
in daily life to describe someone very positively and favorably by saying
"He/she/they is/are *yangban*." It is also used as an honorific reference term,
as in "My boss is a busy *yangban*." One likewise hears "*uri jib yangban*"/ 우리
집 양반, which means "my husband." Yet another common expression is "He
cannot be a *yangban*," which is used in a situation in which a person arrives
just when he or she is being spoken about; this usage is somewhat similar to
the English expression "Speak of the devil."

We must stress that the concept of *chemyeon* has a hierarchy-oriented
semantic component. Its concept is applied to all types of social parameters,
including age, gender, family and social roles, and seniority of all kinds, and
one is expected to show, give, and maintain appropriate *chemyeon* according
to his or her own status and the situation in which he or she is in. We often
hear Koreans say, especially when *chemyeon* is about to be damaged, "As an *X*,

chemyeon an seoji" (meaning "As an *X, chemyeon* is lost"). The *X* could be an elderly person, a man, a father, a boss, a senior, and so forth; the *X* is always a person with a higher rank in age, gender, or profession vis-à-vis the interlocutor or the addressee. One would not say, "As a young person, *chemyeon* is lost."

Deok/덕

Deok and **Cheol.** *Deok* is a most challenging, yet embracive term covering various important points in life. It embeds a dynamic moral force that one may acquire through cultivation, inasmuch as it is associated with an orientation toward self, others, and the community/world. This concept refers to a need for human beings to look outward toward the challenges and opportunities of being a person dwelling in a community or world of ongoing social transformation. It frames a way of life that is responsive rather than merely reactive to events. It is a way of life in which persons are participants in various changes rather than passive spectators or targets of such change. That is, one would need to maximize one's abilities and determine the path of one's life, which appears to be parallel with the concept of "self-actualization," the fifth and final category that Maslow discusses in terms of basic human needs.

As we have already mentioned, the concept of *deok* differs from "self-actu-alization" in some ways, even though reaching self-actualization and finding self-fulfillment are highly desirable and respected across cultures. One of the major distinctions lies in the question as to whether there is an end-product of actu-alization. This question leads to the concept of *cheol* (roughly meaning "discre-tion," "wisdom," or "good sense"), which is closely related to the concept of *deok*.

Cheol is "whole-person oriented," in that it requires "mindfulness for the difficulties" that lie ahead, which could be beyond and/or irrelevant to one's aptitude, and thus hard to measure. It is a native Korean word, used colloquially and applied to all ages. One says to a child who seems very mature, "She's got *cheol* already." Similarly, one says to an adult who seems silly, "*Ije jom cheol-deuleoyaji; nai gab haera*"/이제 좀 철-들어야지; 나이값 해라 ("You ought to get *cheol*; you should know better; act your age"). In other words, one is supposed to have *cheol* with age, as life's fruit gets ripe with time. Lee Eo-ryeong (2002) cites a passage from *MoMo* by Michael Ende (1985) to illustrate the meaning of *cheol*: "We need eyes to see light, ears to hear sound, but what do we need to feel time? That is heart. If we can't feel time because of absence of heart, we can consider that time does not exist" (our translation from Lee, 2002, 12). In this passage, Lee underlines the key question and answers exactly what the concept of *cheol* implies.

Cheol, which deals with time, through heart leads to another closely related concept—namely, *deok* (marginally translated as "virtue, moral goodness, moral excellence, kindness, mercy"). Although these terms share some similarities, there are differences in meaning. Both are desirable traits that one wants as time goes by. Yet, while all adults are supposed to have *cheol* after a certain age, not every adult is expected to have *deok.* While the word *cheol* is an informal term used casually in daily life, the word *deok* is formal and is used less frequently, as it carries much more weight and displays an important normative value. Whereas *cheol* is something that is expected to be acquired naturally in normal upbringings and circumstances, *deok* is something that is cultivated throughout one's life.

Characteristics of a Person with *Deok*

It is significant to note that *deok* is associated with, to a large extent, all of the other concepts discussed in this chapter. Although building *deok* is a lifetime undertaking, let us describe a person with a high degree of *deok* to further explain this concept.

- A person with *deok* sees himself or herself as a son/daughter, brother/sister, husband/wife, or father/mother, but rarely as an individual.
- A person with *deok* is a responsible self, fulfilling one's own duties; he or she is aware of his or her position in family, society and the world; is sensitive to his or her position as above, below, or equal to others; and thus performs said duties accordingly.
- A person with *deok* sees the self as involving multiple layers of relationships supported by cultural values, such as filial piety and loyalty as well as dignity and integrity.
- *Deok* places more stress on one's inner goodness than on one's great achievements or visible outcomes.
- The skills of a person with *deok* are developed in such a way that its fruits and outcomes are beautiful and meaningful to others.
- The cultivation of *deok* is closely connected to the self's orientation to others' needs, wishes, and expectations; in other words, from the perspective of *deok,* skill/talent/great mind–related outcomes become beautiful and meaningful only if they serve others rather than one's own needs.

Just as Maslow places "self-actualization" at the final level of his hierarchy of basic human needs, so we locate *deok* as the last of our key cultural words, since its semantic features include all kinds of virtues, including the aforementioned *jeong, chung, hyo,* and *ye.* In light of its various qualities, its meaning denotes one's "cultivation" rather than one's achievement. In other words, while self-actualization is closely related to one's aptitude (what an individual is born to do and its realization in society), *deok* is something that people hope and are encouraged to cultivate, and practice by doing good regardless of their innate abilities or their potential until the last minute of their life.

PEOPLE WITH A HIGH DEGREE OF *DEOK* IN TRADITIONAL SOCIETY

Although *deok* is very discreet and not something to be pompous about, there are a large number of great people with a high degree of *deok* of whom society is very proud. Traditionally, a person with a high degree of *deok* is called a *gunja/군자,* which originally meant "royal son"' but whose extended meaning refers to a "person of virtue"—a person with wisdom, courage, and understanding of natural laws and a deep appreciation of humanity, a person who is exemplary to all. It is by and large agreed that Great King Sejong of the Joseon dynasty is a great example of a *gunja.*

King Sejong (1397–1450), a scholar, philologist, musician, poet, and skilled swordsman, is the only Korean king to have been given the title "Great"; thus Koreans call him *Sejong Dae Wang/ 세종대왕* (meaning "Sejong Great King"). His name is known throughout Korea, not simply due to the great scientific achievements in agriculture, medicine, and astronomy that took place during his reign, but more importantly because of his great wisdom and the remarkable care and attention he extended to everyone in his kingdom. He established the notion of People of Heaven, and revered everyone as being divine. His goal was to "share in the joys of living with the People of Heaven." When his people were hungry, King Sejong starved with them and offered prayers to heaven. He also considered the rights of prisoners and ensured that their living conditions were proper. Furthermore, believing that people have limitless potential, he felt that the duty of a king is to look after them and help them transform themselves and realize their potential at a higher level. His strength of character and remarkable intellect were combined with genuine humility. King Sejong always attributed the way he was or would be to what he had learned from his family, friends, and teachers. Even with respect to his training with the sword, he stood ready to defend his lineage, family, friends, and blessed country (Diamond Sutra, 2008).

One of King Sejong's most outstanding achievements was the creation of the Korean alphabet, *Hangeul* (Young-Key Kim-Renaud, 1997). He thought that Chinese characters were incapable of capturing uniquely Korean meanings. Therefore, many common people had no way to express their thoughts and feelings. Out of his sympathy for their difficulties, he commissioned a group of scholars to devise a phonetic writing system that would represent correctly the sounds of spoken Korean—an alphabet that could be learned easily by all his people, including commoners. Previously, only the privileged people had learned classical Chinese, and borrowed Chinese script for literary purposes as well as historical records.

Traditionally, *gunja* refers to a man rather than to a woman. Nevertheless, there are a large number of women with *deok* who have been highly praised in Korean history. Sin Saimdang (1504–1551) of the Joseon dynasty, an accomplished painter, calligrapher, and poet, is most exemplary (Kang, 1987). She has been commonly known as "*Eojin Eomeoni*"/ 어진 어머니 (meaning "Wise Mother") for her excellent mothering skills, having raised seven children, one of whom was Yi Yulgok, a most preeminent scholar of Korean Confucianism. As a daughter from a family without any sons, she took care of her aging parents. (In accordance with traditional Korean culture, the oldest son of the family cares for his parents, usually living in the same household with them even after marriage.) As a wife, she provided her husband with much guidance in his professional dealings. As a person whose father had invested in her good education, she felt that producing the fruit of her education was one of her filial duties. She thus painted landscapes and garden scenes, and made calligraphic-style monochrome grape vine renderings in ink.

It is important to note here that the great quality of Sin Saimdang's paintings was well recognized during her lifetime. However, she did not want to sell her work because she considered painting to be an art to cultivate her mind. Nevertheless, on one occasion, she helped a poor woman by allowing her to sell one of her paintings. In the story of this event, the woman is wearing a skirt that she has had to borrow because she does not have an outfit appropriate for the social occasion where she has met Sin Saimdong. Unfortunately, the skirt becomes stained by drops of soup as she goes in and out of the kitchen, and she is overwrought that her poverty will prevent her from replacing the garment. Sin Saimdang paints on the woman's soiled skirt, and the stains turn into bunches of grapes that appear most enticing with their fresh green leaves. Sin Saimdang suggests that the woman sell it so that she can buy a new skirt (Cho, *Young-Jin*, 2000). This anecdote illustrates well her great humanity as an artist.

A Fictional Character in Pursuit of *Deok*. The lives of both Great King Sejong and Sin Saimdang are noble examples illustrating that the building of *deok* is a lifetime undertaking. Although everyone cannot be like them, one can be inspired by them. Nevertheless, one can also easily veer off track while building *deok*, wandering around and giving up on or changing original goals. One's struggles can be endless, especially if one lives in unfavorable situations and conditions, Here, we must note that, given that King Sejong was born into a royal family and Sin Saimdang into the *yangban* class, their starting points for building *deok* do not compare with those of most people. In other words, building *deok* is much more strenuous for commoners and those who have been born into an unfortunate situation. For instance, *Hong Gildong Jeon* (The Tale of *Hong Gildong*), the first novel written in the Korean alphabet by Heo Gyun (1569–1618), a radical intellectual writer, illustrates the conflicts and wrestles of people who were born ill fated, and thus rebellious vis-à-vis society; its story (Jong-Mok Jeong , 2003) has been well read and studied among young people.

Hong Gildong Jeon tells of Hong Gildong, who is born an illegitimate child, and hence is not accepted by his father and family. He becomes a bandit leader, stealing from the rich only to give to the poor. His popularity within the peasant society soars, and many view him as a hero. Therefore, the government offers him the position of Minister of War, which he accepts. But later Hong Gildong realizes that the people still suffer. He departs for Nanjing to seek out truth. On his way, he discovers by chance the nation of Yul-do, which is oppressed by demons. He defeats the demons and is elected king. Upon hearing the news of his father's death, he hurries back to Joseon. After the three-year obligatory mourning period for a father, he returns to Yul-do, where he lives happily as a king and hero. Although the main themes of this tale are social discrimination against the lower-class people and the transformation of society into a fair world, the tale implies that building a utopia is a lifetime undertaking, which requires all features related to *deok* (e.g., skills, talents, inner goodness, diligence, filial piety, other-oriented caring mind and action). It also reveals that *deok* can be pursued by a non-*yangban,* a person like Hong Gildong. In other words, *deok* is not a virtue confined to the upper classes; anyone can pursue it in various ways.

Deok in Modern Society

Compared to traditional society, modernization is a utilitarian pursuit of material interests and desires, which inevitably has led to the loss of traditional morality. Thus, the process of modernization raises such questions as the relationship of values and virtues to culture. Its analysis examines whether, in contemporary society, traditional moral virtues have lost their vitality, and if so how these can be renewed and constitute foundations for contemporary moral life. In other words, what is the position of traditional virtues in contemporary social life? To what extent do changing values provide the additional resources needed for a global ethics?

Some people argue that the cultural terms based on traditional Korean society and illustrated through old stories do not reflect contemporary Korean culture. South Korea, a nation of technophiles, has been changing dramatically in the past four decades. Its economics, rapid high-tech development, urbanization, smaller nuclear families, and staggering profusion of mobile communication are astonishing. Young people are becoming much more independent and now demand a high degree of freedom, rejecting the way of life that their parents and grandparents followed. By taking charge of their own lives, they are becoming far more proactive.

Nevertheless, although everyone thinks that it is very hard to build *deok,* it is widely accepted that one's social status should be the result of the amount of virtue that one can demonstrate rather than that which is inherent due to one's birth. Given that today's young people are motivated and encouraged to become leaders, human rights activist Ham Seok Hon, who was selected as a national cultural figure in 2000 in South Korea, underscores the importance of the *deok* that leaders should have. Ham (2003) defines *deok* as "*jagi sokeseo jeonchereul cheheomhaneun geos*"/자기 속에서 전체를 체험하는 것 (roughly translated as "experiencing the whole public in self") (495). He stresses that leaders should have cultivated *deok* before building their capabilities and self-confidence.

In more moderate words, *deok* is regarded as more important than technical knowledge or skills. Although the term *deok* is not frequently used in daily dialogue, it is the quality that people look for first in their work-related contacts. People feel that without this quality in a relationship, it is hard to do business or collaborate with the individual involved; that is, people view *deok* as a dynamic moral force through which a harmonious relationship is developed.

Going back to the self-actualization concept identified by Maslow, we now see that it parallels *deok* in the sense that both are related to self-development. However, as we have discussed, its starting point is completely different. While self in Maslow's concept is an individual self, self from the perspective of *deok* is an other-oriented self—that is, *self* is denied for the good of others. Self-development from the perspective of *deok* does not take a shortcut. Rather, it takes "sincerity," "truthfulness," "humility," and "humanity" as essential moral virtues for the cultivation of character and as ideal traits to be inculcated. This means that an individual person's flourishing is valuable only as a means of ensuring the flourishing of society as a whole; a single person's life is, ultimately, not important or worthwhile in itself, but is valid only as a means to foster the success of the society, community, and/or group to which one belongs.

Chapter 3

Cinema, Culture
and Key Words

Why Cinema? Why Culture?

What is the relative weight of film, in comparison to written language, as a tool for an in-depth understanding of a given culture? And, by extension, how does an in-depth understanding of a culture open doors to film viewing? Written literature, indeed, provides such a vehicle. Yet a literary text allows for a great deal of divergence in readings. We are free to imagine, to envision characters and to place ourselves as we see fit based on the cultural, sociological, and historical baggage we bring to the reading experience. We are also free to skim over or skip altogether passages that displease us.

If we simply look at the brief description in Boris Pasternak's *Doctor Zhivago* of the final disappearance of Lara—itself imagined by another character, who presumes that she ultimately dies as "a nameless number on a list that afterwards got mislaid, in one of the innumerable mixed or women's concentration camps in the north" (Pasternak, 1958, 503)—we can all have different visions of the protagonist's clothing (which is not described), the configurations of the street (also not described), and the concentration camps that most readers have, one hopes, never seen (Pasternak, 1958, 503). But David Lean's 1965 film provides us with a *concrete* image of a woman walking through a Moscow street. We see her simple clothing and the starkness of the street, and note the absence of other characters. In both our reading and viewing of *Doctor Zhivago,* our own context comes to play in the diversity of our experiences. Have we come from a safe upper-middle-class background? Are we political refugees? Have we ever been to the Soviet Union? But film, unlike literature, lays something down. Although much recent film theory has dealt with multiple and negotiated readings of films, the medium at least starts with a tangible image that the viewer is forced to confront. At the very onset of the film experience, a viewer is already positioned "one step closer" to the cultural context of the film. As discussed earlier, film is a direct and immediate experience that is especially conducive to eliciting visceral and emotional reactions.

Despite the immediacy of film, something may be missing. How we answer the preceding questions will, in part, reveal how close we are to the original cultural context of the film. What we know historically and culturally about the Soviet Union's early decades, for instance, will determine how we read Lean's film. An understanding of the cultural concept of "Mother Russia," as envisioned by Pasternak and brought to the screen by Lean, will lead us to a deeper appreciation of what the disappearance and assumed incarceration and death of Lara imply. We must recall that *Doctor Zhivago* was a film made neither in the Soviet Union nor by a Soviet director; this was obviously due to issues of political censorship. It was filmed primarily in Spain, Finland, and Canada, and was made for the consumption of international audiences. Nonetheless, if we can grasp the subtleties of its references, we can better apprehend its nuances and ellipses—and, with a good sense of humor, take note of its limitations (and bloopers!).

If the viewing of an international blockbuster can be enhanced by a deeper understanding of the culture depicted, then so much more will this understanding enrich our viewing of a film indigenous to a given culture. A case in point is Dušan Makaveyev's *WR: Mysteries of the Organism* (*WR: Misterije organizma*) (1971), a Yugoslavian film that intersects the work of psychiatrist and philosopher Wilhelm Reich with the quest for sexual liberation in the Eastern bloc. One must understand the sociopolitical context of Tito's Yugoslavia and its economic and political divergences from other Eastern European countries. One must further understand the importance of the Orthodox religion and Serbian cultural ties to Russia. Once such understanding is in place, Makavejev's innovative hybrid of documentary and fiction can be better grasped. But this is only the first step! The film then takes on a deeper dimension and allows the viewer to penetrate the complexities and paradoxes of Yugoslav society.

This chapter provides a theoretical framework for the representation of key cultural concepts through film. This framework is primarily intended for non-film specialists, and consequently cinema scholars may find it rather general or obvious. Nonetheless, such hackneyed discourses are necessary for readers new to cinema studies who wish to delve into the elucidative power of film. Given that the major thrust of this book is on the intersection of cinema and key cultural concepts, as concretized through key cultural words, we first examine the notion of language and cinema, focusing primarily on how these codes are similar and different, and highlighting issues related to the signification process. We then look at language *in* cinema, an area that has been grossly understudied. A subsequent discussion outlines how key cultural words provide an anchor for film viewers. We next flesh out issues related to the viewing experience and cultural understanding. In a final section, we cycle back to Korea and offer both a historical perspective on Korean cinema and an introduction to both the New Korean Cinema and the cinema of North Korea.

Prior to our discussion on cinema, a caveat is in order. The theoretical perspective of this book is culturally driven, and consequently lies outside of the scope of discussions of political economy. Such discussions as those by Thomas Guback (1974) and Graham Murdock (1982), although insightful from a socioeconomic perspective, are not of particular consequence to our argument. Rather, like the work of Eungjun Min, Jinsook Joo, and Han Ju Kwak, we focus more on the cultural product itself. However, unlike these authors, whose *Korean Film: History, Resistance, and Democratic Imagination* (2003) constitutes a vital study in the understanding of Korean cinema, we are interested more in the site of reception than that of production; more specifically, we intend to posit ways in which such reception can be reshaped and repositioned.

Language and Cinema

Language and Cinema: Commonalities and Divergences

When approaching a film in conjunction with key cultural concepts, the implications of the cinema for understanding a culture are most evident. To grasp the importance of such a relationship, some words are in order regarding the nature of the signification process, both in general and in regard to the cinema. In his early discussions of *semiotic*—the "s" in *semiotics* was allegedly added by Margaret Meade—Charles Stanley Peirce divided a sign into three components: (1) iconic (visual, audio, or other resemblance to its represented object, such as a depiction of a man or a woman on the door to a restroom); (2) indexical (relationship/reaction oriented, such as smoke indicating a fire); and (3) symbolic (independent of shared quality—a heart representing love). In an application of Peirce's triangle to the cinema, Peter Wollen (1972)— argues, "The richness of the cinema springs from the fact that it comprises all three dimensions of the sign" (141). He further stresses that, in the cinema, the most powerful aspects of the sign are the indexical and iconic elements. Likewise, a key cultural word can have all three dimensions. Its indexical meaning, however, may be alien to a neophyte, given that he or she cannot sense the connections the word implies within its culture. Moreover, its cultural meaning is particularly problematical. One cannot argue, as a remedy, that the combination of key cultural words and the cinema reflects the totality of a sign, since both are complete in and of themselves. But the cinema can provide, especially at the iconic and indexical levels, a reinforcement that allows viewers to sense a cultural concept more viscerally. When linked to a key cultural word, the reinforcement offered by the cinema plays out most completely on the iconic and indexical levels.

These problematic aspects can be illustrated with an example. When viewing Victor Salva's 1989 horror film *Clownhouse,* we do not have to work hard to understand that a young boy's fear of clowns is justified. A clown evokes an iconic funny face, and this, we sense, is indexically linked to such notions as laughter and good times. Yes, as the film progresses, we see that the clown symbolically represents evil, and therein lies the punch to the film. The symbolic meaning forces us to rethink our index. Whenever we see the clown, we know that something bad is about to happen.

This, however, is a very simple case drawn from a B horror film. Let's assume that the image viewed is more complex and nuanced, and that it comes from a culture more or less alien to us. In Almodóvar's *Dark Habits* (*Entre tinieblas*) (1984), the images of a mother superior snorting cocaine and gazing amorously at a nightclub *chanteuse* are likely to be interpreted by viewers as sacrilegious. But when seen within the context of Madrid's 1980s *movida,* they take on deeper meanings of unrestraint, freedom, and the celebration of diverse sexual identities. (Historically, one must consider in the viewing of Almodóvar's film the five centuries of repressive hold that the Catholic Church had on Spanish culture and education.) Film images and sequences can thus be misunderstood from the point of view of the original cultural frame.[1]

Returning to Baudry's discussion of suture, we must recall that the process of connecting the viewer to the space of the film, and by extension, to its ideology, is an *unconscious* one. The same phenomenon applies to Mulvey's paradigm of identification. Can a viewer truly connect unconsciously with a new culture that she understands, in part at best, exclusively through the formal processes of the classical cinema?

To answer this question, we first turn to a brief exploration of the medium and the processes through which it engages viewers. A starting point is the analogy between a word and the cinematic shot, as articulated by Christian Metz (1974b). In his discussion, Metz refers to words in general, yet his arguments are well in line with our discussion of key cultural words. Metz finds a certain parallel between a word and a shot, yet emphasizes a major distinction. First, while a word comes from a finite paradigm, given the limitation of a lexicon, a shot is chosen from an infinite paradigm—there are no limits to the imagination of a director. Second, shots are invented by the filmmaker, which is usually not the case for a speaker's choice of words, since most preexist in a lexicon. Third, a cinematic shot offers much more tangible information than a word. One need only think of the deep focus used by Orson Welles in *Citizen Kane* (1941) and the highly textured complexity of shots whose details are apprehended only through multiple viewings. Finally, Metz describes a shot as an "actualized unit" since it has already been pronounced, in contrast to a word, which a speaker can utter as he sees fit, depending upon the circumstances and the intent and mood of the speaker.

In the case of key cultural words, however, we see that Metz's argument is oversimplified. The concept that a film shot can offer more information than the word becomes problematized, particularly inasmuch as such words are often highly nuanced and multidimensional, having linguistic, contextual, and cultural levels of meaning. The difference in complexity between words and shots is thus reduced when one considers the multiple layers of key cultural words. The analogy of the deep focus shot works well here since a viewer of a foreign culture must come to grips with the many shades of meaning, some overt and others less evident, of a key cultural word. Words and shots can be much more intimate bedfellows than Metz envisioned! Nonetheless, it is necessary to go well beyond such basic units of signification to grasp the broader ramifications of the cinema as an expression of culture—that is, of a specific culture in time and space.

If we attempt to draw analogies between the layers of meaning of a key cultural word and the cinema, such an enterprise can yield surprisingly cohesive results. The *linguistic* level of a word is not unlike a cinematic *shot*. We see a character light a cigarette and move across the screen. The meaning we grasp is exactly that: "she has lit a cigarette and is walking toward her left." We can further draw an analogy between *the contextual* level of a key cultural word and a film *sequence*. Through a combination of shots in which, say, the woman finds lipstick on her husband's collar, lights a cigarette, and then walks to the bedroom, where she further discovers an unrecognized phone number in his wallet, the meaning of the character's smoking becomes clearer. She is calming her nerves while searching for evidence of her husband's affair, which she has intuited. If we equate the *cultural* level of a key word to an entire film, we see that, in the case of the cinema, this level, like those of key cultural words, is the most problematic. A foreigner viewing Almodóvar's *Volver* (2006) may understand the story and its main themes, but the deeper manifestations of cultural concepts such as *sangre* are most likely lost. The viewer indeed finds meaning in the film, but it is not the original one. Explicit knowledge of the key cultural concept can help orient the viewer toward the original cultural meaning.

Metz's studies led inevitably to his assertion that cinema is a *langage* (often translated as "language") rather than a *langue* (often translated as "language system"). His main reason for rejecting the art form as a system is that the cinema does not allow for two-way communication. Rather, it permits only *deferred* communication (e.g., through the difference in time between the making of the film and its reception). In addition, Metz argues that film lacks the

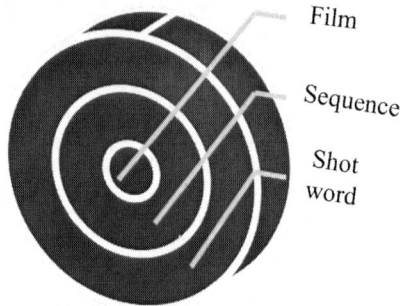

Figure 3. Words and Film.

arbitrary nature of the linguistic sign, relying instead on "pro-filmic" dogs that serve as signifiers for a cinematic critter on the screen. He terms this cinematic relationship as *motivated* rather than arbitrary (Metz, 1974b). It is clear, in this distinction, that Metz was thinking about the cinema as a text and not as part of a broader sociopsychological phenomenon. A cinematic text may, indeed, have parallels with a human language system, but whether it *is* one is not of particular consequence to our argument here. Rather, what is at play is how one views a film as a part of social intercourse and what transpires before, after, and during the film viewing.

More recently, attempts have been made by such scholars as Michel Colin (1995) and Dominique Chateau (1987) to explore the relationship between film and language through the lens of Transformational Generative Grammar, as elaborated by Noam Chomsky. Chateau posits the existence of cinematic competency, which corresponds to the assumptions of the universality of language competence. Nonetheless, like Metz, he argues against the existence of a standard cinematic language, due largely to the "inadequacy in film of supposed ordinary communication" (26). In response to Chateau, Warren Buckland (2000) has outlined filmic constructions that are (1) grammatical and acceptable, (2) ungrammatical and acceptable, and (3) ungrammatical and unacceptable, linking these respectively with the verbal utterances "a year ago," "a grief ago," and "a the ago" (122–123). The grammaticality refers to the *film,* evidenced by its structure and internal cohesiveness. The acceptability is in the mind of the *viewer,* and takes into account the level of viewer cognition and willingness to explore difficult contexts.

Examples of films that are grammatical and acceptable are those classical Hollywood films that foster viewer identification. Events in these films are normally presented in a chronological manner and the film recurs to suturing devices, as discussed earlier. The viewer finds such films acceptable in that there is no rupture in visual pleasure. He or she is simply drawn into the cinematic world. Regarding the second category, ungrammatical and acceptable, Buckland cites a sequence from Godard's *Pierrot le fou* (1965) in which shots of the protagonists fleeing an apartment are interspersed with those of the same characters later on in their journey. Such a sequence is considerably more difficult for a viewer to grasp than a chronologically ordered sequence from the classical cinema. It is challenging, but a sophisticated viewer, nonetheless, can apprehend it. Regarding the third category, Buckland compares a semantic sequence that cannot be uttered by a speaker with a hypothetical filmic sequence that cannot be produced (124–125). In sum, Buckland concludes:

> These predictions [regarding the grammaticality of film sequences] in turn confirm the cognitive reality of filmic sequences as analyzed by the cognitive film semioticians, for they suggest that frequently used sequences [Hollywood] are more easily comprehended than difficult sequences [French *nouvelle vague*], and some sequences are not employed at all because spectators cannot process them [2000, 135].

If we extend Buckland's comments to the interplay between key cultural words and film, sequences in which such cultural concepts appear in a relatively mainstream or classical film, be it visually or through dialogue, will probably assume, for the cultural learner in the early stages, a position somewhere between "grammatical and acceptable" and "ungrammatical and acceptable." The cultural learner is unlikely to understand the true message of certain segments of the film. Oblivious to deeper meanings, he or she recognizes that it is "acceptable," at least *somewhere.* As the viewer grows in understanding of the key cultural concept, other layers of meaning emerge. In contrast, were a filmmaker to articulate such a concept in an abstract, avant-garde manner, the cultural learner may consider this, from his or her perspective, "ungrammatical and unacceptable," whereas someone much closer to the given culture may read its ungrammaticality with some difficulty. It thus seems that the avant-garde is not the best vehicle for the illustration of key cultural concepts, unless the viewer's cognitive skills permit an appreciation of the avant-garde in a more familiar culture. For this reason, in the application chapters in Part II of this book, we will deal primarily with relatively mainstream Korean films that have been well received by Korean audiences. Even the more "art-house" films that we will discuss, such as Im Kwontaek's *Seopyeonje/서편제* (1993) and *Painted Fire* (*Chihwaseon/취화선*) (2002) and Lee Changdong's *Poetry* (*Si/시*) (2010), although constituting open texts, are not examples of experimental or avant-garde films, and hence will not be overly taxing to the Western viewer.

But we must recall that Buckland's argument plays out on a purely cognitive level. What is absent in his theory of grammaticality is the *cultural* level. The grammaticality of a film notwithstanding, a viewer may find a film acceptable or unacceptable depending on her or his knowledge of the given culture. We need only note the extent to which Veit Harlan's *The Third Sex* (*Anders als du und ich*) (1957) was received very differently in New York City than in Berlin. The former audience, oblivious to the subtleties of German family structure and social norms, turned the film into a cult phenomenon. The reactions on the part of German audiences were more restrained, perhaps due to the film's ambivalent positioning of German culture. Such points of contestation went unnoticed by American audiences.

Another recent positioning of the relationship between language and cinema has been Stam's (1989) revisiting of Bakhtin's notion of speech tact and exploration of its ramifications for the cinema. Defining tact as the set of codes that govern discourse, Bakhtin and Medvedev (1986) stress that this phenomenon is "determined by the aggregate of all the social relationships of the speakers, their ideological horizons, and finally, the concrete situation of the conversation" (95–96). Stam argues:

> The notion of "tact" is extremely suggestive for film theory and analysis, applying literally to the verbal exchanges within the diegesis, and figuratively to the "tact" involved in the metaphorical dialogue of genres and discourses within the text, as well as to the "dialogue" between film and spectator [Stam et al., 1992, 219].

Tact is, indeed, contextualized. A neophyte will not necessarily understand the contextual and cultural codes implicit in the relationship among onscreen characters, nor will he or she grasp the relationship between the film and the spectator in the same manner as a viewer native to the given culture. Something is needed to mediate the experience. Key cultural words can serve as a vehicle through which a cultural learner can more closely approach and experience the tact involved in a particular film.

Language in Film

As seen from the preceding discussion, the focus of studies that have linked language and cinema have brought to bear on the language *of* the cinema and not the use of language *in* the cinema. For a discussion of key cultural concepts, the latter is also of importance inasmuch as key cultural words can be *spoken* in a film as well as visualized. To date, only a few scholarly articles have dealt with this relationship. In an article published in 1985 entitled "The Cinema after Babel: Language, Difference, Power," Shohat and Stam attempted to open a debate on this subject, but the topic went, for the most part, ignored. Their argument explored a wide array of issues ranging from difficulties in translation to language choice. We can extend Shohat and Stam's argument to assert that an in-depth knowledge of key cultural words can allow a viewer to disregard mistranslations, however gross. In other words, high competence in key cultural words can override language short-circuits.

More recently, this issue has been explored by such critics as Nataša Ďurovičová (2004, 2010) and Bruce Williams (2002, 2003, 2005). Discussing the difficulty of conveying concepts between languages, Ďurovičová explores how the notion in translation theory known as "functional equivalent translation" attempts to move a text in its totality from one context to another. It has as its goal the effacement of all evidence of the site of production and the translation process. Ďurovičová describes this as a "reassuring for-me-ness" (2010, 112). In other words, the text appears to have been written *just for* the new reader. Functional equivalent translation appeals to the universal side of a key cultural word—that is, what it has in common with the cultural learner. At the same time, it erases all trace of what we could term the local, specific meaning—the meaning essential for gaining a deeper level of knowledge of a culture. Once again, knowledge of key cultural words provides an alternative to functional equivalent translation, or at least can allow a viewer to reach beyond it. Simply stated, our enterprise here is to go against the grain of functional equivalent translations and bring the "me-ness" to which Ďurovičová refers much closer to the original point of utterance.

Williams (2003) explores issues of language and cinema from a sociopolitical point of view. Examining in depth two distinct *bilingual* versions of María Luisa Bemberg's *Miss Mary* (1986), he demonstrates how one version of the film speaks to an international audience, where often more explanation is needed, and the other version to an Argentine audience, where much is assumed without speaking. Again, one of the most significant points made in the article is that both versions are bilingual, one Spanish dominant and the other English dominant. Although Williams has not studied the Spanish version from the perspective of the presence of key cultural words, if these are indeed present, they could orient the viewer more closely to the original cultural context of the Spanish-dominant film.

One of the most obvious gaps in the debate on language and cinema is the virtual absence of the study of this relationship from a linguistic point of view. The debate has been saturated by analyses originating from the domain of cinema studies. Such a phenomenon can, in part, be explained by the fact that cinema studies is an infant field as opposed to linguistics, and has drawn heavily upon the lessons of its grandmother. The latter has not felt the need to learn from its offspring. Peter Wollen offers another argument that sheds light on this imbalance. He argues that explorations that seek analogies between cinema and verbal language are motivated by "the desire to validate cinema as an art" (1972, 140). Forty years after the publication of Wollen's seminal *Signs and Meaning in the Cinema,* we can add that film theoreticians also drew upon the analogy to justify cinema studies as an academic discipline. Linguistics need not defend itself. Although our book does not aim to undertake a reverse analysis of language and cinema, we will develop here a model from a linguistics perspective that will assist in understanding the use and importance of key cultural words in the context of the cinema.

Words in Film

Let us begin with a brief analysis of the use of words, and especially key cultural words *overtly* included in film dialogue or titles. Returning to the example of Victor Salva's *Clownhouse,* we note that most speakers of English understand the generalized meaning of the word "clown." They grasp its dictionary meaning and conjure up notions of a painted face, a wig, and silly actions. Thus, they easily lock in the *principles* of meaning. As mentioned earlier, the word "clown" can be further indexed to laughter and happy times. But it is important to remember that what is involved in a "sign" is a *mental representation,* not a *tangible "thing"* in the external world. Even at the level of icon, "clown" may not signify a real-life guy from Barnum and Bailey. Rather, depending on one's context, it could evoke a fuzzy stuffed toy, an entertainer at a birthday party, or a tragic hero of an opera. On a symbolic level, the word "clown" can even suggest a colleague behaving in an immature manner. Thus, the presence of *parameters* allows us to extend meaning in a restricted domain. Of course, symbolic meaning can be used ironically. When the *pagliaccio* in Leoncavallo's opera sings, "Laugh, clown, laugh," we know the opposite is happening. The jolt in Salva's film occurs when icon, index, and symbol are reconfigured to reference something different than expected. This plays out not only at the level of images, but also at the level of words. As the film progresses, the word "clown" becomes increasingly menacing. If so many visual images can be conjured up by a somewhat more *tangible* word such as "clown," one can imagine how complex the signification process may be when *intangible* cultural concepts are at stake.

In Leitão de Barros's historical drama *Inês de Castro* (1944), the Portuguese word *saudade,* a key cultural word in the Luso-Brazilian world, is used. On a surface level, this term may be simply understood as "missing someone," which is appropriate to the film's tragic tale of the murder in 1355 of a royal mistress; its deeper meaning, evoked even in the film dialogue, implies "homesickness," "longing," or a "fatalistic sense of loss." All of these fit within the context of the film. Nevertheless, a German speaker who knows some Portuguese but is not yet culturally entrenched might easily misunderstand the use of *saudade* here. She may equate it with the term *Sehnsucht,* which has a much heavier, more philosophical meaning, and which combines the notion of "yearning" with that of "addiction" (*Sucht*). In such a case, the reading of the film may be much more ponderous and abstract than originally intended. Conversely, a Brazilian, familiar with some German, may grasp only in part the meaning of the title of a film by Rainer Werner Fassbinder, *Die Sehnsucht der Veronika Voss* (1982). By not apprehending the more abstract levels of the German term, he may equate it unequivocally with *saudade* and, therefore, may expect a more romanticized story than the director's bleak film proffers. As an anonymous Internet blog comment quips, "You can get a B.A. in *saudade* but only a Ph.D. in *Sehnsucht.*" It is very interesting to note that the English title of the film is simply *Veronika Voss,* thus avoiding a sticky translation issue.

Indeed, we hear words spoken in a film not unlike the way in which we hear words in a natural conversation. As we know, a verbal exchange in language implies a speaker and a hearer. Such an exchange is governed pragmatically by the intentions of the speaker and the hearer, the situation, and the cultural context. With regard to film, the issue is far more complex. Within the film's diegesis, verbal exchanges between characters may be governed by the same pragmatic contexts. But we must also consider the relationship between the film as "speaker" and the viewer as "hearer." Does the viewer simply eavesdrop on the on-screen characters' verbal exchanges? Or is there something deeper at play? Recall that, despite Metz's discounting of cinema as a language system, in part due to the deferred communication it offers, the art form needs an audience (hearer) for its mere existence. We can ask ourselves, at least with regard to talkies, "If a film is not heard, does it exist?" Indeed, a great deal of communication between a film and its hearers involves the need to convey information or provoke a reaction. In all actuality, the viewer can alternate among the first, second, and third grammatical persons throughout the course of the film experience, depending upon how the film positions him or her at a given moment. We must recall Grodal's cognitive theories regarding how spectators seek to construct a character's perceptions and ultimately react emotionally and subjectively. The verbal discourse on the screen can elicit a reaction on the part of viewers, although their own verbal response is either subvocalized or, in contrast to legitimate theater, does not reach the diegetic character. We can thus posit two levels of dialogue, between onscreen characters and between the film and the spectator.

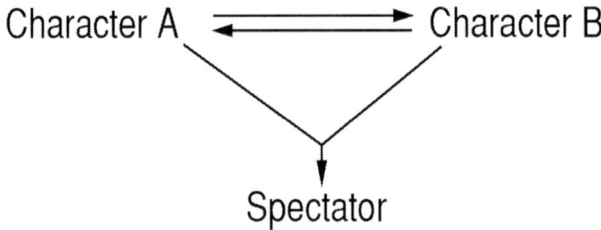

Figure 4. Two Levels of Discourse.

Yet there is a third level, one that is usually ignored in film theory—that of the verbal exchanges among film viewers now that the physical space of the viewing situation has been altered so drastically. We are no longer always in the realm of Metz's darkened cinema space, but rather often view films in the comfort of our living room where we can fast-forward, pause, and *talk*. All of the previously mentioned levels can be applied to key cultural words, as these may be explicitly articulated or the related concepts reflected in film dialogue.

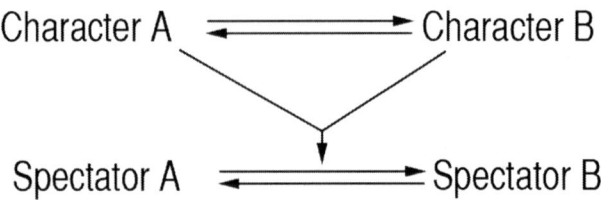

Figure 5. Dynamics of the Group Viewing Experience.

The viewer, moreover, may react to the actual words or implied concepts, with silent or vocal response reflecting her or his own level of understanding of the culture. As will be discussed more completely later, viewers engaged in the same viewing experience can also enter into dialogue over the cultural concepts.

Film and Cultural Theories

Let's return briefly to a purely cognitive perspective. When Grodel argues that a spectator's identification with a film character is a major component in the identification process, he fails to point out that the viewer is inevitably culturally bound in outguessing the character's decisions and actions. Most likely, the viewer has little understanding of how a character is likely to react within the scope of the original culture of the film. In the case of a foreign film, for instance, it is easy for a viewer to construct a character's perceptions, but such construction will be a reconstruction, a transpositioning of these perceptions to a space with which the viewer is more familiar. Such a phenomenon is well in line with post–1970s discussions of multiple spectatorial identifications and with recent examinations of how films travel transnationally. Thus, assuming that a viewer is truly attempting to understand the autochthonous culture in which a film was conceived, made and initially received, his or her reading of the work may still fail to apprehend major cultural components that inform the work. Once again, an in-depth knowledge of cultural words is a valuable tool in understanding the film and the culture it represents.

As early as the late 1970s, such critics as Janet Bergstrom (1979) articulated that viewers can assume multiple identificatory positions during a film viewing. In other words, we do not assume the perspective of a white male protagonist in pursuit of a woman as our exclusive approach to a film. Viewers can become African American, Latino, gay, lesbian, or anything else pursuant with their positioning vis-à-vis the film. Recent film theory, moreover, takes full account of what a viewer brings to the film experience from her own background. A Holocaust survivor, for instance, will have a much different reading of Spielberg's *Schindler's List* (1994) than will a suburban high school student for whom the film is required viewing. Likewise, viewers who grew up in Communist Albania will understand the sociopolitical ramifications of Kujtim Çashku's *Kolonel Bunker* (1998) much more clearly than those viewers who perceive the Balkan nation as distant and exotic. Often, today's transnational critical discourse focuses on how films cross borders and how they are received outside their place of birth. Such a reception may build upon shared experience among diverse groups, be it a postcolonial context, a revolutionary struggle, or some other background. Nevertheless, such a transnational experience obviously allows for readings somewhat divergent than those emerging from the original culture. In this case, we can return to the notion of *principles* and *parameters* that we have seen in the process of signification. A general idea can be easily transplanted, but will often be recouped in terms of parameters distinct to the new viewing context.

In no way does this argument suggest that such new viewings are invalid, for, like the 1950s traveling photography exhibition *The Family of Man,* they shed light on issues universal to the human experience, allowing us to approach contexts that are new to us and to exit our cultural frame for a moment. Today's digital world facilitates such adventures. As early as 1994, Shohat and Stam stressed how electronic media in particular foster a sense of a transnational community:

> The media play a role in shaping identity in the postmodern era. By experiencing community with people never actually seen, consumers of electronic media can be affected by traditions to which they have no ancestral connection. Thus, the media can normalize as well as exoticize other cultures, and can even fashion alternative communities and identities [347].

Shohat and Stam (1994), moreover, have spoken of the ways in which "[m]edia spectatorship forms a trialog among texts, readers, and communities existing in clear discursive and social relation to one another" (347). In a reworking and undoing of Benedict Anderson's paradigm, they envision not a local community, but rather a transnational "imagined community." Their arguments were impressively visionary for 1994; then, it was hard to imagine how easily blogs and social networks could jump borders without passport control and create new virtual communities. Shohat and Stam assert:

> Central to multiculturalism is the notion of *mutual and reciprocal relativization,* the idea that the diverse cultures placed in play should come to perceive the limitations of their own social and cultural perspective.... Each group offers its own exotopy (according to Bakhtin), its own "excess seeing," hopefully coming not only to "see" other groups, but also, through a salutary estrangement, to see how it is itself seen [1994, 359].

Shohat and Stam overtly abandon the notion of authenticity, instead calling for a language of "discourses," which draws upon community affiliation and intertextuality. Considering Bakhtin's notion of discourses, they claim, "Finally, the privileging of the discourse allows us to compare a film's discourses not with an inaccessible 'real' but with other, socially circulated cognate discourses" (215). Hence, the cultural doors opened by an *a priori* conceptualized word are not of great concern to their highly valid and transnational project.

In a manner not unlike that pursued by Shohat and Stam, Hamid Naficy explores at length issues of the expression of cultural identity through film. Focusing on exilic and diasporic filmmaking, his 2001 study defined an "accented cinema" as one in which filmmakers are highly aware of two contexts: "[Accented films] are created with awareness of the vast histories of the prevailing cinematic modes. They are also created in a new mode that is constituted both by the structures of feeling of the filmmakers themselves as displaced subjects and by the traditions of exilic and diasporic cultural productions that preceded them" (22). The focus of Naficy's work, however, is more upon the site of *production* than upon the site of *reception*. His project involves the *expression* of cultural identity.

In the mutual and reciprocal viewings discussed by Shohat and Stam as well as in the case of exilic and diasporic cinema, we must question the extent to which we actually grasp the autochthonous principles of the original viewing context. The community fostered by the convergence of transnational spectators is an impressive tool for the mutual understanding of new and shared experiences, but it is not necessarily one that fosters in-depth cultural knowledge. To arrive at a possible alternative, one must take into account how films are viewed today.

One of the most up-to-date discussions of issues related to transnational readings of films is a 2010 collection of essays edited by Nataša Ďurovičová and Kathleen Newman. Garnering the 2011 award for the Best Edited Collection from the Society for Cinema and Media Studies (the world's foremost scholarly organization in the field), *World Cinemas, Transnational Perspectives* explores such issues from divergent perspectives. In this collection, Lesley Stern examines the reconfiguration of Hong Kong kung fu movies in Zimbabwe. Her premise is to look at "how films circulate, how they are exported and imported, distributed and exhibited, but also ... how they move over time (or how their meanings change over time and according to location—where and how they are viewed)" (188). Although evocative and thoroughly researched, Stern's essay focuses on the "mutation" of films as they "migrate and contribute to the forging of new sensibilities and socialities" (212).

In an essay on world cinema, Dudley Andrew distinguishes the ironic, corrosive, and philosophical underpinnings of the French *nouvelle vague* with the so-called Korean Wave, which has largely "been an artifact of national promotion" (82). He further stresses that, while the *nouvelle vague* was conceived from and lent itself to written criticism, other new waves are measured by the number of films produced and box office grosses. Andrew concludes his discussion by reassuring readers of the existence of films that, "while situated in one place and one time, reach viewers elsewhere, all situated differently, all out of phase with themselves and with each other" (86). One can infer from Andrews's argument that a film's ability to reach another context may be largely a product of universal cultural principles that resonate in many contexts. The coincidence and alignment he suggests could well be strengthened so that diverse *parameters* present in cultural concepts can help viewers get in tune with the local as well as the universal.

Fredric Jameson, in an exploration of Kar Wai Wong's *Happy Together* (1997), a film that travels between Hong Kong and Argentina without any reference to the United States, describes the film from a U.S. perspective:

> The United States is left out of this, which is between China and Argentina, the Southern Cone and the Pacific Rim, and this is equally suggestive for the spectators, excluded along with their superstate centrality and their new world hegemonic language. This is not for you! This is between us! At best, you will be allowed to overhear, to be the voyeurs of this relationship, which oddly defamiliarizes our mental map of the world today all the while deploying two of its other major languages [318].

What is most significant about Jameson's brief discussion is that he envisions a cinema in which Hollywood and the English language are totally ignored, and does so from a transnational perspective. He recalls in his essay Stanley Cavell's 1971 remarks that the fascination of film entails the way the "screen shows us the world *without ourselves* and, as it were, without our point of view (Jameson, 2010, 319). One must question whether the effacing of a U.S. context altogether will force viewers to delve more deeply into the cultures presented. In his argument, Jameson does not address how American spectators understand and interpret the film.

For our purposes, the most suggestive study in Ďurovičová and Newman's seminal essay collection is that of Mette Hjort, who fleshes out a typology of cinematic transnationalism. Among the modalities she identifies are "epiphanic transnationalism," in which the emphasis is on "those elements of deep national belonging that overlap with other national identities to produce something resembling deep transnational belonging" (16) and "affinitive transnationalism," which involves "the tendency to communicate with 'those similar to us,' with similarity being understood in terms of ethnicity, partially-overlapping or mutually intelligible languages, and a history of interaction giving rise to shared core values, common practices, and comparable institutions" (17). Our project is relatively distinct from the second modality. We are encouraging viewers to go beyond affinity and to communicate with those *different* from us in language, ethnicity, and core values. Likewise, although key Korean cultural concepts relate to Western values (as will be demonstrated as mentioned in Chapter 1), we do not aim to develop "transnational belonging" per se. Rather, we hope to provide a blueprint through which viewers can reach as closely as possible to a new and strikingly different culture. For now, we will call our particular modality of transnational viewing a "bridging transnationalism." By viewing Korean films through the lens of key cultural words, Western spectators are encouraged to step outside their own cultural frame and appreciate the core values and practices of a society very distinct from their own.

Although not drawing extensively upon key cultural words, two specific studies go against the grain of contemporary discourses on transnationalism and seek to facilitate a deeper understanding of a film's original cultural context. One of these even does so via the vehicle of a key word, though this word is not necessarily a key *cultural* word in the terms we have discussed earlier. In his extensive study of Indian cinema, Patrick Colm Hogan (2009) agrees with our theories here in asserting that understanding must begin with the universal. He argues, "Our understanding of Indian cinema—or, for that matter, say cinema—must first of all be based on universal principles, on ideas, sensibilities, impulses that we share, whatever our national origins or cultural milieu" (6). He further emphasizes:

> If the main purposes of art—including film—are to communicate emotions and themes, usually by way of narrative, then we are still left with the problem of how we experience these emotions or understand these themes and narratives *in particular cases* [emphasis added]. In other words, we need more detailed, more fully specified universals. We need precisely articulated principles of emotion, theme, and narrative that we share cross culturally [7].

Such universals notwithstanding, Hogan's agenda is to "link the other culture with the universal principles [and do so] by way of cultural specificity, not making the error of assuming that universal principles are particularized in the same way from one society to another" (254). Hogan envisions his book primarily as a guide to understanding Indian cinema rather than as a roadmap to fathoming culture. Nonetheless, understanding cinema is a ticket to exploring a culture. Our enterprise essentially repositions Hogan's goals and develops first and foremost the notion of film as a portal to cultural understanding at a deep level. Our marriage of key words and the cinema enhances Hogan's theories, particularly when the emphasis is shifted from film to culture. Undeniably, our model can be applied to virtually any cultural context.

Although whether *sangre,* or "blood," may be deemed a key cultural word in peninsular Spanish culture remains in question, Marsha Kinder has viewed it as a term that opens doors to many aspects of history and society. In her title "*Blood*-Cinema," she evokes García Lorca's *Blood Wedding* as well as Carlos Saura's 1981 film adaptation (through the vehicle of flamenco) of this play. Kinder emphasizes that the notion of blood is tied to the graphic depiction of violence and the obsession with incest in Spanish cinema (1). On a national level, she links it to "the bloody repercussions of the Spanish Civil War, the glorification of death under Franco, the Inquisition, and the conventions of the Counter-Revolution that fetishized the bleed wounds of Christ and other martyrs" (1). Kinder, in her book, melds both the universal and the culturally specific. On the one hand, she questions whether any national cinema carries traces of its own history, culture and blood. On the other hand, she explores in detail Spanish micro-regionalisms. Nonetheless, Kinder stresses that such terms as "cinema," "nation," and "national cinema" are "increasingly becoming decentered and assimilated within larger transnational systems of entertainment" (440).

Like Hogan, Kinder develops an agenda focused primarily on understanding Spanish cinema, not on understanding the culture of Spain at large. Yet her employment of a single key word elucidates a great deal of cultural concepts. Her study clearly attests to the true potential of such words. When the words used are truly key cultural ones, an even deeper penetration of a culture can occur.

Key Cultural Words as Anchorage in Film Viewing

In search of a remedy to misreadings of culture through film, one can return to Roland Barthes's 1977 essay "Rhetoric of the Image," in which the notion of *anchorage* is outlined, and apply these discussions to our intersection of key words and the cinema. Barthes describes "anchorage" as verbal devices within an image that orient it toward a preferred reading. Barthes provides the example of an image of fruit scattered around a ladder, an image that might indicate "bad harvest" or "high winds." Yet, when a caption is added that reads "as if from your garden," the image is intended to convey the notion of "freshness" (Stam, Burgoyne, and Flitterman-Lewis, 1992, 29). Such anchoring devices can be simple and direct, as in this case, or subtle and textured. In Tomás Gutiérrez Alea's *Memories of Underdevelopment* (*Memorias del subdesarrollo*) (1968), for instance, the protagonist, an upper-middle-class intellectual who has opted to remain in Havana in the wake of the Castro revolution, walks in front of a movie theater during one of his daily perambulations through the capital city. We catch an ever-so-brief glimpse of a poster for Alain Resnais's *Hiroshima, mon amour* (1959). At least for an educated viewer, the poster evokes the notion of memory, which, key to Resnais's film, orients us toward the insistence on the part of Alea's protagonist that Cubans bear a collective memory of colonialism and oppression.

Like written cues in a film image, key cultural words can serve to anchor the viewer. At times, they may appear in actual film dialogue or be seen as written slogans. (The latter is particularly common in the films of China and Albania during their respective cultural revolutions.) More frequently, they serve as a stimulus that the informed viewer brings to the film experience. What happens is dialectical in nature. The viewer can be drawn into the film through the unconscious semiotic and psychological processes of the classical cinema, assuming the film in question is fairly conventional in structure. Subsequently, the presence or evocation of a key cultural word can trigger a conscious response, a recognition of the cultural concept as presented in or implied by the film. This can occur at all levels of meaning—linguistic, indexical, and cultural. (Such a process is not unlike Mulvey's attempts to educate spectators as to the manipulative nature of classical cinema and hamper their visual pleasure.) Not only will the film and key word work together symbiotically to allow for the spectator's deeper appreciation of both, but with time such a process can lead the neophyte to experience more deeply the culture at large.

Viewing Experience and Cultural Understanding

Once again, we can no longer think in terms of the idealized viewer in the darkened movie house, acting as a monad, transported by the film image. Instead, film viewing can be construed as a social, interactive phenomenon. Film theory of the 1960s and 1970s failed to take into account the "discourse" of the film viewing experience and the use of language *per se* among fellow spectators, both within the confines of a local community, or in a broader context.

Today's film viewer is likely to watch a film on a small screen, or even a computer. This is particularly the case in the United States when foreign films are involved. The concept of the 1970s-style "art-house cinema" where foreign, classic, and avant-garde films were announced by a newspaper-sized monthly schedule, from which audiences planned their nights out weeks in advance, is a thing of the past. Rather, we have become a society of instant gratification, streaming films from such online sites as YouTube and Netflix whenever possible. Film viewing now is in part parallel to the television viewing experience. In the privacy of their homes, viewers can talk and comment on what they are seeing without fear of disturbing fellow viewers. But today's experience is far more complex than that of TV. As mentioned earlier, a film viewing can be interactive; we can pause, rewind, fast forward, and ask each other for clarification about what we have seen. An individual viewer who is approaching a foreign film through the lens of key cultural words can, if experiencing the film in the company of a native who is familiar with the film's cultural context, ask for explanation and contextualization.

Furthermore, if one takes into account what occurs prior to and after the actual viewing, one encounters a great deal of social interaction, which can even cross borders. A viewer is often "prepped" by someone who has already seen the film, and utterances such as "You've gotta see this" and "This is wild" are familiar to her ears. Following the viewing, a spectator can return to her recommenders with such phrases as "It was interesting, but ... ," and an extended debate over the film's relative merits can ensue. We can thus open the sphere of the film experience to embrace the overall experience, which includes social interaction before, during, and after the viewing itself. And herein lie the ramifications for an intersection between film and key cultural concepts.

Let us suppose that we have gained an "academic" familiarity with the meaning of a key cultural word, but this word remains abstract and distant. We may have grasped intellectually the complexity of, for instance, *han,* but it is not yet real to us. If our determination to approach Korean culture encourages us to seek out associations with Koreans having an in-depth understanding of their own culture, then we can make best use of the viewing experience. Assuming our Korean companions have seen the film or are willing to view it with us, we, as cultural apprentices, have excellent guides, who can help anchor the viewing experience and orient it toward an explanation of the key cultural concept. To a certain extent, this interrupts much of the unconscious processes of the film experience. In Mulveyan terms, visual pleasure has been short-circuited. In a manner similar to the way in which Mulvey sought to bring viewers toward greater recognition of the gender dynamics at play in the classical cinema, the viewing experience can now alert viewers to a particular cultural aspect.

Things, however, need not be so grim. A viewer can soon come to "intuit" a cultural concept through film viewing and social interaction. She can learn to "find it" and "feel it" more naturally. Pleasure can thus be restored to the film experience, in contrast to the irreversible rupture with male gaze that Mulvey sought to foster. In other words, there can be a return of the unconscious processes of film viewing, but this time informed by a deeper cultural knowledge. A cultural learner can thus develop an "informed unconscious."

It is of particular consequence that the viewer and cultural guide(s) need not be in the same room, nor need they have met in person. The doors opened by digital communities have established new paradigms through which fellow spectators can interact. Film viewing experiences can be shared on blogs and social networks such as Facebook. Spectators can interact via instant messages, chat, or Skype. Expanded in these ways, transnational social networks can provide a useful mediation between key cultural words and film viewing. This is of particular importance when a cultural

Unconscious Viewing
(Pleasure)

↓

Conscious Viewing
(Reduced Pleasure)

↓

Informed
Unconscious Viewing
(Pleasure Recouped)

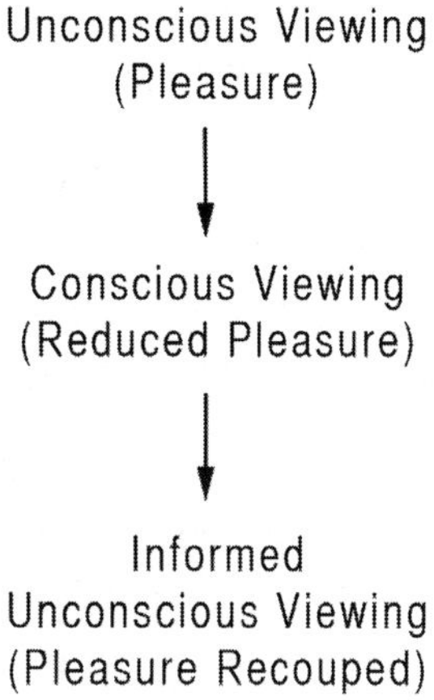

Figure 6. Path to an Informed Unconscious Viewing.

learner has no local and easy access to natives of a given culture. For this reason, in the application part of our book, we will discuss more completely the pre- and post-viewing experiences that come to play in the combination of key cultural words and the cinema.

What Is Korean Cinema?

Our Object of Study

Having established, at least from a film perspective, our approach to Korean cinema, it is essential to say some words about our object of study. Until recent years, Korean cinema was relatively unknown in the West, and such lack of exposure was due, in large part, to historical factors—among these the Japanese occupation, the Korean War, and the military government, which lasted from the coup of 1961 to 1979. In the days of the classical cinema, Seoul, as a film center, was eclipsed by both Shanghai and Tokyo. Korea, moreover, was a late bloomer when it came to film production. Indeed, the notion of motion pictures arrived in Korea only two years following the invention of the new medium. Min, Joo, and Kwak trace the first film shown in Korea to a short film focusing on an oil company made in 1898 by an American businessman in Seoul, who screened it to the public in "a rented bar on South

Gate Street using gas lamps" (2003, 26). The authors state, "Admission was a piece of nickel or ten empty cigarette packs, which was intended to promote the sales of a new brand of cigarettes" (26). Nonetheless, production was slow to catch on. Min, Joo, and Kwak assert that the next known screening took place on June 23, 1903, when the Hansung Electric Company showed a short French film to advertise electric streetcars. In any case, the normal growth of a film industry was delayed by the Japanese invasion of 1910. According to Min et al., under the Japanese occupation, the Korean film industry was unable to accept investments from individuals or from the Japanese government; hence, its growth was severely retarded. As production slowly grew, film production was still subjugated to Japanese censorship (26). Nonetheless, as the number of imported films from the United States and France increased, one saw the spread of a number of cinema houses throughout Korea, most of them owned by Japanese. Note Min, Joo, and Kwak, because such movie houses were mostly owned by private individuals, the proceeds never flowed back to film production (27).

In 1919, the first Korean film, *Royal Revenge* (*Uirijok Guto/의리족 구토*), was produced. Min, Joo, and Kwak explain that the film was financed by the "only Korean businessman" in Korea, and was directed by Dosan Kim, the leader of a theater troupe. It was necessary to use a Japanese cameraman, since it was difficult to find a qualified technician and equipment in Korea (27). The authors describe the work as a "kino-drama," consisting of a film coupled with a play on a stage. They affirm, "The first form of a motion picture in Korea, kino-drama, was favorably accepted and recognized as a Korean film by the audiences who had been familiar only with Western films" (27). According to Jeong Jong-Wha (2008), South Korea, in 1966, established October 27 as the "day of film" in homage to the first performance of *Royal Revenge.*

In 1923, the first Korean feature film (as opposed to kino-drama), *Promise under the Moon* (*Wolhaui Maengseo/월하의 맹서*), was made to promote the notion of saving money in a bank.[2] The first screening of the film occurred in the Seoul Kyeongseong Hotel on April 9, 1923 (Jeong, 2008, 28). During this period and the years that followed, Japanese producers and directors embarked on productions with Korean topics. In or around 1923, a film was produced titled *Chunhyangjeon/춘향전*, which focused on the plight of a young woman, the daughter of a *gisaeng* (female entertainer), in love with the son of a *yangban* (man of the upper class), who is imprisoned out of loyalty to her lover and who is subsequently freed by him once he has attained an influential position. (This story has seen numerous cinematic adaptations in both South and North Korea.) In 1926, Na Un-kyu, a 25-year-old director, made *Arirang,* a protest against the Japanese occupation that drew its name from a folk song, which, as Tom Vick (2007) asserts, would become the "anthem of the Korean resistance" (145). Vick explains:

[The film] depicted a man driven mad by torture at the hands of the Japanese authorities. It inspired others to make similar cinematic calls for independence, which led to stricter censorship from the Japanese authorities, who by 1930 were approving only films with safe subjects, such as melodrama, costume dramas, and pro–Japanese subjects [145].

In 1935, another version of *Chunhyangjeon* was financed by the Japanese and became Korea's first sound film. Unfortunately, as Vick clarifies, upon the 1937 invasion of Manchuria by Japan, "the Korean film industry was converted wholesale into a pro–Japanese-propaganda machine, and in 1942 Korean-language films were banned entirely from being produced" (145).

Following the surrender of the Japanese in 1945, there was a rebirth of Korean cinema. On October 21, 1946, in Seoul's Kugje Theatre, *Hurah! Freedom* (*Jayu Manse*/자유 만세), a fervently anti–Japanese piece produced by a Korean crew, premiered. According to Jeong (2008), the film was criticized for being rather remote from reality. Nonetheless, it was loved by audiences (90). According to Vick (2007), another film of considerable importance during this period was *A Hometown in Heart* (*Maeumui Gohyang*/마음의 고향), a story focusing on a young widowed mother, an orphan, and a monk set in a remote Buddhist temple on a mountain. The original 33-mm negative was found in the Japanese National Film Center in 2005 (Jeong, 2008, 96).

South Korean Cinema

In a 2002 introduction to the work of Im Kwontaek, Kyung Hyun Kim asserts that Western ignorance of Korean cinema is mainly due to its inaccessibility. Such lack of accessibility has to do not only with patterns in international distribution, but also with historical factors. As Kim explains, most Korean films made before 1943 have been permanently lost (James and Kim, 2002, 20). Moreover, the heritage of Korean cinema was further complicated by the move of the film industry to Pusan, to minimize the proximity to the Korean War. Thus, one can argue that the early phases of South Korean cinema constituted a fragmented phenomenon. In the wake of the war, Kim argues, "A national culture that valued humanity was lost, thus opening the door to a gene ration of brutal military dictatorships in South Korea" (James and Kim, 2002, 20). Such a condition favored an industry that was subjected to heavy censorship, so as to maintain control over public ideology. Not only were

South Korean films rarely seen in the West from the 1950s through the early 1980s, but moreover there was virtually no critical discourse on the subject.

One of the first references to South Korean cinema occurred in Roy Armes's 1987 *Third World Film Making and the West,* a seminal analysis of the cinemas of Latin America, East and Southeast Asia, Latin America, and the Middle East and Africa. (The inclusion of the nation in this discussion seems particularly ironic today, given Korea's powerful economic status.) Stressing that the economies of Taiwan, South Korea, Hong Kong, and Singapore witnessed over 50 percent of the growth in Third World industrialization in the 1960s and 1970s, Armes argues that "All four [were, in the early 1980s] fragmentary states produced by the vagaries of war, colonialism, and decolonization," with South Korea having witnessed both war and foreign intervention (154). Armes briefly explains how the quota system, which established the ratio between domestic and foreign films shown in South Korea, was highly detrimental to the film industry inasmuch as, through this vehicle, the government increased its regulation of the film industry from the days of the post–Korean War economic miracle to the 1980s. He cites Kai Hong's 1981 assessment of South Korean film, which indicts the government for its policies vis-à-vis the film industry:

> Korean society and government is determined to keep Korea as insular as possible and turn its citizenry into well-behaved conformists. This deliberate policy is applied with particular high-handedness in the strict regulation of the film industry, perhaps in recognition of the democratizing and liberalizing tendencies of the film medium. No country has a stricter code of film censorship than South Korea—with the possible exception of North Korea and some other Communist bloc countries [241].

At the time of his essay, Armes stressed that South Korean films were rarely shown abroad, and that the few films screened in London in 1984 were "very introspective melodramas, often ending in spectacular self-immolation" (156).

Tony Rayna (2002), along similar lines, argues that in the early 1980s, South Korean cinema had abandoned anti-communist motifs, but relied instead on "martial arts movies, melodramas and ubiquitous soft-core sex scenes to counter the appeal of television" (6). He emphasizes that the reliance upon such "tired genres compounded tendencies to accept low technical standards and hopelessly dated acting styles" (6).

To rebuild the film industry following the Korean War, cinema was granted a tax-exempt status. As Vick observes, this incentive was combined with foreign technology and equipment, and through this, the cinema was reborn. An audience for Korean films was built through early action film and melodramas (146). (A connection cannot be definitively drawn with further audience research on the relationship between the popularity of melodrama in what Vick terms the "Golden Age" of Korean cinema [1953–1973] and the status of this genre as acceptable under the Japanese invasion. Nonetheless, it appears that audiences were predispositioned in favor of melodrama.)

Among the most significant directors of the Golden Age was Shin Sang-ok, who brought a number of the tenets of Italian neo-realism to Korea, including location setting and the unabashed depiction of social issues. His 1958 *A Flower in Hell* (*Jiokhwa*/지옥화) tells the story of a prostitute who entertains American soldiers and is torn between two lovers, one a gangster and the other a young man recently arrived in Seoul. In 1961, Shin made *The Mother and the Guest* (*Sarangbang Sonnimgwa Eomeoni*/사랑방 손님과 어머니), a film that Vick describes as influenced by Jean Renoir (150). This work is a melodrama focusing on the relationship between a young widow in love with her tenant, and exploring how this relationship runs afoul of the norms of Confucian society. *The Mother and the Guest* was awarded Best Picture at the 1962 Asian Film Festival. The star of a number of Shin vehicles was actress Choi Eun-hee, who was also the director's wife. The couple's life was not without adventure. Following her divorce from Shin, Choi alleged that she had been kidnapped by North Korean agents in 1978, and Shin made a similar claim later the same year. Pyongyang has fervently denied the allegations, stressing that the couple came to the North voluntarily. Shin asserted that following a five-year period in prison, during which time he was separated from Choi, he was given an impressive budget to make films in the North and to help take the North Korean film industry to new heights. .One of his most famous films from his Pyongyang period is *Pulgasari* (불가사리) (1985), often known as the "North Korean Godzilla film." Shin and Choi sought refugee status from North Korea in 1986 during an official visit to a film festival in Vienna. Both received political asylum in the United States, and Shin continued his career for a few years under the name Simon Sheen, making ninja films. He died in South Korea in 1996.

Another major figure of the Korean Golden Age was director Lee Man-hee, who is best known for such patriotic war movies as *The Marines Who Didn't Make It Home* (*Dolaoji Anhneun Haebyeong*/돌아오지 않는 해병) (1963) and *04:00–1950* (*1950 nyeon 4si*/1950 년 4 시) (1972). Man-hee also directed psychological horror movies and works reminiscent of *film noir*. In contrast, director Yu Hwon-mok's films deal with socioeconomic issues in the wake of South Korea's industrialization and societal transformation. His films *The Coachman* (*Mabu*/마부) (1961) and *Daughters of Pharmacist Kim* (*Kim*

Yaggugui Ddaldeul/김약국의 딸들) (1963) are of particular consequence. It is significant that such excellent films were produced during a period of military rule. Such a phenomenon can be compared to the excellence of those Brazilian *cinema novo* films made following Brazil's military coup in 1964.

Vick (2007) has cited a 1973 revision to the Korea Motion Picture Act, which drastically increased censorship, coupled with the rise of television, as factors leading to the decline of South Korean cinema. He argues that, during this period, Korean directors, as under the Japanese occupation, were forced to make "either blatant propaganda or innocuous genre flicks" (152). According to Vick, "Audiences, accustomed to the more sophisticated fare of the 1960s, increasingly turned to other forms of entertainment" (152). Nonetheless, there were a number of significant directors working during the 1970s. Among these were Lee Jang-ho, whose work offered a strong indictment of the military government, and Im Kwontaek, whose *The Deserted Widow* (*Jabcho*/잡초) tells the tale of the hardships undergone by a widow in the wake of social transformations following the Korean War. Im's work grew in quality, and his film *Seopyeonje* (1993) was a key work of the early stages of the New Korean Cinema. The importance of this film has been noted by Chi-Yun Shin and Julian Stringer as well as by Jinhee Choi (2010), who notes that post-*Seopyeonje* cinema marked a radical departure from the early 1980s (6).

Tony Rayna (1994) offers his own account of the development of the New Korean Cinema. He discusses the Film Act of 1987, which abolished the quota for domestic production versus foreign importation of films, and served to loosen authoritarian state control on the industry. Such measures, notes Rayna, went hand in hand with South Korea's "desperate desire to present a more 'liberal' face to the world" (5). This climate led to the birth of what has been termed the "Korean New Wave."

From an economic standpoint, Brian Yecies (2007) analyzes the distinction between the U.S. approach to films as "goods" and the Korean notion of film as "cultural expression." Yecies posits that the liberalization of the quota system and the increased presence of foreign films in Korea have actually served to foster the growth of the domestic market. He argues, "With the onslaught of foreign films since the late 1980s, new cinemas had to be built and a whole new generation of moviegoers was born" (27). Assessing Hollywood's efforts to pressure Seoul to limit the number of domestic films screened, Yecies concludes that, despite U.S. gains in the Korean market, "the history of cinema in Korea has proven the local film industry is an economic and cultural asset worth fighting for—for both sides of the negotiating table" (27).

As Jinhee Choi highlights, there has been much debate as to the exact timing of the birth of the New Korean Cinema. Nonetheless, she stresses that there is a strong level of concurrence that the movement is associated with directors born in the 1950s who began their work in the second half of the 1980s (2010, 6). These directors were quickly followed by what Choi (2004) has defined as the "386 Generation," "a term borrowed from computer chip technology, which refers to the generation who were born in the 1960s and educated in college in the 1980s, one of the most politically traumatic periods in Korean history" (xii). Choi defines the 386 Generation as literary, film-school-educated, and self-conscious of film style (xii). Rather than focusing on the "newness" of the New Korean Cinema, Choi (2010) frames the phenomenon in terms of a second renaissance in Korean film, which is characterized by social consciousness, aesthetic experimentation, and industrial boom (6).

Choi's exploration of the 386 Generation implies a trend toward modernization is present in the Korean New Wave, a position shared by Frances Gateward. In her introduction to *Seoul Searching: Culture and Identity in Contemporary Korean Cinema,* Gateward notes that modernization is a major theme in Korean art, literature, and film, in that it reflects "the rapid and radical transformation of the nation" (2007, 7). She opens her book with a taxonomy of plots—a Vietnam veteran plagued by memories of his past; working-class teens faced with life choices; a love affair brought about by a misdirected letter; a prostitute and a taxi driver who vow revenge on local gangsters; a deaf young man who kidnaps a child to help provide a kidney transplant for his dying sister. Gateward argues that, despite the fact that these premises seem integral to Hollywood cinema, they represent the diversity of today's South Korean cinema (6–7). She further ventures that Seoul has replaced Tokyo as the "center of 'cool' popular culture.... In less than twenty years, Korean cinema, once a local cinema on the verge of collapse, has emerged as an international economic and cultural powerhouse, becoming the most dominant cinema in Asia" (2).

The New Korean Cinema has gained a good deal of attention from the U.S. popular press. These discussions serve as indicators of the extent to which American audiences have attempted to view Korean films from an autochthonous perspective, versus whether more universal, cross-cultural readings have come into play. The North American press has tended to base its discussions of Korean cinema on festival screenings and releases of individual films in major metropolitan centers. Although a good number of the reviews are very insightful, particularly in terms of the films of the Korean New Wave, the tendency has been to downplay cultural distinctness in favor of making the films more accessible to a U.S. audience. Our cursory examination of these discussions will look at articles—albeit often extremely brief—that have dealt with the Korean film phenomenon in broader terms. They stem from major newspapers as well as a trade publication, *The Hollywood Reporter.*

Among the most prevalent themes in the more general discussions are the exoticism and inaccessibility of Korean films. For instance, in a *New York Times* discussion of a 2004 Lincoln Center retrospective, "The Newest Tiger: Sixty Years of South Korean Cinema," Manohla Dargis (2004) observes how this cinema tradition has gone from "relative obscurity on the world stage to hotter than hot," and laments the fact that most South Korean films never receive U.S. distribution and, therefore, must be seen at festivals and university screenings. Dargis, however, provides little insight into what viewers might expect from the festival, mentioning only the names of a few of the directors of the 40 films to be screened and highlighting that *Low Life* is the 99th film of Im Kwontaek.

As can be expected, mentions of the South Korean film industry are highly oriented in favor of U.S. interests, particularly in what concerns the quota system and box office trends in South Korea. In a May 2011 article in *The Hollywood Reporter,* Hyo-won Lee explores the patterns of film-going in South Korea, stressing that older audiences often go to films that young people have talked about, and quoting a senior film distribution executive who argues that younger audiences often rewatch films with their parents and grandparents. The dearth of films that appeal to older audiences, however, has forced department stores to host "silver cinema" events. Lee cites cultural critic Lee Moon-won, who explains, "Regardless of age, many moviegoers are tired of provocative thrillers and scandalous melodramas and want to see feel-good movies" (Hyo-won Lee, 2011). Such comments, elucidative as they are for issues of domestic marketing, downplay differences between Korean films and Western genres. "Thrillers" and "melodramas" are the order of the day.

The title of a recent popular-press article in the United States, "Discovering Korea through Film," promised a discussion of the role of film as a vehicle for understanding Korean culture, yet remained at the level of anecdote. Hannah Stuart-Leach's July 2011 article in *The Korea Herald* chronicles the career of Darcy Paquet, a Slavic linguist trained at Indiana University, who became, through a combination of circumstances, one of the foremost specialists on Korean cinema in the United States. Having studied in Russia, Paquet ended up traveling back and forth to Korea, reporting for *Variety* and working for the Korean Film Council. Paquet has identified a number of characteristics evident in recent Korean film that he feels differentiates this cinema from other film traditions. He emphasizes that Korean filmmakers are more likely than others to have a tragic ending to their tales or to leave loose ends open. Their works focus more on character and are "more evocative." Paquet concludes that Korean films "have a very strong emotional impact ... and directors aren't afraid to push that as far as it will go" (Stuart-Leach, 2011).

North Korean Cinema

An extensive catalogue of North Korean film is to be found in a colorfully illustrated volume simply titled *Korean Film Art* and published in 1985 by the Korean Film Export and Import Corporation. The volume divides North Korean film production into several closely related themes: (1) feature films adapted from the immortal classics; (2) feature films on the theme of revolutionary traditions; (3) feature films on the theme of the socialist reality; (4) feature films on the theme of the fatherland liberation war; and (5) feature films on the theme of intelligence and counterintelligence.[3] According to this work, North Korea took its first step toward building up its film industry in 1949 with the production of *My Home Village* (*Nae Gohyang*/내고향), a film directed by Kong Hong Sik, which focuses on the "joy and emotion of the Korean People who are now liberated [from] the colonial yoke of Japanese imperialism" (*Korean Film Art,* 1985, np). This work was exemplary of the ideological underpinnings of North Korean cinema, as expressed by Kim Il Sung himself: "Like the leading article of the Party paper, the cinema should have great appeal and move ahead of the realities. Thus, it should play a mobilizing role in each stage of the revolutionary struggle" (*Korean Film Art,* 1985, np). Kim Il Sung is credited with having had "a deep insight into the great role of the cinematic art in the development of literature and art" and with having "built up the ranks of movie workers, laid the material and technical foundations for film production by appropriating an enormous amount of funds for it, and ... shown the way for the cinematic art to go in each period and each stage of the revolution" (*Korean Film Art,* 1985, np).

Among the most famous North Korean films are *The Sea of Blood* (*Pibada*/피바다) (Choe Ik-gyu, 1968), the story of a simple mother in the 1930s who is awakened to the need for revolution and becomes actively engaged in the struggle; *The Flower Girl* (*Ggoch Paneun Cheonyeo*/꽃 파는 처녀) (Pak Hak, Choe Ik-Gyu, 1973), a film that introduces the tragedies of the Korean people under the Japanese occupation through the story of a young woman who, due to her father's debt and her brother's imprisonment, must become a servant in her landlord's home; *Unsung Heroes* (*Ireumeobneun*

*Yeongungdeul/*이름없는 영웅들) (*Ryu Ho-son and Ko Hak-lim,* multiple parts, 1978–1981), an espionage film that played an important role in the celebrity of American defectors James Joseph Dresnok and Charles Robert Jenkins in North Korea; and of course, Shin Sang-ok's *Pulgasari* (1985), which has gained an international cult following.

   Kim Jong Il surpassed his father in his passion for the cinema as a revolutionary art form. Closely involved in film production, in 1973 he published *On the Art of the Cinema,* a lengthy treatise on diverse aspects of filmmaking—among these, directing for the camera; actor and character; camera and image; screen art and fine art; scenes and music; art and creative endeavor; and guiding the creative process. Kim draws a parallel between the North Korean "speed campaign" and film production, asserting:

> The speed campaign in the creation of works of art and literature is a fundamentally revolutionary mode of creative work providing the basic structure for artistic endeavor. It allows writers and artists to fulfill the requirements of the Party's ideological work promptly, by encouraging them to display the maximum of political awareness and creative enthusiasm and produce successful works of high ideological and artistic quality in the shortest possible period of time [291].

   Kim focuses a good deal of his discussion on strategies through which North Korea could rid itself of outmoded approaches to film production and criticism. He argues that works of art must be "examined in a spirit of solidarity and cooperation" remain "strictly in accordance with the Party policy" (310). Only in this way can they "be developed soundly and quickly to serve the Party, the revolution and the people" (310).

   Although North Korean films do often focus on historical themes and societal issues, they also pay homage to traditional music and dance, and to Korean cultural heritage. In this respect, although in a very different manner than their southern counterparts, they lend themselves to an examination of key cultural concepts. It can be assumed that in North Korean cinema, where the role of the individual is significantly downplayed in favor of that of society at large, such concepts will take on a more politicized role.

   In the following chapters, we explore key cultural words through individual films and, in turn, films through key cultural words, taking into account how these cultural concepts overlap and intersect. The layering of key cultural concepts and explicit or implicit visualizations thereof will prove to be strategic for obtaining a deep and multilayered understanding of Korean culture.

Introductory Remarks

The second part of this book comprises in-depth readings of select films that illustrate the key concepts articulated in the previous chapters. It also briefly examines the critical reception of these films and provides short plot summaries. The discussions weave together analyses undertaken by the Korean and American authors, both mediated by the key concepts under consideration in each case.[1] The films to be analyzed here include, in chronological order, the following works Im Kwontaek's *Seopyeonje* (서편제) (1993); Park Chanwook's *Joint Security Area (J.S.A.)* (*Gongdong Gyeongbi Guyeog*/ 공동 경비 구역) (2000); Lee Changdong's *Oasis* (오아시스) (2002); Im Kwontaek's *Chihwaseon* (취화선) (Painted Fire) (2002); Kim Kiduk's *Spring, Summer, Fall, Winter ... and Spring (Bom, Yeoreum, Gaeul, Gyeoeul, ... Bom*/ 봄, 여름, 가을, 겨울, ... 봄) (2003); Kang Jegyu's *The Brotherhood of War (Taegeukgi Hwinallimyeo*/ 태극기 휘날리며) (2004); Lee Junik's *The King and the Clown (Wangui Namja*/ 왕의 남자) (2005); Bong Joonho's *Mother* (마더) (2009); Lee Changdong's *Poetry (Si*/ 시) (2010); and Kim Kiduk's *Pietà* (피에타) (2012). Of particular consequence in this selection is that, despite their invaluable role in illustrating key cultural concepts, a number of these films have not yet made their way into Western scholarly discourse.

Chapter 4 consists of an examination of the venting of *han* through performance, as viewed through the lenses of *pansori,* a genre of traditional Korean music, in *Seopyeonje* and *gwangdae nori* (folk performance/farce) in *The King and the Clown,* and the venting of an intricately entwined, co-dependent *han* in *Pietà.* Chapter 5 presents an analysis of the irrational aspects of *jeong* through discussions of *Mother, Taegeukgi: The Brotherhood of War, Joint Security Area,* and *Oasis.* Chapter 6 draws upon *Spring, Summer, Winter, Fall ... and Spring, Chihwaseon,* and *Poetry* to flesh out the concept of *deok* from the perspective of progress.

In addition to these 10 films from South Korea, three films from North Korea are examined in terms of key cultural concepts as mediated by the lens of *juche* (주체) ideology in Chapter 7. They are, in chronological order, Rim Changbom and Jon Kwangil's *On the Green Carpet* (*Pureunjudan Wieseo*/푸른주단 위에서) (2001); Pho Kwang and Maeng Choimin's *Pyongyang Nalparam* (평양 날파람) (2006); and Jang Inhak's A Schoolgirl's Diary (*Han Nyeohaksaengui Ilgi*/한 녀학생의 일기) (2007).

Chapter 4

Han in Venting

Cinema, *Han* and *Han*-Venting

Film scholars dealing with South Korean film have previously emphasized the importance of *han* in understanding this cinema tradition. In his introduction to the section on Korea in *Asian Cinema: A Field Guide* (2007), Tom Vick argues that Korea's history is "Bound up with influences—not to mention invasion and subjugation—from both [China and Japan]" (143). He further attributes "Korean cinema's long history of tragic, melodramatic works" to the foregrounding influence of *han* (143). Likewise, in an examination of *Seopyeonje*, Kim Kyung-Hyun (2004) explores the importance of *han* in Im Kwon-taek's film. He explains:

> Usually positioned as one of the most actively mobilized referential idioms in Im Kwontaek's films, the significance of *han* is intensified in *Seopyeonje* as [the protagonist] and his family are pushed to society's periphery without the recognition of their talents and determination to preserve national aesthetics [63].

These critics have enhanced our understanding of *han* in Korean cinema. Yet, our grasp can be further refined by examining it from another angle, that of *han*-venting. We consider, as discussed in Chapter 2, that *han*-venting is just as significant as *han*-bearing in Korean culture. An analysis of a film that reflects *han* from the perspective of venting will enhance our understanding of this complex cultural concept.

The following discussion focuses on the presence of *han*-venting in *Seopyeonje*, *The King and the Clown,* and *Pietà*. The first two genres through which the process occurs are the *pansori* in *Seopeonje* and the farce/comedic mockery in *The King and the Clown*. Both occur as performances within a performance—in other words, a diegetic performance within the films' performances. In the former film, emphasis is placed on the *han*-venting of the performer; in the latter, the process occurs for both diegetic performer and spectator. The large difference between the genres notwithstanding, both require "truthfulness" on the part of the artist.

A performance must be sincere and real for *han* to be vented. However, with respect to *Pietà,* the process of *han*-venting is not as transparent as in the two films dealing with performance. It is much more complex in that it involves two main characters who are co-dependently venting their *han*. Moreover, such co-dependence is intriguingly intertwined. Emphasis is placed on one character's suppressed *han* and its emergence and on the hidden plot involving the other character, whose *won-han* turns into *jeong-han*.

We sometimes are told, "Don't take what he or she said personally; that person was just venting." That is to say, the receiver of someone's griping and moaning, by virtue of the acts of talking and listening, could function (unwillingly or unwittingly) as an outlet that improves the psychological health of the grumbler. If we were not allowed to vent, it is said, we would bottle up our emotions, leading to countless side effects. We, as listeners, can therefore become more or less an outlet for someone else's psychological well-being. Nonetheless, the speaker is not necessarily seeking advice, nor is advice always warranted, which is one of the ironic aspects of venting. Similarly, *han*, as something that is psychologically or psychosomatically stagnant in the heart, needs to be vented from time to time to maintain its bearer's health. Just as talking to someone can be a coping mechanism that allows an individual to rationalize and validate his or her own concerns, worries, dreams, and hopes, so there are a number of ways through which people can vent their own *han,* regardless of its validity. This chapter aims to provide a further understanding of *han* by analyzing three films from the perspective of *han*-venting, specifically by examining what is involved in this phenomenon, how it is exhibited, and what interpretation is plausible. As each film is so distinctive in various ways, the analyses take a unique approach and enlarge the realm of *han* and its venting.

Seopyeonje

The film *Seopyeonje,* based on a short story by Cheong Jun Lee (1976), tells of an itinerant family of singers who are struggling to preserve the disappearing *pansori*, a traditional form of vocal music accompanied only by drums, as well as trying to make a living during and immediately following Japanese colonialism. The older protagonist, Yubong, is the leader of a troupe of musicians, consisting of his adopted son and daughter, who is dedicated to preserving this age-old musical genre. The son, Dongho, who lacks the talent of his father and sister, Songhwa, eventually abandons the itinerant life to seek stable employment. Much later, as a middle-aged man, Dongho develops a growing interest in his past and sets out on a search for his family, with this search constituting the framing device of the narrative. Dongho learns that Yubong is dead and that his sister, Songhwa, has been blinded by her father to make her a better singer. Brother and sister are briefly united, and they spend a night performing *pansori,* although each pretends not to recognize the other. Given the depth of her *han*-venting in the presence of her brother, Songhwa performs her best *pansori* that night.

Han-*Venting of the Three Main Characters*

In Chapter 2, we discussed three approaches to *han*-venting; while *han*-venting is situation specific, it is vented (1) through reliance on super-nature; (2) through others, especially children, grandchildren, and siblings; and (3) through the building up of inner strength and persistence. To explore how these approaches play out, we will describe the three main characters, Yubong (father), Songhwa (adopted daughter), and Dongho (adopted son), in terms of their *han.*

YUBONG'S *HAN*-VENTING: COMPULSORY TRAINING

Yubong is doubtless very disturbed, and his disorders are first exhibited through the film's backstory, in which he is expelled, despite his great musical

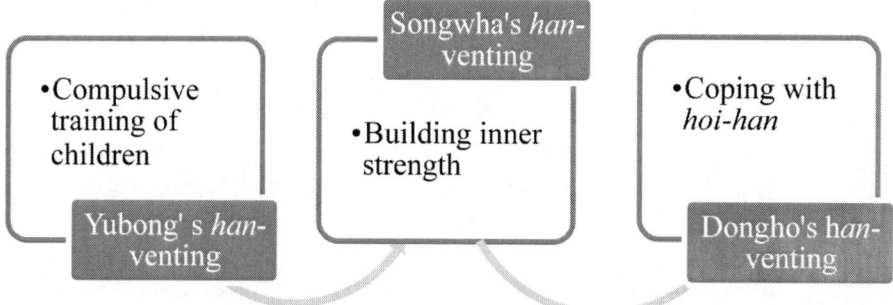

Figure 7. *Han*-Venting of the Three Main Characters.

talent, from a *pansori* school as the result of his affair with his mentor's mistress. Two key factors contribute to his disturbance. First, it can be attributed to the weakened position of a man during the transitional period from the Japanese colonization of Korea to the beginning of modernization. Men, especially of a low social class, lost their male chauvinistic, patriarchal image under colonialism; this circumstance, which resulted in the dwindling of the power of Korean men during this period, as we have seen, is well illustrated in the short story "Wings" by Yi Sang, as well by Choi Jisoo, a character in *Toji* (*Land*) by Park Kyung Ni.

The second factor contributing to Yubong's mental state is the decline of *pansori,* his true passion, during this colonial period, and thereafter. Yubong appears to be one of the most talented trainees/performers in the *pansori* school, according to what one of his old colleagues says over drinks. Even though he was expelled from the school and is now aware of the difficulty of making a living through *pansori,* he cannot give it up. When his friend, a street-painter, suggests that he have his children learn painting from him for a living, he refuses the suggestion bluntly, and exercises his authority over the friend (and all those who do not respect *pansori*), by replying with a pun, "*Pansori* will *panchida*" (*Pansori* will have a great deal of influence).[1]

These two factors, which account for Yubong's troubled behavior, plant a seed of *jeong-han* in his heart, in that he is not in a position to be able to fight against society and challenge societal cultural norms. Nevertheless, Yubong's *han* is released, to a certain degree, through *pansori* performance (as shown in scenes of the family singing on the road and Yubong's performance at a local party). But that is just a momentary relief. As the popularity of *pansori* declines, the opportunities for performance dwindle; moreover, Yubong is growing old. The only way of venting his *han* is to achieve the highest level of musical beauty, and thereby restore the popularity of *pansori,* through the vehicle of his adopted children, the second approach to *han*-venting.

Since Yubong's desire to revive *pansori* through the production of the best-quality performance cannot be actualized given the reality to which he is confined, he insists on attaining this goal through the means of patriarchal force and male chauvinistic violence. He exploits his children and uses them in his *han*-venting. However, from his perspective, his cruel behavior does not constitute exploitation. For Yubong, it is part of the nature of *pansori* training. It has been noted that "the training to express the difficult vocal skills includes many years of personal practice in an isolated place, including activities such as shouting against a roaring waterfall and performing vocal exercises in mountains" (Han et al., 2001, 366). Yubong pushes and forces his children to endure extreme privation, believing that is the best way to achieve the best *pansori*. His firm affirmation of hardship is implied throughout the film.

Yubong's most inhuman act is preparing for Songhwa, who has become ill following Dongho's departure, a medicinal concoction that will render its recipient blind. Even this unforgivable action is closely linked to Yubong's *han*-venting. As he is dying, he confesses to having blinded her, yet justifies his act by stating that his cruel deed had been intended to plant *han* in Songhwa's mind, so that she would be capable of producing *pansori* of the highest order. According to him, *han* is an *a priori* condition for the attainment of *pansori* beauty. This suggests a paradoxical allegory, inasmuch as cruelty and beauty coexist.

This allegory is well reflected in a scene where Yubong is badly beaten by a local man because he has stolen a chicken to feed Songhwa, who has grown physically weak. In spite of the terrible pain from the beating, Yubong instructs Songhwa in issues of sound production. He says to her, "What a voice he made! That kind of sound has to be produced when performing Sim Bongsa (the father of Simcheong)." Songhwa subsequently sings the musical role of Sim Bongsa, after which Yubong proclaims, "Finally, you are able to carry *han* in your voice." After confessing that he has made her blind, he asserts, "If you had considered me as your enemy, *han* should have been reflected in your voice, but there was no trace of *han* in your voice." He continues, "Now, you need to conquer your deeply seated *han* and bring it out of your heart, and produce sounds that conquer *han*.... If *han* is conquered, one can only produce sound of attainted beauty."

Here, from the perspective of *han*-venting (which paradoxically carries a conundrum), Yubong intensifies not only Songhwa's *han,* but also his own, through his bitter and hurtful action. In other words, the second approach to *han*-venting for Yubong is highly challenging, intricate, and difficult. As stated in Chapter 2, usually it is children who initiate the venting of parental *han* out of filial piety. In the case of Yubong, however, it is the father who initiates the *han*-venting process in both Dongho and Songhwa. From this point of view, *han*-venting is distressing and painful for Yubong as well. Thus, *han,* as made implicit in Yubong's blinding of his daughter, must prevail for *pansori* to shine. *Han* provides the "method" to the acting, the merging of one's own emotions with the emotions of the song.

Songhwa's *Han*-Venting: Building Inner Strength

Of the three characters, Songhwa's situation is the most vulnerable inasmuch as she is a girl/woman who must assume a submissive role in traditional society. Songhwa is an adopted child, which implies that her foster father could exploit her via a sexual relationship; at the same time, as a daughter, she must show the highly valued and expected filial piety. The *jeong-han* (self-compliant *han*) that has been instilled in her due to her lack of a biological family, her foster father's maltreatment and severe training in *pansori,* and the societal expectation for a female during that period is further enhanced by Dongho's departure. This *jeong-han* later becomes deeply rooted, by virtue of her blindness, which has been induced by her father, whom she cannot challenge.

Songhwa's *han*-venting is actually unthinkable. Yet, one observes that she is coping with the situation in an amazing way. She feels sorry for her foster father, who has been left out of the mainstream and who became marginalized during the country's capitalistic development. When Dongho, her adopted brother, decries Yubong and their under-respected, under-paid lifestyle, she defends their stepfather and even admonishes Dongho for his lack of understanding of their father's condition. Songhwa undertakes excessive practice and tries to cope with agonizing situations, including performing at a *gisaeng* party as well as on the street to earn bread. She takes the third approach to *han*-venting, building inner strength, to fulfill what is expected of her from Yubong and from herself as a person who loves *pansori.* Songhwa articulates to Dongho that she can forget all the hardship when performing. Her *han* is becoming extremely intense, severe, relentless, harsh, and even cruel. Nonetheless, inasmuch as the positive aspect of *han* generates inner strength rather than physical strength, Songhwa is becoming more resilient.

The moments in which she feels the happiest are doubtless those in which she and her brother Dongho sing "*Chunhyangga,*" the best-known and most-loved story of all *pansori* repertoire. Even after Dongho has left, she goes to the enormous tree under which they sang the piece, hoping that her brother will return. Again, this is a passing release of her *han.* The tree is thus related to the close bond between Songhwa and Dongho.

An especially critical moment follows her blindness. During a sunset, Songhwa and Yubong discuss what she no longer can see:

SONGHWA: Did the sun set?

YUBONG: Not yet.

SONGHWA: Is there an afterglow of sunset?

YUBONG : Ya, the sky is reddish. It looks like it's windy.

SONGHWA : Ya, cold wind is blowing. The moon will come out soon.

YUBONG : Ya, it will. And the stars.

SONGHWA : Ya. Will I ever see the sky, sun, moon, stars?
YUBONG : (Sighs in silence.)
SONGHWA : Am I becoming blind?
YUBONG : (Sighs in silence.)
SONGHWA : I'm cold.
YUBONG : Come inside and I'll give you a blanket.

Immediately following this exchange, Songhwa asks her father to teach her "Simcheongga," a story (discussed in Chapter 2) that focuses on a young maiden named Simcheong and her blind father. In the story, Simcheong dies at sea so that her father can regain his eyesight, a classic example of filial piety. At this moment, Songhwa appears to fully accept her fate; she acknowledges her blindness as a means through which Yubong has planted *han* in her voice so that excellence in *pansori* can be attained. Although the blindness in "Simcheongga" is present in the father, not the daughter, both dyads reveal filial piety. The singing of "*Simcheongga*" constitutes a turning point, in that Songhwa allows her *jeong-han* to bud and grow in an affirmative way.

At the end of the film, Songhwa, who has been living in a small tavern, is found by Dongho. Since she is blind, she does not recognize him at first. However, when she performs the *pansori* of Simcheong, she recognizes him by his style of drumming. In this sequence, we hear her voice up to the moment in which Simcheong implores her father to open his eyes. The remaining portions of the song are not heard; the film's main theme substitutes Songhwa's singing. Native Korean viewers can "fill in the blank" due to their familiarity with the song. As mentioned earlier, the *pansori* at once describes and reverses Songhwa's relationship with Yubong. Thus, Songhwa, by virtue of her own blindness and having taken on the *han* of her father, can expressively play both roles. In this performance, her voice reaches a sublime level, and her *han* seems to be fully vented, at least temporarily, which leads her to begin a new journey.[2] In the morning, Songhwa's lover asks her if she had recognized her brother. She affirms that she did, indeed, recognize him through the way in which he played the drum, which was similar to that of Yubong.[3] When asked why the siblings failed to acknowledge each other, Songhwa states that they needed, instead, to keep their *han* alive.[4] From the standpoint of *han*-outcome, Songhwa's attaining a sublime level in her art and moving forward on a new journey is similar to Lady Hyegyeong's memoirs, discussed in Chapter 2. Although these two women's backgrounds are totally different, both of their lives are extremely painful. Furthermore, they are both able to reach literary/artistic excellence.

DONGHO'S RETROSPECTIVE *HAN*-VENTING:
  COPING WITH *HOI-HAN*

Although Dongho's *han* leads to considerably less drama that that of Yubong or Songhwa, it nonetheless provides the film with its framing device. Dongho's rebellious attitude toward his foster father and his ultimate departure can be attributed to a number of factors, including the cause of his mother's death, the family's poverty, his father's irrational and cruel behavior, and, most importantly, the maltreatment of his foster sister Songhwa, for whom he really cares. Although Dongho ultimately finds a decent profession, he feels guilty about having deserted Songhwa to make money and build his own family. He senses something missing in his life and longs for his childhood family, especially his sister. In Dongho, we thus find *hoi-han*/ 회 한 (roughly translated as "remorse or "repentance"), which spurs him to search for his sister. When he finally meets his sister, he beats the drums rhythmically and passionately as the two spend the night performing *pansori,* although they themselves are the only intended audience. His *hoi-han* is freed by turning into tragic joy as they part, without overtly revealing themselves to each other.

Han *and* Han-*Venting: A Prerequisite to the Sublime*

Sandra Webster (2002, 2003) and her students have investigated how Koreans have developed not only a specific emotional coping style to protect themselves from the chronic stress they have experienced as a people, but also a vehicle through which they have built Korean character, both nationally and individually. *Seopyeonje* can be viewed as an illustration of Webster's findings. In it, adversity fosters positive character, as evidenced by Yubong's merciless training of Songhwa and the latter's heart-breaking endurance and painstaking practice. Although some may view Yubong's way of teaching to be an exploitation of the vulnerable Songhwa, others may consider it to be an example of how *han* provides the prerequisite to reaching beyond one's perceived limits. Certain situational constraints are necessary for an individual to move from chronic stress to the development of a strong character that will reach an inspiring, uplifting, transcendent level. From a Christian perspective, *han* can be viewed as paralleling the mystical concept of the pathos of Good Friday in relationship to the Resurrection.[5]

Importance of Pansori *in* Han-*Venting*

One of the reasons why *Seopyeonje* has enjoyed such great appeal in South Korea as well as in diaspora may lie in the fact that Koreans have been contemplating whether their culture-based sentiment still exists, the extent to which it has been transformed, and how it will evolve. To this effect, the film, while revealing an aspect of Korean cultural beauty through the harsh life of a commoner, aims to reflect the sublime sound of two longing souls encountering each other after a long and difficult life-journey. It illustrates the primal importance of *pansori* as an art form with respect to the *han* and *han*-venting of Koreans.

More specifically, *Seopyeonje* demonstrates that *han* is a driving force that can be sublimated into a great form of art. It further suggests that this concept is always linked to a longing for the past and a desire to search for future meaning. This is made manifest through Dongho's adult journey from *sorije jumak*/ 소리제 주막 (roughly translated as the "Tavern of Minstrel Height"), where Dongho meets the first woman whom Songhwa had trained. *Han*-venting in *Seopyeonje* is thus centered on *pansori*, which holds a different meaning for each character. For Yubong, it is the reason for his existence; yet at the same time, it incarnates his failure to attain a high level of art. For Songhwa, it is a prop for building inner strength to endure the suffering that leads to artistic excellence. For Dongho, it is a medium through which to search for his past. Regardless of their individual relationships with *pansori*, all three use it as a vehicle to vent their *han*.

Having observed the importance of *pansori* in *han*-venting, a further investigation of *Seopyeonje* in terms of *pansori* is in order. *Seopyeonje* is a school of *pansori*, an operatic performance art, often involving passionate love stories, that developed in Korea in the late 19th century. It is epic in nature inasmuch as it delivers a long story, sometimes taking two to eight hours to perform. In *seopyeonje*, the singer's voice is light and decorative, employing minimalist melodies that result in a light and florid style of singing; its melody is soft, yet pathetically sad and beautifully mellow, and the phrase ending is prolonged. This stands in contrast to *dongpyeonje*, another style/school of *pansori*, in which the singing begins with great weight and the phrasing ends stiffly. The singer must have a strong voice and deploy energetic pronunciation, using little decoration to project the grandeur of sound for its beginning and forceful ending. Both the music styles of *seopyeonje* and *dongpyeonje* are conducive to protecting *han*. A *pansori* is performed by two persons: a *gosu*, who makes long and short beats on a special drum, called a *buk*, and a *sori-gwangdae*, who sings the long poems (sometimes combined with passages of narrative speech), usually with a long folding fan in her hand. The training required to express the difficult vocal skills takes many years, and vocal exercises are performed in isolated places such as roaring waterfalls and mountains. Furthermore, "to reach the position of *gwangdae*, disciples don't mind undergoing difficulties including eating dung and coughing blood" (Han et al., 2002, 366).

Pansori has been described by Tony Rayna (1994) as "a musical sublimation of South-West Korea's collective grief and suffering—in other words, a kind of blues" (30). Like the blues, a *pansori* performance allows for a considerable amount of improvisation, yet must be bound to highly controlled parameters. Given the nature of the stories told, a great deal of emphasis is placed on emotion, and one of the hallmarks of an excellent *pansori* performer is the ability to genuinely sense and transmit the feelings of the story sung and its characters.

Another noteworthy aspect of *pansori* is that its origin can be traced to *hereditary shaman* chants (Daeseok Seo and Peter Lee, 2005, 297), whose singers came from hereditary shaman households. As the musical elements of these songs became more polished, the artistic conventions and standards of the genre took shape, the musical skills of its singers improved, and a colorful and versatile body of work developed. Despite being primarily a folk art, *pansori* appealed to some members of the upper class. Although it was barely maintained during the colonial period due to the pre-influence of Japanese music, which was called *sin-pa,* and American pop music, it was revived in the late 20th century. Its revitalization and popularity can be attributed not only to its aforementioned unique musical styles, but also to its narrative themes, which are derived from legends, folk tales and novels to which its singers and listeners can relate. It is worthwhile to note that "*O Jeok*" (Five Bandits), a satirical poem that depicts the political situation of the late Japanese colonial period, written by Kim Ji Ha (1941), adopted stylistic features of *pansori*.

The King and the Clown

Lee Junik's *The King and the Clown* focuses on Jangsaeng and Gonggil, two male street entertainers (and the latter a female impersonator) who arrive in Seoul, hoping to further their career. Together with an extended group of artists, they concoct a performance that mocks the king and his concubine. Upon their arrest, the two are given an ultimatum: they must make the king laugh or be beheaded. Ultimately Jangsaeng and Gonggil succeed and are welcomed to the court, the king having become obsessed with the transvestite. The king uses the performers to stage a play depicting the murder of his mother at the hands of jealous concubines. Following this performance, he executes the perpetrators of his mother's death. Palace conspirators, alarmed by the king's friendship with Gonggil, distribute inflammatory flyers against the king, which are written in an excellent forgery of the performer's handwriting. Jangsaeng assumes the blame to save his friend and is ultimately blinded as a punishment for his subversive acts. When Jangsaeng is ordered by the vindictive king to walk the tightrope blind, Gonggil ascends to join him. They muse upon their fate while balancing above the palace, agreeing that, were they to live again, they would want to continue as clowns. As angry crowds storm the palace in protest of the despotic ruler and his court, the two artists jump from the rope.

Han-*Venting in* The King and the Clown

Han reflected in *The King and the Clown* is much more complex than its counterpart in *Seopyeonje*. The main characters of *The King and the Clown* belong to two extremely different social classes, while the protagonists of *Seopyeonje* are exclusively from the lower class. Consequently, the type of *han* and the roots thereof depicted in *Seopyeonje* are distinct from those explored in *The King and the Clown*, inasmuch as the latter circulate through vastly different social classes. Our analysis will be structured as follows: we will first focus on the two *gwangdaes* with regard to the endangerment and regaining

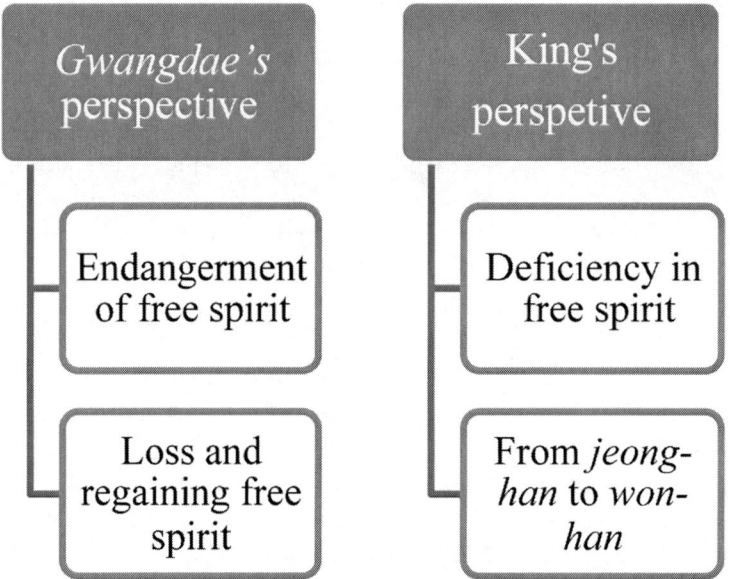

Figure 8. *Han*-Venting in *The King and the Clown*.

of their free spirit. We will subsequently deal with a king's deficiency in free spirit and his two types of *han* (*jeong-han* and *won-han*).

A Gwangdae's *Perspective*

THE ENDANGERMENT OF THE FREE SPIRIT OF JANGSAENG AND GONGGIL

Han can be generated by defeat of the country; foreign invasion and colonialism; the oppression and exploitation on the part of ruling classes; and the loss of land, or the loss of a beloved, among numerous other causes. Inasmuch as Jangsaeng is a *gwangdae*/ 광대 (roughly translated as "folk-performer; merrymaker"), his *han* would immediately be assumed to have taken root in the class status of a minstrel, the lowest rank in the Korean dynasties; that is, he may experience *jeong-han,* an unresolved sentiment of self-compliance.

The film opens with loosely connected shots depicting the dish-spinning tricks and other games of a street performance. We observe vitality, warmth, and a twinkle in the eyes of the performers. The energy of the performers foments a connection with their diegetic audience: all are laughing or smiling, and living in the present. Both artists and audience partake in the enthusiasm, fun, and excess of mirth. The diegetic spectators as well as the artists appear to let go of whatever burdens they are carrying. The form of performance depicted is termed *gwangdae*[6] *nori* (hereinafter referred to as *nori*/ 놀이) and is posited not only as an art form, but also as an instrument for the venting of *han,* inasmuch as it allows the performers to generate the "free spirit" essential to the process.

We soon observe that Jangsaeng is burdened by an unrevealed secret, that of his affection and feelings for his effeminate male *gwangdae* colleague, Gonggil. Jangsaeng aborts his tightrope act when he notices a *yangban* gazing at his companion's beautifully feminine body during his performance. After saving Gonggil from sexual harassment on the part of the upper-class man, the two *gwangdaes* flee from that town, opting to go to Hanyang, the country's then-capital. Although their flight implies a desire to maintain the free spirit of a *gwangdae,* such a state of mind becomes more endangered in the capital, where Jangsaeng must confront the power of the upper class. This experience generates *jeong-han,* inasmuch as he experiences sorrow and grief at being forced to comply with his vulnerable situation and limitation vis-à-vis the dominant class.

After having performed a skit mocking the king and his mistress, Jangsaeng is dragged to the royal guard and accused of having ridiculed the monarch. To thwart punishment, Jangsaeng places his life at stake and requests that he be allowed to make the king laugh, agreeing to die if he fails. A laugh on the part of the king watching a play about himself and Noksu, his favorite mistress, will indicate that the play is not meant to ridicule them; instead, it will underscore that the performance is an example of *mobang yesul* / 모방 예술, or the art of imitation. In the theatrical art of imitation, art is art and is divorced from reality. One can enjoy a performance on its own terms. The king's laugh, moreover, will confirm that he is king while the *gwangdae* is a *gwangdae,* thereby upholding the traditional hierarchical structure. From this perspective, Jangsaeng's betting his life on a play constitutes a vehicle for venting his *han.*

Jangsaeng is successful in that the king has a good laugh not only while watching the play, but also when imitating it with Gonggil in his private chambers. However, the positive feeling that Jangsaeng gains from the outcome of his artistic impulse is transient. After having enjoyed the play, the king, despite strong objections on the part of court officials, orders Jangsaeng's group to remain in court and to continue to perform. For the *gwangdaes,* "staying in court" implies that their "free spirit," which allows them to vent their *han,* will no longer exist, as they will be rendered puppets of the king. In other words, their free spirit will be trapped by a state of mind that acknowledges their unfortunate condition.

In the wake of the horrific incidents generated by the politically charged plays they have performed for Yeonsan, and the latter's cruel and mortal turmoil, Jangsaeng falls into a political trap. Although he wants to leave the court with his troupe, he is ultimately blinded in punishment for having saved Gonggil from a scheme devised by Yeonsan's mistress. This blindness implies the endangerment of his free spirit while living in the court. He is no longer able to vent his *han,* despite the better social position and material goods given to him in court. He is, moreover, obliged to display his *chung* (i.e., loyalty to the sovereign, official morality, group consciousness), a concept deeply embedded in the Korean psyche during the Joseon dynasty. Recall that such a concept involves situational ethics in the traditional Korean sense rather than ethics based on unchanging principles.[7] This conflicting situation will be discussed later.

What makes Gonggil stand out from the other minstrels is his ambivalent gender and sexuality. In the court, Gonggil cannot distance himself from the performances he must undertake, so his free spirit becomes endangered due to the fact that his ambivalent gender has embroiled him in court intrigue. In his performance as well as in the mind of Yeonsan, he assumes the role of the king's mother, who had been ordered to commit suicide by a jealous concubine, still residing in the court as the "Queen Mother."

When the king's jealous concubine conspires to have Gonggil killed during a hunt, his life is spared, but other *gwangdaes* and ministers die. Following the hunt, the king retreats to his chambers with Gonggil and, in a frenzied moment revealing his growing madness, asks him to shoot him with the bow and arrow. When Gonggil fails to respond to his order, Yeonsan grabs a servant who has come to serve tea and asks him to shoot her instead, decrying the woman's wickedness. Gonggil slowly raises the bow and arrow and shoots. Although the performer misses both potential targets, the trajectory of the arrow indicates that his intent was to shoot the king. This sequence reveals that, like Jangsaeng, Gonggil has become endangered: he, like his friend, is now the puppet of the king.

Loss and Regaining of Free Spirit

Gwangdae-nori conveys, in an exhilarating way, one's emotions through physical language as well as words, often accompanied by music. It spreads dynamic energy created by an excess of mirth and elevates the spirits of spectators, bringing a convergence of tension and relaxation. It can also generate and reinforce a "free spirit," which allows one to—at least temporarily—let go of *han.* In contrast, *nori* can be a source of conflict, confusion, and danger when the *gwangdae's* performance becomes an investigation of inappropriate behavior or an intolerable incident. The *gwangdae* would perform a skit satirizing these individuals, a performance intended to generate tremendous tension. From this standpoint, the *gwangdae*, underneath his mask, experiences a paradoxical conflict between reality and imitation, his principal role as *gwangdae* becoming blurred.

Living in court, Jangsaeng and Gonggil have lost their freedom. Jangsaeng faces conflicts between himself, the court officials, and the king; his spirit of freedom has become a spirit of conflict as he must uphold class status and meet bodily/material demands. Jangsaeng breaks the principal maxim of a *gwangdae*, that of keeping distance from reality, which is essential to the performing art of *nori.* He fails to maintain his identity as a performer not only due to his lack of power, but also because of the complexity of his inner feelings toward the relationship between Gonggil and Yeonsan, which he dares not reveal.

Jangsaeng, now blind, delivers a revealing speech, structured around *gwangdae-nori,* while balancing on a high wire. He asserts that he was blind to the *gwangdae's* rhythmic beats when he was child; he was blind to the excited culmination of *gwangdae-nori* when he became a performer; and he was blind to losing his sweetheart when he was at court. Nevertheless, he would still want to be a *gwangdae* if he were to be reborn. He wants to perform *nori* in a risk-free place where he can speak and act freely. Thus, he desires to regain his identity as one blessed with free spirit, the return to which would necessitate leaving the court. For him, the sense of freedom, joy, lightness, and openness is a natural state. He wants to remove a lid that has been placed on top of his true self. His desire to leave is similar to that of Hong Gildong (discussed in Chapter 2), who departs on a quest for utopia, where everyone lives in harmony and everything is for the best.

The utopia for Jangsaeng may be a place where he can vent freely not only his low-class-related *han* through the art of imitation, but also the *han* resulting from his inability to publicly reveal his attraction to Gonggil. That is, the mask that Jangsaeng has been wearing has served not only as an item in service of Art, but also as a means to hide his feelings toward his companion. As he does not want to accept his homosexuality, both self-deceit and external societal rules have prevented him from loving. He longs for a utopia free of conventional social norms, a place where a free spirit can be contagious and supportive.

Jangsaeng walks a high wire, a last performance before leaving the court, and Gonggil, who had attempted suicide when he became cognizant of the difficulty implicit in leaving the court, joins him in the performance. While walking on the rope, both express a wish to be reborn as *gwangdae* of "free spirit." They want to get rid of the lid limiting their lives and be in full connection with their spirit. The image of their two bodies suspended in the air is a metaphor of such freedom. The subsequent code, in which members of Jangsaeng's *gwangdae* group, including those killed in the hunt, allude to the fact that they will regain their "free spirit of *gwangdae*," reminds us of the liberty necessary for *han*-venting through authentic and carefree performance.

The King's Perspective

YEONSAN: DEFICIENCY IN FREE SPIRIT

Yeonsan's *han* may have started while growing up, since it was forbidden to speak at court about what had happened to his biological mother. Breaking this rule and challenging the authority of his father and grandmother was unthinkable. During his early reign, Yeonsan revealed himself to be a wise and capable administrator, strengthening national defense and seeking ways of helping the poor—that is, he might have been wearing a mask of *jeong-han* so as not to reveal it. Nevertheless, he also displayed some signs of a violent streak, most likely because he needed breathing space. Gradually, he developed abnormal behavior, especially when he discovered precisely what happened to his mother, at which point his *jeong-han* (self-compliance *han*) became a *won-han* (justice- and revenge-oriented *han*) toward those who were involved in the incident. In this state, he is totally deprived of the opportunity for free spirit.

When Jangsaeng's group starts to perform a small play, they are all nervous and make numerous mistakes. However, thanks to Gonggil's witty act, Yeonsan finally enjoys a good laugh. Furthermore, Yeonsan (with his mistress) relishes imitating what Gonggil played later in his private place. He has come to enjoy the fruits of *nori,* accepting the art form on its own terms. Thus, he can temporarily release his *han.*

However, the free spirit he demonstrates while enjoying *nori* turns evil when *nori* is deployed as a political tool. Yeonsan's *han* gets increasingly more severe and leads him to tyranny. His apparent *han*-venting is no longer such, inasmuch as the desire to control others precludes free spirit. In other words, whereas Yeonsan could continue to enjoy *nori,* tragically he and especially his subject, Cheoseon, are also clever enough to realize that the performance genre can be used to uncover the government officials who have been involved in a political stratagem as well as in his mother's death. The *nori* that Jangsaeng's group performs depicts vividly the political crisis and the conflicts between Yeonsan and the officials, serving as an efficient means for detective efforts. Those who cannot laugh at the performance, since they feel the *nori* represents themselves (rather than thinking that it is just a play), must have been involved in the incident. Unable to keep distance between themselves and the play, they appear to identify with the characters depicted. Their failure to laugh at the play provides Yeonsan with an excuse to kill them for their past acts, which ultimately leads to two historical literati purges, which occurred in 1498 and 1504.[8]

From the perspective of Yeonsan's need, a *nori* performance in which the king crawls under his concubine's skirts symbolizes his longing for his mother, making it a device for venting his *jeong-han.* In other words, the concubine plays an important role in Yeonsan's compensation for the lack of his biological mother's love. Similarly, his special feeling toward Gonggil appears to be a way of venting his *jeong-han,* in that Gonggil makes him re-feel his childhood sentiment; subconsciously, he may consider him to be another young mother. Here one could argue that the fact that the king bestows on Gonggil higher status as compensation for having made him happy implies his desire to restore his mother's title and position posthumously. One could also consider that the decadent, self-indulgent spirit Yeonsan displays with both his concubine and Gonggil is attributable to his lack of biological maternal love. At a subconscious level, he may not be able to distinguish between mother and lover, conflating his women, including Gonggil, with his mother.

FROM *JEONG-HAN* TO *WON-HAN*

Upon learning what actually happened to his mother, another type of *han* emerges in Yeonsan's mind—namely, *won*-han vis-à-vis those who had supported the laws and regulations that his father had established, and who were involved in his mother's exile and death. Thus, as his *han* becomes more complex, he proportionately becomes more inhumanly cruel. His tyranny can be viewed as a path toward venting his *han* against his father's laws and regulations. However, the two-sidedness of his *han* (*jeong-han* and *won-han*) was far from vented from a historical point of view. Although this outcome is only suggested in the film, from historical anecdote we know that a group of officials plotted against Yeonsan, launching a coup, demoting him to prince, and sending him into exile, where he died. Similarly, his mistress, considered the key person in encouraging Yeonsan's misbehavior, was beheaded.

With respect to the link between Yeonsan and *nori*, the king enjoys *gwangdae-nori* early in the film. This demonstrates that he understands satire and has a sense of humor. While a *nori* spectator, he appears to let go of his *han* and has a good laugh. What could be more important for him than to free himself from the unnecessarily burdensome *chemyeon* (socially prescribed rules) and overt appropriateness to which the upper class must adhere? As indicated in "The Tale of Heosaeng" in Chapter 2, there is an empty aspect to *chemyeon;* the upper classes, including the royal family, are expected to care a great deal about their behavior, following rules with consideration for their responsibilities. However, as Park Ji Won's "Tale of a *Yangban*" satirically implies, the status of a *yangban* is far from desirable, and one can be a much freer person without it. This is clearly what Yeonsan might have felt when he burst out laughing while watching Gonggil's quick-witted performance. Yeonsan's need for *nori* to free himself from the *chemyeon* boundaries that constrain him is complex. *Gwangdae-nori* can be a mirror of reality—but it can also be a narcissistic mirror in that the audience identifies with the performer. Yeonsan, while recognizing reality, also enjoys becoming a performer who wants to pursue narcissistic joy through the play. As a spectator, he is captivated by Gonggil's charm and invites him to his room, thus becoming unable to distinguish reality from *nori*. He makes a transition from Yeonsan, the audience-king, to a *gwang-*

dae. In other words, there is a reversal of roles; the king becomes a *gwangdae*, and the *gwangdae* becomes king. This narcissistic behavior can be attributed to Yeonsan's *jeong-han.*

A more serious link between Yeonsan and *nori* lies in a negative aspect of the function of the latter—that is, *nori's* role as a device for detecting something about one's previous involvement. The *nori* functions as a summons being served, thereby losing the fundamental freedom it implies and becoming a device for political action. As Yeonsan's *jeong-han* turns into a growing *won-han,* his relationship with the popular performance genre is reversed.

When Jangsaeng is blinded, Gonggil, having overheard his companion's lament, returns to the king's chambers to stage a puppet show, repeating to the king the words he has overheard. The motif of the puppet show recalls an earlier comment by Jangsaeng, who questions the role the performers have assumed in the palace, wondering whether they have become mere puppets. Such a sequence not only textualizes Gonggil's lack of free spirit, but further recalls the performance devices that are now preventing Yeonsan from venting his *han* and facilitating his more complete descent into his twisted realm. Moreover, the very friendship between Yeonsan and Gonggil, although initially appearing subversive in nature and failing to be constrained by conventional notions of gender and protocol, contains both men, pre-empting the venting of *jeong-han* and forcing, particularly in the case of Yeonsan, *won-han* to gain in prominence.

Han-*Venting Is Possible for* Jeong-han, *But Not for* Won-han

As Jangsaeng and Gonggil regain their free spirit at the end of the film, Yeonsan seems to return to the position of a spectator enjoying the performing arts. The last close-up shot of his smiling face watching Jangsaeng and Gonggil astride the high wire presents a number of possible interpretations. As the two minstrels once again enjoy free spirit, the king may be envious of their status. The bodies of the *gwangdae* appear light and relaxed, and they seem to trust in the power of free spirit. While watching, Yeonsan may wish to transcend his blocked *han*-venting via their free spirit. He may wish to let go of his deeply written burdens by looking high in the sky where two individuals communicate freely. Inasmuch as he is able to smile, his *jeong-han* seems to overrule his *won-han* at that particular moment. This suggests that *jeong-han* can be vented but *won-han* cannot.

Another point to be made here is the incompatibility of *han*-venting with power. Jangsaeng and Yeonsan appear to need each other. The *gwangdae* provides Yeonsan with *nori,* which is entertaining, but which can also be used as a political tool. Yeonsan, a most powerful person, raises the class status of Jangsaeng by giving him a position in court. Unfortunately, their relationship is clouded by conflict of interest inasmuch as they both have deep feelings for Gonggil. In such a case, it is usually the person with a lower rank who is the loser in the deal; at the same time, a *won-han* is formed in the loser's mind. Unless Jangsaeng had not died, there could have been another whirlwind of battle given that one *won-han,* in turn, results in another *won-han.*

Pietà

The film *Pietà* is an intensely haunting story involving two main characters, Gangdo and Miseon; Gangdo was abandoned as an infant and now works for loan sharks, and Miseon is a mysterious woman (whose name is revealed only late in the film) who claims to be his mother. It is set in an unfriendly neighborhood with small machine shops, where Gangdo goes to collect payments from debtors. He treats the money borrowers mercilessly, which results in the terrorizing of countless victims. Miseon persistently follows him, showing motherly care to prove her maternity in spite of Gangdo's execution of numerous atrocities to deny that she is his mother. Nevertheless, he is ultimately convinced and accepts her as his mother, slowly transforming himself and leaving his job to live a decent life with her. However, he has made many enemies while working for the loan shark; due to what he did to them in the past, he is afraid that their revenge will cause him to lose his mother, who has just entered his life. Meanwhile, the woman proceeds with her plan, the end goal of which is to make Gangdo miserable by forcing him to experience the loss of a beloved family member. Although her plan is carried out successfully, Miseon dies feeling sorry for him. Having experienced the terrible pain coming from the loss of his mother, Gangdo departs from life.

Han-*Venting in* Pietà

Pietà, the title of the film, refers to a masterpiece of Renaissance sculpture by Michelangelo, which depicts the body of Jesus Christ lying across the lap of his mother, the Blessed Virgin Mary. This reference may seem to allude to the connection between the film's theme and the Christian meaning of redemption, yet viewers will agree that this film has hardly anything to do with Christianity.

Nevertheless, *Pietà* is a good place to explore other aspects of *han*-venting given the paradoxical conundrum of *han* described in Chapter 2. This is especially true in conjunction with the view of *han* as a great asset for faith in all religions, inasmuch as its core aspect is characterized by "sorrow and hope." We recall the comments of Kim Paul Tchang Ryeol (1986) that *han,* in reality, is a blessing. When applied to *Pietà,* these remarks do not imply that the film makes viewers want to search for God, although this is falsely alluded to by the remote background of its setting. We see a cross on the top of a church, along with a banner that says "Hallelujah will be eternal" (author's translation). Nonetheless, revisiting Kim Paul Tchang Ryeol's words allows us to consider how an aspect of *han* reflected in *Pietà* is so atypical and nonconforming that its venting appears enigmatic and intriguing. We will examine *han*-venting from the perspectives of the two main characters, Gangdo and Miseon, whose *han* is intertwined.

Han-*Venting from Gangdo's Position*

Suppressed *Han*

Gangdo lives alone in a neighborhood that is populated with small machine shops. He is a money collector working for a loan shark who charges outrageous interest (10 times the principal per month). To guarantee the payment of the interest, debtors sign an insurance policy that pays benefits for industrial accidents and permanent disability. Part of the cruelty of Gangdo's job includes forcing the debtors to sign for the insurance.

When Gangdo sees the repayment is late and almost impossible, he threatens and attacks his clients. He injures the affected debtors to the extent

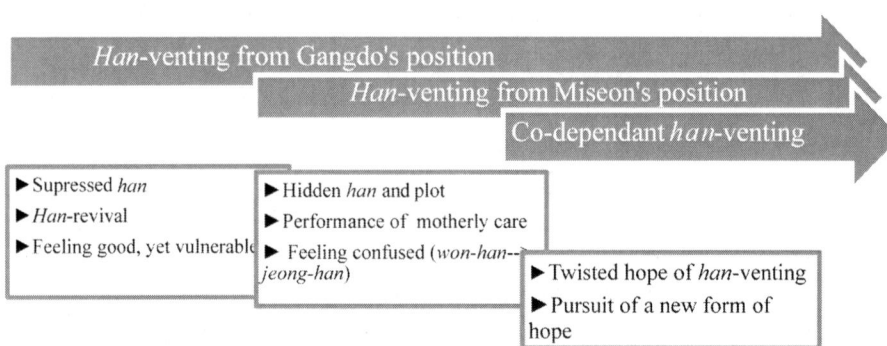

Figure 9. *Han-***Venting in** *Pietà.*

of the insurance coverage to pay for what they owe. What is disconcerting and disturbing is that Gangdo treats this as a routine job without displaying any sentiment. He is brutal, merciless, and unyielding.

Gangdo's lack of sentiment can be associated with what Sang-Chin Choi and Ki-Beom Kim call "self-involved meta-cognition" (2011, 119). They note that *han* is not abstract unhappiness. For unfortunate factors (e.g., poverty, low class status, discrimination, war, betrayal) to develop into *han,* one has to experience sorrow and grief in one's unhappy and miserable self. In other words, if "self-involved meta-cognition" is lacking, *han* is not developed. From this perspective, Choi and Kim argue that the experiential psychological mechanism of *han* is less developed in the minds of young people, who are self-centered and thus uninterested in others' assessment of them, as compared to members of the older generations. Yet we might argue that other people may have developed the mechanism, but suppressed it unconsciously for various reasons; that is, *han* is at the subconscious level and cannot be felt, yet can be acted out mechanically. Before leaving his apartment, Gangdo indulges in the ritual of pulling a dagger out of a painting of a woman's breast attached to the wall; this ritual implies that his *han* is suppressed.

Given that human nature can yield either norms of conduct, thinking, feeling, and acting or undesirable dispositions, which constitute obstacles and even lead to violence, a question arises: what does it mean to be human to Gangdo, given that he appears devoid of all sentiment? Consider the following reply of Gangdo to a debtor's wife:

THE WIFE OF A DEBTOR: Damned piece of shit. You'll pay for this.

GANGDO: Irresponsibly borrowing money and not paying up. Unlikely ... (*seolma* ...) Folks like you are shit. [By saying, "unlikely" and then stopping, Gangdo seems to imply that the couple is thinking that it is unlikely that anything will happen to them if they don't pay up.]

From the perspective of Gangdo's lack of sentiment, he is totally right in that the debt should be paid off; thus, his brutal actions are justified. A collector for a loan shark may be considered a representative of capitalist exploitation, but cannot be viewed as an actor of depravity on a personal level. The attribution of his pitilessly cruel behavior to capitalist society can be sensed through the contrast between the luminous buildings in the center of Seoul and the dismal area full of machine shops, and between the high-rise apartment buildings and rundown houses. Nevertheless, Gangdo may not want to be cognizant of his social deprivation, nor does he want to think of himself as heartless. The best way for him to sustain himself is to suppress any *han* he may have.

Han-Revival

The seemingly suppressed *han* slowly emerges, however. One day some-one knocks on the door. Gangdo, with a suspicious look on his face, grabs the aforementioned knife and opens the door. A strange, middle-aged woman forces her way in despite his slamming the door on her fingers three times. She cleans dishes and puts leftovers and the disgusting internal organs of a chicken he has cooked in the garbage bag, all without saying a word. Gangdo, so stunned and even angry, yells at her, curses, and pushes her out of the apart-ment, throwing the knife erratically and breaking the window. Give that Gangdo has never experienced such care, it is inconceivable for him, and he cannot tolerate it. To him, it may appear as an act of being carried away by ill-advised bravery. He goes out to retrieve the knife, whereupon he sees the woman approaching him, stepping on broken pieces of glass, and holding out her hand with the knife. Gangdo roars at her again: "Do you have a grudge against me? Stab me!" Such a series of sequences implies that there has been suppressed *han* in Gangdo's heart, which is about to emerge.

The next morning as he leaves home, the woman, who has waited for him all night, follows and calls his name, even adding his surname: "Gangdo, Lee Gangdo." She begs and kneels down, asking for forgiveness for having abandoned Gangdo when he was an infant. Gangdo shouts at her, ordering her not to call him by his name since he has no one. He slaps her strongly on the cheek, treating her as some sort of eccentric. When Gangdo notices that the woman, who has been watching his pitiless actions (i.e., forcing a debtor to jump from a third-story ledge, he says angrily, "Do you want me to make you jump off?" She replies, "Forgive me, it's because of me. I don't mind being killed by you." At this, Gangdo once again becomes outraged and curses her.

One evening, Gangdo is drinking at home; it seems that he feels some-what lonely. He gazes at a sizable fish bowl in which there is a fish that the woman has brought to him. The fish has a nametag around its neck, on which is written her name and phone number. He dials the number and disdainfully inquires: "Are you sure that you are my mother who abandoned me? You shouldn't play with me, me who lived 30 years without mom. If I see you, I will tear you up since you stirred up my heart." He hangs up, but then calls her up again, madly inquiring, "Are you the mother who left me in the hospi-tal?" He then hears the woman singing a lullaby over the phone, which tells of an island baby who is left home and falls asleep when the mother goes out to the sea to get oysters, but who returns immediately when she hears a seagull's cry. The woman is actually at his door. He lets her in and forces her to undergo a trial of sorts, expecting her to pass three troublesome tests to prove that she is his mother. The first test concerns his birth mark, which the woman refutes, claiming that she was only a young, frightened girl at that time and remembers nothing. The second test is about eating his excrement, which appears to make her bleed. She passes this test. In the third test, Gangdo threatens her, saying that he wants to go inside her where he came out from. After much corporal struggle, the room is filled with the painful cries of the woman, and the test is passed. Gangdo, sitting next her, seems to mull over what has just happened. It appears his *han* is now fully emerged from his heart and does not what to do.

The next morning, he sits at the table eating food prepared by Miseon, who smiles at him as if nothing had happened the night before. Gangdo does not eat, maintains his silence, and gets up. He folds the knife. (It is the first time that the viewer has seen him fold it.) He goes out, and from the street, he looks back up at his apartment window, from which the woman is gazing down at him. This scene constitutes a sign that he is beginning to feel something—something that has been lying in dormancy for the past 30 years. He may well feel how horrible life has been without a family, especially a mother. The *jeong-han* that has been deeply rooted in his heart is revived; sentiment turns on, and this is turning point for him in his life.

Feeling Good, Yet Vulnerable

Gangdo has not had any normal human interaction with anyone until the woman comes into his life. The arrival of the woman (whom we will call "the mother" from now on) and its consequences have made him feel something deep within his heart.

A prerequisite of *han*-venting is an experience of *han*. If one does not feel *han*, there is no point of doing something to vent it. Consequently, *han*-venting had not even been an issue for Gangdo until the arrival of the woman. Now, the light of his sentiment is on; he is entitled to find ways to vent it. Nevertheless, *han*-venting involves more than just the good feelings that all human beings continuously want to preserve; it also makes one feel vulnerable and fearful, as seen in *Seopyeonje* and *The King and the Clown*. Gangdo, as he starts to let the woman into his life and accepts her as his mother, experiences a variety of feelings.

Feelings of Care and Their Expression. One day, Gangdo goes to a guitarist debtor who is willing to be disabled by having both hands cut off so that he can borrow more money. Gangdo asks why he wants to make money. The man says he needs money to support his soon-to-be-born baby. Gangdo replies, "I envy you." The debtor asks "Why?" Gangdo replies, "The mind that cares for his baby," reacting, "Aren't all parents supposed to be that way?" Before having his hands amputated, the musician wants to play the guitar for one last time. Gangdo allows him to do so. After the man has played, and when everything is ready for the terrible act, Gangdo stops suddenly, returning the insurance paper and stating, "Play the guitar for your baby." He leaves.

Gangdo, passing a clothing store, looks at the window displays and buys an outfit for the mother. The mother, who has been preparing for him, dons it. At the table, Gangdo asks her in a warm tone. "What did you do before meeting me?" She is silent and continues her crocheting. Gangdo asks, "Do I have siblings?" She remains silent but sheds tears. Gangdo asserts, "Today is the last day. Anything you need? Anyone you want to kill?" Here, we must note that killing someone for the mother is Gangdo's genuine way of expressing his caring for her. Gangdo experiences further feelings of tenderness when he walks hand in hand with his mother during an outing that she has requested. When a man on the street sneers at Gangdo's childish behavior, the mother reacts strongly, defending her son's pure expression of joy. In turn, Gangdo protects her against the man whose violence has been spurred by the mother's eccentric behavior.

Feeling Vulnerable. While Gangdo is, for the first time, experiencing something good around him, what he has done in the past forces him to face his vulnerability. One day, the mother, while crocheting, asks how today's debtor is. Gangdo replies, "He jumped." She utters, "He may be dead." Then, Gangdo asks her, "What is money?" She replies, "Money is the beginning and the end of everything—love, violence, anger, hate, jealousy, revenge, and death." Gangdo inquires in a startling tone, "Revenge?" The mother states, "Yes, revenge." Then, Gangdo instructs her very fearfully, "Don't open the door when I am out. If a bad guy comes, give me a call immediately."

In fact, an incident does occur. A disabled debtor who has seen Gangdo with the mother threatens her with a knife at the door of Gangdo's apartment. At the same time, the wrathful debtor, holding a match, commands Gangdo to pour a big bottle of gasoline over his body, which will make him burn to death when he lights it and throws it toward Gangdo. Gangdo holds his hands up, kneels down, and shouts that the mother has not done anything wrong. Disagreeing with him, the mother says that it's she herself who is culpable. To save the mother, Gangdo is about to follow the disabled man's command, but the mother intervenes by biting the hand of the debtor. Thus, both are able to escape from danger. The next morning, Gangdo, who is very still scared, says to the mother, "I'm very afraid of your sudden disappearance. I would no longer able to live alone."

One day, Gangdo comes home with a cake that the mother asked him to buy since it is his birthday, but the mother is not at home. After waiting for a while impatiently, he goes to a loan shark for whom he used to work, thinking that he might have kidnapped the mother given that Gangdo has stopped working there. He furiously claims that it may have been one of the disabled men who has kidnapped her out of revenge. Gangdo returns home to check the list of the debtors who might take the mother hostage. At this point, the mother returns home. Gangdo angrily asks where she has been, and reproaches her for not having taking her phone. He seems so helplessly vulnerable in preserving what he has just found, something highly valuable to him.

Han-*Venting from Miseon's Position*

Now that we have observed *han*-venting from the perspective of Gangdo's position, let's examine how *han*-venting occurs in the case of Miseon, the subject of whose *han* is Gangdo. While Gangdo's *han* is described as *jeong-han,* Miseon's *han* appears to be *won-han.* Thus there ensues a mixture of *won-han* and *jeong-han.* In this section, we intentionally repeat numerous plot details here, yet we do so from Miseon's perspective.

Hidden *Han* and a Plot

In Korea, it has been said that the most terrible lack of duty to parents is to die before them. Traditionally, parents do not attend their children's funeral; the child is buried not under the ground, but in the parents' heart. This means that the terribly painful sorrow from losing a child cannot even be compared with all other kinds of sufferings. Furthermore, the parents' pain turns into *won-han* if their child's death is due to an injustice incurred while the child was living.

Miseon has lost her son; he has committed suicide. The cause of the suicide is not known, but the film implies that it has something to do with a debt, and possibly the dreadful threats he had received from Gangdo. Because debt collection is legal, and a threat from the debt collector is not illegal, Miseon cannot sue Gangdo. She bears hatred toward Gangdo, but there appears nothing that she can do to console the soul of her son and mitigate her terrible pain. For Miseon, the best way of *han*-venting appears to be forcing the cruel debt collector to feel the loss of the person whom he most dearly loves. As a Korean proverb, "Grief is best pleased with grief's company," implies, she might have thought that her *han* would be released when Gangdo experiences a painful grief similar to what she has been through. Yet, it is a highly challenging task to make such a heartless person feel that way. Miseon must devise a meticulously intricate plan that involves herself. The film, however, does not reveal just how she has come up with it. Even so, the viewer comprehends that her plan requires painstaking strategizing and astounding performance. Following is our examination of the self-authored play in which Miseon is the lead actress. Given that her plot involving Gangdo and his *han*-related behavior has already been described, the following depiction of her part is relatively brief.

Performance of Motherly Care

Miseon has to make Gangdo believe that she is the mother who abandoned him as an infant. There is no concrete evidence for this claim. Since she is not his mother, she cannot request a DNA examination, which today would be the norm for establishing a blood relationship between a parent and a child. The only means she has at her disposal "motherly care," a psychologically powerful tool. Here, motherly care does not mean just cleaning, cooking, and feeding the child, but real self-sacrifice for the child. Given that care is meaningless to Gangdo, a hardened person in whom sentiment is dead, Miseon faces numerous obstacles in demonstrating motherly care.

Determined to pursue her plan, Miseon visits Gangdo's apartment. She knocks on the door, but it is obvious that Gangdo will not let a strange woman in his apartment She succeeds in entering, despite Gangdo's having slammed the door repeatedly. Once inside, she cleans dishes and dirty floors, and places disgusting things in a garbage bag, things that most mothers do at home. Later, after having been shoved out, she retrieves a knife that Gangdo has thrown out of anger toward her bizarre behavior. When Gangdo emerges to retrieve the knife, Miseon treads on broken glass to hand it to him. This is the first door of many doors she must open to gain the title of mother and enter Gangdo's inner sphere.

The next morning, Miseon is sitting on the stairs of Gangdo's apartment waiting for Gangdo, who will soon leave for work. When he is out, she follows him, claiming that she is his mother and begging his forgiveness for her abandonment. She continues to follow Gangdo despite his slapping her on the cheek and cursing. She persists. When a debtor curses Gangdo as he is trampled underfoot by the latter, Miseon also steps on his foot, ordering the debtor not to curse at him. She wants to demonstrate that she is on Gangdo's side no matter what. Miseon brings a fish for dinner; around its neck she has placed a tag with her phone number. At this point, she has probably anticipated Gangdo's puzzlement at her motherly lie determination and hopes that he will call her for whatever reason. As she expected, Gangdo calls. This represents a second door leading into Gangdo's inner world.

Upon the second call from Gangdo, Miseon, who is already at his door, sings him a lullaby, the previously mentioned song about an island baby. As Gangdo lets Miseon in, she faces three tests ordered by him to prove her being his mother. Miseon refuses the first one, which concerns his birthmark, stating that she had been too young and terrified at the time of his birth to notice any mark. The second test involves eating his excrement, and she undergoes it, despite her revulsion. The third test entails her accepting him into her body. This is an unbearable, heart-breaking act for Miseon, who has prepared herself to do anything to make Gangdo believe her maternity. She struggles, both against Gangdo and against her own moral standards, and cries out. Yet she reaches the thorny gate leading to the Gangdo's inner state.

FEELING CONFUSED (*WON-HAN* TO *JEONG-HAN*)

The morning after this horrible night, Miseon behaves as if nothing had happened. She prepares breakfast for Gangdo. As he goes out, she stands by the window and looks vacantly at him walking on the street. She ponders Gangdo's subtle, yet significant change in behavior as he turns and looks up at Miseon. This is a turning point for Miseon, in the sense that her *won-han* takes on a color of *jeong-han;* she begins to feel something toward Gangdo. At the same time, gazing at Gangdo with an abstracted air may indicate just how much she misses her own son.

Miseon's *jeong-han* is "temporally" vented. One day, Miseon suggests that she and Gangdo go out together to have a mother-son date. On the street, they walk hand in hand cheerfully in free spirit. At least at that moment, Miseon seems to be freed from her fake performance. In a restaurant, she asks him to open his mouth and puts a piece of food in it, saying, "Does it taste good?" Gangdo performs the same act, placing a piece in Miseon's mouth with a warm smile; both seem contented. At a shop, Miseon puts a pair of glasses on Gangdo's face, and Gangdo does the same thing. Both look together themselves in a mirror, seeming highly pleased. At a public square where a clown is making heads with balloons, Miseon seems to enjoy watching Gangdo wear a hat made by the clown. This outing may well express just how much Miseon misses her son, with whom she can no longer enjoy a date of this type. Nonetheless, even though this outing may be a part of her plot to make Gangdo feel more terrible in the end, it still appears genuine.

One evening, Miseon gazes at the sleeping Gangdo, who is exhausted from a dreadful incident with a debtor who had tried to force the collector to kill himself. She lies down next to him as if she pities him for his vulnerability. As he masturbates, she caresses him (as a mother cuddles a child who is physically and emotionally sick). Even though she is feeling pity toward Gangdo at this time, she gets up suddenly; washes her hands thoroughly, as if she has done something shameful; and notes her reflection in the mirror. She appears confused.

Miseon returns from the place where her son committed suicide, lights the candles on the cake she has asked Gangdo to buy for his birthday, and sings "Happy Birthday!" to him. She then asks a favor of him, to plant a tree near by a river. They go out and do so. Miseon thanks him, and requests that he bury her under the tree when she dies. Gangdo yells at her, "Don't say those unpleasant things; I feel very bad." She replies, "Everybody dies." Gangdo says rather angrily and innocently, "But death, it's still far away." At that moment, Miseon gazes him with a warm, yet sad smile.

Co-dependent Han-*Venting*

In this short section, we examine the narrative from the perspectives of both Gangdo and Miseon. In this way, the co-dependency of their *han*-venting can be better sensed.

Twisted Hope of *Han*-Venting

On the one hand, Miseon has successfully fooled Gangdo by persistently displaying motherly care, accepting terrible tests given by Gangdo, and performing what a real mother is capable of. Her hope is now to make him experience something terrible, similar to the pain and grief she has endured since the loss of her son. On the other hand, Gangdo, thanks to Miseon's outstanding care and performance, has discovered sentiment in himself—a feeling of love for someone else, feeling loved, and feeling scared and vulnerable, all fundamental attributes to a human being. His hope is now to preserve the feelings he gained through Miseon; to do so, he must protect her. However, their *han*-venting goes beyond the realm of a mismatched, twisted hope; it is heading in a direction devoid of a navigator due to the emotional co-dependency of two people for whom a normal relationship is impossible in this world.

Gangdo falls asleep on a chair in the place where Miseon's son has committed suicide; he has visited the site while searching for the mother, who has suddenly disappeared. Miseon, who has just appeared, approaches Gangdo and stares at him, bitterly and silently chastising him: "I can't forgive you; you are an evil person who tests human beings with money. You will experience what watching a family member die is like. No need to cry now, a poor little monster!"

Miseon's final dramatic performance is intricately staged as a revenge killing, inasmuch as she pretends that one of Gangdo's bosses is threatening him. Nonetheless, her feelings toward Gangdo are conflicted. To lure him out to the designated place where she will jump to her death, she goes to the office of the loan shark and slaps the agent for whom Gangdo had worked on the cheek so that he will get furious and loud. She then calls Gangdo to make him think she is in danger. Miseon sends Gangdo a photo of an unfinished building where she plans to have him watch her jump and die. She ascends to the fourth floor of the building and contemplates the area where they have planted the tree. She cries out very sadly, speaking to Sanggu, her son: "Sanggu, you've waited for long. His soul is going to die. If he sees me die in his sight, his life will be so miserable, like an empty shell. Sanggu, this feeling was not meant to be this way though, I feel so sorry. He is so pitiable; Gangdo is so pitiable."

Gangdo has received the call from his mother, who sounds very threatened; he hears dreadful noises and is terrified. A photo of an unfinished building near by the spot where he planted her tree appears on his phone. When Gangdo arrives hastily at the bottom of the building, Miseon is screaming from the veranda of the fourth floor that she is afraid. She shouts to Gangdo not to come up, conveying that someone is threatening her life. Gangdo desperately shouts out for her to beg for forgiveness, kneels down, prostrates himself, and fearfully shouts out: "Please forgive me, I'm the one who is guilty. My mom didn't do anything wrong. Please, I beg you to let her go. Please save my mother's life. Take my life instead of hers."

Miseon looks very painfully at Gangdo and jumps to the earth in front of him. She has accomplished what she had planned. Gangdo, after having cried out frantically, digs the ground where he had planted the tree. There, he notices a dead body with the sweater that the mother was crocheting, which he had assumed was a gift for himself. A shot of three bodies lying down on the ground is shown: Gangdo wearing the sweater and hugging the mother by placing his left arm in her right, Sanggu wearing his shirt. This image implies how much Gangdo loves her, even though he now discovers she is not his mother. They all appear to sleep peacefully.

PURSUIT OF A NEW FORM OF HOPE

The culmination of the co-dependent *han*-venting is subtle, yet astonishing. Early in the morning following the fatal incident and the discovery of Sanggu's body, Gangdo heads to the house of a crippled victim. We must recall how mercilessly Gangdo had treated the debtors, and how they, in turn, had hated him. On one occasion, the man had threatened Gangdo's life, and his wife had screamed that she would like to run him over with her truck. Gangdo gazes at the couple through the window of their house. Although they had had marital problems, it seems that their problems are now resolved. Gangdo lies down under their truck. He puts a heavy metal chain around himself and attaches the hook to the truck, which will drag him—an act that recalls the pre-title sequence in which Miseon's son commits suicide. The wife boards her truck and drives innocently along the road, without being cognizant of what is under the truck. This image of heartbreaking horror turns into a mystic metaphor of hope.

The highway appears very peaceful and even serene, which implies an invisible, yet significant landmark in a long journey. The pain caused by the loss of a loved one has brought closure to an entwined *han* and its venting. The intangible landmark raises a question: does this imply "hope lost" or "hope found"? Perhaps there will be a new chapter of amalgamated *han* for the three souls. They will be freed to pursue a new form of hope, as *han* is meant to generate hope.

Conclusion: *Jeong-han* and Free Spirit

The historical aspects of *han* development and its two-sidedness (*jeong-han* and *won-han*) as discussed in Chapter 2 would make for a good photo montage. *Han,* as reflected in *Seopyeonje, The King and the Clown,* and *Pietà,* is like an image created by the blending of its multiple images: the *jeong-han* of Yubong and Sonhwa, and the *hoi-han* of Dongho in *Seopyeonje;* the *jeong-han* of Jangsaeng and Gonggil, and the *won-han* and *jeong-han* of Yeonsan in *The King and the Clown;* and the suppressed *han* of Gangdo and its emergence, and the *won-han* and *jeong-han* of Miseon. That is, the image of *han* varies as it traverses across the pantheon of characters, social classes, and contexts in the three films. Nonetheless, in the diversity of this photo montage, one finds connection. *Jeong-han* and free spirit are interconnected in that the former is a prerequisite for reaching the sublime, which may well be unidentified and intangible. All the same, *jeong-han* needs to be vented, at least occasionally or momentarily, through free spirit. *Han*-venting is, therefore, a life journey in which a free spirit can come and go, and its control lies in inner strength, which is manifested differently across individuals.

Songhwa has built inner strength and will finally be able to produce the great sounds of *pansori;* yet she does not remain in one place and moves on in spite of her blindness, implying her wish to preserve a free spirit. Similarly, although *The King and the Clown* does not depict the process of *gwangdae* training, which could serve as the subject of another dramatic story similar to *Seopyeonje,* it demonstrates a significant point resembling that of its companion film. Jangsaeng has finally realized that his original identity as a *gwangdae* can be regained outside the court, in a space in which a free spirit can be restored. Like Songhwa, he desires to move on. It may be coincidental that both Songhwa and Jangsaeng become blind, yet blindness in this case implies that free spirit can be better felt in the absence of physical sight. Comparably, Gangdo's way of ending his life under a truck driven by a victim of his own suppressed *han* implies his yearning for a free spirit that will bring the deep sentiment of which he dreams. Similarly, Miseon's approach to her own death—a tree planted by Gangdo, the burying of her own son under the tree, and herself being buried there by Gangdo—alludes, beyond the tragedy of her plot, to her wish to have a free spirit that will allow her to bear both Gangdo and Sanggu in her heart. The shot of the three bodies together lying on the ground underscores their right to free spirit.

Chapter 5

Jeong in Irrationality

Preliminary Discussion: Cinema, *Jeong* and Irrationality

Cinema as an art form is in part defined by the irrational. Its illusion of movement created by still frames allows the brain's rational perceptions to be short-circuited, thereby inviting the viewer to delight in the realm of the intangible. Furthermore, the "I am at the movies, but this is real" condition permits two contradictory states to coexist, and suspension of disbelief invites the irrational to take hold and transport the viewer. Not only is the very nature of the film experience predicated on a break with the rational world, but its visual pleasure stems, to a large extent, from the irrational behavior of on-screen protagonists. Part of the thrill of a movie is watching a protagonist behave in a twisted manner and outguessing her next moves. The irrational must be present in all cultures in one form or another, for there is something universal in the notion of violating accepted psychological and social norms. But is this rupture, like key cultural concepts, rooted differently from one culture to the next?

The attraction to the irrational is largely derived from the undisputable fact that human relationships themselves are often illogical. These relationships can frequently be labeled as examples of Freudian disavowal, caught between "I know he is not right for me" and "I love him more than anyone." Indeed, emotional bonds can override rational choice, and such a dynamic can rear its head from Sarajevo to Seoul. Nonetheless, human bonds—be they between parents and children, siblings, friends, or lovers—may also echo the discrete culture in which they have grown.

A *jeong*-based life can be wild, turbulent, and incomprehensible to certain people given that *jeong* involves both an affective, social–psychological mind rather than a rational, cognitive mind. Some attributes of *jeong* include the following: it often overrules logic; it habitually neglects out-group members; it pushes away privacy; it is deemed unbreakable. Moreover, it is an important factor in the etiology of *hwa-byeong* (sickness of anger from the betrayal of *jeong*). Due to this aspect of irrationality, the concept of *jeong* is very hard to explain to non–Koreans, especially to people informed by Western logic. The films we will analyze here show how irrational *jeong* is and illuminate what underlies its irrationality. Furthermore, they let us see how the irrationality of *jeong* touches the human condition positively or negatively, and how the concept leads us to reexamine our own way of being as well as those of others.

This chapter will draw upon Bong Joonho's *Mother,* Kang Jegyu's *Taegeukgi: The Brotherhood of War,* Park Chanwook's *Joint Security Area,* and Lee Changdong's *Oasis* to explore *jeong* and consider its irrational side, which in the case of each of the films examined, is a defining aspect of dramatic tension.

Mother

Traditional Korean Motherhood and Mother

A mother is the first person whom babies encounter, and the latter develop both a trustful dependence and the belief that nothing bad will happen through the mother's care. This growth of good feelings is probably one of the most natural ways through which a baby starts to learn about love and the value of personal contact. Yet, each culture seems to have its own characteristic features of "mother"; we often hear stereotypes of Jewish mothers, Chinese mothers, and Italian mothers, to name but a few. But what are the characteristics of a Korean mother?

The song "Mother's Heart," as discussed in Chapter 2, stresses that nothing could be greater than *mo-jeong,* or motherly love. Non-Koreans, however, might refute the notion that there is anything culturally specific about *mo-jeong,* as unconditional motherly love is a universal phenomenon and stories focusing on the great love of mothers abound in many cultures.

However, the film *Mother* lends us to think about just what *unconditional motherly love* implies to the child, to others, and to society. More importantly, we must ponder what it means to the mother who must deal with many obstacles. We often neglect to consider the difficulties that unfortunate mothers experience due to their socioeconomic status or problems related to their child. For instance, when a child is cognitively disabled in traditional Korean society, he or she is the brunt of much discussion. Nonetheless, by and large, these children's needs are brushed off. Beyond the glowing, fulsome aspects of *mo-jeong,* there may be many battles for mothers to confront, battles that may lead to error and guilt.

The film *Mother* is set in a small town in South Korea's southern region. Its protagonist is a middle-aged widow, who earns a meager living by selling medicinal herbs and performing unlicensed acupuncture. The unnamed mother learns that her slightly retarded son has been accused of the murder of a young schoolgirl. Unsatisfied with her lawyer and the legal process, she sets out to investigate, on her own, the background of the victim and the circumstances of the crime. While trying to draw upon acupressure to help her son recall the events of the fateful night, she unwittingly triggers his memory of how, when he was a small child, she had attempted to kill both of them in a murder/suicide. The mother ultimately murders a possible witness, who believes he saw her son with the victim.

Jeong *in Irrationality in* Mother

The film opens as a woman walks through a wide-open field and breaks into a slow, rhythmic dance. Especially in light of the solitary figure in a sparse environment, with the image lacking a clear context, the sequence is enigmatic. As she proceeds with the dance, the woman puts one hand on her eyes and reveals her teeth; one can wonder whether the woman is laughing or crying. She then covers her mouth with her hand. When the dance concludes, the woman puts her hand inside her jacket as if to suggest a pain in her heart. Reading the film in terms of the Western avant-garde or even somewhat mainstream film, the dance sequence appears disconnected, non-diegetical. Over the concluding image, in which the woman stands still with her hand on heart, is superimposed the title *Mother.* We assume the woman to be the mother in the film, and the gesture, which betrays the initial emotionless appearance, implies that she suffers severe anguish from *mo-jeong.*

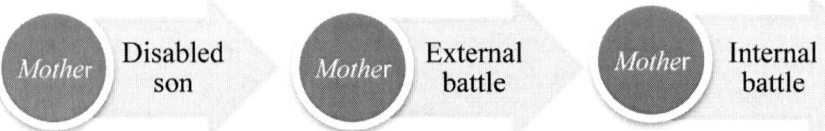

Figure 10. Mother's *Jeong* in Irrationality.

A Mother and Her Cognitively Disabled Son

The unnamed woman[1] is a single mother, who has a special acupunctural skill of making bad memories disappear by puncturing a spot on the inner thigh. Living with a mentally challenged 27-year-old son named Dojun, Mother is faced with three major social handicaps: a marginal living, single motherhood, and the parenting of a cognitively disabled son. Of these, the last is obviously the most painful to bear. In his jail cell, Dojun recalls that his mother had tried to kill him as a child. He misreads her true intentions, not understanding that her pain had been so torturous and unbearable that she had thought of taking his life. In actuality, her plan was for him to die first by consuming a poison-laced soft drink and then to follow him in death by the same means. (Some Korean mothers say to their most troublesome and rebellious children, "You die; I die; let's die together." In most cases, such an expression is a sign of mere venting.)

To most Korean mothers, a child is always a child about whom they will worry, regardless of age and ability. Koreans often quote the example of an 80-year-old mother says to her successful 50-year-old son, "Dear child, please watch out for cars when crossing streets." If an elderly mother harbors such concerns about her "normal" adult child, then the preoccupation of the mother of a cognitively impaired child must be much greater.

In an early scene, Mother casts worried glances at her son as he goofs off across the street while she busily chops herbs with a big blade in her darkened shop.[2] (This activity is physically very dangerous—she could easily cut her fingers off with the blade.[3]) Sometimes, Mother places a piece of food on Dojun's spoon while eating, as a mother does to a baby. She sleeps next to him, as the mother of an infant sleeps next to her child. Mother scolds him for hanging out with Jintae, a young man whom she thinks is not good for him. She watches her son urinate as a mother would watch her baby's urination. While gazing at the act, she may also be wondering whether Dojun can function properly as a man. Yet, her son's well-being is her priority; he is the centerpiece of her heart, as illustrated in an early shot of the dim interior and bright exterior that accentuates his body.

In the penultimate scene, when Mother is resting before boarding a bus for a filial piety trip, Dojun brings some snacks and drinks. When she inquires why he has bought so much, he encourages her to share with others and not to spill. Mother smiles at him, despite her internal turmoil in the wake of the recent traumatic events, and the smile seems to imply that she is happy about Dojun's generosity toward others. To Mother, any small good deed that her cognitively impaired child can do is greater than anything else.

Mother's External Battle for Her Son

It is natural that Mother wants to believe in the goodness of her child, regardless of the level of his cognitive ability. Although traditional Korean mothers are not good at praising their children in public, they are so proud of them that they have great difficulty in digesting remarks made by others regarding their children's weakness, even if these points are meant to be constructive. Furthermore, nothing can stop a mother from fighting for her children. Korean mothers' methods and persistence in this regard are sometimes extreme and irrational. Dojun's mother is no exception.

One night, Dojun goes out to a local bar to meet Jintae, his trouble-making friend; on his way home, he has a brief encounter with a schoolgirl. The next day, the girl's body is found on a rooftop in town. Based only on circumstantial evidence, a local police officer arrests Dojun, whose mother is horrified, unconvinced that her fragile son is capable of murder. Although Mother immediately hires a lawyer, she is forced to take matters into her own hands when her attorney proves incompetent and when the police refuse to look at other suspects. Mother gets involved in unraveling the details of the murder and the background of the victim in an attempt to prove her son's innocence. She kicks furiously into full-battle mode, rooting around the village in search of the killer. At one point, Mother sneaks into Jintae's apartment, thinking that he may be the real perpetrator. When this proves false, she enlists the young man to find other leads. She tracks the girl's cell phone, which might help her identify a potential killer. In that attempt to flush out other suspects, Mother uncovers a world of sexual promiscuity and intrigue beyond anything she bargained for. Yet, this doesn't faze her. Her investigation and search for the real murderer take her to an old man, the town's junkyard keeper.

When the junkyard man hints that Dojun may have actually committed the girl's murder, Mother, in a fit of hideous rage and denial, kills the old man and burns down his shack. This sequence stands in stark contrast to a scene in which she walks slowly behind a junk-cart pulled by an old junkman and takes an old umbrella from the cart, paying the junkman for it courteously, even though he is not aware of her having taken it out. These contrasting scenes illustrate that a mother's genuine goodness can turn to evil when the well-being of her vulnerable child is at stake. In an earlier scene in which she visits Dojun in prison, Mother says to Dojun, "You and I are one." This statement seems to confirm the possibility of her change in nature, from good to bad, for the sake of her son. However, such a change would doubtless cause a mother to harbor even more inner conflicts and pain.

MOTHER'S INTERNAL BATTLE

Winning the external battle for her son leaves Mother with another struggle, which can be deemed even more serious. She has lost confidence in her own judgment and faith in her son's naivety. Her previous righteousness is illustrated in two scenes. First, when she informs the victim's family that her son didn't commit the murder, her eyes are so electrically charged that the viewer is led to believe her. Her firm belief is further evidenced in a second scene in which she finds a blood mark on a golf club in Jintae's room. Holding the club on her shoulder, she makes her way most gallantly toward the police headquarters without knowing whose blood it was or whether it indeed is blood. The viewer observes an aura of pathos generated by her face and her speedy steps.

Upon the arrest of Jongpal, another young man, for the crime, Mother cannot reveal any of what she has learned to anyone. She meets with the new suspect, gulps down her tears, and asks, "Do you have parents? Do you have a mother?" When he replies that he does not, she cries out internally as well as externally, not only for him, but probably for herself as well given that she is now so helpless. For a moment, her intense love for Dojun is transferred to the imprisoned youth, and her tears suggest that she firmly believes in the importance of a mother. It is at this point that the film's conundrum is most evident; we are profoundly aware of Mother's genuine caring, and we must reconcile this with her actions.

As the plot unravels, one can view Mother's unemotional appearance as a sign that she is psychologically devastated. When Dojun mentions the reason why he thinks the killer may have left the girl's body on the rooftop, she is not agitated, which suggests the dullness of her heart. Later, prior to her boarding the bus, her son brings her a small box containing her acupuncture needles, which he has found at the site of the junkyard murder. At this point, her dormant heart returns to its original state of internal battle. She dashes out frantically to the bus platform, wanders about, and finally boards the bus. While other women dance in the corridor of the bus,[4] she takes a needle and acupunctures the fleshy inside of her thigh, which supposedly banishes troubled recollections. The film ends in a manner similar to its opening: she dances away her burdens.

Source of Mo-jeong in Irrationality

Mother relates the story of a maternal love carried to horrific extremes. It is not about the mother's heroic love, but rather raises the question as to who is responsible for the freaky nature of love, the dreadful manifestation of love. Who is entitled to judge the irrational, yet heartbreaking *mo-jeong* of a single mother who fights for her marginalized cognitively disabled son?

We must also consider the film from Dojun's perspective. Society is often oblivious to the position of people with cognitive disabilities, and herein lies the importance of self-advocacy. After an incriminating golf ball is found at the scene of the crime, Dojun is brought in for interrogation. He remembers little of the night in question, only vaguely recalling the encounter on the way home. The fast-talking police officer pressures him into signing a confession instead of trying to hear him out. To Dojun, society is absurd. After being freed from the jail, he asks his mother a question, and answers his own: "Mom, I thought of something; why did Jongpal put the body on the rooftop? I think it's because he wanted the town's people to take the bleeding body to the hospital, for which reason he had to put the body on a place from which people can see well." Such an observation throws into question the film's unseen narrative. Dojun's memory seems lucid and logical, but it is unclear whether he is imagining things from Jongpal's perspective or whether he moved the body himself. Dojun's cognitive ability allows him partial memory, but due to the lack of completion in his recollections, both Mother and society are prone to brushing off his thoughts.

Dojun may want to be heard and have his memories understood from his perspective. Although Mother asks her son to try to remember something about the terrible night, her intention is to hear what she needs to hear to prove his innocence and not to explore or help clarify his partial memories. Unfortunately, she misjudges the actual level of his ability, which leads to her become victim of her illusions. To Mother, Dojun is so vulnerable that his self-advocacy in public is not possible; hence, she values their "oneness" as construed exclusively from her own perspective.

This film illustrates how little mothers know their own children, and this lack of knowledge is attributed to their unawareness of and inability to listen to them. The expression, "We deliver a child's body, not his or her mind," which Korean mothers use upon realizing the deceptions they have harbored regarding their children, is applicable to this film in that it illustrates how maternal illusions can be a catalyst for the irrational.

Taegeukgi: The Brotherhood of War

The highly intricate storyline in *Taegeukgi: The Brotherhood of War* is framed by present-day events in which an elderly Korean, who has learned that human remains have been unearthed that are believed to be his own, travels to the excavation site, confident that it is his brother's body that has been found. His suspicions are confirmed, and he retrieves a silver pen that he had lost while a military prisoner and that he had entrusted to his brother. At their last meeting in North Korea, the brothers had promised that the pen would be returned to him in times of peace.

The majority of the film takes place as a flashback, where we learn that Jintae is working as a shoe-shiner to pay for the education of his brother, Jinseok.[5] Upon the North Korean invasion, Jinseok is conscripted into the military. In an attempt to rescue his brother, Jintae boards the train carrying the soldiers to the front and, in the ensuing confusion, is drafted as well. After being informed by a superior that if he earns the Taegeuk Cordon for military honors, his brother can be sent home, Jintae embarks on a serious of extremely dangerous missions and ultimately receives the medal. A series of unfortunate coincidences subsequently occur. The brothers happen to be present at the execution of Jintae's fiancée, who has joined the Communist party, and they are imprisoned because of the connection. When Jintae believes that Jinseok has died in a prison fire, he defects to North Korea, but is later tracked down by his brother, who has also fled across the frontier. When the two meet, Jintae does not recognize his brother and attempts to kill him, but is struck instead by a bayonet. Despite his injury, Jintae wards off North Korean soldiers so that Jinseok can escape. He dies, gazing at his brother's desperate flight.

Fraternal Jeong *in Irrationality*

The Brotherhood of War opens near the 38th Parallel, where the excavation of human remains from a Korean War battlefield is under way so that a memorial site can be established. The army excavation team phones an elderly man to determine whether some remains bearing the name (Lee Jinseok) might be his. The elderly man asks whether the identity of the remains and artifacts might not be that of Lee Jintae, his brother, for whom he has been searching for half a century. His granddaughter alludes to his visit the previous year to Yeonbyeon,[6] during which he had hoped that he might learn something regarding his brother's whereabouts or fate.

Immediately prior to driving to the site with his granddaughter, Jinseok goes to an old desk where, in a broken-glass frame, we see a family picture of a mother with two sons. He subsequently opens a cabinet and retrieves a box containing something wrapped in white paper. Unfolding the paper, Jinseok gazes at and touches a pair of shoes, repressing his tears. From this series of

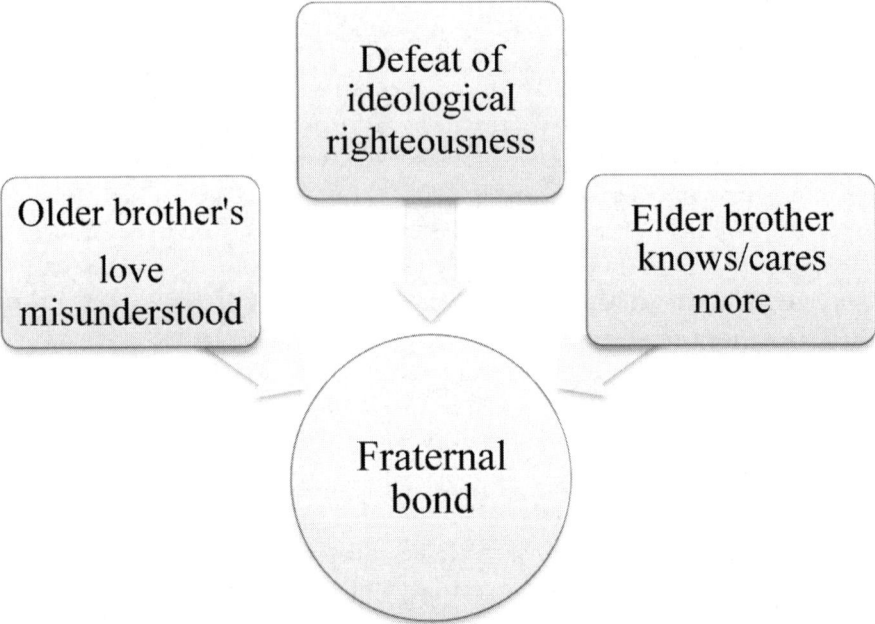

Figure 11. Fraternal *Jeong* in Irrationality.

shots, viewers can intuit that he has an enormous attachment to his beloved brother and that the shoes may be closely related to the latter.

The film flashes back to June 1950, where, in an iterative mode, we witness typical activities in Seoul prior to the onslaught of the war. Stylishly clad women board a street car; children dance to popular music; Jintae peddles shoes and frolics in the street with his brother. As the two gaze at a pair of shoes made of Italian leather on display in a store window, the iterative slips to the specific as Jinseok describes the heels he would like to have on a pair of shoes. Jintae then presents his brother with a pen, a symbol of the latter's quest for a university education. We become aware that the deep bond between them has led Jintae to make tremendous sacrifices to send Jinseok to school. The two brothers share an ice cream bar, something they will remember clearly as they suffer a dearth of food in the trenches. Later, kneeling in front of the *jesa* table dedicated to his late father, Jintae speaks of how his brother's studies at the university will make his father proud. The subsequent carefree play of the two brothers in a river marks one of the final moments of their antebellum existence.

This film invites the viewer to contemplate a traditional concept of brotherhood. A Korean saying, translated as "Elder Brother knows and/or cares better or more," does not question the degree of caring. Rather, it conveys recognition and appreciation for what an older brother has done for his younger brother, as well as for family and social expectations in a hierarchical, traditional society.[7]

THE LOVE OF AN OLDER BROTHER MISUNDERSTOOD

Despite extensive scenes of battle, *The Brotherhood of War* is primarily centered on the deep personal bonds of the brothers, and in particular Jintae's relentless efforts to obtain his brother's release. The brotherhood, as the title indicates, is one of war, however. This bellicose reference speaks not only to the historical tragedy that the brothers must face, but also to the growing hostilities between them.

The intensely emotional reaction of Jintae as he boards the train bearing new conscripts in search of Jinseok, whom he believes has been wrongly drafted, reveals his genuine concern for his brother. When we learn of the policy that two brothers from the same family cannot be conscripted, we realize that what has happened to Jinseok and Jintae is an anomaly. Jintae implores that he and his brother remain close; when this request is granted, he stays faithful to his promise to protect his brother. His passionate attachment to Jinseok is evidenced by the valor he demonstrates while saving the life of his brother in the Battle of Nakdong.

Following the first artillery strike, during which Jinseok nearly dies, Jintae is told by his commanding officer that his brother can be sent home only if he can earn the highest award, which implies taking on many dangerous suicidal missions. He accepts this challenge, in spite of Jinseok's objection, thinking that this is the only way of releasing his brother. As he tries to convince Jinseok of the plan's value, Jintae cracks a smile at his younger brother in an attempt to reduce the latter's fear. In the subsequent Battle of Pyongyang, he captures an important North Korean captain and is finally awarded the medal. However, a close friend has died in the process, which enrages Jinseok. There then ensue numerous horrific incidents, massacres, and chaotic escape attempts by prisoners. Yeongsin, Jintae's fiancée, is shot and killed by anti-communists, and the two brothers are arrested for trying to rescue her. Jintae is later brought in for questioning by a security commander. He implores officials to release his brother, but his request is denied. During a Chinese artillery strike, the commander orders the prison in which Jinseok is being held to be set on fire. Trying to rescue his brother, Jintae loses consciousness; he wakes up believing his brother has died in the fire.

While Jintae has manifested his genuine love and protection for Jinseok, his brother does not fully understand this. Loving his brother and showing genuine affection for him, Jinseok knows that Jintae is the only person to whom he can turn in the wake of his father's death and his mother's subsequent muteness. He loves his brother and shows great affection toward him. Moreover, Jinseok recalls how the brothers had lived happily until the onslaught of the war.

To Jinseok, Jintae is a father figure. At the same time, just as children do not understand parents, so Jinseok does not understand Jintae's genuine wishes, concerns, and related behaviors. While he loves and respects Jintae, and appreciates deeply what he has been doing for him, he views some of Jintae's decisions and actions as irrational, and even as signs of a selfish desire for glory. This is particularly the case when Jintae volunteers for increasingly suicidal missions, which would bring him the necessary medal. Jinseok is deeply hurt by his brother's behavior on numerous occasions. When Jintae and others want to execute a group of North Korean soldiers in a tunnel, he argues that if they kill unarmed prisoners, they will be no different from those who massacred civilians earlier. Moreover, when Yeongseok, whom Jinseok had taught, is killed in a crossfire caused by Jintae while a group of prisoners are making a stand with a hostage, Jinseok is devastated. Likewise, when Yeongsin—Jintae's girlfriend, who signed up for the Communist Workers' Party to get food for the family—is shot in their presence by anticommunists and her body thrown into the trench along with the other executed prisoners, he cries out in anger. In jail, Jinseok quietly ridicules Jintae for Yeongsin's death.

Defeat of Ideological Righteousness

It is only when Jinseok reads an unopened letter written by Jintae, which the latter had tried to send home, that he fully recognizes and deeply feels his brother's unconditional and genuine caring for him. Jintae had been saved by a soldier, who had promised to convey a letter that he had written to their mother. The soldier claims that Jintae was never found and that he doubts that the hero had deserted. Jinseok is somewhat indifferent toward both the letter and his brother's uncertain fate. The next day, he learns that his brother has defected to the North Korean army and is now a leader of an enemy unit. Jinseok is furious and temporarily disowns his brother. Jinseok believes Jintae's defection is motivated by medals—he still cannot accept that his brother's suicidal missions and life-risking choices have been carried out for his sake. Later, he reads Jintae's letter sent to their mother: "Mom, I miss you. We are OK. I'll send Jinseok back to you at the risk of my life.... I will return and open a shoe store and make you happy." The letter is full of spelling errors, which implies its author was not even able to go to elementary school because he had been the breadwinner since his father's death and the onset of his mother's disability. Jintae's own schooling at the expense of his brother's education was unthinkable. Jinseok now understands the source of Jintae's wish.

Jinseok is denied the right to fight at the 38th Parallel, so he escapes his camp and runs to the North Korean site. He fights his way through the soldiers before the "Flag Unit," commanded by Jintae, arrives to reinforce the North Korean lines. After slaying a number of South Korean soldiers, Jintae attempts to kill Jinseok, not recognizing his brother's face covered with mud. Jinseok begs his brother to recognize him. At the moment when Jintae is on the verge of shooting Jinseok, he is badly wounded by a bayonet strike; his brother, who is also injured, tries to remove him from the battlefield. When Jinseok talks to him about his promise to return home, making his mother proud by owning a shoe store, Jintae finally recognizes his brother. Although Jinseok initially refuses to retreat without his brother, the latter finally convinces him to escape, promising that he will meet him back at home.

Jintae removes from his inside pocket a silver pen that belongs to Jinseok, which had been his gift to his younger brother when they were still hoping to send him to college. Jinseok asks him to give it back to him when they meet again in times of peace. He also reminds his older brother that he must return home to finish the shoes, which were intended to be worn when he set off to the university. Jinseok retreats while Jintae holds off the North Korean infantry with a machine gun, providing cover for the retreating South Koreans. Jintae, struck down in a barrage of bullets, after giving one last look to his fleeing brother, dies on the battlefield. The brotherly *jeong* linking Jinsoek and Jintae has finally triumphed over the former's lack of understanding and ideological righteousness.

The intimacy of the brothers is especially felt in the return to the excavation site following the extensive flashback. We learn that Jinseok has traveled to China in search of his brother, and this search remains unresolved. When the army excavation team suggests, due to objects found on the battlefield near Jintae's skeletal remains, that they have located the body of Jinseok, the we-ness of the brothers is once again textualized. Such we-ness reaches the level of true pathos when Jinseok emotionally speaks to his brother's bones, recalling the promises they made at their last meeting. As his granddaughter looks on, Jinsoek prostrates himself over the remains. The sequence is quiet and contemplative, in sharp contrast to the complexity and explosive violence of the war sequences.

Following the return to the present day, the film concludes with a coda, which details Jinseok's return to Seoul in the wake of the armistice. Embraced by family and friends, he goes to an armoire and retrieves the shoes that Jintae had been making for him. The sequence is phantasmagorical inasmuch as the shoes appear to have been completed, with the heels that Jinseok so desired.

ELDER BROTHER KNOWS/CARES BETTER AND MORE

The literal translation of this film's title is "Waving the Korean Flag." Yet, its viewers see that main theme is not closely related to the South Korean flag. As we have discussed previously, it focuses on family love, especially the love between two brothers, and its themes are better expressed in the English translation, *The Brotherhood of War*. That is, this film seems to attempt to analyze and understand the fundamental meaning of the Korean War from a human perspective in Korean culture.

We can compare this film's story to the painting known as "*Hyeongje geubnando*," in which an elder brother has saved both his own life and that of his younger sibling. If it had been the elder brother who had been wounded, we would question what he would have said to his younger brother to assure that, at least, the latter would escape safely, and whether his brother would have heeded his advice. Such a comparison recalls a dialogue between Jintae and Jinseok in a battlefield sequence. When Jintae insists that Jinseok has to be left alone without him, the younger brother replies, "Are you kidding? Getting the medal takes life. Even if you got the medal at the expense of saving my life, how can I face mother and Yeongsin?" Jintae, who tries to make his brother understand, stresses, "I won't die; I have to make you live and send you home. You are a student and ill." Jinseok retorts furiously, "I'm a soldier. We live and die together." Jintae concludes, "Listen carefully.... If one of us gets to go, I want you to live." During this stretch of dialogue, Jintae is calm and even smiles at his brother, while Jinseok is livid. Jintae might have hoped that his calm and smile would make his brother feel at ease. In this case, Jinseok's outrage appears to be primarily self-centered. The apparent irrationality notwithstanding, the deep caring of the elder brother reflects a longstanding notion of *jeong* between siblings.

Joint Security Area

In *Joint Security Area* (*JSA*), Sophie Jean, a Swiss–(North) Korean and neutral army major arrives in Panmunjom, the village jointly occupied by North and South Korea, to investigate the slaying of two North Korean soldiers at their military post and the injury of a South Korean soldier on the demarcation line. Neither of the surviving witnesses, North Korean Sergeant Oh and South Korean Sergeant Lee, is willing to discuss the events. Through the investigation, we learn that Sergeant Lee had inadvertently crossed the demarcation line while urinating and stepped on a landmine. When he was subsequently rescued by his North Korean enemies, a deep bond of friendship developed, and Lee and another Southern soldier undertook nightly trips across the Bridge of No Return to visit their North Korean counterparts, where the enemies cum comrades partook in ritualistic male bonding, drinking, and the abolishment of artificial boundaries. By day, however, they feigned hostility as they guarded their respective sides of the demarcation line.

During one of the night meetings, the friends are apprehended by a North Korean soldier, who is shocked to find South Koreans at the post, and the shootings that lead to the international incident ensue. Following the discovery of the truth, Sergeant Lee commits suicide, and we are left to contemplate whether this is due to the revelation of his friendship with the enemy or to the exposure of the circumstances that led to the shooting and killing of his North Korean friend.

U-jeong *in Irrationality in* Joint Security Area

There are many ways in which people categorize and conceptualize their relationships with others who are not family. One category would be "mutual liking," which Serpell (1989, 116) claims to be an essential feature of "friendship." Nevertheless, as Wierzbicka (1997, 32–124) argues, the concept of "friend" is culture-specific. In Korea, as we have already observed, a basic concept of human relationship is *jeong,* which applies to all categories including those characters in the film *Joint Security Area.* Based on Park Sangyeon's novel *DMZ* (1977), the film's storyline must be viewed as pure fantasy inasmuch as the events could never happen in real life.[8] The film, nonetheless, lets the viewer contemplate the true meaning of *jeong* between/among human beings.

Koreans might well consider the possibility of friendships between civilians from the North and South. As in the case of any civil war, families and friends have been unduly separated for some six decades.[9] However, given the state of war between the nations, for military personnel to fraternize with the enemy would be simply fraternizing with the enemy. Such behavior would be unimaginable and would doubtless produce highly visceral responses. If we extend the notion of in-group/out-group dynamics to a national level, these friendships would be especially unspeakable, for friends would have been selected from a prohibited paradigm. Given the tense relationship between the Koreas, the mere mention of bonds between enemy soldiers would constitute a deeply rooted social taboo. Thus, one is frequently confronted in South Korean cinema with stereotypical images of North Korean soldiers. In sharp contrast, the North Koreans in *Joint Security Area* are most likeable.

The focus of the investigation conducted by an impartial military officer is not on what happened—who shot who—but rather on why the incident occurred and how it developed. As is revealed at the end of the film, such a process can be attributed to the breaking of ground for *u-jeong,* its cultivation, and its ultimate endangerment. As the story jumps back and forth between the present and the past, the truth about the incident and the development of a forbidden *u-jeong* gradually come to light.

Breaking the Ground of U-jeong

One night a South Korean soldier, Sergeant Lee, goes out to a field to urinate, and is terrified when he learns that he has stepped on a North Korean landmine. His crossing into North Korea is articulated in such a way as to render the border invisible. As we see him approach the line, an innovative circular pan, which violates the 180-degree law of cinematography, gives the illusion that he has reversed direction. We never see him actually crossing the border in a long shot. But we know, as the sequence progresses, that he has entered

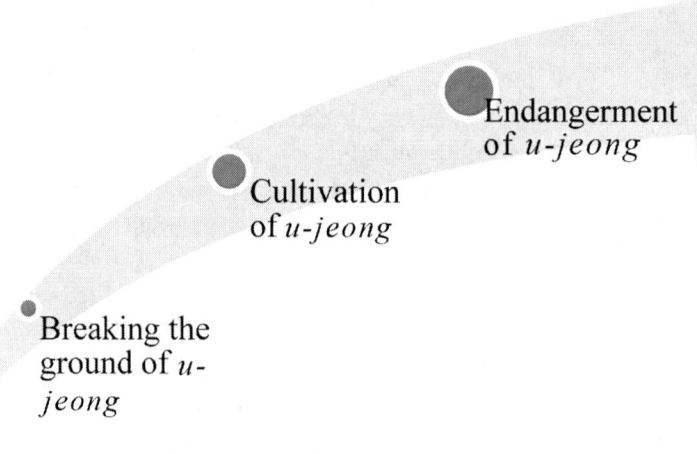

Figure 12. *U-jeong* in Irrationality.

North Korea. The illusory reversal of direction functions metaphorically to underscore the need for return—the need for an end to separation—and constitutes a visual trope for the future we-ness, the brotherhood of the enemy soldiers.

Sergeant Lee then sees a dog, and subsequently North Korean Private Jeong, at whom he aims his gun. North Korean Sergeant Oh appears from behind and tries to capture him. Sergeant Lee shouts for the enemies not to come closer, cautioning them that if they do, he will trip the wire. As the two North Koreans leave him, he cries out for help. North Korean Sergeant Oh returns, carefully removes a mine from the ground, and gives it to Sergeant Lee, stating, "Take it; it's a gift." Sergeant Oh and the other North Korean soldier take out cigarettes and begin to smoke. Oh whistles softly, telling Lee to watch out for himself, and then makes his way back toward the other soldier, who is concerned about the mine. Oh scolds him for his thinking of saving only his own life. This scene suggests the insemination of *jeong* in the hearts of enemies.

Two additional sequences indicate that *jeong* will be developed. In a scene atop a snow-covered hill, both South Korean and North Korean soldiers are standing in lines, face to face, yet far from each other. Oh spies Lee in the South Korean line, acknowledges him, and whistles softly. In a counter-shot, Lee cracks a smile and then lowers his head. Both soldiers leave their respective formations to share a cigarette. The muted exchange of cigarettes is extremely poignant in its silence.[10] In another scene in which both Lee and Oh are on guard duty face to face on the outside of the jointly occupied border house, the North Korean says to his counterpart, "Your shadow is over the line." When he repeats the admonishment, Sergeant Lee steps back without saying anything. This can be read as each soldier's attempt to claim his own right, but the implied humor in the encounter suggests the interconnectedness they are beginning to feel.

CULTIVATION OF *U-JEONG*

U-jeong is finally seeded by follow-up actions initiated by Sergeant Lee, who writes a letter of thanks to Sergeant Oh for having saved his life. In the letter, he asks the North Korean if he can have permission to call him "brother." The letter is put in a tiny box and thrown to the North Korean side of the border. Oh likes being called "brother," given that he has been always called only "comrade." Such an exchange indicates that the cultivation of *jeong* between them has begun. Lee sends music tapes to the North, in response to which Oh asks "pleasantly" whether he has tapes of a female singer; the Southern soldier feels ready to move one step further.

One night, Sergeant Lee crosses over to the North Korean border post, responding to a letter written in jest by the North Korean Private Jeong. Oh is astonished by his friend's coming over and reads the letter of "invitation." The North Koreans do not ask Lee to leave; rather, this event marks the start of their fun and games together at the Northern post. Later, Lee invites his companion in arms, Private Nam, to join him because the latter seems to feel lonely, especially given that Lee is scheduled to leave Panmunjom. Nam is bewildered by what Lee has been doing and is hesitant about joining, but accompanies him nonetheless. A Korean expression, "*Chinguttara gangnam ganada*/ 친구따라 강남 간다" ("Follow a friend wherever the friend goes"), can be applied to this situation. Here, a friend does not mean just any friend, but rather a friend for whom *jeong* is felt.

When both Lee and Nam enter the North Korean post, Oh vigorously hugs Nam, who is obviously terrified. While holding him his arms, Oh says to Nam, "You are warm." Upon hearing this, Nam seems relieved. (Here, "warm" implies not only body temperature, but also welcome.) From this moment on, both South Koreans enjoy the crossing, and they bring such things as a lighter, shoe polishers, and *Playboy* magazines. The soldiers play different games together; they show pictures of their girlfriends; they even make jokes about landmines, shooting styles, and saving lives.

Following a subsequent bombing alert, Lee suggests to Nam that they should stop crossing over. He stresses that Nam should not go there alone after Lee's discharge from military service. Nam requests that both return to the North one last time to say goodbye and give a birthday gift to Private Jeong. At the North Korean post, the soldiers discuss what would happen were hostilities to truly break out and whether they would shoot each other. They also make small talk, toast, and take a picture. Oh, quietly smoking a cigarette, begs Lee and Nam to leave, even though parting is heartbreaking for all of them. Nam polishes Jeong's shoes one last time.

ENDANGERMENT OF *U-JEONG*

In the midst of the heightened emotion, the doorbell rings. A North Korean soldier enters and is stunned by what he sees. All soldiers except Sergeant Oh take out their guns as if to shoot immediately; Oh makes lame excuses, clarifying that the South Korean soldiers are there because they are considering defecting to North Korea. He also tries to convince both parties not to shoot, and has all three lower their guns slowly and simultaneously. Nonetheless, shooting occurs. After the North Korean soldier who entered the room and Private Jeong are killed, Oh instructs Lee and Nam to take a gun, shoot at him, and leave. He also advises them not to reveal that Nam had been there, further informing them that he will claim that the South Korean soldier, who had been captured, had escaped. As both Lee and Nam leave, Lee shoots at Oh, wounding him superficially and thereby creating an alibi.

Nam's ultimate suicide is the result of a polygraph test, through which it is learned that he has been lying. The Swiss officer, who has met with both Lee and Oh, has brought the former to the verge of revealing the truth. Oh feigns anger over the incident to prevent Lee's confession. After being ordered to halt the investigation, Sophie asks Lee to tell the truth, as she has evidence that the enemies had been together for a long period of time. Lee, who does not care whether he goes to jail, asks what she can do if he tells the story. She promises that, to save Oh, for whom Lee genuinely cares, she will not submit another report.

In a subsequent encounter between the investigator and Sergeant Oh, the two share cigarettes.[11] Sophie then inquires whether the North Koreans can forgive the South Koreans for this incident. Wise Sergeant Oh, who loves his country, yet fully understands its flaws, asserts that he would have shot first had the incident occurred in the South Korean border house. His statement clearly illustrates an aspect of *u-jeong*; *jeong* between friends is accompanied by *uiri/*의 리 (the principles of righteousness). When the investigator asks whether he has something to say to Lee, Oh lights a cigarette and whistles, giving the lighter to her after lighting her cigarette.[12] In a subsequent sequence, the investigator informs Lee that Oh, in contradiction to formal versions of the story, has claimed that Jeong was killed by Lee, not by Nam. She further suggests that Oh has perhaps remembered the events wrongly. Oh's assertion might have been intended to protect Lee, inasmuch as it would be the latter's expected duty to kill a North Korean. Despite all that has transpired, Sergeant Oh has demonstrated immense loyalty to Sergeant Lee. At this point the viewer can observe loss, sadness, and anger in Lee's face. He exits and shoots himself.

Jeong *Has No Frontier*

If we substitute the word *jeong* for "love," the Korean expression "Love has no frontier" can apply to this heart-rending story. The notion of intimacy and mutual affection between North and South Korean soldiers is impossible in reality. Yet, *Joint Security Area* illustrates that *jeong* is a common denominator of Korean culture, regardless of the political division between South and North. In other words, the cultural *jeong,* seeded in Korean ethos over the course of its long history, still resides in the hearts of North and South Koreans. It is evident as a sense of faithfulness and solidarity, as well as a willingness to take care of one another, and further follows the gradual, beautiful, and dangerous growth of the friendship in *Joint Security Area*. By contrasting the similarities of the four men with the conflicting ideologies of their native lands, this film neatly encapsulates the components of one nation at war with itself. The adversarial relationship between the two halves of the Korean peninsula and its ultimate pointlessness are reduced to cigarette exchanges and harmless adversarial games and teasing.

In this film, many of the characteristics of *jeong* discussed in Chapter 2 are displayed; *jeong* is manifested through commitment, without validation or reason. Interactions, whether formal or private, often carry the assumption of noncontractual commitment, as greater value and significance are placed on maintaining *jeong*. *Joint Security Area* shows how *jeong*, while overruling logic, incorporates loyalty, which is implicit in the noncontractual nature of the commitment. Here, one observes a *jeong* that functions as an important mechanism in controlling personal relationships. It bridges the emotional isolation and separateness between human beings, and establishes an emotional connectedness that encompasses all sorts of feelings, including joy, anger, affection, sadness, and fear. Bonded by *jeong*, collective efforts toward a common goal, overcoming crises, and survival are fortified.

The lack of frontiers implied by *jeong* was exemplified by the recent visit of South Korean President Lee Myungbak to Washington, D.C. At a state dinner held on October 13, 2011, U.S. President Barack Obama toasted Lee by referring to the relations between the United States and South Korea as a manifestation of *jeong*, which he described as reflecting "a deep affection, the bonds of the heart that cannot be broken and that grow stronger with time" (Wilkie, 2011). President Lee responded that Obama epitomizes "the characteristics of *jeong*, in that he is humble and very strong inside." Lee further asserted that when he sees the U.S. president, he feels that Obama has an oriental, positive *jeong*, which is a (special) quality (Kim Dong Kuk, 2011). Such mutual respect in the political arena recalls the relationship between Sergeants Oh and Lee. If in *Joint Security Area*, Sergeant Oh represents a prototypical North Korean soldier, and if Koreans on both sides have the same feeling of great respect toward him, the film is successful in that the delicate emotion that transcends opposing ideologies is well illustrated.

Oasis

The story in *Oasis* focuses on the relationship between Jongdu, a social outcast, and Gongju, a woman suffering from a palsy that has left her in a perpetual state of convulsion. Jongdu had served time for the death of Gongju's father in a drunk driving accident, although we later learn he was innocent. Contrary to all social expectations, Jongdu looks in on the family of the accident victim to see how they are doing and to apologize. Although he is sorely rebuked for his action, he catches sight of Gonju, who intrigues him. The two develop a bond divorced from all societal norms. Although Gongju's handicap impedes conventional speech and body language, the two generate pet names for each other and laugh and frolic within the enclosed space of the apartment. Jongdu demonstrates his usual antisocial behavior by, at one point, forcing himself upon her. The relationship, however, does not remain in the confines of the apartment. Jongdu attempts to take Gongju to the outside world, yet they are turned away, first at a restaurant and later at a formal birthday party for his mother. During a surprise visit by Gongju's brother and sister-in-law, the lovers are caught having sex, and Jongdu is returned to prison on charges of rape.

Ae-jeong *in Irrationality*

In the cinema, two characters linked by mutual attraction are usually presented as visually appealing, particularly in light of the cinematic gaze. In contrast, the protagonists of *Oasis* are far from being amiable at first sight. Nonetheless, the film seems to tell us that the beautiful fruit of *jeong* is beyond what ordinary people can picture.

Oasis begins with a man named Jongdu wearing summer clothes in midwinter. He is a social misfit—squirmy, snuffling, and simple-minded. His carefree behavior suggests mental illness, particularly given that he has just finished serving his third prison sentence, this time for manslaughter in a hit-and-run, drunk driving accident. He is now searching for his family.

Neither Jongdu's mother nor his siblings know that he is back on the streets; they have moved from their former home without leaving a forwarding address. Jongdu flaps around and ends up in police custody for nonpayment of a restaurant bill, being bailed out by his somewhat-sympathetic younger brother. However, he is greeted with suspicious hostility by his family, who reluctantly takes him back in. Here, there arises a question about *jeong* among family members. Traditionally, families are expected to show their love and care for each other. When a family member is in prison, he or she is visited on a regular basis. Thus it is very unusual that Jongdu was not informed of their move; moreover, the way in which the family greets him is out of the ordinary. The elderly brother treats Jongdu insolently; his sister-in-law informs him in a calm, but very cold way, "I dislike you. Sorry to say that it was so great when you were not around." The treatment Jongdu receives is especially unwarranted given that he had actually taken the rap for an accident caused by his older brother. Jongdu had wanted to protect his brother's status and name; after all, the brother had a professional career while Jongdu did not. Later in the film, Jongdu's family becomes even more repulsed when he is charged with rape. Similarly, Gongju, the female protagonist with severe cerebral palsy, is not treated decently by her brother and sister-in-law. When they move out of the apartment, they leave her in the care of neighbors while they use her disability pension to supplement their own lifestyle.

We may ask whether *jeong* exists only for people deemed "normal" and "good" by society at large. Most people would argue that it involves everyone, regardless of any mental or physical abnormality. On the one hand, those who do not have to live with a person like Jongdu or Gonjgu might judge that the families of the lovers are immoral and unethical. On the other hand, those who live with a person similar to Jongdu or Gongju in terms of cognitive, social, or physical disability may understand, at least to a certain degree, the uncaring and even heartless behavior of the families. In other words, they would appreciate that it is very hard to live with a severely disabled person in Korean culture. Nevertheless, there is something about their attitude that makes the viewer very uncomfortable.

Jongdu's family may well have strived to set him on a proper path, yet he has likely brought lifelong torment to his family. Similarly, Gongju's family may have tried to provide good care. But, as implied in what Koreans often say—"Filial piety does not work for parents with a long-term illness"—the proper care over a lifetime of a disabled person may be too much for ordinary people. While understanding the difficulties encountered by their respective

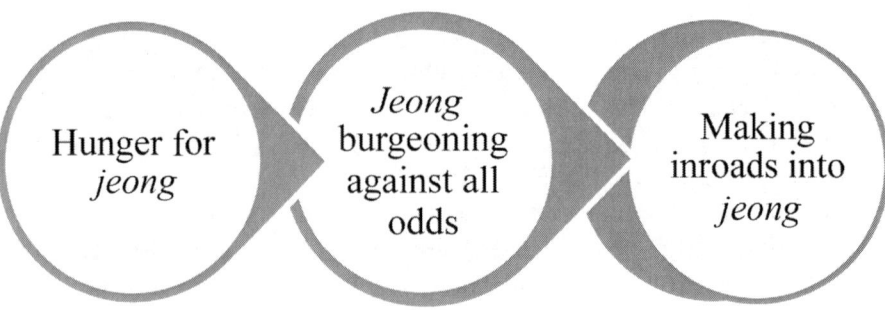

Figure 13. *Ae-jeong* in Irrationality.

families, it is heart-rending to observe what Jongdu and Gongju lack and how they search for what is lacking. The viewer's sympathy moves back and forth between these individuals and their families, wondering where these socially, mentally, and physically limited individuals turn for *jeong*.

HUNGER FOR *JEONG*

It has been said that no one manages to live without *jeong* in Korean culture. Many argue that no Korean would contest that *jeong* is a common denominator of Korean life. However, the two main characters in *Oasis*, social outcasts as they are, seem to have been surviving without *jeong* for a considerable amount of time, considering how ruthlessly they are treated by their families and how badly they are perceived by those around them. Despite reactions to Jongdu's marginality, social disapproval of Gongju's public appearances is even more clearly inscribed. The young woman's body tests perceptions of "normality," and she is treated like a grotesque creature, threatening socially constructed concepts of decorum and attractiveness. This point is underscored when, subsequent to Jongdu's arrest for the attempted rape of Gongju, the police ask him if he is a "pervert." During the interrogation, the officer alludes to her deformity by questioning Jongdu as to whether he is excited by the handicapped woman.

Earlier in the film, after a half-hearted reunion with his family, in an awkward attempt at reconciliation, Jongdu makes an impromptu visit to the home of the family of the drunk driving victim. As a friendly gesture, he brings along a fruit basket. From Jongdu's perspective, it is a genuine act that implies his willingness to make new friends. To no one's surprise, Gongju's family is horrified at Jongdu's intrusion and orders him to leave. As Jongdu does not have a sense of boundaries, it seems that he did not imagine that he would be unwelcome. Moreover, the family is in the process of moving out of the apartment and is leaving Gongju behind in the care of neighbors. The viewer, nonetheless, can sense that the care provided to her is minimal and heartless.

Despite the nasty and repulsive reaction to his visit demonstrated by Gongju's family, Jongdu is intrigued by Gongju, who is more or less confined to her room. She barely talks and most of the time is ignored. Her cerebral palsy is so severe that she cannot make herself understood. Shortly after meeting Gongju, despite being thrown out of the family home, Jongdu takes an interest in her. He resolves to return when he knows she will be alone. He decides to entice her by sending flowers, secretly taking a key to her apartment and entering the room. While trying to reassure and pacify Gongju, who is greatly frightened, he loses control and starts to impose himself on the helpless woman.

Their awkward physical contact precipitates what appears to be a clumsy, awkward sexual ventilation, although it is unclear whether penetration has occurred. This is a most appalling scene in that Gongju is not just a disinclined victim; she is so vastly disabled that she can't even control her own body, much less turn aside an assault.

Gongju passes out in terror. Jongdu flees, yet leaves behind his phone number in her room so that she would know where to find him; this act is unthinkable to "normal" people. However, the act of leaving a phone number indicates how naïve and simple-minded Jongdu is. He seems to want to express his sincere feeling toward Gongju. In other words, he is hungry for *jeong,* and searches for *jeong* in his own unique way.

JEONG: BURGEONING AGAINST ALL ODDS

Jongdu works in his brother's auto repair shop, after being fired from his delivery job for crashing a scooter, and also sleeps there at night. Eventually, Gongju surprises him by calling in the middle of night. (Jongdu's visit was the first time anyone has paid attention to her.) Despite her difficulty in engaging in physical movement, Gongju manages to place the call and invite Jongdu into her life.

A passionate bond develops; after a number of secret encounters and outings, the two misfits become inseparable. He calls her Gongju (which means "princess"), lavishes her with compliments, and carries her out of her shabby apartment on delirious excursions through the city, during which, fortified by their love, they shrug off the scorn and prejudice of the outside world. Jongdu reads Gongju's mind and apprehends what she cannot express.

In Gongju's apartment, there is a picture labeled "Oasis," which obviously depicts South Asia. In it, we see a woman in a sari, a small boy wearing a turban, and a baby elephant. At times, the branches of a tree outside of Gongju's window cast an eerie shadow across the picture, which frightens Gongju. To the viewer, this shadow may appear natural, devoid of the strangeness the handicapped woman ascribes to it. Yet Jongdu is never belittling of his companion's fears; at one point, he stands in front of the picture, pretending to be a musician who can erase the shadow. In sharp contrast to the dark patterns superimposed over the "oasis," Gongju seeks to embellish her domain with light. One of her favorite pastimes is to play with a hand mirror and create reflections of light on the wall and ceiling. At one point, these images turn into butterflies or a dove. In the mirror sequences, there is cinematic refutation of this point of view. It is unclear whether the transformations stem from the woman's imagination or whether they are real.

On their adventures outside of their limited place, the lovers are faced with the harsh reality of a discriminating society. Yet they are comforted by the innocent sanctity of their *jeong.* In a very candid act, Jongdu brings Gongju to his mother's birthday celebration in a restaurant. However, his family is stunned and infuriated; the last thing Jongdu's elder brother wants is for him to be socializing with a family member of the man who died in the accident in which he, the brother, was involved.

Gongju, for her part, wants to feel and be treated like a woman. She invites Jongdu back to her apartment, and they have sex. When her brother arrives on an unexpected visit, pandemonium ensues. Jongdu is arrested and charged with raping a helpless, handicapped woman. No one is interested in asking about or hearing their side of the story. Indeed, the young woman's family diverts their attention to the amount of money they will request of Jongdu's family in compensation for his act.

Jongdu's genuine caring for Gongju is exhibited in the form of one final burst of passion. He escapes from the police and rushes to Gongju's apartment. The pair manage to reaffirm their *ae-jeong* (i.e., *jeong* between lovers) when Jongdu fulfills his promise of making the frightening shadow cast by the branches against the picture disappear. Jongdu climbs the tree adjacent to her apartment and cuts the branches off before falling and being dragged off to prison.

MAKING INROADS INTO *JEONG*

Oasis focuses on two individuals who might well be deemed dislikable and miserable: a man socially limited by his post-prison existence who can offer little and a woman imprisoned by her uncontrollable body. The film does not magically deliver these two from their isolation, nor does it portray them as holy innocents. Yet, it leads its viewers to witness a romance filled with resonance and whose protagonists are both overcoming the confines of their surroundings.

Jongdu gives Gongju (who has been warehoused in a grimy apartment by her neglectful family) access to the world outside, which she never sees. She, in turn, offers him a nest in which he is not entangled with social norms that he fails to understand. If we read *Oasis* in terms of the traditional domestic space allocated to women in narratives, then Gongju's apartment epitomizes confinement; by virtue of her handicap, Gongju is a prisoner within these walls even more so than most women. Moreover, the film takes place in the narrative space of the melodrama, given that Gongju and Jongdu have essentially established a "home." Nonetheless, inasmuch as the film's title is *Oasis,* the picture on the wall is of particular consequence. Through this picture, Gongju is able to escape from the enclosed environment in which she spends her days. As the relationship between the two outcasts develops, Gongju's apartment assumes the opposite resonance. It provides the oasis where the friends can live, laugh, and love. It is in this space that their special bond develops over an unspecified number of days or weeks. Jongdu's ultimate return to prison is softened by his knowledge that he has an "oasis," or absence of prejudice, to which to return where he can share *ae-jeong*.

Jongdu is a gentle, childlike soul. The scene in which he cuts the branches remind us of the boy in Hwang Soon-won's short story "Rain Shower" (1959), which depicts the brief, but heart-rending love between a boy and a girl. Here, we could associate the boy with Jongdu through the naïve, ingenuous love and caring that he offers to Gongju. Similarly, Gongju's emotional state parallels with the mood of Hwang Jini's poem "Longest Night of Winter," which we examined in Chapter 2, as well as another of her most famous poems, "*Cheongsanlee Byeokyeosuya*/ 청산리 벽계수야." We can make the following transformations in the poems, with italics showing possible substitutions, to describe the film's lovers: "*Were I only to grasp the core of this longest of winter nights/And gently crease it into the breath of a spring quilt (Gongju's heart)/And lovingly unravel it the night my lover returns…Venerable Byeok Gyeosu (Jongdu), flaunt not your easy departure/When you reach the sea (the world outside of Gongju's apartment)/Your return will be arduous./When the bright moon envelops the hollow mountain/Why don't you just come in and rest?*" (Yeo, Sangdeok 2013).

Although the two limited characters of the film, the story, and the poem manifest significant differences in terms of background and situation, they are all alike in that they illustrate well that the turf of *jeong* can be very ugly, cold, and insensitive. Yet its building process is moving; all of the protagonists seem to eventually achieve a sense of triumph through the transformation of misery into its opposite.

Conclusion: *Jeong* and a Most Persevering Human Tie

Psychologists tell us that there are vast empty spaces in every individual's existence that only emotional connection can fill. At the same time, sociologists characterize this world as being filled with *narcissistic anxiety* (i.e., care and concern that is chiefly focused on ourselves). Listening to contemporary writers and artists leads us to think that we are inhabiting a planet of monsters.

Assisted by technology, a new kind of warfare has emerged that is impersonal, mechanized, brutal, and socially enforced. Where, then, do we turn—where do we look to find those tender, gentler forms of existence, of human connection, which psychology tells us are the requirements for our well-being? Surely, one might expect to find this in the relationships built on the basis of *jeong,* one of the most important ingredients that renders our lives enriched and meaningful.

The four films we have analyzed seem to shatter these kinds of expectations because we are not acknowledging reality when we impose "expectations" on life. Despite those expectations, life has its own way of proceeding. This irrational aspect of *jeong* is further characterized by the strength that it provides to its possessors.

The protagonist of *Mother* has a sense of honorable justice, which stands out, at the beginning of the film, in comparison to the conventional and traditional sense of honor that surrounds her and that society upholds with all its powers. Contrary to the traditions regarding women and their vulnerability, it is Mother's belief in her child (what may be considered as "blind motherly *jeong*") that adds to her strength. At every turn in the action, it is not her own torture, but rather her motherly feelings about her son's innocence, that fill her mind and direct her care, assuring us of her continued strength. Even after Mother finds out what has happened, she exhibits a capacity to recharge her inner force, as symbolized in the final scene in which she dances with other women after self-acupuncture aimed at forgetting the past.

The Brotherhood of War sets up a contrast between circumstance and the wider range of possibility to give its philosophical perspective on brotherhood. While Jinseok is doubtful about what Jintae does, both brothers believe in the possibility of dreams. They believe in each other's *jeong;* as long as they hold onto *jeong,* their goals are possible. That is, their *jeong*-based belief in each other is a firm source of strength and courage and is needed to survive all perils. Inasmuch as Jintae's death is extraordinarily difficult for Jinseok to accept, the viewer observes the shattering of life-supporting continuity in the harsh, yet new environment of the penultimate scene: Jinseok opens the shoes that Jintae had made for him. This suggests that the price for *jeong* that Jintae had to pay was immeasurably high; its outcome is everlasting in that Jinseok will be recharged to continue to live as Jintae wished.

Joint Security Area implies wonderful, but never-reached potentials and possibilities. We are told that in man, there is everything, the greatest to the lowest. Everything coexists in us, an unlimited number of realities. We live in a world without limitations, of infinite possibilities to be explored. The risky interactions between the South and North Korean soldiers are contrasted with the philosophical dimensions of the film, which seem to say that we can find greatest level of existence. We can find positive emotional connection, which fills the dangerous spaces and bathes our existence with feelings of shared warmth—namely, *jeong*. Measured against better possibilities, sorrow and suffering are always perceived as more painful and yet, ironically, less absolute and unavoidable. The unspoken, unrevealed fruits of *jeong* between the North and South soldiers will be the source of strength for Sergeant Oh as he continues to live after the dreadful incident.

Finally, *Oasis* shows that, although we are all to some extent vulnerable to misfortune like Jongdu and Gongju, we are also all part of a world where possibilities for good exist. This possibility for "good" is clearly tied not only to the ability to feel love/*jeong*, but also to the capacity to give love/*jeong*. Caring and love exist exclusively through shared experience, regardless of the obstacles. Just as an oasis in a desert is supplied with water or a spring that reaches up from beneath the ground, so the relationship between socially isolated individuals is well supplied with *jeong*, which comes from and goes deep into the heart. In spite of all barriers and human cruelty, *jeong* provides them with the strength for living, longing for, and hoping for the greatest.

In all four films, *jeong* is seen in all its extremes. It is illogical, unreasonable, crazy, and seemingly groundless. Nonetheless, it is a most persevering human tie providing continuity in Korean culture.

Chapter 6

Deok in Progress

Preliminary Discussion: Cinema, *Deok* and *Deok/Cheol*

The positive hero or heroine who has attained self-actualization in the Western sense or who is on the lifetime path of cultivating *deok* in the Korean context is not exactly the stuff that movies are made of. Part of what makes film characters interesting is when they yield to temptation and fall. We relish in their lapses into obsessiveness, carnality, or pure evil. Simply put, virtue and selflessness can be boring. Extraordinary creativity is needed to render a work predicated on such a principle as *deok* riveting. American actress Lillian Gish, speaking primarily about the virtuous women and selfless "goody-goody girls" she portrayed during the silent era, has commented on the difficulties implicit in making a positive character interesting: "Those little virgins, after five minutes you got sick of playing them.... To make them more interesting was hard work. Give me a harlot and half the work is done!" (Sanders, 1988). In D. W. Griffith's films, the "goody-goody" needs a counterpart. Gish's nameless, but good little American virgin living in France in Griffith's *Hearts of the World* (1918) is offset by a character played by the actress's sister, Dorothy Gish. Again unnamed, this character is a street singer from Paris, simply called the "Little Disturber," who provides comic relief and an intimation of sexuality to the film.

From the perspective of the New Korean Cinema, it goes without saying that to make a character on the path to virtue at all engrossing takes the same ingenuity that Gish employed in creating her "little virgins," as well as tremendous flair on the part of writers and directors. Inasmuch as *deok* implies an ongoing process and the absence of conclusion, it lends itself particularly well to an open-ended cinematic discourse, not only in terms of an open ending, but also with regard to narrative threads that are never fully knotted.

Before approaching *deok,* we should return to a closely related concept discussed in Chapter 2, *cheol* (figuratively and roughly meaning "discretion, good sense"). While not all adults are expected to grow in *deok,* all are supposed to have attained *cheol* at a certain age. *Cheol* is an informal term and is used casually in daily life, while *deok* is a formal term, employed less frequently; it carries much more weight and displays an important normative value. *Cheol* is expected to be acquired naturally under normal upbringing and circumstances, whereas *deok* is a never-ending process.

We can compare *deok* with "knowledge" to better conceptualize the term, since the cultivation of the former is not unlike the acquisition of the latter. No one can fully acquire "knowledge" given that its sphere is infinite and its areas are innumerable. Even a highly prominent scholar's knowledge is limited. One can be knowledgeable in that one can know about something *to a certain degree.* Yet there is always more to learn, more to flesh out. Thus, learning is a lifelong task, just as is the cultivation of *deok.* As we learn things (which could be useful or harmful) every day, every week, every month, and every year, consciously or subconsciously, we are all in the process of cultivating *deok,* knowingly or unknowingly. For this reason, we have opted to title this chapter "*Deok* in Progress."

A further comparison between *deok* and knowledge can be made in terms of our observation of a person's knowledge. We can scrutinize and discuss such individual knowledge in general terms or, alternatively, from the perspective of one's particular field. Yet, we can argue that the degree of knowledge that a person is perceived to have is subjective; one looks very knowledgeable to certain people, but not to others for various reasons. Similarly, we can observe and talk about a person's *deok* in general or from the perspective of the particular life that individual lives. The same person can also be perceived positively, favorably, or unfavorably in terms of *deok.* This further comparison leads us to mention the aims of this chapter. It is not intended to assess whether characters in the films are on the right track toward cultivating *deok,* but rather to make the viewer contemplate what *deok* means from various angles, given the complexity of its meaning.

As *deok* and *cheol* are tightly interrelated and since the concept of *cheol* is more easily approachable, it seems logical that this chapter should begin with the examination of a film through the lens of *cheol.* Thus, Kim Kiduk's *Spring, Summer, Fall, Winter, ... and Spring* will be approached within the framework of "getting *cheol.*" This analysis will be followed by a discussion of

Im Kwontaek's *Chihwaseon,* which will address the "cultivation of *deok.*" Finally, Lee Changdong's *Poetry* will be viewed in the context of "*deok* in germination."

Spring, Summer, Fall, Winter ... and Spring

Of the films we are exploring here, following *Seopyeonje,* Kim Kiduk's *Spring, Summer, Fall, Winter ... and Spring* has been the most widely explored in scholarly discourse outside of South Korea. Highly allegorical in nature, the film follows the life cycle of a Buddhist monk, from his apprenticeship with his master to his ultimate role as master to another young boy. It chronicles, through the trope of the changing seasons, the spiritual progression and worldly experiences of a man whose apprenticeship as a monk is interrupted by both sexual experience and murder. "Spring" marks the young boy's learning of responsibility and atonement. In "Summer," the youthful apprentice explores his sexuality and leaves the monastery in the arms of a young woman, who has come there for physical and spiritual healing. The apprentice ultimately kills her in a rage of jealousy, although this event is never depicted (the film's setting never leaves the monastery). In "Fall," the bitter disciple revisits his master and the monastery, where he learns to control his anger, yet is arrested for his crime. Upon his release from prison and his return to the monastery in "Winter," the former apprentice learns that his master has died in an act of self-immolation. Now a master, he adopts a young disciple. Thus begins a new "Spring" and a new apprenticeship.

Cheol *in Progress with the Seasons*

In the initial sequence of the film, a wooden gate opens on a mountain lake. In the center of the lake, we see a floating monastery. The mountains are reflected in the lake, and the landscape is thereby redoubled. Reflection in the physical world connotes reflection in the spiritual realm. The monastery is serene and appears so undisturbed that it gives the impression that those who inhabit it live a simple, peaceful, worry-free life. From the tranquility of the initial shot and the film's title, we immediately sense that the elderly monk will move toward death and the child monk with pass through boyhood and manhood to a period of preparing for death and renewal. The film alludes to the distinct seasons of one's life that bring something new. But most interestingly, the title names the four seasons, yet adds one more.

Here, it is worthwhile to recall that the literal meaning of *cheol* is "season." On the one hand, a common admonition to an immature person is "*ije jom cheoldeuleoyaji; nai gab hae-ra*" ("you ought to get *cheol*; you should know better; act your age"). This expression conveys that one is expected to have *cheol* with age, in the same way that fruit gets ripe with time. On the other hand, there is another expression that Koreans use when finally becoming sensible and wise: "*cheoldeulja mangryeong*"/철들자 망령 ("being in one's dotage right after becoming sensible"); this implies at once the importance of timely *cheol* as well as regret at becoming wise and sensible too late. These Korean expressions suggest that questions about the stage of one's *cheol* arise as time passes.

Spring: Committing Errors in Naivety

The "Spring" section of the film reveals that, although children may unwittingly commit gross errors, they must, nonetheless, become accountable for them. In an early sequence, the young apprentice is seen gathering herbs. A snake approaches him, and he grabs it, hurling it forcefully into the air.

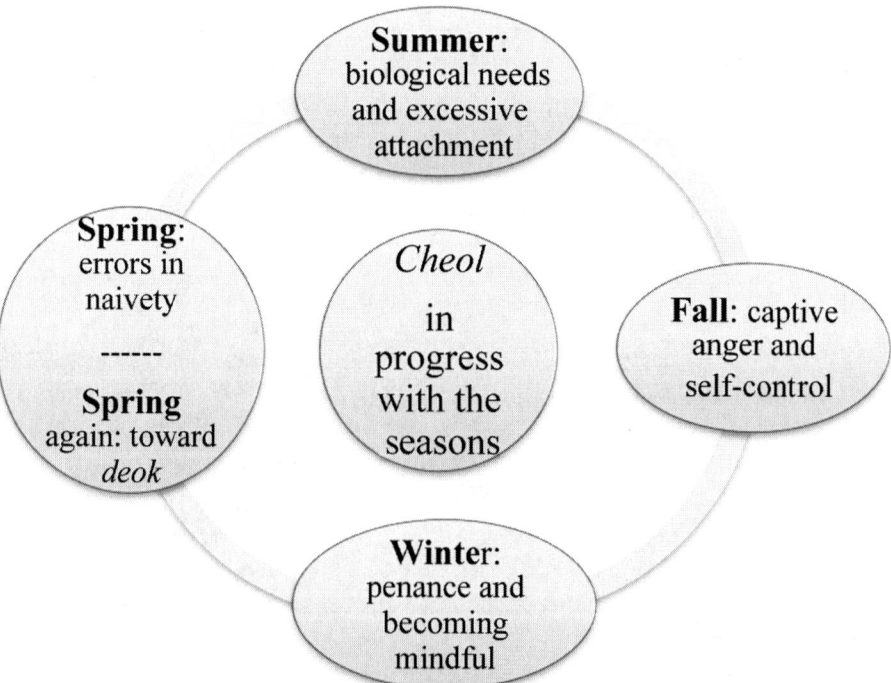

Figure 14. *Cheol* in Progress with the Seasons.

Upon returning from this outing, the master explains that one of the herbs is deadly. Thus, amidst the good there is also the bad—a lesson that the young disciple will eventually learn through his future life experiences. One afternoon, the child monk, who seems so naïve, casually torments animals; he catches a fish, ties a stone to it, returns it back into the water, and seems to enjoy watching it try to swim. He performs similar acts on a frog and a snake. These horrible deeds are in sharp contrast to his fair-skinned, soft, and gentle appearance. Moreover, the torturing of the snake recalls the presence of the snake in the earlier sequence. Hence, the evil implied by the herbs denotes the boy's own cruelty to the animal. The boy laughs as he commits the acts, and his expression is distinct from an earlier image in which he stands on the shoulder of an enormous statue of the Buddha at the top of a mountain, his tiny face reflecting the serenity of that of the statue. The master, who has been seen in soft focus watching the boy torment the animals, ties a rock to the child. The next morning, when the child asks him to untie the rock, the elderly monk instructs that the child should undo the rock he tied to the fish, frog, and snake first.

The child monk is able to rescue the frog, but the fish and the snake have not survived the torture. He buries the fish tenderly and sadly, but when he finds the dead snake, he cries out in desperation. The image is ambivalent. On the one hand, it may reveal the boy's repentance over the death of the snake. On the other hand, it may express his fear that the rock (i.e., torture and agony in its metaphorical and symbolic sense) will stay with him indefinitely, as the old monk has asserted. In this way, the master teaches valuable lessons regarding the nature of cruelty and guilt to his disciple. The "Spring" sequence implies that a modest act can bring forth terrible consequences, and that the simple choices we make ultimately result in changes in who we are becoming. The episode further suggests that everyone carries a stone with them, either in their head or in their heart, and that this can be either harmful or productive, inasmuch as carrying yesterday's burden can be tomorrow's hope.

Summer: Meeting Biological Needs and Excessive Attachment

"Summer" brings sexual initiation and a separation from the monastery. In this film, each season is a chapter in the child monk's life, separated by a decade or so. In "Summer," the child monk of "Spring" becomes a teenager whose biological changes are inevitable. Early in the episode, he gazes with fascination as two snakes mate, then ascends to the immense Buddha on the mountain. He is then shown standing on the Buddha's left shoulder, the opposite side as in the "Spring" sequence; he is now as tall as the statue's face. From this vantage point, he observes the arrival of an attractive young woman, who has been sent to the monastery to recover from physical sickness and to find spiritual support. The image, in which the apprentice aligns his gaze with that of the Buddha, reveals both his orientation as a disciple and his anticipatory embrace of the sexual exploits that lie ahead.

The lovers' first act of copulation occurs in an outdoor, natural setting and suggests the "nature" of the world outside of the monastery.[1] Their subsequent encounters change venues, and we see them together on the rowboat, which links the monastery to the outside world, and inside the monastery itself. Thus sexual activity provides a bridge between the hermitage and the external realm, to which the disciple will soon flee. As the couple begs forgiveness of the master, the latter is shown inside the monastery facing inward. The lovers are outside on the deck, and they are seen through the open door. The proscenium effect places them in a different world. While the monk is focused on his interior world and contemplative, the couple is surrounded by nature, and once again the humanity of their bond is underscored.

After the short period of sexual involvement, the young woman seems to be cured. While the fact that she finds comfort in the arms of a teenage monk may be deemed ironic, the elderly monk views it as a natural happening. Yet he admonishes, "Desire leads to excessive attachment; excessive attachment engenders murderous intent," and dispatches the young woman from the monastery. The teenager monk, struggling between spiritual and physical needs, follows her. Upon departing, he retrieves a small Buddhist statue in front of which he used to pray; this suggests that the next phase of his life will consist of an attempt to merge the secular and the spiritual.

FALL: CAPTIVE ANGER AND SELF-CONTROL

The English word "fall" is highly evocative in this film. The apprentice has fallen from grace, and returns to the monastery following his lover's murder, where he is arrested. "Fall," moreover, denotes "falling leaves," and these may well be the residue of an obsessive body and mind. One morning, the elderly monk happens across a newspaper article telling of a fugitive who has killed his wife. His facial expression suggests regret. Soon thereafter, an adult, who was the teenage apprentice of "Summer," returns to the monastery. The elderly monk greets him and remarks, "You have grown up a lot. Did you live happily?" Contemplating his apprentice's angry face, he continues, "Was the mundane world so painful?" The now-adult apprentice replies irately, "I didn't do anything wrong, but love. She was the only person I loved, but she liked someone else." The old monk replies, "The mundane world is like that; what you like is likable to others as well"—a statement that is neither a reprimand nor a consolation. In the case at hand, it fails to reach the mind of the adult monk, who cannot control his anger.

The elderly monk, so furious at the childlike behavior of the adult disciple, beats him and suspends him with a rope. While corporal punishment is not his way of teaching, this violent action seems to indicate his despairing realization that he may have failed both as a monk and as a guardian in his upbringing of the child apprentice. He writes *Banyasimgyeong*/ 반야심경 (*Prajna-Paramita, Sutra*)[2] on the wooden floor for his disciple to carve out, an act intended to pacify his emotion and erase the thunderstorm of anger he holds in his heart. The elderly monk explains, "One may easily kill others, but one cannot easily kill oneself." Two policemen come to capture the apprentice, and the monk bids them to wait until the young man finishes carving the text. The disciple carves *Prajna-Paramita* (*Sutra*) all night, becomes exhausted, and throws himself to the floor.

Early in the morning, while he is sleeping, the elderly monk and the police paint his carved characters with materials the monk has concocted himself. When the disciple awakens, the apprentice is amazed at the hewn and painted characters, and contemplates the artistry. He finally seems to know how to cope with his anger, and acknowledges this by bowing to his master monk. The boat taking him along with the police officers does not move until the old monk waves, which symbolizes a "sign of blessing" for his disciple's having attained *cheol*.

After the departure of his disciple, the elderly monk covers his eyes, nose, mouth and ears with four pieces of a paper on which he writes the Chinese character 閉, translated as the verb "close"; this act denotes that he is closing all processes of life, from which he will now disconnect. He subsequently immolates himself on the boat that once ferried him to shore. This series of acts is very ritualistic, implying that what we see is not a suicide. The monk's death is juxtaposed with an image of a slithering snake, which, in light of the dead animal that had led is child disciple to cry out in anguish and the later copulating snakes, suggests rebirth. In Buddhism, an enlightened monk knows from where he has come, to where he is going after death, and when it's time to die. The immolation implies that the elderly monk realizes that it is time to depart now that he has dispatched his adult disciple, who has finally learned to manage anger. The carving of *Prajna-Paramita* (*Sutra*) was the climax of his path toward attaining *cheol*.

Winter and Spring Once More: Penance
   and Becoming Mindful

"Winter" alludes to a period of self-reflection. The adult monk returns
to the monastery years later, following his release from prison. He appears
ready to proceed with his own spiritual transformation, as suggested by the
highly disciplined movements, akin to martial arts, that he practices early in
the morning.[3] One day, he breaks through the icy area where his master had
immolated himself, retrieves some relics, wraps them in red cloth, makes a
Buddha statue of ice, and inserts the objects into a hole in the statue's forehead.
In another defining sequence, which visualizes his asceticism, he ties a stone
to himself and carries a Buddha statue to the peak of the high mountain over-
looking the lake on which the monastery floats. As he passes, we see both a
fish and a snake with stones tied to them, yet they are alive. The monk drops
the statue once on his arduous path to the summit, but retrieves it and continues along his path. The act suggests an act of penance not only for his childhood cruelty, but also for his violence as an adult. At the top of the mountain,
he and the Buddha sit side by side as they gaze down at landscape below, where
we have followed the life cycle of a human from child to adult. This time, he
and the statue are the same size; we no longer see the gigantic Buddha of the
earlier episodes. Such a transformation reveals the spiritual growth the monk
has attained. The child apprentice is tiny in comparison to the Buddha's
enormous face; the young man's stature is equal to the face; and finally the
former disciple, now a master, is depicted as virtually on even turf with the
Buddha.

In the "Winter" sequence, the monk's penance is carried further following
the visit of a hooded woman, who arrives with a small child. When she clan-
destinely attempts to leave the monastery at night, she is mired in a ditch. The
next morning, her baby, upon discovering her body, cries out. The monk comes
to him and realizes that the boy is now his disciple.

In "Spring," the cycle is renewed. The elderly monk of "Winter" sketches
a portrait of a child disciple, who was the baby of "Winter." He appears to
have found inner peace, and is consequently mindful of what the apprentice
will go through. In fact, the boy monk feeds a stone to a fish, frog, and snake,
and giggles.[4] What is intriguing here is that the elderly monk watching the
child is not shown; rather, we see an aerial shot of the island from the backside
of the Buddha statue on the high mountain, as if to suggest that the Buddha
is observing the child as a proxy for the monk.

One Step Further toward Deok: *Sensing Time*

The film shows that our life is similar to the seasons in that it undergoes a series of transformations. The film's painterly framing is coupled with extensive moments of silence, which allow the viewer to contemplate a very simple story, one that depicts various stages of life and the movement toward enlightenment. The contemplative rhythm of the film suggests the critical moment of transition is when one can "sense" time and do the right and proper thing at a given age. If one cannot sense time, one's maturing is meaningless.

Despite the vivid sensory experience of *Spring, Summer, Fall, Winter ... and Spring,* there are two similar, yet contrasting scenes of the covering of sense organs. The adult disciple of "Fall" covers his eyes, nose, and mouth, but interestingly not his ears, "out of anger"; the fact that he leaves his ears uncovered expresses that he is still attached to the world around him and to his inner rage. It is only in "Winter," when he returns to the monastery following his imprisonment, that he finally does penance on his own. The elderly monk, in contrast, covers all his sense organs, including his ears, in a very serene manner. He desires to "feel time," time for his adult disciple to stand alone without his spiritual assistance. In other words, he feels that it is time to leave. Eo-Ryeong Lee (2002, 12) cites a passage from Michael Ende's *MoMo* as a foreground that implies the importance of being able to feel time. In this film, the elderly monk feels time for the adult monk to become mindful, and the adult monk feels time for himself to live with compassion for those on the path toward *cheol.* Ultimately, the adult monk will enter a gate leading to a path toward *deok.*

Chihwaseon: Painted Fire

Although very distinct in structure and style from *Seopyeonje, Chihwaseon* shares the common motif of the quest of the artist for authenticity. This film relates the story of 19th-century Korean painter Jang Seungeop, deemed to be one of the major figures who transformed Korean art during the Joseon dynasty. Encouraged by a mentor, who, by coincidence, has seen the artist's childhood drawings, Jang opts to pursue a lifetime in art, yet understands his own need to progress from a mere copying or imitation of Chinese masterpieces to the development of his own unique talent. Becoming an itinerant artist in search of his own direction, Jang turns to excessive pleasures, indulging in alcohol and frequent sexual encounters with women. As he cries out at the royal court, "How can I paint without an erection?" The film thus details the enigmatic combination of artistic pursuit and hedonism, which leads Jang to produce works that will gain international recognition.

Chihwaseon, which jumps back and forth in time, not only presents an examination of Jang's life, but also examines the sociopolitical transformations of Korea. Set during a 40-year period during which Korea was striving to find its own identity despite Chinese and Japanese imperialism, the film's diegetic time encompasses the anti–Catholic persecution of 1866 and the peasant revolts of the 1890s. Jang Seungeop's tumultuous behavior thus encapsulates the stormy transformations of Korean society during the latter half of the 19th century.

Deok *in Process in* Chihwaseon*: Struggles*

Diverse Perspectives on Our Path toward Deok

Viewing *cheol* as feeling time and becoming mindful, one would ask how to describe *deok,* whose cultivation implies lifelong understanding. The film *Chihwaseon* takes its viewer on a walk through a life of Jang Seungeop, a painter born into the lower class in the late 19th century. Because he has not achieved the fame of many other Korean painters, and details of his life are not readily known, a number of aspects of the film are most likely fictitious.

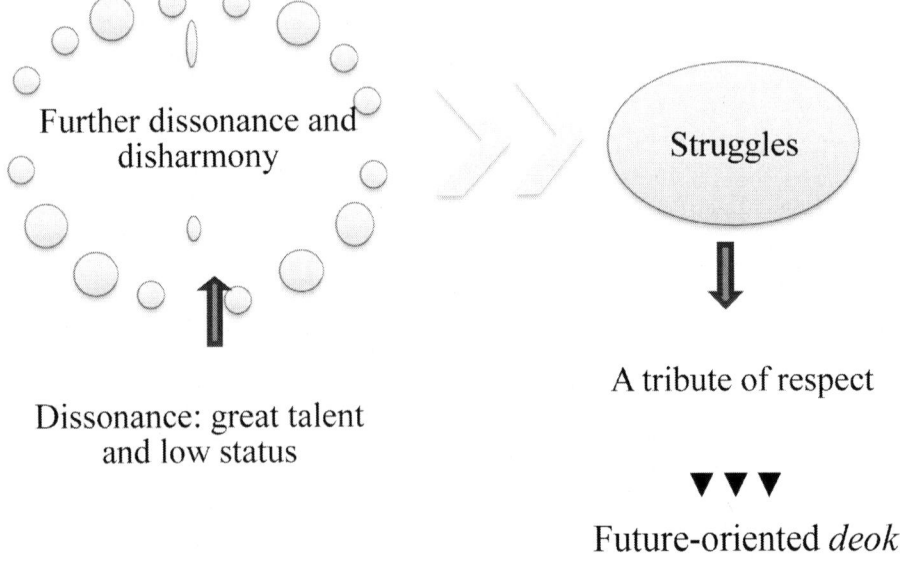

Figure 15. *Deok* in Process in *Chihwaseon*: Struggles.

A number of well-known critics, both popular and academic, have provided interesting analyses of the film from different perspectives. A. O. Scott of *The New York Times* (2002) views the film in terms of the political imbroglios that surrounded the artist and reads it on the level of national history. Moreover, a volume titled *Chihwaseon* (Yoon Jinhi, Nayeong Yu, and Kyeonghwa Yang, 2004) presents six articles on the film, three from a Korean perspective and three from a non–Korean perspective. The Korean contributors—Chungmoo Choi, Soyeong Kim, and Hyangjin Lee—look at the film from the (meta) perspective of Korean political history and Korean film history. Kim and Choi explore it through the lenses of Korean cinema history and the melancholy of male subjectivity, respectively. Lee deems it a work dealing with the conflict between the public film and the director's film, and examines the contrast between societal criticism and aesthetic achievement in the context of contemporary Korean film history. The non–Korean contributors—Adrien Gombeaud, David James, and Jungha Yu—explore the film from aesthetic angles and focus on issues of Jang Seungeop's art. Acknowledging that film has an innate similarity to painting and that the painter's work is artistically vivid, Yu raises an intriguing question as to how *Chiwhaseon* would be viewed if it were presented through animation, considering that the animation genre brings "liveliness."

These critics offer valuable insights into the film and lead interested observers to further look into it from a perspective that has not been given consideration in the past. What we discuss here is substantially different from the aforementioned commentary, given that we are approaching *Chihwaseon* in the context of *deok*.

Dissonance: Great Talent and Low Status

The opening of the film plays with the notion of *deok* inasmuch as it presents two seemingly incompatible factors (i.e., prodigious talent and low class status) from the societal perspective of the particular time depicted. It presents a close-up of a low-class–looking painter moving his brush frantically and chaotically across a thin sheet of paper; the artist creates images in great haste. At this early point, one cannot tell whether this short sequence expresses an impatient creation of the artist or a leisurely consumption of the work by its patrons. This scene is followed by another close-up of a person who makes tea in a very laborious way with slow motions. These two scenes are contrasted in terms of the consumption of time—the painting by a commoner done at a fast pace, and the tea-making by an upper-class man (namely, a *yangban*) at a slow pace.

This contrast alludes to the discrepancy of social class, which is shown in the following scene. The *yanbans* give compliments on the artist's painting, yet their compliments are left-handed. A *yangban* says (in literal translation), "It follows rules while it appears to break them." Seungeop replies, "One stroke is ten thousand strokes; ten thousand stokes is one stroke. How one can talk about rules." The *yanban* gets furious at his reply and reproves Seungeop for his allusion to rules (which are not the domain of the low class). He reprimands the artist by saying that he will deceive himself throughout his entire life due to his superficial talent in strokes.

When Seungeop meets with a Japanese art collector who admires his prodigious painting, the film flashes back to his childhood. Seungeop was born poor and became an orphaned beggar at an early age. One day Kim, a merchant, sees him being beaten by his beggar boss. Kim intervenes and takes the boy home. The boy shows a drawing he made for a woman who was badly treated by the beggar. Here, one observes two of Seungeop's traits: the drawing attests to his talent, and the act of drawing implies his refusal to bend to the chain of command. In fact, soon after he comes to Kim's house, he runs away. According to Kim's wife, he appears not to be able to cope with the *yanban's* rules.

A few years later, Seungeop again encounters Kim in an art supply store where he works for a living. As Kim notices that the local store is ready to take advantage of a new discovery (Seungeop's talent), he provides the young artist with the means to pursue his art, free from worry about obtaining the basic necessities. He introduces Seungeop to an art teacher, who instructs the youth in the basic techniques of drawing and has him practice strokes extensively, to the extent of developing nose bleeds. Furthermore, his literacy skills are developed. A year later after his teacher dies, he returns to Kim. Kim brings him to a *yangban* and arranges for Seungeop to stay in his house as a servant as well as a person who can be asked to draw as needed. He copies numerous famous paintings marvelously and draws nature in an exquisite way. Yet, his prodigious talent and low-class status do not work constructively for Seungeop, but rather lead to his departure. That is, from the perspective of *deok,* his early stage of development seems to present a dissonance, a lack of compatibility between his talent and his constrained social class. Thus, Seungeop may have felt that it was time for him to leave to nurture his artistic skills in a nonconfined setting.

FURTHER DISSONANCE AND DISHARMONY: EMPTY FAME AND NARROW PERSPECTIVES

Despite his humble beginning and the war-torn times in which he lives, Seungeop becomes widely renowned for his impeccable imitations of known masters; he gains a reputation for infusing meticulous copies of old Chinese drawings with his own exquisite melancholy. During the phase in which he is imitating Chinese painting, he begins to make small modifications. At one point, he adds an extra bird to a landscape, and this bird appears lonely and dismal. Such an artistic touch recalls advice given him by his master, who, in an analysis of a painting, explores the mental and emotional state of the sole human figure. Seungeop, as an apprentice, is taught that imagination gives a painting fire, and that what is important is what lies between the strokes. His gift of having a photographic memory helps him remember details of paintings by the masters; more importantly, he actually improves upon their techniques.

Bumping along in an episodic chain of events, Seungeop discovers objects and forms in nature that are telling instances of an artist's quest, suggesting where the mystery of inspiration comes from. The cinematography beautifully captures lush, gorgeous images of nature throughout the film. Seungeop quickly rises in the artistic ranks and is asked to produce paintings for nobles and even the king's family. At one point, he is asked to determine whether a given painting is his own or a fraud. He identifies it as a fraud. When later questioned as to why he has done this when the painting is obviously his own, he stresses that he had given it to a friend for the latter's father's birthday. The friend, however, used it as a bribe. This betrayal rendered the work a fraud.

As his talents are highly regarded, Seungeop's fame and dominance in the art market expand and he becomes known as an exponent of readily sold commercial works-to-order. Nonetheless, Seungeop's problems with upward mobility are exasperated by his discomfort in negotiating art and commerce. More seriously, he strives to distance himself from the masters he is accused of copying. He is so uncomfortable within his own flesh and so tortured by his constant frustration that his carnal indulgences divert him from his path toward an indefinable transcendence.

As the traditional style of painting becomes more and more inadequate for his aesthetic vision, Seungeop sets out to find his "true art" instead of simply enjoying fame. A disciple asks Seungeop why he wants to change his art so much. "People find in my pictures what they expect," he explains. "If I don't change, I'll always be their prisoner."

Thus Seungeop appears to experience a cognitive disequilibrium; since he cannot attain what is expected of him, he reduces his dissonance by criticizing other people and by finding other means of escape such as alcohol, sex, and violent behavior. He appears to believe that a deliberate disordering of the senses is necessary to produce art. Consequently, he never denies any desire—as if suppressing it would choke off his artistry as well. Furthermore, he argues with his patrons as he seeks commissions. Though idolized and celebrated by colleagues and contemporaries, Seungeop refuses to capitalize on that prestige, sometimes insulting his employers or tearing up his own paintings. Along his journey, he experiences some rather tormented relationships with women, mostly courtesans, and discloses an explosive personality given to destructive outbursts. Difficulties with commitment and his tendency toward emotional contradiction are reflected in many scenes, which imply an empty aspect of his fame.

This is underscored by his lack of broader perspectives. To go beyond his ability to copy old masters and find his own style, Seungeop needs sociopolitical insights to be able to discern and understand what is transpiring, especially in an era when only the "learned" are considered to be talented. Even though he goes to great lengths to prove how good an artist he is, he is not taken seriously, given that his literary perspectives are very limited. Moreover, he has an unconstructive attitude toward the socially valued literacy expertise; his literacy skills are presentable, thanks to his previous art mentor, but he is not prepared to be a well-read intellectual.

One could defend Seungeop in that his lack of broader perspective is attributed to his unprivileged background as well as to the historically turbulent period in which he lives. He was born disadvantaged; the conditions of his growing up precluded the development of a keen sense of political and societal changes. He meets with numerous political figures, but they are only transient actors in his life. Even though Kim tries to help him, Seungeop can neither read the flow of changes nor ascertain their meaning. While his inky black brush strokes burst into cascades of flying birds or coalesce into lovely garden landscapes, he slides from patron to patron, from mistress to mistress, soaring to heights of fame and adulation, ruining his career with tantrums, and finally sinking into squalor and homeless wandering. In other words, there is no past and the future is uncertain. Seungeop lives only for the present, as the moment appears to be all he has.

A Tribute of Respect to Jang Seungeop

The final scene in the pottery factory leads the viewer to contemplate the possibilities of assessing Seungeop's life in terms of honor. Seungeop seems to face a divine existential truth; his staring into a kiln generates an intriguing mood for the film's conclusion and raises a fundamental question regarding "fame" and "tribute" in the context of *deok*.

From the perspective of society at large, Seungeop has lost "fame" since he has not established his own voice. His skills have been developed in such a way that its fruits and outcomes do not appear to be very meaningful to others. He has been disdained by other Korean artists (who not only tended to be well read in the Confucian classics, but also were of high class) because he was "unlearned" in the ways of art. He overlooked various voices—those of elitists, who view scholarship as a base for the arts; those of literary artists, who stress the importance of meaning in painting; those of revolutionaries, who call for the true depiction of life in arts; and those of merchants, who promote the commercial aspects of painting. Furthermore, Seungeop does not seem to be aware of his position in society—that is, sensitive to his position as above, below, or equal to others—and thus does not seem to perform his duties accordingly. He does not involve himself in the multiple layers of relationships, supported by cultural values such as loyalty and integrity. Based on the traditional way of conceptualizing *deok,* Seungeop seems to be far from a person with this cultural trait, especially from the perspective of the *yangban* of the Joseon dynasty.

From an inner perspective, one could argue that Seungeop searches for a kernel of *deok,* in that he takes bitter stimulants in pursuit of soul-generated simplicity in the midst of chaos. While the cultivation of *deok* is closely connected to the self's orientation to the needs, wishes and expectations of others, this concept also emphasizes one's inner goodness, which leads to the renewal of oneself as well as one's surroundings, despite prevailing chaos, which is one of the themes of *Chihwaseon.*

We observe that Seungeop lives outside of society and produces works of classical simplicity that contradict the chaos of his world and life. He is like a depraved champion fighter under a dictatorship, ignoring the moral conflicts and constraints of life. Yet he captures birds and flowers so movingly in his paintings and drawings. Seungeop destroys the furnishings in his surroundings, yet he takes pains to pursue a higher vision by tearing up his most sellable work. He sleeps with numerous courtesans and becomes violent if he feels them to be disloyal. Alcohol distracts him from his dissatisfaction with his own progress, yet sometimes leads to new expression. He is tormented by the thought that his work is nothing but copies of the masters. That his soul is so misunderstood and tortured is well typified in a scene where a bare-chested Seungeop charges out into the middle of a raging thunderstorm.

To play the devil's advocate, we can argue that, as Seungeop learned early on in his apprenticeship, a painting is never finished. A work is perpetually in development; the creation of art is a never-ending process. Not unlike the development of a painting is the growth of the artist himself. An artist must always avoid repetition, for in repetition there is death. Seungeop articulates that for him, each day brings deeper renewal. His goal is to make progress every day. But such a process is other-oriented. When Seungeop's master sees that his apprentice has exceeded the master's own talents, he reminds his student that it is the artist's responsibility to foster the talent of others. After all, the blue extracted from indigo is more beautiful than the indigo itself. Seungeop, in turn, must be like indigo and serve as a model for future artists. The artist takes this advice to heart. Pointing at a black rock, he explains to other artists that, in the painter's eye, the rock must be alive to be dynamic.

Despite his numerous vices and peculiar behavior, Seungeop is able to outshine his enigmatic talent. He finally creates a simple piece that fuels the soul of the Korean people who have endured the civil battles of the conservatives and revolutionaries of that particular time, the former supported by China and the latter by Japan, as both countries have had eyes on the Korean peninsula. Seungeop's last painting on the white porcelain and his subsequent disappearance carry significant weight in that its viewer is left to reflect on whether a tribute of respect to Jang Seungeop should be given in the context of *deok*.

Future-Oriented Deok

As the film portrays a person in dissonance and disharmony due to his prodigious talent and low class status, we must raise a fundamental question: can *deok* be a virtue expected from commoners, especially during a period of foreign invasion and/or political corruption? Traditionally, *deok* is a virtue of a *yangban* who pursues *chemyeon* (socially prescribed rules) as implied in the stories of *Yangban* and *Heosaeng* in Chapter 2.

Seungeop exhibits the opposite characteristics that a person with *deok* would be expected to exhibit. Nevertheless, a further examination of the film leads us to reorganize our thoughts on why the artist behaves and talks in the way he does. He appears to be madly self-indulgent, but not in his work. He tries to see life with ardor and show it with clarity. Seungeop exhibits negative attitudes toward those who deal with areas that he cannot understand, which may come from his superiority complex in terms of his artistic talent. The negative attitude can be viewed as a childlike behavior, a denial of self-deception that could serve as a base for fostering genuine elements for developing goodness.

As a young artist, Seungeop displays a positive learning attitude when he is introduced to a mentor. As he gets older, he is fascinated by a stone that symbolizes enduring life. After having led a roving life, he appears mellow and serene, and visits Kim, his lifelong mentor, who is now disappointed by the revolutionary movement and lives quietly in a remote area. Finally, Seungeop reaches his ultimate destination, a pottery shop where he ends his life. He makes strokes with a brush on white porcelain, with his calm manner standing in contrast to his frenzied painting in the first scene of this film, where he moved his brush frantically and chaotically across a thin sheet of paper. The picture he draws is of a person standing on the edge of a boat. It is so unadorned and unpretentious that many people would not recognize its real value. Seungeop seems to express who he is now by finally creating his own unique style that he may have searched all his life.

Just before he enters in the flaming kiln, he asks a ceramist which type of porcelain he expects. He replies, "A painter would expect a lively image, an enamellist a well-polished product, the kiln owner prominent porcelain—but it does not depend on the ceramist, it is the fire that determines." Seungeop nods at the ceramist's statements, and especially at the last one, as if he remembers what the Japanese art collector once said. Seungeop had encountered him again on a street, where people sadly watched the procession of General Jeon being sent to custody after the failure of a political movement. The collector remarked, "The Joseon dynasty is dying out, and your painting will be the only flame to survive." The artist stares at the fire and crawls in the kiln, thereby planting a seed for the future cultivation of *deok* by other artists.

Seungeop's vagrant childhood and the mystery of his disappearance remind us of the story of *Hong Gildong* by Heo Gyun (1569–1618), a radical intellectual writer who illustrated the conflicts and struggles of people who were born ill fated and, therefore, rebelled against society. As mentioned in Chapter 2, this story was written in a feudal society, yet described a utopia devoid of rank. Similarly, Seungeop's life, although tragic in that his prodigious talent is dissipated, particularly in light of the chaos and horror of the times, could be pictured as a utopia where an artist's life flashes within his brush strokes, where one experiences the passion behind the legend.

Poetry

Like so many films of the Korean New Wave, *Poetry* defies classification. Incorporating elements of the melodrama, crime drama, and inspirational fiction, it nonetheless thwarts all attempts to confine it within generic norms. The film relates the story of Yang Mija, a grandmother who learns that she is suffering from Alzheimer's disease and that the malady is no longer in the earliest stages. She enrolls in a poetry class in a community center and begins to keep notes on what she perceives in the world around her. Her motivation for studying poetry may be dual in nature. Mija genuinely displays a love for the art form and seeks a vehicle for her self-expression. At the same time, writing poetry provides her with a chance to exercise her mind and to retard the progression of her degenerative disease.

Another plot thread deals with Mija's grandson, for whom she is the primary caregiver. The son is involved with a group of five other friends, who, over the course of a number of months, repeatedly raped a female classmate, who ultimately committed suicide by throwing herself from a bridge. The grandmother is summoned by the fathers of the other boys and is asked to contribute to a fund to be offered to the victim's family to avoid a police investigation. Mija is expected to visit the girl's mother, bond with her, and initiate the contact. At the same time, it is assumed that she will come up with her share of the bribe. She visits the mother, but forgets her mission. To come up with the bribe money, Mija has sex with and later bribes an elderly man for whom she provides care and housekeeping on a part-time basis. The two narrative threads tie together as Mija writes her first poem, an ode and farewell to the girl who has died.

Deok *in Process: A Far-Reaching Path*

As previously mentioned, the term *deok* was employed by and for certain people of the upper class during earlier Korean dynasties. In contemporary society, however, the word *deok* has been used by and for all individuals. Ham Sok-Hon (2003, 495) defines *deok* as "*jagi sokeseo jeonchereul cheheom haneun geos*" (roughly translated as "experiencing the whole in self"). Although he considers the term in the context of what leaders should have cultivated, Ham views *deok* as more important than technical knowledge or skills, and as a special trait that people should first look for in their work-related contact. His stance implies that the property of *deok* is not confined to certain areas and classes, but rather encompasses all areas and all lifestyles. That is, one can find *deok* germinating in any given ordinary life in which one interacts with various people; experiences joy, anger, sadness, and sorrow; faces conflicts; tries to mitigate tension; and strives to find a solution if problems arise. Thus, we approach *Poetry* from this far-reaching perspective of *deok*.

A SEARCH FOR A GEM IN AN ORDINARY LIFE

The film opens by presenting an image of a river with a bridge in the distance. From the shore, a group of boys playing on a riverbank catch sight of

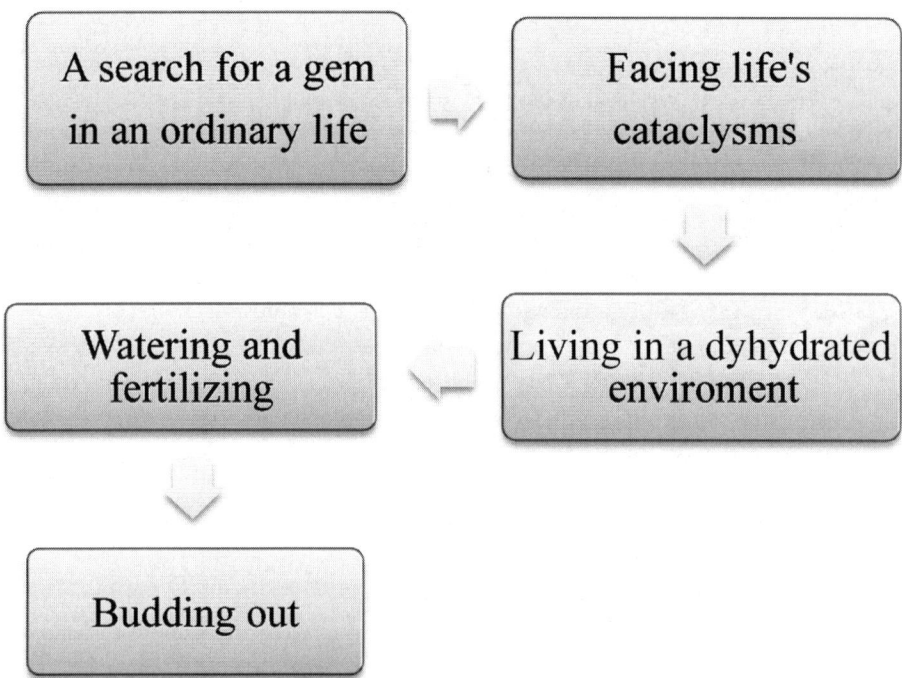

Figure 16. *Deok* in Process: A Far-Reaching Path.

the body of a girl face up in the water, floating towards them from the bridge. Superimposed over the image of the body, which we later learn to be that of Agnes, the young rape victim, is the film's main title, *Poetry*. Poetry is thus linked to death.

The time span of the film covers two major losses experienced by Yang Mija. When we are first introduced to her, she is in the waiting room of a hospital. On the television is a news report covering the discovery of young Agnes's body. Mija appears to have no reaction as she watches the events, which later will be of great consequence to her. In the doctor's office, she discusses her loss of memory, yet disavows the doctor's concerns. In a subsequent appointment, the woman is informed that she is suffering from Alzheimer's disease, and that it is well along its course. Mija explains to the physician that she is forgetting nouns. The doctor responds that this will soon be the case with verbs as well. Mija is asked whether she knows what verbs are; she responds "yes," but states that nouns are more important. The physician agrees, but intimates that verbs will gain in importance. From the standpoint of language, it is important to note that Mija first begins with nouns in her poetic explorations, through the observation of everyday objects. Verbs, in contrast, vibrantly appear in her ultimate poem.

Mija's life appears to be carried along by a stream of circumstances. Every day, she makes breakfast and dinner in a cramped, cluttered little apartment. She lives with her resentful teenage grandson, whose mother, Mija's only daughter, has moved to another town for work. She has a part-time job as a caretaker for a demanding, senile, old man who has suffered a paralyzing stroke; through this work, she makes a little money. In term of daily activities, Mija is typical of individuals with a low-middle-class lifestyle, living on a governmental stipend and residing in less than desirable circumstances. Yet, her floral outfits, tidily arranged scarves, exceedingly ladylike hats, and somewhat breathy or deferential manner of speaking suggest that her mind is floating in a dream world. When the daughter of the old man gives her a compliment on her outfit, she replies shyly, "Do I look chic?"

On the way home from the doctor, Mija notices a poster advertising literature classes in a local community center. This discovery establishes thematic echoes that resonate throughout the film. Mija decides to take a poetry class. We are not sure of her real motivation; it may be a delayed follow-up to a suggestion that she become a poet made by her elementary school teacher more than 50 years earlier. It may be her noble attempt to make art out of the words she still has left before they all go away. She may also think that focusing on language will slow the process of forgetting words.

Mija's seemingly arbitrary interest in poetry is registered as a kind of existential panic. Out of fear or confusion, she keeps the diagnosis to herself and almost from herself, telling neither her grandson nor her daughter. Instead, she wears a poet's cap. She says, "Yes, I do have a poet's vein. I do like flowers and say odd things" when chattering somewhat cheerfully on the phone with her daughter, who seems to be the only person with whom she communicates on a regular basis.

Ironically, the poetry teacher emphasizes that poetry is really about sight—about truly seeing what's in front of our eyes. In the first class, he asserts, "Until now, you haven't seen an apple for real." "To really know what an apple is, to be interested in it, to understand it," he adds, "that is really seeing it," As the teacher exhorts his students to look at objects as if they've never seen them before, Mija goes looking for poetry in flowers, fruit, trees and clouds. She has a clear, open face, demure with a touch of befuddlement. In some shots, she is like a dainty and inquisitive child. At one point, Mija asks her poetry teacher with almost comic innocence, "Where does 'poetic inspiration' come from? ... Where should I go?" she persists. He replies that she must wander around, see it out, but notes that it's there, right where she stands.

As the camera settles on Mija sliding into a seat in first class, the word "apple" appears to be a symbolic term for daily life, in that it could be very ordinary or marvelous, depending on how one sees it. This symbolic term seems to suggest that, as Mija struggles to write a poem, she is able to see the invisible world through facing, dwelling, searching, and painful handling of what occurs in an ordinary life. When Mija returns home, her grandson is in his bedroom with his friends, and she is left alone in the kitchen. The grandmother takes an apple and begins to contemplate it in the *chiaroscuro* of the room. Even though she may be losing the ability to name things, she is able to see more clearly and to scrutinize the world. When asked if she wants to become a poet, she responds that, for the time being, she only wants to write one poem. Such a modest response suggests that poetry, for Yang Mija, is a process. It is most likely viewed as growth over time rather than as a single goal.

FACING LIFE'S CATACLYSMS

The film connects two stories: the dead girl's silence and Mija's incurable cognitive impairment. The first one involves her lazy, uncommunicative grandson, who betrays no remorse or strain over the consequences of his deed. The second one is concealed; the gradual loss of language sends Mija into a panic. She senses that she must somehow find a new way of seeing, of remembering, of being. The pursuit of poetry may sound like a divine activity, a delightful distraction from a mundane existence. However, to Mija, its process is not glowing, in that it involves the exercising of a mind that could slip slowly away from a cruel situation in an unknown direction, as evidenced by her encounter with the young girl's mother. One afternoon, the father of one of her grandson's friends contacts her for a meeting with other fathers. At the meeting, when a father says, "Although I feel sorry for the dead girl, now it's the time for us to worry about our own boys," Mija sits wordlessly. She then drifts outside, looks at cockscombs, opens her little notebook, and proceeds to write. A father comes out to see what she is doing. She responds that the language of the cockscomb flower is "a shield that protects us." Her statement implies that something dreadful will happen, and thus she will need something for shelter.

Whereas Mija appears clueless to others, what is increasingly clear is that her loss of words is both a medical condition and a metaphor, inasmuch as her voice has been muted by the condescension of the fathers of the boys. Her voice is valued merely as a conduit to the grieving, impoverished single mother. From the fathers' standpoint, this gracious and accommodating old woman could go with the river's flow and let the girl's story die with her. However, from the perspective of Mija's desire to write a poem, the film suggests that the painful concessions she has made (pleading with the girl's mother, secretly paying up a large sum of money) and her struggles with the early stage of Alzheimer's disease will lead her along her path.

More specifically, the film presents Mija as an enigmatic person around whom two discrete points emerge. Her interest in her appearance and floral outfits are in stark contrast with the shabby rooms in which she lives and the ordinary streets she walks. Her girlish manner, poetic spirit, and naïve and unsophisticated mind can be compared to the brutish behavior of her grandson, who has been implicated in the death of a classmate, a desperate girl, victimized first by her classmates (Mija's grandson and five other boys) and then by society. Mija is speechless at the crime she cannot fathom, and her description of the cockscomb as "blood-like red flower" contrasts with the stance of the boys' fathers, who treat the crime merely as a hurdle in their sons' careers. Considering these two dichotomous aspects of Mija's character, the parallel between her inevitable cognitive impairment and the death of a desperate girl elevates the dreadful issues to a poetic level. Here, we note significant meaning in the happenings in the ordinary life of a woman living in an uncaring environment.

Along with her quest for poetry, Mija finds another mechanism for coping with the horrific events that surround her; she seeks to come to know the victim in a way similar to that in which she has come to know an apple. This process is the converse of that in *Mother*, in which the protagonist attempts to ascertain the true, negative character of a murder victim. In the case of *Poetry*, Mija's quest is one of affirmation. She eavesdrops on a requiem mass for the girl and steals a small photograph of her. The girl becomes an obsession, and Mija textualizes the loss of the girl she has never known through the poem she ultimately succeeds in writing. Although we can consider the atrocity her grandson has committed a loss of sorts, it becomes relatively unimportant over the course of the film. Mija's attention is diverted from the pay-off intrigues to something of far greater value.

Living in a Dehydrated Environment

The opening sequence, in which children clustered on the riverbank return Agnes's body to the water, serves as a metaphor for the numbing and uncaring environment in which Mija lives. The children appear very indifferent; the death is not of consequence to them. When the girl's hysterical mother cries out in front of the hospital where her daughter's body has been brought, no one offers her any help or comfort. People merely stare at her curiously and proceed along their way.

The absence of normal relationships in Mija's life is striking. She talks to her daughter on the phone, but never tells her anything. She has neighbors, but apparently no friends. Her relationship with her grandson seems remarkably shallow; he agrees to play badminton with her outside their small house, but quickly escapes when his friends show up. Her doctor diagnoses her symptoms routinely without showing any warm concern, while Mija speaks to him in a friendly manner, with a smile. The old man for whom she cares treats her with resigned contempt. At one visit, he pleads with her to let him feel like a man one more time, the nonjudgmental tone of this scene suffusing the film. Although Mija is repelled by the man's action, he does not appear revolting, just selfish and determined. The old man's daughter speaks to Mija routinely as the latter goes in and out of her house. The fathers of the other guilty boys are pragmatic rather than apologetic about paying the girl's mother a bribe for her silence so that neither the school nor their sons will suffer long-term harm.

WATERING AND FERTILIZING

Living in an unassuming environment devoid of normal relationships is depressing and psychologically dangerous to a single, elderly, and powerless person, who could easily become rude and insensitive. Nonetheless, Mija speaks very politely and smiles. Her inner strength is evidenced by the fact that she holds her tears within herself. Only in two scenes does she allow her tears to gush out in front of others. The release of these tears is akin to the watering of hearts that have dried out. In her poetry class, she weeps as she reveals the first beautiful moment in her life, a precious memory from when she was three or four years old. One day, her sister, who had been taking care of Mija due to the illness of their mother, stood by a half-open reddish curtain and called out for Mija to let her dress her. As Mija approached her sister with an unbalanced gait—this due to her tender years—she felt dearly loved and elated. Her tears and raindrops begin to water her heart, which has dried out owing to the dreadful issues she has confronted in such a parched environment.

The second outpouring of tears occurs outside of a restaurant where a poetry recitation party is taking place. This gathering follows an unexpected meeting with the girl's mother and the boys' fathers, which was terribly embarrassing in that Mija had made a frightful mistake in a previous encounter with the woman. The fathers had sent her to meet with the girl's mother to discuss a possible solution for mitigating their sons' responsibility for Agnes's death. On her way to the field where the woman worked, Mija had enjoyed the encounter with nature so much that she forgot to prepare the mother to accept the bribe. Instead, she spoke to her about the apricots and flowers she had observed, and conveyed her good wishes for the outcome of the harvest. Observing the fallen apricots, Mija commented on how these give forth new life. Such remarks reinforce the link between Agnes and poetry. On the way back, Mija remembered her task and provided a false report to the fathers. Her tears outside of the poetry gathering indicate her need to water her heart, which was drying out through her fight against her internal wounds. That is, Mija is unable to release all of her hidden sorrows regarding Agnes, the mother, and her own helplessness triggered by her Alzheimer's disease. Prior to stepping out from the restaurant, she had asked her teacher, "How to write a poem? Didn't you say everyone hold a poem in one's heart?" Her tears appear to be a good fertilizer.

BUDDING OUT

The watered and fertilized heart is able to feel a rose's thorn and find a way to remove it. Mija goes to the old man, with whom she has recently had sex, and asks for money, without revealing the reason for her request. After delivering the funds to the boys' fathers, she seeks out her grandson, buys lunch, and has him take a bath and cut his toenails, reminding him that "a clean body makes a clean mind." Mija plays badminton with him, and watches as the boy is taken away by a policeman. Finally, she sits at her desk and composes a poem, leaving it with flowers on the poetry teacher's platform. As the film's final episode opens, we see the poetry classroom, where it appears that Mija is the only student who has successfully written a poem. The teacher opts, in her absence, to read the work to the class. The poem speaks of death, of regrets of things unsaid and undone, of wondering whether the next world is similar to this one. It is a heartbreakingly beautiful tribute to Agnes; through her poem, Mija speaks for the girl's young victimized soul, assuring that her death will have repercussions of light, and positing that leave-taking will lead to a blessed rendezvous. Stemming from the heart and highly revelatory in nature, the poem is the fruit of the honesty with which Mija has written notes to herself. We hear the majority of the poem through Mija's voice, although she is not present in the class to read it. In its final stanzas, in which goodbyes are expressed, these are first uttered by Mija, and subsequently by the voice of a young girl, possibly Agnes. The poem is superimposed over moving shots that revisit key places in the lives of both Agnes and Mija. We see a classroom in the grandson's school, which most likely was that of Agnes. We return to the homes of both Mija and Agnes, and revisit a park where the former has spent time observing and writing notes.

Finding a Little Path

Poetry demonstrates that beauty lies in how we live truthfully, regardless of the terrible things we might encounter. The film connects two destructive threads (a girl's suicide and an incurable cognitive impairment), and the individuals surrounding Mija exhibit neither violence or hostility, nor any moving affection. *Poetry* shows where creative inspiration derives from, and suggests that it is possible to create beautiful art while living a life of tragedy and inner torment.

Mija finds a narrow path that leads her through the two damaging parts of her life, and follows this conduit faithfully in the pursuit of writing a poem. She brings to light the concept that poetry is a natural part of our lives. She makes herself a visionary through what is transpiring around her. Mija searches herself, and takes in all the spiteful, nasty, hurtful elements that humans exhibit; she cultivates her soul and tries to render it rich. Her struggles to write a poem bring her to the point of discovering on the page something that she had not known until she wrote it.

Losing ourselves in a poem is one of the best ways of finding out who we are. Consequently, we are immersed in Mija's poem, and discover something that we did not know we knew. We are all born poets in the sense that we enjoy the sounds of language. This is what is meant by "discovering the beauty in ordinary life." A discovery of this kind attests to a new, far-reaching concept of *deok*. The aforementioned definition of *deok* by Ham Sok Hon (2003, 495) is applicable to Mija's case in that she is the only one who has completed the course's assignment despite the large number of students; she has emerged as an invisible leader of the class.

The film's ending reiterates the relationship between poetry and death suggested by the title sequence. As the recitation of the poem concludes immediately prior to the end of the film, we see shots of the school bus and then one of the bridge that may reflect the point of view of either Agnes or Mija. Agnes, standing on the bridge, gazes pensively at the camera, as if returning the look of another person. The lack of an orienting counter-shot to ground her look suggests the absence of Mija. Earlier in the film, Mija walks to the center of the bridge, the site of Agnes's suicide, and contemplates the waters in which the girl had died. When the wind blows her hat away, it floats downstream, exactly as Agnes's body had. In the final sequence, the destinies of Mija and Agnes appear conflated. Such a relationship is exemplified by the two voices that read the concluding poem. Does the grandmother's empty apartment, her failure to read her only poem in class, and the water under the bridge signify that she, too, has chosen death? In any case, the completion of the poem has been a major feat, given her progressing Alzheimer's disease, and it has allowed Mija to see the beauty of the world, even under the worst of circumstances.

Conclusion: *Deok* and Dying

As *doek* is something that is cultivated throughout one's life to one's dying breath, it is closely related to death, in that the prospect of the latter prompts us to rethink life. Death is present in all of the films we have analyzed here: the elderly monk's death, that of the painter, and that of the teenager (and arguably, Mija). This death presence leads us to raise a number of questions, such as how death can be viewed from the perspective of *deok,* what meaning can be added to one's life before we die, and how we prepare for our death and thereby make life more rewarding. There may be innumerable answers to these questions: praying, helping others, giving to charity, completing certain things, being the best person one can be—and the list goes on and on. Yet, these films seem to suggest that the best way to prepare for death from a perspective of *deok* is "to live" in a noble way.

Dying for the elderly monk (and the adult monk) seems to be a time of deepening faith and commitment to spiritual beliefs and practices; it is not the end of everything, but rather a gateway into another life. Self-immolation is a positive and ethical action leading to rebirth. Dying for the painter Jang Seungeop constitutes a heightening of his awareness of what is important in life as he nods in agreement with the ceramist's statements before entering the kiln. Death for him is not something to be feared, but rather brings understanding and the transformation of suffering. Dying for Mija provides an opportunity to gain insight into her true nature and that of all things. Death for her is a time of making connections, healing, and letting go, as conveyed in her poem. These observations reinforce the view that the cultivation of *deok* is a lifelong endeavor, a process that melds preparation for death with spiritual enlightenment.

Chapter 7

Key Cultural Concepts as Viewed from the North

The Korean peninsula is home to the only nation in the world so completely divided, and for this reason, it has become a political hotspot for forces from the outside world. North Korea (Democratic People's Republic of Korea [DPRK]) and South Korea (Republic of Korea) are so drastically separated from one another that the Cold War division of Germany pales in comparison. It is hard for outsiders to grasp completely the historical and political factors that have led to this partition. One can only wonder how one Korea perceives and understands the other. How would North Koreans view the films we discussed in Chapters 4, 5, and 6? Considering the extreme curb on cross-national exposure between South and North Korea, we can merely speculate as to how such films and cultural concepts would be read in North Korea today or by former North Koreans were the two halves of the peninsula to reunite. The ideology of the South Korean cinema is clearly in opposition to North Korean ideals, which explains the absence of these films north of the 38th Parallel. Yet, the key concepts are so deeply rooted in Korean culture that they are likely to transcend political barriers, albeit in reconceived and transfigured forms given the 60 years that have separated the Koreas. (The song "Arirang" was used by the DPRK as a symbol of separation and reunification in the Mass Games performed frequently between 2002 and 2013.) But what about films made in North Korea? Can these be viewed in terms of the cultural concepts we have explored in South Korean cinema?

The cinema of North Korea is decidedly less well known internationally than that of its southern counterpart. It is arguably one of the world's least viewed cinemas, although an impressive array of films are now available for online purchase, a number of which have English subtitles. The world's relative unfamiliarity with this film tradition is due largely to the fact that the country makes films primarily for the ideological education of its citizens. Over the course of some six decades, it has been less concerned with disseminating its films abroad. Two noted exceptions are Shin Sang-Ok and Chong Gon Jo's *Pulgasari*, which has gained cult status in the West, and Jang Inhak's *A Schoolgirl's Diary* (2007), for which limited international rights were sold at the Cannes Film Festival ("N. Korea Film Hunts Buyers at Cannes," 2007). It is possible that the increasing international presence at the Pyongyang Film Festival may serve to bring North Korean cinema to the world. The challenge is that, in light of the ideological role this cinema plays domestically, it must be viewed in terms of the sociopolitical underpinnings of North Korean society. Nonetheless, like the cinema of South Korea, it invites an analysis drawing upon key cultural concepts.

This chapter is structured somewhat differently than the previous three in that it provides an introduction to both North Korean political ideology and the inner workings of its film industry. Such discussions are necessary given that North Korean cinema has a very different didactic role than does its southern counterpart. Contextualization of its broader scope will provide a framework for our analysis of those key cultural concepts that are still unmistakably present, albeit in various forms and to differing degrees.

North Korean Film, *Juche* Ideology and Traditional Cultural Concepts

Kyung Hyun Kim opens his 1996 study of the discourse of the nation in the North Korean film *Sea of Blood* with a quote from Bruce Cummings (1992), an American academic who has traveled to North Korea. Cumming writes:

> North Korea has one undeniable freedom, a freedom disallowed during the colonial era, attenuated by the Sinified elite in the 500 years of the Yi Dynasty, and a freedom less easily exercised in the South, the freedom to be Korean [207].

Cummings views national identity as paramount to North Korean society and life. Kim further highlights the country's desire to protect its national identity, particularly in light of South Korea's pursuit of modernity or post-modernity, by attributing this phenomenon to North Korea's *juche* ideology.

The principle of the *juche* philosophy was elaborated by Kim Il Sung with the assistance of Hwang Jangyop; the latter had studied in Japan during World

War II and later majored in philosophy at the University of Moscow during the Korean War (Oberdorfer, 2001, 400). Hwang was one of the most prominent officials of North Korea and was the "principal authority on *juche,* which became the official credo of the DPRK in the 1972 constitution" (Oberdorfer, 2001, 401). (Hwang Jangyop had been accorded special responsibility, while a professor at Kim Il Sung University, for the education of Kim Jong Il [Oberdorfer, 2001, 401].)

The literal meaning of *juche* (주체) as given in a dictionary can run the gamut from "the subject," "the main body," "the core," or "independence." As Grace Lee (2003) notes, foreign scholars often describe it as "self-reliance" (105). Nonetheless, Lee views its meaning as much more subtle and distinctive, in that *juche* implies being the master of revolution and reconstruction of one's own country, from a political, economic, and military standpoint (105). The Korean Friendship Association, an international organization founded in 2000 to foster ties with the DPRK, describes the major elements of *juche* ideology: *Juche* implies:

> maintaining an independent and creative standpoint in finding solutions to the problems which arise in the revolution and construction. It implies solving those problems mainly by one's own efforts and in conformity with the actual conditions of one's own POLITICS.... The realization of independence in politics, self-sufficiency in the economy and self-reliance in national defence is a principle the Government maintains consistently [Korean Friendship Association, 2011].

Lee (2003) argues, "The fundamental tenets of *juche*—that man is the master of all things and decides everything, and that an ideological consciousness determines human behavior in historical development—do not strictly hold Marxist–Leninist principles in view of several factors, one of which is the advocacy of Kim Il Sung's regime regarding a single leader-headed revolutionary hierarchy" (111). She affirms that authoritarianism is an inherent part of *juche* ideology: the presence of an "exceptionally brilliant and outstanding leader" is inseparable from the mobilization of the working class (111). In his study of North Korean cinema history, Johannes Schönherr concurs with Lee, but adopts a different perspective. He notes that, although *juche* was based on Marxist–Leninist doctrine, it nonetheless "placed absolute North Korean self-reliance in all political, economic, ideological, and national defense matters at the center" (Schönherr, 2012, 35).

The Democratic People's Republic of Korea,[1] unlike the Republic of Korea, has a centrally run film industry that constitutes a major governmental agency. The notion of independent production does not exist, and both Kim

Il Sung and Kim Jong Il took great interest in the film industry's development. As mentioned earlier, the Japanese occupation was a major impediment to the development of a Korean film industry in the 20th century. Nonetheless, following the division of the country, the South Korean film industry could be viewed in terms of a continuum with the past, particularly in light of the growing importance of Seoul as a film center. The industry in the DPRK, however, needed to be built from scratch. This task was foremost on the government's mind in 1949. The Korea Film Export and Import Corporation describes this cinematic tradition:

> Our cinematic art, which entered a new stage of upswing in the 1980s, presents the true aspects of the revolutionary cinematic art of the *Juche* era in the philosophical depth and range of the ideological substance and in direction, acting, shooting, music, décor and other methods of representation, techniques, and search for original cinema forms [Korea Film Export and Import Corporation, 1985, np].

When Kim Jong Il discusses "original forms," his meaning is sharply different from that assumed in South Korean cinema. Articulating such narrative principles as "conflicts should be settled in accordance with the law of class struggle" (66), "each scene must be dramatic" (77), "the best words are full of meaning and easy to understand" (91), and "the mood must be expressed well" (98), Kim Jong Il (1973) outlines the principles of narrative development. Defining "originality," Kim stresses, "Only those who can see life with their own eyes and describe it well by applying their own distinctive artistic talent and skill, are capable of producing original images" (106). He adds, "A writer who has chosen his seed must create an image with definite characteristics, conforming to the seed's requirements. If the theme and characters are hackneyed, although the seed is fresh, this means that natural logic has already been distorted" (108). He contrasts revolutionary art with bourgeois art since the former does not advocate "individuality for individuality's sake" (116).

In what is arguably the most extensive academic study of North Korean cinema, Hyangjin Lee (2004) identifies three principles that govern the making of films in North Korea: (1) the seed theory, (2) modeling, and (3) the speed campaign. The first is tied to the subject matter, which must "treat ... material and themes that feature the revolutionary thoughts of Kim Il Sung" (33). The second involves the portrayal of "the struggles of the working class to achieve class and national liberation" (33). The third is intended "to meet the demands of the Party to make films of high ideological and artistic quality rapidly and to strict schedules" (33). Lee also identifies two salient themes of North Korean cinema: the revolutionary tradition of class struggle and films on the Korean War and unification. With regard to class struggle, she discusses at length O Pyŏngch'o's *The Untrodden Path* (1980), which she describes as "[dramatizing] the process of establishing a working class in the newly emerging socialist state" (150). The film, as Lee explains, portrays a steel factory worker who returns to a factory that had previously been unsafe under Japanese control so as to "participate in the nation-building by producing much-needed steel" (151). Among the films related to the Korean War and unification, Lee discusses O Pyŏngch'o's *Ch'oe Hakshin's Family* (1966) and Ch'oe Kyŏngsan's *Wŏlni Island* (1982). These were "selected by the Party as the best and 'representative' war films, which raised the standard for artistic expression of the North Korean's fighting spirit and patriotism" (43).

Kyung Hyun Kim has offered a different taxonomy of themes in the North Korean cinema, specifically as seen through *Sea of Blood,* which includes (1) the Party, (2) the leader, (3) the family, and (4) the nation. He posits that a primary goal of the film is to endorse North Korea's national unity (1996, 102). Kim's stated agenda in his analysis is to explore "how North Korean cinema intervenes in the discourse of the nation." Drawing upon the work of Benedict Anderson, he looks at the ways in which *Sea of Blood* imagines a unified and liberated nation-space (86).

Hyangjin Lee presents an especially astute examination of cultural traits that are preserved in North Korea:

> Under the observable differences between South and North Korean films, however, my analysis also uncovers the sustaining power of the cultural homogeneity among the Korean people, which has not been entirely lost despite their four and a half decades of political confrontation [188].

She further stresses that, despite the preeminence of the cinematic depiction of tensions between the two Koreas, the cinemas of both North and South display "a similar use of the cultural legacy of their shared past" (191). Lee asserts:

> [The cinema's] fundamental root goes back to the enduring cultural traditions that have survived among the people.... In this sense, the cultural homogeneity of traditional Korean society can be said to constitute a common undercurrent in these films, although their surface narratives capitalize on the ideological difference between the two states [191].

Lee offers considerable insights into both the production of films in North Korea and their reception. She stresses the importance of the training and reeducation of film professionals, mentioning the founding of the Pyongyang Drama and Film University in 1953, which became the Pyongyang Film University in 1973. Pointing out that prior to the late 1970s, the majority of films did not list the names of individuals who participated in the filmmaking process, Lee underscores that films are deemed collective efforts of "creative workers" (41). She offers insights into the division of the Korean Film Studios into 10 subgroups, and notes the presence of several workshops, each of which, at the close of the 20th century, produced two to three films per year. Lee explains that another unit, called the Korean 4-25 Film Studios, is run by the Korean People's Army. Its primary focus is to produce war films. Regarding film reception, Lee foregrounds the importance of screenings at workshops, cooperatives, and factories (41). She stresses that film viewing constitutes the most important political education of North Koreans (41).

What one immediately notes, when comparing the cinema of the DPRK to that of the Republic of Korea, is that revolutionary films tend to be very straightforward. The open discourse that characterizes so much of the New Korean Cinema is, by and large, not present. Narratives tend to be clearly presented and neatly tied to *juche* ideology. Burning questions are usually answered in the films' final sequences. Thus, the open-endedness of South Korean cinema would be inconceivable in the North, particularly in light of film aesthetics as developed in Pyongyang over the course of the past seven decades. *Han, jeong,* and other cultural concepts in these films, as we will explore in this chapter, are embedded into *juche* ideology. Nonetheless, these concepts are very distinct in that they circulate among characters, always with an eye toward society at large and revolutionary struggle. They are frequently tied to cultural and national issues, and the focus is on how these issues serve to foster a genuine national discourse.

For these reasons, the close readings in this chapter are considerably different from the earlier discussion of South Korean films. They focus less on the importance of cultural concepts as depicted through an individual character, which might be too bourgeois for revolutionary cinema. Instead, the emphasis is always on broader sociopolitical and ideological perspectives.

This chapter explores how cultural concepts and ideology meld in three films set in contemporary North Korea and a historical drama that takes place at the onset of the Japanese occupation: Rim Changbom and Jon Kwangil's *On the Green Carpet* (*Pureunjudan Wieseo*/푸른주단 위에서) (2001), a film focusing on Pyongyang's famous mass gymnastics spectacle); Jang Inhak's *A Schoolgirl's Diary* (*Han Nyeohaksaengui Ilgi*/ 한 녀학생의 일기) (2007), a story of the sacrifice of a personal life for the broader needs of society, and Pho Kwang and Maeng Choimin's *Pyongyang Nalparam* (평양 날파람) (2006), a martial arts film. These films have been selected not only for their thematic use of cultural concepts, but also because they were produced in recent years and, therefore, correspond at least temporally to our discussions of South Korean films.[2]

On the Green Carpet

On the Green Carpet is set in Pyongyang in 2000 during the preparations for a mass gymnastic display to be staged in celebration of the 55th anniversary of the founding of the People's Party. Mungyu is an assistant choreographer charged with managing a group of young children, and Hyonhui is a young woman who has been appointed vice chief of the Mass Gymnastics Creative Group. The pair, who once knew each other as child performers, have opposing ideas regarding just what the children are capable of doing. Mungyu advocates for a difficult move that Hyonhui believes impossible. Over the course of the film, we learn that Mungyu's determination to include the number stems from his desire to create a very special performance for Kim Jong Il. As a child, he had arrived late at a performance before the Dear Leader, and now dreams of doing something very special to please him. When a child in the group is injured and it is unlikely that he will be able to perform, Hyonhui visits the boy and learns of his dream to perform for the General. Her heart is softened, and she comes to share Mungyu's faith in the children. The vice chief not only approves of the risky forward tumbling, but recasts it as an even more difficult and complex maneuver. The performance is a great success, and Kim Jong Il congratulates (off screen) its creators.

A Hidden Han

The film opens with an image of a mass gymnastics performance, followed by a shot of fireworks above the stadium in which the event is held, although, for the moment, this shot seems unattached to the narrative that follows. We then see Mungyu on his way to work. Walking along a Pyongyang street, he is greeted by a busload of children, who we subsequently learn to be members of the "chapter"—a segment of the mass performance that depicts a specific historical or ideological theme—that he is coaching in the mass performance. Mungyu catches sight of a woman who has paused briefly to listen to a children's band conducted by a young girl. Recognizing her as his childhood gymnastics partner, he rushes after her, but she disappears down the steps of a metro entrance. As Mungyu rides a trolley with his sister, who questions him regarding the woman's identity and reminds him that it is due time for him to marry, little does he realize that he and his former partner, Hyonhui, are actually headed to the same destination, a field where preparations are under way for the 2000 mass gymnastics event.[3] The opening sequence is key inasmuch as it brings together a number of the thematic foci of *On the Green Carpet*—namely, a teacher's love for his students, children in performance, and the sacrifice of personal life for a higher goal.

Hyonhui reports to work as the new vice chief of the mass performance, and is introduced to her creative team. She recognizes a woman from her childhood, who is now a creative leader and Mungyu's direct superior. The woman mentions to Hyonhui that Mungyu is one of the trainers of her "chapter" and that he is in the field. Hyonhui remembers her former partner, who had been known to their team as "the donkey." She is anxious to see him in the field.

As Mungyu arrives to work with his children, we note the special care and attention he devotes to them. He stays abreast of their individual academic performance in school subjects and is concerned about their health and well-being. Mungyu explains to the children that they will be learning two difficult moves: backward tumbling and forward tumbling with a partner. If approved by the board, these moves will become a part of their chapter. The children applaud enthusiastically. Nonetheless, Hyonhui is not convinced of the feasibility of such additions. Having read about the proposed moves, she expresses to the creative leader her concerns: backward tumbling is extremely difficult, and forward tumbling in groups of eight is so risky that, if one child performs badly, the entire chapter will fail.

Hyonhui and Mungyu rekindle their friendship, but their relationship is not unstrained. She visits him at home and they enjoy a pleasant evening together, yet their professional life is fraught with tension given the vice chief's lack of confidence in the assistant choreographer's creative choices. Moreover, Mungyu vividly remembers how Hyonhui brutally rebuked him as a child for having arrived late to a performance before Kim Jong Il. The vice chair, for her part, recalls having blamed the boy for their chapter's last-place finish in the competition. At this point, it is unclear to Hyonhui that the young assistant choreographer's determination to implement the challenging moves is part of a deeply rooted *han*.

Hyonhui approaches her new position with fervor and dedication. She is meticulous with all performance details, including the appropriate background for each chapter. As she watches Mungyu during training sessions and notes how a good number of the children stumble and fall, she is more convinced than ever that the chapter will never be able to perform the forward tumbling. The vice chief thus takes drastic measures. Hyonhui transfers the senior creative director to another stadium and offers Mungyu the opportunity to direct his own chapter, which consists of a women's marching band. The young man firmly protests this decision. His children, having heard rumors of his departure, express their severe distress over the change. Their stance encourages Mungyu to refuse the offer firmly, and to convey to Hyonhui that he is willing to sacrifice a promotion to keep working with his children. The vice chief still fails to understand the true nature of Mungyu's *han,* the origin of which will be explained later in the film.

Han, *Leader and Nation*

As part of their training, Mungyu takes the children to a planetarium, where he demonstrates to them how planets revolve around the sun as satellites. The sun provides the warmth that allows the planets to live. The children immediately recognize the metaphor: they are planets and satellites that surround the Dear Leader, Kim Jong Il. This is what the tumbling movements are designed to illustrate; the children will tumble as satellites surrounding the sun. This is the first time in the film that the metaphor behind Mungyu's choreography is completely articulated, and it will be up to Hyonhui to grasp and condone it. But before that, she must understand the assistant choreographer's *han*. The seeds of her ultimate acceptance are planted by the creative director, who, during a night walk, describes to the vice chief an incident that had transpired during a period when the latter had been gaining an international reputation and hence was separated from her former teammates. When a group of children were on the "green carpet" (the mass gymnastics field) to perform for Kim Jong Il, a thundershower broke out. The leader retreated from his place in the stadium, stressing that if he had remained there, the children would have been soaked while performing for him in the rain. He reminded his entourage of the love and respect his father had had for the country's youth. Moved as she was by the story, the creative director has yet to understand how performance and *han* are connected for Mungyu.

In a subsequent meeting, Hyonhui and the creative director watch a rehearsal on the green carpet. The director tells the vice chief that she had actually visited Mungyu at home following his late arrival. On this occasion, she had learned that Mungyu's mother had just died. Despite the protests of his family, who felt that any single performer could replace another on the green carpet, Mungyu had run to the stadium, declaring that nothing could replace the desire in his heart to perform for Kim Jong Il. Hyonhui now begins to understand and accept the *han* that drives the assistant choreographer.

Her change in heart is further solidified when a young child—one of the most awkward in the children's chapter—is severely injured. Mungyu remains by the child's bedside, and his dedication encourages the hospital staff to find an alternative to surgery so that the boy can continue to perform in the chapter. Hyonhui, however, is not convinced that the child will recover and orders Mungyu to find a replacement. Upon meeting the child herself and hearing that the latter had dreamed of performing for Kim Jong Il, who in turn applauded his work, Hyonhui sees a direct link between the boy's desire to perform and Mungyu's passionate work with the chapter. She now understands the secret *han* that has driven her former partner and that must be vented through the creation of dynamic choreography. Alone, she maps out graphically the motif of the sun and planets, and prepares to defend the difficult moves at a board meeting. In an encounter with Mungyu on the rehearsal field prior to the meeting, she asks him if he is preparing himself to defy her. He, in turn, states his intention to do so. All present are dumbfounded when, rather than rejecting the forward tumbling altogether, Hyonhui declares that, as is, the movement fails to convey adequately the intention of its creators. The vice chief suggests, instead, that the movement be accomplished with groups forward tumbling in different directions. Only this way can justice be done to the intent of the creative team.

The concluding sequences of *On the Green Carpet* present portions of the mass performance and its aftermath. For the first time, we see the tumbling in its full metaphorical context, and we ascertain how it represents the importance of the strong leader as a central force in *juche* ideology. The children perform flawlessly. Their movements are coordinated, and they move as one, which is closely aligned with the *juche* ideal of the oneness of the nation. The synchronized movements of the children reflect the unity of the entire performance. In the background, thousands of people hold placards and move them in perfect harmony to create slogans, maps, drawings, and an image of Kim Il Sung. Such harmony is noted several times in the lyrics to the song that accompanies the children's performance, which repeat *ilsimdangyeol*/일심단결 (literal meaning "one heart unity"), a phrase that also appears visually in the stadium background. Fireworks exploding above the stadium recall the film's opening image. Alone on the green carpet, Mungyu is approached by Hyonhui, who asks him whether he has heard the good news: Kim Jong Il has not just loved the children's performance, but has deemed it a masterpiece. The children reappear on the field and dance with their teachers.

Han *Release and Artistic Expression*

Mungyu's *han,* which has at last been released, might superficially appear individualistic in nature—that of an artist in search of recognition. Yet it is, in reality, strongly collective. The recognition desired is that of the chief of state, and by extension, of all of the satellites that surround him. The entire performance metaphorically celebrates patriotism, revolution, and the *juche* notion of national culture. Over the course of the film, the reported—but never seen—actions of Kim Jong Il are always closely in line with the doctrines and principles his father had developed. In turn, Kim Il Sung is viewed in terms of historical factors, as part of a continuum that has extended to the present day from the birth of the People's Party, which the 2000 mass performance celebrated. One thus encounters in *On the Green Carpet* an implicit equation among the two successive leaders and the people of the DPRK. Through his desire to create a performance that reflects the North Korean people and their leaders, Mungyu's *han* has become political in nature. His individual *han* is tied to the nation, and is expressed on numerous levels of the story through the subjugation of personal interests and desires in favor of the revolution. Mungyu is one of many satellites that revolve around the sun.

A Schoolgirl's Diary

The protagonist of *A Schoolgirl's Diary* is Suryeon, a young girl who lives with her mother and paternal grandmother near Pyongyang. Her father, a scientist, is absent most of the year and makes only rare visits to his family. Her mother is a librarian, but spends a great deal of time translating scientific material to help her husband's research. Suryeon's dream is to move from their small house to an apartment block, and she resents her classmates whose fathers have earned doctorates or other titles of prestige, and, as a consequence, have been offered apartments. In addition, she is taunted by a classmate whose father has completed his doctorate and who asserts that Suryeon's father is a failure. In light of the father's absence, an uncle has assumed a paternal role for Suryeon and her sister, an aspiring soccer player. Yet Suryeon desperately misses her father and feels betrayed by him.

The situation is worsened for Suryeon when her mother is diagnosed with cancer. In an attempt to inform her father of the mother's illness, the young woman travels to his workplace, only to see that he is working as a laborer. We later learn that the father is indeed a research scientist; he is most likely working in a menial position so that he can better understand the manufacturing process. He is, in fact, leading a team that is developing a computerized assembly line. When the team succeeds in meeting their goal, Suryeon is proud of her father and follows in his footsteps, entering into an academy of science. Her mother misses her matriculation due to her health, and her father is unable to attend because of his work and doctoral defense. Nonetheless, Suryeon now understands that her father, like the Dear Leader, must be absent from his family to fulfill his duty to the state. She appreciates the deep bond her parents share, despite their frequent separation, and opts to follow in their footsteps.

Fatherly Jeong *Missed*

The events of the narrative comprise excerpts from the diary of Suryeon, a girl who desperately longs for her father, Kim Sanmyong, a research scientist who visits his family only on rare occasions. The film opens as young Suryeon is struck by a paper airplane launched from an apartment in the multistory building where she longs to live. She is headed home from school for lunch, and she continues alone to her small house as her classmates enter the apartment complex. For Suryeon, an apartment implies the presence of a father, since all of her classmates' fathers live with their families. The young girl not only misses her father, but also envies her classmates whose families, due to their fathers' success, have been relocated to modern apartment buildings. She feels that her own father is a failure, since so many other fathers have earned their doctorates but hers seems not to have made any progress toward this goal. Suryeon focuses merely on his absence. In all actuality, the young girl is surrounded by *jeong*. She lives with her mother, grandmother, and sister, and the four are deeply attached to one another. Nonetheless, she misses her father and understands neither the deep commitment that her mother has for him nor the symbiotic tie that binds her parents.

When her classmates help repair a broken chimney on Suryeon's house—a job that typically would have been performed by a father—her mother prepares for them a special dinner. One of her friends announces that he has just volunteered for the army, and that he will soon have to trek through wet snow. Suryeon, in his honor, sings her favorite song, accompanying herself on the guitar. The song tells of a father who is walking through snowy mountain paths near the front; as it progresses, we learn that the father in question is the father of the country, Kim Jong Il. The song wishes the General a safe return. Singing about a father, Suryeon is most likely thinking about her own father. Despite her love for the song, she does not yet make the connection between her own father's work and that of the Dear Leader. Suryeon is, therefore, unable to sense the ideological connection between the notion of fatherhood and that of the nation.

Jeong *among Spouses and* Chung *for the Nation*

Given her strong emotions toward her father, it is hard for Suryeon to understand the special *jeong* shared by her parents. The latter's love is also romantic in nature, as brought forth in an awkward moment during one of Sanmyong's infrequent visits home, when the sisters inadvertently break down the door to their parent's bedroom. So intense are their feelings for their father that they fail to understand their parents' need for privacy. The visit, as can be expected, is cut short by Sanmyong's early departure.

Sanmyong is almost continuously separated from his wife, yet she is instrumental in the success of his scientific pursuits. Although she is a librarian and not a professional translator, she spends her nights translating materials that will help him. (The language or languages of origin are not specified.) Even when she is recovering in a sanitarium from cancer surgery and against the better judgment of her nurse, she continues to work as part of this effort. Thus, both Sanmyong and his wife are making tremendous sacrifices for the growth of science in the nation. The bond between the couple has grown deep over the years, despite their rare meetings. Having witnessed an audience applauding her father's victory, Suryeon writes to her mother, who is still away at the sanitarium, that she now understands the deep bond between her parents and that their hearts burn with love for the General. The parents are shown gently embracing as they share an umbrella on a stroll near their new apartment. We once again hear Suryeon's favorite song and realize that her parents are now keeping step with the General, as evidenced by their new apartment. In the film's final sequence, Suryeon has accompanied her parents to the train station, where she watches as her mother bids her father farewell, running alongside the departing train and waving. As Suryeon is now embarking upon her own life, her parents are the models she will emulate. The last words of her diary state, "[The] future will prove the worth of her life." Suryeon is now feeling the deep *chung* for her country that has guided her parents' lives and sustained them through countless long separations.

A Life of Hard Work and Loyalty

Sanmyong is deeply committed to his scientific research, and wishes to take the long road to research that will truly benefit society. He emulates the Dear Leader, who himself must be absent from his family while he sees to the good of the nation and visits soldiers at the front. A line is drawn not only between the workplace and the military front—after all, both are inseparable from the well-being of the nation—but also between Sanmyong's passion for his work and Kim Jong Il's love for the Korean people. Sanmyong's dedication to the Dear Leader is a form of filial piety (*hyo*), which in turn represents a strong sense of loyalty to the nation (*chung*). Suryon, for her part, fails to understand her father's position and mistakenly assumes that he is nothing more than an assistant to other workers, a perception she gains when she visits him at the factory where he is employed. Little does she know that being actively engaged in the work process enhances the scientist's research by allowing him insights into processes that can be changed and improved.

On a subsequent visit to Sanmyong's workplace, Suryeon and her sister are able to catch a glimpse of the final simulation session for a computerized assembly line. The team of researchers is successful, and Sanmyong is not only lauded by his peers, but, as we learn from a newspaper photograph, is visited by Kim Jong Il himself. The researcher's ongoing dedication to his work is evidenced by the fact that, after his victory, he does not return to hearth and family, but rather continues along his own research path. Such commitment will ultimately inspire Suryeon, who has already become an expert in computers, to undertake university studies in science.

Suryeon's understanding of her father's loyalty to the nation occurs late in the film when Sanmyong, unable to attend her university matriculation, sends her a small cassette player with which he has recorded himself singing the song as a special gift to his daughter. Following the song, he explains to Suryeon its deeper meaning. This moment is decisive in reinforcing the young woman's understanding of her father's impassioned *chung* for his country.

Jeong *Interwoven with National* Chung

Toward the end of the film, Suryeon throws her own paper airplane from the balcony of the apartment that her family has now earned. In contrast to her earlier linking of an apartment with the presence of a father, she is able to appreciate the new living accommodation without her father, now that she understands his dedication to the nation. She now grasps the national *chung* that is closely tied to her fatherly *jeong*. Sanmyong's special type of fatherly *jeong* is demonstrated by showing his daughter the importance of loyalty to the homeland. Suryeon has also come to appreciate the ongoing nature of Sanmyeong's *chung*. This is expressed visually by cross cuts between Suryeon's matriculation and her father's continued work on the assembly line, even after his well-received success. We thus see that the intersection of *jeong* and *chung* has come to fruition. Any resolution felt by the viewer is only partial, however, because the characters must continue to strive, each in their own way, for the continued transformation of society.

A Schoolgirl's Diary is a relatively closed narrative, leaving very few gaps or fissures for the viewer to ponder. Yet despite its narrative closure, it implies that social transformation is an ongoing, open-ended process. The commitment of Suryeon's parents to their own continued work reflects Kim Jong Il's theories on the cinema. Kim views the training of professionals as not just for artists and technicians in the early phases of their careers, but as a lifelong process. Kim writes, "Writers and artists who are determined to work for the Party and their fellow citizens must, without exception, strive throughout their lives to improve their skills" (Kim Jong Il, 1973, 287). He emphasizes the long-term, ongoing nature of the development of revolutionary artists:

> Writers and artists must not be half-hearted in their efforts to revolutionize themselves, nor must they give up the effort after only a short crash programme. A man cannot become a revolutionary in a couple of days, nor can he become revolutionized by reading a few books or by making a few innovations in his work and his life. The struggle for revolutionary transformation must be waged with stubborn patience to the last [Kim Jong Il, 1973, 278].

Pyongyang Nalparam

At the onset of the Japanese occupation of Korea, the invaders are determined to uncover all four volumes of a manual that collectively detail the timeless Korean martial art of *taekkyeon*.[4] Their intent is to gain control over the art so that their own judo, which has been defeated by *taekkyeon*, can be the superior martial art in East Asia. The story focuses on Jeongtaek, a young master of Pyongyang Nalparam, the most evolved form of *taekkyeon*, who is set to marry Sokyeon, his former childhood playmate. The fathers of both Jeongtaek and Sokyeon have been actively striving to prevent the manuals from falling into the hands of the Japanese. After Jeongtaek is forced to feign marriage to a Sokyeon imposter, who has murdered his father, he meets his true fiancée, and the two join in an intricate series of attempts to thwart the Japanese claim to Pyongyang Nalparam. Ultimately, *taekkyeon* proves its superiority over judo as Jeongtaek publicly fights his Japanese counterparts. The victory is short-lived. A Japanese platoon shoots the lovers to death, along with a number of *taekkyeon* devotes. Miraculously, however, the four volumes of the manual are returned to Korean hands.

A Door to the National

The film opens in present-day Pyongyang as Mr. Ko, an elderly "gentleman from abroad," arrives at an archive late at night. We see the lights inside the library turn on, and it is obvious that his visit is a private one and most likely highly official. The lavish archive claims to possess all four volumes detailing *taekkyeon.* As we later learn, to understand the martial art, it is necessary to read all of the volumes—individually, they are meaningless. A woman clad in a traditional Korean dress, obviously an archivist, greets Mr. Ko and names several of the subcategories of *taekkyeon,* to which the visitor adds Pyongyang Nalparam. The guide leads him to an escalator, which takes them to the archive's book stacks. Mr. Ko apologizes, stating that he will understand if the library really does not have the volumes. The archivist simply replies, "Seeing is believing," and uses an electronic code to unlock a door. Mr. Ko enters a special collection where the four volumes are housed under glass in a side-by-side arrangement, with one open to the first page. As the guest reads from the open manual, we begin a flashback to the life and experiences of Jeongtaek. This sequence appears to constitute a framing device, and we expect to return to Mr. Ko at the end of the film and understand his relationship to the events depicted during the early days of the Japanese occupation. This, however, does not occur. An image of the outside of the archive at the close of the film notwithstanding, we do not return to the story of Mr. Ko, whose identity remains a mystery. We know only that he is "from abroad."

The sole reference in the main narrative to anything outside of the Korean/Japanese context occurs when a practitioner of *taekkyeon* indicates that he intends to emigrate to Russia to escape from the Japanese presence, but this plot line is soon dropped, and we later learn that no one has actually emigrated. Although he is elderly, Mr. Ko is certainly not old enough to have been one of the film's protagonists, who were likely born in the late 1870s or early 1880s. Whatever the case, Mr. Ko has a vested interest in the martial art, and it is likely that one of his primary goals in life has been to find that the volumes are safe in Korea. However noble this intent, Mr. Ko's quest does not constitute an important plot line of the film.

Rather than returning to Mr. Ko's archival visit, the film's closing image is merely a daytime exterior a Taekkyeon-do Center, in front of which a statue depicts the kicking movement of *taekkyeon*. Nonetheless, if we view the film through the lens of a combination of cultural concepts, we see that Mr. Ko encapsulates the love and passion for Pyongyang Nalparam that drives the actions of the main characters.

Jeong *Nurtured in Absence and Subsequently Displaced*

In the flashback, we see Jeongtaek as a young man recalling how he, as a child, had been introduced to Sokyeon, and we hear what appears to be Mr. Ko's voice presenting himself to the young girl, who replies in her own voice. Their names—*taek* as in *Jeongtaek* and *kyeon* as in *Sokyeon*—reflect the components of the name of the martial art *taek-kyeon,* and it is implied that, as children, they were both well on their way toward mastering the art. The two children become inseparable, and their affection is best illustrated by a swing tied to a tree, where they play side by side. The time comes, however, when they must part. Jeongtaek's father has decided to send him to Seoul, where the seeds of *taekkyeon* can flourish. The two children are consequently separated for the rest of their childhood and adolescence. We understand that Jeongtaek, as a young man, has become not just a master of *taekkyeon,* but specifically is one of the most adept at Pyongyang Nalparam, a variety of the martial art developed near Pyongyang on Mount Taeseong.

Jeongtaek and his friends visit the Pyongyang market, where he purchases a yellow jade ring for Sokyeon, their engagement having been arranged by their fathers. At the market, the group has an altercation with another set of martial arts practitioners, who obviously covet the knowledge contained in the carefully guarded volumes. We learn that the fathers have refused to turn the last volume of the manual over to the occupying government, an act of treason that could lead to their death.

Before Jeongtaek arrives home for the wedding, his father receives a visitor. A young woman claiming to be Sokyeon explains that she has come ahead of her father so that she can meet her fiancé. She offers the older man a glass of wine that her mother has fermented especially for him. She then excuses herself to go outside to wait for Jeongtaek. The father sips the wine, and instantly falls dead. When Jeongtaek discovers the body and subsequently meets the imposter, he realizes the deception, and an intricate game of mutual deception ensues. The woman claims that the murder was committed as revenge for her own father's death, and that the double tragedy has resulted from the fathers' contradictory positions regarding the disposition of the fourth volume. Convinced that the murders are actions taken by those who wish to turn the manual over to the Japanese, Jeongtaek pretends to believe that the imposter is Sokyeon. In reality, she is Mieko, a Japanese woman who has been raised in Korea.

The *jeong* that has been nurtured through absence has thus been displaced. Jeongtaek appears to feel genuine affection for his future bride, and the two are depicted within their domestic space as a young couple. When the groom is summoned to retrieve the manual, which is hidden in a cave known only to him and Sokyeon, Jeongtaek presents the jade ring to his future wife and promises that, when he returns, he will put it on her finger. The episode with the fake Sokyeon thus fulfills a special function in the development of the genuine *jeong* between the childhood sweethearts. Jeongtaek senses the reawakening of this affection, and he realizes how inseparable it is from the quest to save the manual from the Japanese and the dire need to preserve Pyongyang Nalparam as a superior martial art.

When the young man arrives at the secret cave, he finds that he is not alone, and believes that the woman who confronts him is his enemy. Standing at a distance, she proves her identity as the true Sokyeon by simulating *taekkyeon* moves. Her in-depth knowledge of Pyongyang Nalparam leaves no doubt in Jeongtaek's mind that he has met his fiancée. The *jeong* that grew through childhood play and through the linkage of the two families through *taekkyeon,* and that was later rekindled through the imposter, has now come to fruition. It is soon evident, however, that the affection between the two lovers is not the focus of the film.

Esteem for Tradition, Chung for Nation

The love displayed by the couple for the martial art that is their mutual namesake is every bit as intense as the passion displayed by Mr. Ko in the opening sequence. *Taekkyeon* is an inherent part of Korean tradition, something that must be preserved lest Koreanness be eradicated by the occupiers. It is directly tied to national identity, and the division of the manual into four volumes constitutes a jigsaw puzzle of sorts that protects the secrets of the art from being easily revealed. *Taekkyeon,* as a martial art, is considerably different from judo. While the latter is primarily characterized by hand-to-hand grappling, which leads to the winner's grabbing and forcing the opponent to the ground, the former consists of punching and kicking to the head and upper body. Much more akin to karate than to judo, *taekkyeon* is not the best art for protecting oneself on the street, as its high kicks render it somewhat slower than other martial arts. Such a peculiarity of the art is articulated by Jeongtaek, who stresses that it is degrading to deploy *taekkyeon* on a street corner. It is of special significance that the film contrasts *taekkyeon* with judo rather than karate in that, through this juxtaposition, a greater distinction between Korea and Japan is articulated. The uniqueness of this martial art, and specifically of Pyongyang Nalparam, establishes it as a national treasure, something that Koreans under the occupation must defend by any means to preserve their cultural heritage.

In the cave, the lovers first recognize each other owing to their knowledge of *taekkyeon*. A flashback to their childhood ensues, and we see young Jeongtaek bite his companion on her hand while playing. Sokyeon chides her lover for having been slow to recognize her, and the latter replies that he cannot mistake her for anyone else, given that she still bears the scar from his bite. The two embrace and tearfully declare their affection, articulating how much they have missed each other. We subsequently learn that Sokyeon's father died defending the manual from the Japanese, and that her mother was subsequently murdered while shopping for her daughter's wedding at the bazaar. Jeongtaek searches for the volume, which is hidden in a crevice in the cave. Cognizant that the failure to protect the book would constitute treason to his nation, he stresses to Sokyeon that they must take all measures to deliver the volume to a Buddhist monk, who will guarantee its safety. From this point on, the film focuses on this plan, and the love between the childhood sweethearts assumes a secondary role in the narrative.

The remaining hour of the film is replete with fast-paced martial arts action, and the coveted manual changes hands several times. Jeongtaek and Sokyeon are separated, and both strive to find and protect the book. Mieko, who had deceived Jeongtaek in her disguise as Sokyeon, goes mad. In a sequence that seems relatively out of place in the narrative, Mieko speaks to her dead mother and laments her betrayal of the Koreans who have raised her. Her mother's voice reminds her of her Japanese ethnicity. Nonetheless, to certain extent the young woman remains faithful to her Korean friends, as evidenced by a sequence in which she saves Jeongtaek, who has been taken hostage. As the Japanese attempt to assure Mieko's return to Japan, the Nalparam practitioners intercept her journey and find the fourth volume of the manual hidden in a secret compartment under the young woman's make-up.

The practitioners of *taekkyeon* are faced with a new and powerful enemy, a Japanese woman and judo master who is one of the masterminds of all attempts to regain the manual. At one point, she pits her judo skills against

Sokyeon's *taekkyeon* in a flashy match in which their bodies appear to float through the air. The Japanese have now announced full annexation of Korea, and in celebration thereof, a match will take place on Mount Taeseong that will determine the superiority of either *taekkyeon* or judo. Aware that her attendance at the event may imply death, Sokyeon decides to defy danger and lend support to her countrymen. At this point, she recites a poem by Jeong Mong Ju (discussed in Chapter 2), which focuses on loyalty to the nation. During the match, Jeongtaek appears on a roof behind the playing ground, and plunges to the ground below to fight a Japanese master. *Taekkyeon* is victorious.

The celebration of the Koreans is short-lived. They retreat to a meadow, where they meet their companions who had intended to emigrate. This happy moment comes to a sudden end. A Japanese official, backed up by a gun-toting platoon, demands that they lead him to the Buddhist monk who allegedly holds the missing volume. Two of the Koreans claim in succession to be the monk, and both are shot. The platoon subsequently opens fire on the remaining Koreans. As Jeongtaek and Sokyeon leap into the air, we see a still frame of their bodies and hear gunshots. We cut to the lovers, who are obviously gravely wounded, crawling toward each other. In what appears to be a final gesture, Jeongtaek places the jade ring on his beloved's finger. Ironically, through this act, he fulfills the promise that he had earlier made deceptively to Mieko. By offering the ring to his true bride, he asserts their inherent Korean identity. A brief flashback depicts the children on their favorite swing, clad in the red and blue of what would later become the DPRK flag and wearing garlands of flowers around their heads, with Jeongtaek's arm affectionately around his playmate.

The film then cuts to the aforementioned exterior shot of the *taekkyeon* center (*Taekkyeondojeondang/*택견도전당), in front of which a statue depicts a *taekkyeon* fighter. Although nothing is offered to explain just how, the image of the building implies that the four volumes of the *taekkyeon* manual are safe in Pyongyang. Over the closing titles, we see a *taekkyeon* match in a packed stadium in Hungary. The stadium is filled with English-language ads for rent-a-car companies, video equipment, and Malév, the Hungarian national airline. Though not specifically stated, it is clear that the event depicted is the 1988 6th ITF Taekwan-do championship in Budapest, in which the DPRK team was victorious. (The Hungarian setting is emphasized by the use of the red, white, and green colors of the Hungarian flag on both the fighting turf and the medals the victors receive.) The traditional art of *taekkyeon* stands in contrast to the Western-style commercialization of the Eastern bloc states during the waning years of communism there. In opposition to both their opponents and the audience, the North Korean team's dedication to this traditional martial art underscores the nation's dedication to its age-old traditions and customs.

In *Pyongyang Nalparam,* cultural concepts are intricately interwoven, which reflects the complexity and collectivity of the relationships depicted. *Han* and *chung* together appear as overarching themes. Nonetheless, one encounters the *ae-jeong* between the lovers, and *u-jeong* among the Nalparam devotees. Filial piety, moreover, is present through the children's desire to avenge their parents' death. Although the *jeong* between the protagonists is temporarily displaced when Jeongtaek encounters Mieko, the real displacement of *jeong* occurs when the lovers' affection becomes secondary to a national attachment, one that implies the dire need to preserve the martial art, and by extension Korea itself.

Conclusion: *Han* and *Jeong* in Revolution

The first two films discussed in this chapter draw upon contemporary society as constructed in accordance with the principles of the People's Party. The third film is a period piece, but nonetheless reflects the struggle of the Korean people to maintain their identity under the Japanese occupation. *On the Green Carpet* reveals how the traditional concept of *han* can be displaced from the individual to the societal level. Mungyu's *han,* which involves the creation of a dynamic and original performance for Kim Jong Il, is not that of an individual with individualistic goals. The metaphor behind his choreography links the Dear Leader with the Korean people who surround him, and hence the performance is for Korea. Moreover, his work is but one chapter in what would later become known as "Arirang Performance," a spectacle depicting Korean history of the 20th century and the precepts of socialist society. The *han* vented by an artist is thus not that of an individual, but rather that of a country that suffered under occupation, saw itself separated from its southern brother, and has developed its own path toward socialism, all the while maintaining the goal of reunification.

In *A Schoolgirl's Diary, han* and *jeong* are interwoven, but not in the most expected of manners. The father's absence from his family's life, and most specifically when his wife is undergoing cancer treatment, may appear as abandonment to many Western viewers. Nonetheless, the *han* that marks his scientific research is compared, by virtue of his daughter's favorite song, to the "General," Kim Jong Il, who must also sacrifice time with his family for the greater cause of the nation. When the father's dreams come to fruition, the young schoolgirl understands the deep *jeong* between her parents, whose love has flourished despite their separation, yet which has been displaced onto the passionate love of nation. It is the image of this *chung* that allows the young woman to embark on her life's journey. *A Schoolgirl's Diary* constitutes the epitome of originality as posited by Kim Jong Il. It depicts a nuanced context that requires an in-depth exploration of the motivations that drive its protagonists. Of all of the North Korean films we have discussed, it is most likely to be the one that most perturbs Western viewers. Nonetheless, it is replete with expanded meanings, as will be explored in the following chapter.

The diegetical time of *Pyongyang Nalparam* is some four decades prior to the birth of the DPRK, yet its protagonists display a strong *chung* for Korea and its people. Superficially the work is an action film, yet its opening sequence in the archive, its concluding images of the archive and *taekkyoen* statue, and the closing title's use of footage from an international *taekkyeon* championship underscore how the DPRK has succeeded in preserving a passionate *chung* from the past.

Chapter 8

Expanded Viewings

Our analyses of the films examined are far from closed. They do not constitute an overarching interpretation. Nonetheless, the key cultural concepts have led us to envision other possibilities, which are also valid avenues in our quest to understand Korean ethos. One of the essential components of the key cultural words is that they are multifaceted and invite divergent approaches to their explication. In Chapters 4, 5, 6, and 7, we have offered one reading per film, mediated by the cultural concepts discussed. These readings have followed, as much as possible, the films' narrative progression. But, not unlike a narrative film whose gaps and fissures offer new interpretative lenses, our explorations have left behind critical "residue"—residue that reveals the convergence of key cultural words and the cinema is not a closed process. Although our use of key words in the analysis of the films constitutes a unique approach, it in no way implies the rejection of other debates in cinema studies. Rather, it can be deemed a bridge that allows the reader to circle back to ongoing discussions on cinema with an enriched perspective. In the discussions that follow, we seek connections between our cultural-words–based readings and both mainstream film criticism and issues in the field of cinema studies at large, all the while venturing new interpretations.

Mainstream Criticism, Academic Discourse and Expanded Ideas

In the same way that a given scene in a film can be shot with deep focus, in a close-up, or even at a Dutch angle, so it is time to change our lens and rethink how we approach the foregoing films. The three primary key cultural concepts that drove our discussions—namely, *han, jeong,* and *deok*—invite the viewer to probe beyond narrative progression and focus on other aspects of the works. A number of these bear upon either mainstream film criticism or issues in film theory, or both. In any case, they can lead the viewer to fresh and original takes. In this chapter, we will revisit the films previously discussed in earlier chapters. Each discussion will be different in regard to both structure and length, given the specific issues we flesh out. When appropriate, we will draw upon both mainstream and academic film discussions. We will return to the films in the same order as they were dealt with in the earlier chapters.

Seopyeonje

Seopyeonje *and* Han: *Critical Discussions*

The preeminence of *han* in *Seopyeonje* has been noted in academic discussions. Adam Hartzell (2006) has attributed the film's noteworthy critical acclaim to its visualization of *han*:

> Many Koreans commented on how the film represented the purest portrayal of Han they had yet to see on screen. Han, as I repeat ... is a concept ever elusive to non–Korean viewers.

Hartzell stresses that the phenomenal reception of *Seopyeonje* was initially not expected. Given the success of *The General's Son* (*Janggunui Adeul*) (장군의 아들) trilogy (1990, 1991, 1992), Im was granted funding to create a more artistic film, aimed at a more restricted audience. Once it was released, the fact that the film drew more than 1 million viewers in Seoul alone is not very surprising, in that the events of the period depicted are topics in which most Koreans are still interested. Koreans older than age 70 remember the unfortunate and terrible incidents that occurred during the film's diegetic time; those of the 40- to 70-year-old generation grew up with parents and grandparents who had lived through the period; and 20- to 40 year olds have heard and read about stories related to this time frame. Hartzell attributes the success of the film to the "Searching for Our Culture" movement that was present on college campuses in the 1970s. Explaining that students set out to reconstruct and reinterpret traditional Korean artistic discourses, Hartzell (2006) asserts, "*Seopyeonje* was the right film at the right time for just such a South Korean audience searching for something to reclaim about its culture."

The story of *Seopyeonje* and *seopyeonje* music must have provided Koreans with something they could relate to in various ways, as evidenced by the large number of Korean-language reviews, opinions, and related stories on the Internet as well as in newspapers. Film scholars have also been very interested in *Seopyeonje*. Three chapters of a book edited by David E. James and Kyung Hyun Kim (2002) focus on the film: Chungmoo Choi discusses it from the perspective of gender, aestheticism, and cultural nationalism, and compares it with another film by Im Kwontaek, *Jokbo* (*Genealogy*) (1979); Cho Hae Joang investigates its cultural and historical meaning; and Julian Stringer explores issues regarding the inner domain of national culture in relation to the specific case of *Seopyeonje*.

Seopyeonje is arguably the defining work of the Korean New Wave. When initially released, it became the top-grossing Korean film of all time, although its box-office success was subsequently eclipsed by *The King and the Clown* and later by Bong Joonho's monster movie, *The Host* (2006). Like *The King and the Clown*, its story is distinctively Korean, but its setting in the mid-to-late 20th century renders it more accessible to international audiences than the later film. Kyung Hyun Kim (2004) explains its role in the transformation of the Korean film industry:

> Released at a time where the invasion of Hollywood films peaked in the Korean film market, [*Seopyeonje*] became the nation's response to foreign imports. The characters' struggle to resist foreign cultural invasion and to secure p'ansori's spot in the pantheon of national aesthetics resembled the Korean film industry's uphill battle against the Hollywood onslaught [60–61].

Non-blood Lines

To a Western viewer, Yubong's decision to blind Songhwa clearly stands in sharp contradiction to any view of physical safety. Rather, it plays out as an atrocity committed by a tyrannical, patriarchal figure. One could further read Yubong's compulsive training as emblematic of such tyranny. From the perspective of a Freudian feminist critique, Yubong has denied his daughter entrée to the male-dominated visual world. Her physical space has been limited, and she lacks access to the gaze that is so defining of narrative cinema.

We can think of Frank Perry's *Mommie Dearest* and of actress Joan Crawford's tyranny over her adopted children. Nothing in this behavior was productive, except that it spurred daughter Christina to write a highly successful tell-all book. But what about Daddy Dearest? The extreme brutality to which Yubong goes can be viewed, from one lens, as productive in light of the perfection of Songhwa's *pansori*. In the early segments of the film, it is emphasized that Songhwa and Dongho are foster children, not the *pansori* singer's biological offspring. Given the strong inscription of blood lines in Korean culture and the fact that the adoption of children is less accepted in Korea than in the West, one can wonder whether Yubong could have ever deigned to blind a biological daughter. From a narrative perspective, the device of the foster children works especially well in *Seopyeonje;* it permits an extreme act through which Yubong can deepen the venting of his own *han* through the vehicle of Songhwa. In a like manner, one can question whether Dongho's ability to escape from his family is facilitated by the lack of blood ties. His rejection of the dictatorial discipline enforced by the master *pansori* singer is more conceivable given the foster relationship that binds them. From a narrative perspective, his ultimate goal to search for his roots is rendered particularly intriguing given that these are not biological ties. Rather, they have developed around the differing relationship of each of the three characters to *pansori*. It is significant, to this effect, that the first step in his search is a meeting with a *pansori* singer.

The King and the Clown

Han-*Venting and the Carnivalesque*

In *The King and the Clown, han*-venting implies the authenticity of performance. Such performance, moreover, is carnivalesque in nature. Hence, there is an implicit relationship present between the carnivalesque and *han*-venting. The film, grounded as it is in traditional, popular performance, explores one designation of the term *gwangdae,* which although referring to a broad scope of popular genres—ranging from street song, to circus, to acrobatics—can also be employed to denote those performers who provide others with joy or sorrow by making them laugh or cry, respectively.

The film, based on a 2000 play by Kim Tae-Ung titled *Yi* (an honorific given to a king's subject), explores the relationship between a Joseon king and a court jester. Inasmuch as it is based on a historical incident—it is drawn from a passage in *The Annals of the Joseon Dynasty*—rather than on a more contemporaneous story, the tremendous success of *The King and the Clown* is quite surprising. Not only has the sexual ambivalence it depicts been the source of great debate, but it is also a period drama with relatively unknown actors.

The King and the Clown is a decidedly self-reflexive film about performance. Concentrating on the challenges and losses faced by *gwangdaes* as they move from street to court during a period of sociopolitical upheaval, its performance modalities encompass vulgar street skits, tight rope acts, puppet plays, and ritualistic psychodramas. In the film, history, personal destiny, and gender are all the subject of performance, and these theatrical discourses are woven into a complex fabric, in which the distinction between artist and audience is blurred, and in which the very nature of performance is interrogated. The obsession with performance is closely reflected in the Western titles given to the film. Released in England as *The Court Jester,* the British title privileges the theatrical. The use of the word "clown" in the American title functions in a like manner. In contrast, the original Korean title translates neutrally as *The King's Man.*

Films that self-reflexively examine performance have also served to unravel complex moments of socioeconomic transformation. A key example is Carlos Diegues's *Bye Bye Brazil* (1980), in which an itinerant troupe of performers, who travel through the back-lands of Brazil, must come to grips with industrialization and the onslaught of mass media. In this process, they intertwine Brazilian folkloric tradition with gaudy neon and television screens. As Bruce Williams (1995) stresses, *Bye Bye Brazil's* nomadic Carnaval Rolidei fuses the contradictory discourses of Brazilian and North American pop cultures, as it brings Bing Crosby's "White Christmas," complete with actual snow, to the Brazilian *sertão* (49–50). In a like manner, *The King and the Clown* counterbalances traditional Korean performance with intertextual references to Shakespeare. The enactment of the murder of the king's mother mirrors the play staged to indict the murderers of Hamlet's father. Similarly, the film's final words recall the famous monologue from *As You Like It.* Nonetheless, there is a significant difference. While "All the world's a stage" describes the life cycle of a man, from infancy to second childhood, the remarks in *The King and the Clown* are transcendent and suggest an overturning of traditional hierarchies. Such intertextuality is extra-diegetic inasmuch as the two plays by Shakespeare were performed roughly 100 years following the diegetic time of *The King and the Clown.* Nonetheless, Shakespeare and Lee come together in their celebration of the popular. Moreover, street performance becomes elevated, and it serves as a stand-in for the sway of the masses that topple the regime. This process reflects Bakhtin's notion of the carnivalesque, which Robert Stam has described as follows:

> The carnivalesque represents the transposition into literature of the spirit of the carnival—that is, popular festivities in which the people gain brief entry into a sphere of utopian freedom by turning the world upside down. The carnivalesque is profoundly subversive of all that is official and oppressive since it abolishes hierarchies, levels social classes and genres, and creates an alternative second life free from conventional rules and restrictions [Stam, 1992, 167].

The microcosm of the lives of the performers reflects the sweeping transformations occurring on a societal level. In the early sequences of the film, the street performances are vulgar, with a strong emphasis on urination, defecation, and masturbation. Such bawdy humor recalls Bakhtin's celebration of the "lower body stratum" to counter the protocol of king and clergy and to celebrate life in all its worldliness. In *The King and the Clown,* this recoupment of vulgar forms of humor performatively celebrates the Korean masses and provides a vehicle through which social transformation can take place.

Transgression and the Carnivalesque

Our foregoing discussion of *The King and the Clown* had as its center the relationship between the king and Jangsaeng. Nonetheless, of equal importance is the ambivalence of the character of Gonggil, who offers a strong counterpoint to his fellow *gwangdae*. In many ways, he, rather than Jangsaeng, can be read as the "king's man" implied by the Korean title of the film. Gonggil is responsible for much of the transgressive nature of the film. He is an especially ambivalent character, and his effeminacy is paramount to the unraveling of the storyline. This ambivalence plays out on a number of levels. It is never made clear whether there is anything sexual between Gonggil and the king, but the relationship does shatter traditional notions of gender and class. A kiss between the two, which occurs following the hunting incident, further attests to the subversive nature of the relationship.[1] Like the popular front that ultimately dethrones the king, Gonggil's subversive nature threatens all hierarchies. It foreshadows the depiction of the *jeong-han* of the Korean people in the concluding sequences of the film.

The mood of carnival is present in the film's coda, in which, following the implied death of the protagonists as they fall from the tightrope, we see them laughing and joking with their fellow performers at the site of the hunt, where the plot to kill Gonggil had failed. The effacement of the boundary between life and death in this sequence recalls Norman René's *Longtime Companion* (1989), a film portraying the ravaging effects of the early years of the AIDS epidemic on a group of gay males and their friends. In the film's final sequence, all of the characters who have died return for a carefree walk along a Fire Island beach. The similarity between *The King and the Clown* and *Longtime Companion* does not end here. René's film is also about performance. Its characters are the actors, writers, and viewers of a soap opera, *Other People,* which, like the Korean film, presents a controversial male–male kiss.

As the performers mock the king and his concubine, the vulgarities of earlier performances return, and the sexual prowess of Yeonsan is relegated to the level of street humor. In this process, Gonggil's sexual ambiguity plays a pivotal role, as he defies containment by prescribed social roles. In *The King and the Clown,* such recoupment of vulgar forms of humor performatively enacts the *jeong-han* of the Korean masses and provides a vehicle through which social transformation can take place. One of the most ambivalent sequences of the film involves the king's jumping up to dance with the performers. He is carefree and unrestricted in a carnivalesque manner. This act is repeated and, in fact, is one of the primary factors contributing to the ministers' desire to rid the court of the minstrels who have upset its order and balance. Such intentions are in vain; the ultimate storming of the palace depicts the *won-han* of an angered and repressed populace. A despotic regime is overturned, and a new era can begin. In most cinematic contexts, the carnivalesque implies the abolishment of rigid societal categories and permits an undoing of convention. In the case of *The King and the Clown,* the carnivalesque is inscribed even more profoundly in that it is tied to both the individual *han* of the performers and the collective *han* of the populace.

Pietà

Pietà *and Christian Iconography*

The motif of the *pietà,* a subgenre in medieval and Renaissance art that depicts the Virgin Mary cradling the body of the dead Christ, was prevalent throughout Europe, with examples ranging from 14th-century Bohemia to the Spanish Golden Age paintings of Luis de Morales. The most famous of these, of course, is the Michelangelo statue housed in Saint Peter's Basilica in the Vatican. This statue is of particular consequence to our analysis in that the Virgin Mary is depicted as notably youthful. In a similar manner, with respect to Gangdo's age, Miseon is relatively young, an age relationship carefully corroborated by her stories. In the Christian notion of the passion, death, and resurrection of Christ, the *pietà,* closely related to the "lamentation," occurs between the crucifixion and burial of Jesus. Unlike other representations of the lamentation, however, a typical *pietà* presents only the figures of Mary and Jesus, with no one else present. The painting of Luis de Morales notwithstanding, most *pietás* are sculptures. As the majority stem from the Renaissance, they are closely aligned with notions of humanism, evidenced by the deep emotion sensed in the depiction of the Virgin Mary's face. The emphasis is clearly on the pain that the mother feels in the loss of her child rather than on the notion of redemption or in otherworldliness. The use of such Christian iconography, inasmuch as it implies suffering, is directly tied to *han*-venting in the non-spiritual realm.

The film *Pietà* opens with an image of a young man's suicide by hanging. Immediately following his death, we cut to the opening title, which displays *Pietà* in Korean. We hear a scream. But it is not that of a man, but rather a woman. At the very beginning of the film, we are thus positioned to assume that the film will deal, at least in part, with a mother's anguish over her son's death. Later in the film, we see Miseon in the machine shop where her son committed suicide. She opens a casket and gazes at his body, although we do not see it. The anguish of a mother is felt in a manner similar to the *pietà* sub-genre. Her son's body is shown only at the end of the film, when Gangdo starts to dig a grave for Miseon under the tree he has planted in her honor. It is significant to note—in yet another reference to Christian iconography—that the body of Miseon's son has remained uncorrupted, despite the considerable amount of time that has passed since his death. Such a phenomenon may well render him saint-like, and suggests that he is the true object of Miseon's mourning. Nonetheless, Kim Kiduk has complicated the situation considerably.

A Play of Reversing Roles

Simply from the title *Pietà*, we expect the film to revolve around the grief of a mother, a *mater dolorosa*. At first glance, such a role is assumed by Miseon in her mourning for her son. Yet the film's homage to the Christian myth, viewed through the lenses of both Catholicism and Protestantism (although the former is much evoked), is far more complex, and roles are reversed more than once and cross boundaries of age and gender. We must bear in mind that there is very little in *Pietà* that would render the film an allegory of Christianity. If anything, Gangdo is the opposite of a Christ figure. While Jesus is loving and merciful, Gangdo is uncaring and brutal. While Jesus uplifts the Magdalena, Gangdo degrades Miseon sexually. And while Jesus is deemed celibate in most Christian traditions, the debt collector's sexual acts stand in sharp contrast. For her part, Miseon's behavior, particularly during the early phases of her scheme, fails to reflect that of the Virgin Mary, except in the profound grief she feels. Nevertheless, the film opens an undeniable dialogue with Christianity, and does so in a number of ways. As mentioned earlier, in the background of the shabby working-class neighborhood is a church with a cross and a sign that reads "Hallelujah Will Be Forever!" This image evokes Protestantism, a relatively widespread religion in South Korea. Even if we assume that Miseon will never experience the emotions of the grieving Virgin Mary in the case of Gangdo—after all, he outlives her—we nonetheless note that she has begun to care for and pity him. At this point, she becomes like a Christ figure who loves even the worst of mankind. Her death can be viewed as a sacrifice. It is at this point that Gangdo, by reversal, assumes the role of the *pietà,* gently holding his mother's body. Yet another sacrifice is in order. Gangdo himself must die.

Throughout history, the *pietà* has not been a motif of Christianity writ large, but rather a symbol of Catholicism specifically. Protestants eschew, by and large, the representation of the dead Christ and favor that of the empty cross, a metaphor for resurrection. Thus, Catholicism constitutes a stronger offset to the brutal existence depicted. Kim Kiduk's reference to the *pietà* is clear and unmistakable. By inscribing Catholic motifs into the narrative, the director has underscored the emotional and existential plight of the characters and rendered their ultimate redemption more conceivable. Christianity, by nature, implies the hope that constitutes the positive aspect of the *han* conundrum.

Mother

Enigmatic Sequences in Mother, Han *and* Jeong

Bong Joonho's 2009 *Mother* has been read in the United States primarily as a crime drama or thriller, forcing it to be pigeon-holed as a genre film. The catchphrase on the cover of the Magnolia Home Entertainment DVD, "She'll Stop at Nothing," reinforces this reading. Such categorization, however, is unfortunate given the structural complexity of the film and its visual dynamics, which, in essence, refute many of the conventions of a mystery or detective film. Like a number of the films of the Korean New Wave, although it can be deemed a mainstream film in many ways, it is replete with structural discontinuities that resemble international art-house cinema. Thus, balancing between mainstream and art house, *Mother,* even when divorced from Korean culture, is a surprisingly open work inviting many levels of interpretation.

In cinema, when two similar sequences are present in a given film, they normally mirror each other and offer thematic reinforcement. Such is the case of two of the most enigmatic sequences in *Mother*—namely, the title sequence and the final scene. The film's opening recalls the pre-title sequence of P. J.

Hogan's *My Best Friend's Wedding,* in which a bride and bridesmaids, who do not appear in the rest of the film, dance to Burt Bacharach's "Wishin' and Hopin'." The title sequence of *Mother* shows a woman walking through a meadow and breaking into dance, her actions appearing outside of the time and space of the narrative. What distinguishes Bong's film from Hogan's is that the dancer, as we will soon learn, is the film's protagonist. The overall mood of the dance, moreover, evokes a deep sense of melancholy not present in the Hollywood comedy. It is only much later in the film that the sequence is contextualized within the diegetic development. Although we have read *Mother* in terms of *jeong, han* is also present throughout the film and, in hindsight, we can read the woman's dance as *han*-venting.

The mirroring sequence occurs at the end of the film. Aboard the bus for the excursion her son has offered her, the mother rises to dance with the other parents, and the movements recall her own solitary dance in the meadow. Sunlight from outside casts the dancers in *chiaroscuro* as the mother moves forward to the front of the bus, and the dancers seem to vent their *han* collectively.

A third highly open-ended sequence bears upon the *mo-jeong* of the protagonist. Occurring immediately prior to the murder of the junk collector, it plays heavily on point of view and leads to a high level of ambivalence. As the man relates what he saw near the murder site, we are never sure whether the images we see of Dojun pursuing the victim and asking her if she doesn't like boys stem from the junkman's memory or from the mother's imagination. This ambivalence is of special importance, inasmuch as it speaks to Dojun's guilt or innocence. It is never completely clear whether the young man who is ultimately arrested for the crime is the actual perpetrator. Either interpretation is plausible, given that both can explain the irrationality of the mother's *jeong,* her intense rage, and the ultimate murder of the junk collector.

Blood Conspiracy and Jeong

As Marsha Kinder has stressed, Spanish culture at large and its cinema in particular are obsessed with blood, an observation that is especially fitting in the case of the cinematic *oeuvre* of Pedro Almodóvar. In the Spanish director's films, blood ties are essential to the narrative, and are most markedly evidenced through the themes of motherhood and incest. The complexity of the family ties in *Volver* (2006) are crucial to narrative twists and turns. Moreover, the close relationship between mother and son in the early sequences of *All about My Mother* (*Todo sobre mi madre*) provide a blueprint for the subsequent spins on the notion of motherhood the protagonist demonstrates following the death of her child. In *Mother,* the theme of blood is equally overarching, and serves to foreground the *jeong* relationship between mother and son.

The mother's caring for her son is visually linked to the image of blood. While searching for the Mercedes-Benz that has bumped Dojun, Jintae asks his friend why his mother is so attached to him. Dojun fails to respond, but speaks only of the minute quantity of blood he has shed. Meanwhile, the mother visits a pharmacist, who bandages the cut she received to her finger while chasing her son following the accident. The special bond, as indicated by the two images of blood, can be explained by the mother's obsessive care for her cognitively disabled son.

The blood ties between mother and son, and the *jeong* they imply, are reinforced in two sequences in which the two characters serve as each other's proxy. When Mother becomes histrionic and kills the elderly man by repeated blows with a blunt instrument, an implicit conspiracy between mother and son is suggested; he has been accused of murdering the schoolgirl with a similar weapon. Of equal importance is that she succeeds in killing *on his behalf.*

In the related sequence, Dojun and a young woman subsequently visit the ruins of the junk collector's home. If a murderer always returns to the scene of a crime, then the young man does so *as a proxy for* his mother, once again emphasizing their strong bond. There, he finds his mother's set of acupuncture needles (yet another symbol of blood), which she has carelessly left behind. In the same way in which she has fought so hard on his behalf to find the true murderer and thereby set him free, he takes the evidence that would link her to the crime. Once again, it is through blood that mother and son become linked in conspiracy and their *jeong* even more irrational.

Peculiarity of the Mother-Son Relationship in Western Eyes

For a Western viewer, one of the more disturbing aspects of the relationship between Mother and Dojun is the incest it might imply. The fact that mother and son sleep in the same bed may suggest something other than merely the poverty and confined quarters the two share. After having pursued the high school student to what will ultimately be the site of her death, the son returns, undresses to his boxers, and crawls in bed with his mother, who is clad in a nightgown. He assumes a semi-fetal position and gently caresses her. Later, following his ultimate release from prison, we once again see the two of them in bed together. This time, both are fully clad, and the camera, in a medium close-up, focuses on the mother's eyes as she watches over her sleeping son. Despite how Westerners may view these sequences, there is nothing that even remotely indicates incest. The comments made by Dojun's friends about his sleeping arrangements simply imply that he is still a child, a mama's boy. The bed sequences define the mother's over-protectiveness of her son, and through them we ascertain the passion behind her search for the real killer and the histrionics she displays in the murder of the junk collector.

In a like manner, sections of dialogue between them appear sexually charged when read from a cross-cultural perspective. When Dojun returns from the police station following the Mercedes incident, he is seen at table with his mother, who has made him a broth from special roots, which she asserts will be good for his virility. The mother and son engage in a discussion of his determination to have sex with a girl, a foreshadowing of his eventual pursuit of the murder victim later the same evening. The discussion reveals the converse of what Julia Kristeva (1982) has identified as the role of a mother: an authority who maps out the body and defines areas that are proper and clean and improper and dirty (72). We thus apprehend the multilayered nature of the relationship between mother and son, which cannot be described by a single notion of mother-son bonding. Refusing to eat, Dojun declares that he is off to see Jintae. The mother follows him on to the street, where he urinates against a wall. She watches as he urinates, and attempts to feed him the broth. When he departs, the mother covers up traces of Dojun's urine with her feet. Once again, we witness the intensity and obsession on the part of the mother toward her son. The verbal and physical discourse between them is extremely intimate, but we do not fully understand the complexity of what lies behind it.

Taegeukgi: The Brotherhood of War

Border Crossings and the Intensification of Jeong

This film's original title Taegeukgi Hwinallimyeo/태극기 휘날리며 translates as "Waving the Korean National Flag," with the literal meaning of taegeuk referring to the "Great Absolute" in Chinese philosophy, the source of the dual principle of yin and yang. This dual principle is of particular consequence in that it reflects the complexity of the relationship between the two brothers. Such dynamics are underscored by a poster for the Korean release of the film, which depicts the two on opposite sides of the frame, facing toward the camera and away from each other.

Although the title is understood to refer to the South Korean flag, which covers a casket containing the collective remains unearthed from the film's final battle site, the North Korean flag is omnipresent during the actual battle. Thus, each of the flags appears, albeit at different historical times, at the site where the brothers are reunited for the last brief moment. Geographically, *The Brotherhood of War* travels from South to North, and finally back to the 38th Parallel. From its early depiction of the Battle of Nakdong near the southern city of Daegu, it progresses northward to Pyongyang, then to the Chinese border, and finally allows the two brothers their penultimate meeting near the nations' line of demarcation. Hence, North/South dynamics are paramount to the film's development. Nonetheless, in contrast to *Joint Security Area, The Brotherhood of War* is considerably complex in its presentation of the "other." While the former film depicts forbidden bonding and friendship between *de jure* enemies, the dynamics of the latter are considerably more subtle. In *The Brotherhood of War,* both brothers essentially defect to the North, and their decisions to do so are driven primarily by the irrational extremes of their own relationship (*jeong*). For Jintae, the motivation for defection is twofold. First, he has witnessed the death of his fiancée, Yeongsin, at the hands of anticommunists. Second, following the burning of a South Korean prison in which his brother has been detained, he comes to believe that Jinseok has died. Jintae's ensuing despair leads to his rejection of his homeland.

When they are reunited immediately prior to Jintae's death, the now North Korean officer's failure to recognize his brother curtails the latter's defection and provides a short space of time in which Jinseok can flee to the South. When Jintae finally comes to realize who Jinseok is, he offers his brother the pen he had found in the ruins of the burned prison. Jinseok hands the keepsake back to Jintae, entreating him to return the pen in times of peace. Jintae dies from a bayonet wound, but only after he has guaranteed his brother's safe return to the South.

The tragic lives of the two brothers and their border crossings are paralleled by the film's two key objects, a pair of unfinished shoes that Jintae has been making for Jinseok and the silver pen, a symbol of the latter's future education. The latter plays a pivotal role in Jintae's defection. The pen, like the brothers, crosses borders. Jinseok ultimately retrieves the object when he is united with his brother's remains. In contrast, the shoes remain safely in Seoul throughout the war. Before traveling to the excavation site, Jinseok retrieves the shoes from the armoire in which they had been stored for some five decades. Miraculously, they appear complete, with the special soles the young student had wanted. It is unclear as to whether Jinseok opts to wear them to the site, yet this is implied. In any case, on the same day, Jinseok retrieves both objects in an intact form. Brother and brother's body, pen and shoes, all come together, recalling the passionate *jeong* that had united the two during their lives. The dramatic and intricate play of border crossings, moreover, serves to intensify this *jeong*.

Joint Security Area

Enemy Friendships as Jeong

From an initial reading of blurbs regarding Park Chang-wook's *Joint Security Area,* one might be led to believe that the film constitutes another exploration of the hackneyed theme of espionage and the anticommunist sentiment that characterized much of South Korean cinema during the post-war days. But on closer examination, the film is extremely subtle and presents viewers with a very humanistic, non-stereotypical portrayal of forbidden friendship between enemy soldiers. In his discussion of such friendship, Kim Kyung-Hyun (2004) explores the attractiveness of the North Korean soldier:

> An affable North Korean Communist soldier ... arouses desire because he has been devalued by the South Korean state as nonexistent beyond the masses of faceless soldiers who mechanically march to the rhythms of military trumpets and pledge their dogmatic loyalty to their totalitarian leader. Yet this is the very place where his aura—unique and fetishistic—can be uncovered, once his veil is lifted and he emerges as a demystified individual [269].

Faulty Language Dubbing and Jeong

In a *Variety* review, Dereck Elley points out deficiencies in the film's soundtrack as originally cut. He describes the English dialogue that is predominant early on in the film as clumsy, and urges that the film be "re-voiced" prior to its release in the Anglophone world. For instance, Lee Young Ae, the actress portraying Sophie, had great difficulty with the English pronunciation required in the dialogue with the non–Korean characters, which was subtitled in Korean in the original release. Thus, Palm DVD, when preparing the version of the film destined for the English-speaking world, opted to dub it. It is significant to note that the efforts to "Americanize" the film's dialogue may have been too extreme. Yet, for the English speaker, this defect works well in favor of the theme of *jeong*. The American English in the dubbed version seems highly artificial, particularly in the exchanges between North and South

Korean characters. In contrast to the original Korean version, in which accents differ between North and South, no attempts are made to distinguish between these in English. Very colloquial American accents are used for all Korean characters, with both North and South Koreans having a very marked Midwest accent. Thus, it is difficult for viewers to distinguish between players on the two sides. Nonetheless, such an unintentional flaw further serves to flatten the distinction between the enemy camps and heighten the naturalness of the *jeong* the friends develop.

Cardinal Points, Camera Pans and the Development of Jeong

Part of the appeal of *Joint Security Area* both as a thriller and as a political drama derives from the way in which it plays with geography. The film is set in one of the world's most tension-ridden villages, and a number of shots reveal a blue barracks-like structure that straddles the border in which meetings between the enemy nations are held.[2] The buildings at Panmunjom are carefully reconstructed in the film, as is the Bridge of No Return. The geography of Panmunjom reflects the cardinal points on the compass, but in somewhat different ways for Anglophone and Korean viewers. In English, cardinal points are spoken in the order "north, south, east, west," and this process hence privileges the North. The North–South line of demarcation thus resonates in multiple ways to the English speaker. The separation is powerful; we think in terms of hemispheres, of the dynamics of unequal distribution, of the Irelands, the Carolinas and Dakotas, and so on. One can argue that, linguistically, the separation between North and South Korea is more deep-seated for English speakers than was, for instance, that of East and West Germany. The enemy has deigned to occupy our precious North, as it once did in the case of Vietnam. In Korean, in contrast, the cardinal points are articulated as "east, west, south, north." East is thus privileged, as suggested by a phrase that refers to South Korea as the "Land of the Morning Calm." Although the line of demarcation separates North from South, East and West are also present by virtue of ideology—Eastern communism versus Western capitalism.

Visually, the cardinal points are reflected in the film's cinematography. The demarcation line is at times clearly depicted; at other times, it disappears altogether from sight. Such a peek-a-boo device suggests both the need to abolish barriers and the creation of a space where *jeong* can be cultivated. Such a device is echoed in a sequence occurring later in the film and ultimately repeated as the final images of *Joint Security Area*. A tourist from the southern side loses a souvenir cap, which is blown across the demarcation line. It is retrieved by Sergeant Oh, who, with a very human smile, returns it to an out-stretched hand. The film concludes as the camera pans a still photograph of the final image. We see, from the southern perspective, the North Korean soldier standing in front of the jointly controlled blue barracks. As we pan from the image of the northern guards to those of southern soldiers, the camera focuses on the faces of the soldiers. The pan follows the conventions of narrative cinema: East is positioned on the right of the screen and West on the left. Once again, the ground is not shown, and we have the illusion of a borderless geography.

Another geopolitical component that contributes to the appeal of *Joint Security Area* for a Western viewer is its penetration into the forbidden land of the Democratic People's Republic of Korea. For many decades, North Korea, like Albania, was virtually off-limits to Americans. Only recently has guided travel to the "hermit nation" become an option. (Other Western tourists have had more, yet still limited options.) In contrast, travel to East Germany was always relatively easy, as it was to most other communist nations. Thus, although Western viewers may not react as viscerally as Koreans to the forbidden friendship (*u-jeong*) between enemy soldiers, they can sense the dynamic tension implicit in such a relationship.

Oasis

Deformity and the Inscription of Jeong

In *Threshold of the Visual World,* Kaja Silverman draws upon Max Scheler's examination of "excorporative identification" and elaborates a model of identification that leads to "neither the triumph of self-sameness, nor craven submission to an exteriorized but essentialized ideal." Silverman explores what she terms "the active gift of love," through which we can relate in a positive manner to bodies "which we have been taught to abhor and repudiate" (1996, 79). As Bruce Williams points out, Silverman's notion of active love "reassesses non-idealized inscriptions of femininity" (45). He argues, "Silverman's theory, when applied in the context of the depiction of physical deformity in narrative cinema, can serve to interrogate conventional taxonomies of both the feminine and the grotesque and to posit new models for identification" (45). Williams further asserts, "Deformity is a social construct formed through perceptions, words and images and is not a natural phenomenon" (47).

Lee Changdong's *Oasis* is a film that defies social norms and celebrates taboos. Blurbs on the LifeSize Entertainment DVD cover describe it as "a daring heartbreaker" or "a small miracle ... pure magic." The DVD cover also quotes Michael Atkinson of the *Village Voice,* who asserts, "No movie in recent memory has translated so clearly the secret language of lovers." The film shares a catchphrase with *Seopyeonje,* having been deemed the "seminal film of the Korean New Wave." A French-language review by Nicolas Marcadé in *L'Avant-scène du cinéma* lauds the director's ability to "créer la malaise" ("create uneasiness") by adapting the age-old maxim, "Nothing human to me is alien." Marcadé identifies a number of the elements of melodrama present in the film—impossible love, illness, family secrets—yet asserts that Lee "manhandles" these (84). For Marcadé, *Oasis* constitutes "less entertainment and more true experience, a sort of concessionless play with brutal truth" [authors' translation] (84). The very terms used in this critique suggest the intensity of the *jeong* between the lovers.

In Silverman's parlance, Jongdu's feelings for Gongju most likely constitute "an active gift of love." He is able to look beyond her handicap and love the body that society would have him to repudiate. Some viewers may feel that Jongdu's feelings actually go beyond Silverman's concept, for Gongju may well constitute his essentialized ideal. Particularly in light of Jongdu's dissonance with anything mainstream, it is unclear whether he even has a notion of what is deemed "normal" or "essentialized." Herein lies one of the great mysteries of Lee's film.

"Normality" Recouped through Jeong

For a brief moment, let's return to Norman René's *Longtime Companion.* In the previously mentioned coda to the film, two gay partners, who have been spared the affliction of the AIDS epidemic, stroll along a beach as they discuss recent grassroots efforts to bring the need for intervention to officials in New York City. When their friends who have fallen victims to the disease suddenly appear, their bodies free of deformity, the camera makes it clear that the miracle we are witnessing stems from the thoughts of the protagonist.

The case of *Oasis* is more complex. On four occasions, Gongju suddenly appears devoid of her palsy and inexplicably assumes a "normal" form. At one point, she and Jongdu are riding an elevated train. Gongju is seated, while Jongdu stands facing her. Across from Gongju is a young couple, who laughingly tease each other. The woman amicably slaps the man on the face. The camera pans toward Jongdu, and we suddenly see Gongju standing next to him. She has lost her distorted appearance, speaks normally, and slaps him on the face in a gesture reflecting that of the unknown woman. On another occasion, in the auto repair shop of Jongdu's brother, Gongju circles about in wheelchair, creating mayhem as Jongdu attempts to speak to his sister-in-law on the phone regarding business matters. When he articulates that something is "upsetting," Gongju stands next to him in a natural posture and asks why he is upset with her. She then reassumes her convulsions and distortions.

Jongdu tells his companion of a strange dream he has had in which the two are dancing with the three characters from the oasis picture: the woman, the little boy, and the elephant. In a subsequent sequence set in the apartment, the Indian woman enters and dances, as does her son. When the camera pans back to Gongju, she is standing and her dance is devoid of convulsions. It is unclear as to whether the dance is real or a recollection of Jongdu's dream.

The final instance of a return to "normality" for Gongju occurs after a visit to a private karaoke room. Jongdu sings for her, and then implores her to sing as well, which she is unable to do. On the way home, as the two wait for a subway train, Gongju is suddenly seen standing, singing to him a song about oneness in love.

On all of these occasions, it is impossible to determine whether Gongju's corporal transformations from the deformed to the socially acceptable are real or imagined. In most cases, the camera pans away from her, and when it returns, she is erect and articulate. Nothing is present to indicate whether the camera is objective or whether it is attached to either diegetic character.

If we attempt to view the momentary transformations in Gongju's physical qualities in terms of *jeong,* we must recall that, of the two lovers, she is the one whose difference from societal norms is most easily spotted and, as evidenced in both the birthday party sequence and the sequence in which the two are expelled from a restaurant, the most disturbing. The palsy is severe, and her spasms and physical distortions are unceasing. Whenever the symptoms appear to cease, Jongdu is present. Metaphorically, such "normalizing" moments represent the lovers' oasis, the safe haven in which their *jeong* can grow. To each other, they are normal.

Poetry

Cinema, Process and the Development of Deok

Although even the most conventional of classical or commercial Hollywood films have been "read against the grain" to seek out narrative "fissures" that refute facile interpretation, they remain relatively closed texts that leave viewers with a sense of satisfaction that all ends have been tied up. Most readings of the gaps present in the narrative have dealt with race, gender, and social class, using these issues to explore the inherent ideology of the films. Films that lack an overall sense of closure are more challenging to audiences in that they require an "active viewer," one who is ready to participate in the creation and interpretation of the narrative. Since *deok* implies an ongoing process, one that refutes closure, we can posit that the more open a narrative is, the more actively and accurately it can textualize this cultural concept.

As demonstrated in the following sections, *deok,* by nature, lends itself to poetic cinematic discourse, in that such a choice both avoids closure and invites the viewer to consider an ongoing and spiraling play of imagery. Since *Spring, Summer, Fall, Winter ... and Spring, Chihwaseon,* and *Poetry* can all be deemed examples of poetic films, a discussion of each to this effect would be redundant. Therefore, we will limit our examination to *Poetry,* which presents the most subtle inscription of the concept.

A Film Misread

In the United States, popular-press accounts of *Poetry* have failed to explore the film's poetic nature and its refutation of closure. Moreover, they have attempted to reposition the film for international audiences in favor of seeking out something authentically Korean. For instance, at the time of the New York release of Lee Changdong's *Poetry, The New York Times* ran a profile of veteran actress Yoon Junghee. The article explores Yoon's passion for film, her youthful idolization of Audrey Hepburn, her decision to leave Korea to live in Paris (the home of the Lumière brothers), and her relationship with her pianist husband, Paik Kunwoo (Lidz). The profile is personal and reflective, and explores Yoon's relationship to the character she portrays on screen. Nonetheless, the piece fails to mention anything inherently Korean, except for details of Yoon's biography. Yoon is presented as a great actress, one of the truly great artists of the world, who lives a quiet life—*abroad.*

In a review of *Poetry* also appearing in *The New York Times,* Manohla Dargis concentrates on the poignant and heartbreaking plot, describing the film as "a quietly, devastating, humanistic work." Her discussion focuses on the protagonist's progressive case of Alzheimer's disease, which is doubtless one of her motives for exercising her mind through poetry. Exploring the protagonist's questioning of poetic inspiration, Dargis (2011) asserts: "The question that she doesn't ask is the why of art. She doesn't have to because the film—itself an example of how art allows us to rise out of ourselves to feel for another through imaginative sympathy—answers that question beautifully." Once again, the review completely removes a Korean film from its Korean context and focuses on those universal and human aspects that will attract a U.S. audience. For Dargis, *Poetry* seems to transcend its national context, and there is nothing expressed to draw it back to its roots. But now let's examine it both in terms of its poetic discourse and its visualization of *deok*.

The Creative Process and the Cinema

Structurally, the two plot lines of *Poetry* run parallel. As the group of fathers increases its resolve to pay off the suicide victim's mother, the protagonist grows in terms of her love for poetry and in her determination to write a single poem. From her teacher, Mija learns to observe, and observe in detail, even the simplest of things in her life. The title of the referenced review by Dargis, "Consider an Apple, Consider the World," captures the process that Yang Mija learns to emulate. The creation of her ultimate poem may, on a certain level, parallel that of a plot line in John Huston's *Night of the Iguana* (1961), based on Tennessee Williams's eponymous play, in which an elderly man completes, immediately prior to his death, a poem on which he has labored for many years. The similarity, however, is only on the surface. In *Night of the Iguana,* we sense nothing of the inner process present in the creation of poetry; we simply hear the poet as he articulates his poem with false starts and stops. In *Poetry,* in contrast, the creative process is omnipresent, and we follow Mija as she ponders both poetic inspiration and her inner trajectory. A second reference to John Huston's film occurs when Mija visits the victim's mother at her fruit farm. Over the course of the meeting, she discusses only the beauty of fallen apricots that give seed to new life. In this case, her poetic speech is akin to the poem of *Night of the Iguana,* which explores the life cycle implicit in the fall of ripe olives from a branch. Such observations, however, remain at the level of a *poem within a film.* What is of greater significance in *Poetry* is the *film itself as cinematic poetry.*

Cinema and Poetry

Early Russian formalist debates separate "heterotelic" language, which finds its "justification outside of itself, in the transmission of thoughts or interpersonal communication" (Todorov, 1985, 131), from "autotelic," or poetic language, which finds its "justification, and hence its entire worth, within itself; it communicates its own end, and is thus no longer a mean" (131). Russian formalists speak of *zaum,* or "trans-sense, or supraconscious language ... a pure signifier, a poetry of sounds and letters that goes beyond words" (131–132). As Bruce Williams (2001) has observed, one of the hallmarks of a poetic film lies in the "residue" of its images, which we can deem the cinematic counterpoint of sounds and letters going beyond words. "[The process of poetization] is intensified by the failure of the film's images to be absorbed into metaphor. A residue of the image 'in and of itself' remains, defiantly resisting the safe haven of metaphor and story" (36). Williams uses as examples of poetic cinema Dovzhenko's *Earth* (1930), a masterpiece of Soviet cinema that was banned for several decades, and Mário Peixoto's *Limite* (1931), arguably the most enigmatic work of Brazilian silent cinema.

It is not coincidental that Lee Changdong's film is titled *Poetry.* Of all of the films discussed here, it is the one whose images are the least absorbed into story and metaphor. The title sequence and closing moments of *Poetry* are particularly evocative of what concerns poetic cinema. As the camera closes in on a body floating down the river, the film's title is presented. One encounters a juxtaposition of poetry and death, yet the image fails to be completely absorbed into metaphor. We are still faced with the depiction of a girl's body, and the residue of this image, in fact, drives a great deal of the narrative that follows. The film's final images are even more complex. As the poetry teacher introduces Mija's poem, we see places that are important to the protagonist in her own life—her poetry classroom, her cluttered apartment. As Mija's voice reads the poem entitled "Agnes's Song," which deals with separation and death, we see places of importance to Agnes that Mija had visited, such as her humble rural home and her school room. The mirroring of places—Mija's home and classroom with Agnes's home and classroom—mirrors the reading of the poem itself, which is started by Mija's voice and concluded by what we presume to be Agnes's voice. Such devices underscore metaphorically the strong connection between the two. Nonetheless, the point of view is rendered ambivalent. When we learn that Mija is missing from her home, we might be led to assume that the montage of images stem from her revisiting key places in Agnes's life. The shots, however, are unattached to any diegetic character. The camera pan across the interior windows revealing Agnes's classroom appears to be seen from the perspective of someone walking nearby. But who? The point of view could be that of either Mija or Agnes, or it could be neutral, allowing viewers to contemplate the places on their own. In a like manner, not all of the images can be subsumed into the metaphor of the bond between the protagonists. For instance, we see children running on the street and playing hula-hoop, images that Mija had indeed seen earlier in the film. Yet, particularly when juxtaposed with Mija's poem, they appear uncontained by the film's narrative.

On the Green Carpet

Film and Communist Ties

Although there are many differences, significant comparisons can be made between the cinemas of North Korea and Albania, which during the Cold War were arguably the two most isolated nations in the world. Like the government of North Korea, the government of Enver Hoxha forged a path of maximum self-reliance as the nation gradually, but thoroughly broke ties with the communist nations of Eastern Europe, and later with communist China, which had become its closest ally. The break with Eastern Europe, which had begun as early as 1961, was of particular significance for the cinema given that Albanian film professionals had been trained since the late 1940s in prestigious programs in Moscow, Budapest and Prague.[3] In contrast, as Johannes Shönherr claims, the training of early North Korean professionals was accomplished in Pyongyang. In this respect, North Korean film professionals were steeped exclusively in Korean culture, while their Albanian counterparts were more markedly influenced by the film traditions of the Soviet Union and the Eastern European bloc.

Albania and North Korea share another similarity in their cinema histories. Both developed their own national film industries shortly after the end of occupation (Italian for Albania, Japanese for North Korea) and the establishment of their respective communist governments. An Albanian national decree of April 10, 1947, mandated the establishment of an Albanian National Cinematographic Enterprise (Këshilli Ministerial nr. 163), and the New Albania (Shiqipëria e Re) Film Studio was subsequently inaugurated on July 10, 1952. Similarly, Pyongyang's Art Film Studio opened in 1947. Although not specifically addressing the medium of film, Enver Hoxha praised the importance of socialist art (Kinostudio Shqipëria e Re, 1977, 3), and a 1977 manifesto by Kinostudio extended the leader's remarks to the cinema, by stressing the importance of positive heroes with spiritual strength and moral purity who are "completely devoted to the Party, the people and socialism" (Kinostudio Shqipëria e Re, 1977, 9). Kim Il Sung (1958), for his part, underscored the importance of the cinema itself for socialist society, referring to it as "the most important and powerful education means" (9).

There were, however, major differences between the two contexts. First, the studio complex in Albania was relatively contained. Housed on the outskirts of Tirana, its main building in Albania was an ornate red Stalinist edifice surrounded by a number of smaller structures. In contrast, the scale of North Korea's main film studio in Pyongyang is immense. It comprises over 170 buildings, and has streets portraying 1930s China, 1950s South Korea, and European cities, among other sets. There is even a cinema façade displaying a poster of Marilyn Monroe in *The Seven Year Itch*.[4] One must note even a greater distinction between Albanian and North Korean cinema. Neither Hoxha nor his successor, Ramiz Alia, was a die-heard cinema fan, while Kim Jong Il was passionate about the medium. In 1973, he authored a treatise on the art of the cinema and, beginning in 1968, personally supervised all film production in his country (Lee Hyangjin, 2000, 31). State engagement in cinema has thus been much more intense in North Korea than it had been in Albania under communism.[5]

Film, Children and Socialist Education

Both the North Korean and Albanian cinemas have paid special attention to the socialist education of children. During the Hoxha years, the Albanian Young Pioneers would view films and hold discussions of them from an ideological perspective. Of particular consequence in this endeavor were the films of Xhanfise Keko. One of her most celebrated films, *Beni Walks on His Own* (*Beni ecën vetë*) (1975), tells of an overly protected boy from the city who learns self-reliance and the importance of physical work while on a visit to the countryside. Another of her films, *On the Tracks* (*Pas gjurmëve*), explores how even when becoming patriotic child spies and thwarting an attack on a hydroelectric plant, young boys cannot neglect their schoolwork!

In *On the Green Carpet,* the realms of education and cinema merge. Mungyu's *han* is closely linked to his passion for educating the children with whom he works, and such education is present on a number of levels. The rigorous physical training that Mungyu demands of the children notwithstanding, the importance of their academic education outside of training hours is underscored. In the planetarium sequence, the discourses of artistic performance, academic discipline, and ideological instruction converge. *On the Green Carpet* dedicates a considerable amount of attention to a young boy who is determined to perform for Kim Jong Il, despite having sustained an injury. This plot line recalls the importance of self-reliance and determination in Albanian children's films, and particularly the story of Beni, who learns to "walk on his own." The hope implied by Mungyu's *han* thus implies the self-reliance that the children will attain.

On the Green Carpet places special emphasis on the great love Kim Il Sung had for the children who represented the future of the nation and, by extension, on the importance of their education. But the knowledge one must gain through education is not knowledge for knowledge's sake. As Kim Jong Il (1973) asserts:

> The real value of knowledge is defined by its accuracy in reflecting the truth of nature and society and its effectiveness in practical activity. Only knowledge that has been derived from the requirements of practice and the truth of which has been tested in practice can be an effective force for the transformation of nature and society [279].

In *On the Green Carpet,* Mungyu's pedagogy is closely aligned with the practical goals of the state. The mass gymnastics performance is not a purely artistic one. Rather, depicting both Korean history and the ideology of the People's Party, it is viewed as an effective force for the transformation of the society of the DPRK. The same analysis can be extended to the film itself, which unravels the complex workings behind the spectacle in light of both the choreographer's *han* and the ideological message the performance must convey.

A Schoolgirl's Diary

The Subversion of Melodrama: Family and Nation

One of the characteristics of what E. Ann Kaplan has defined as the "resisting" film melodrama is that the genre "deliberately foregrounds the public/male–domestic/female split, making it central to their narrative strategies—a way to make a social comment as against the mere acceptance of such a split in the complicit text" (Kaplan, 1992, 131). In the mother-daughter melodrama, the narrative space of the home is of utmost importance, cases in point being John Cromwell's *Since You Went Away* (1944) and Michael Curtiz's *Mildred Pierce* (1945). *A Schoolgirl's Diary* is clearly set in the narrative space of the melodrama. The film's setting is the home of a married couple, and a great deal of its focus deals with the lives of its female characters. Similar to a good number of Hollywood vehicles set during World War II, one of the salient features of the film is the absence of the father. This comparison becomes even clearer when, by virtue of the young protagonist's favorite song, the father's separation from his family is compared to that of the General (Kim Jong Il) himself. The feminine realm of what initially appears to be a film melodrama is thus transformed as the *jeong* for the absent father is displaced onto the Dear Leader.

Referring to the "complicit" melodrama, Kaplan stresses that "the 'lie' namely that woman must of necessity be subjugated to the Law of the Father, is ... concealed in the dominant Hollywood genre" (Kaplan, 1992, 66). She argues that the film system organized by genre "produced a subordinated set of films functioning as a counter-balance to the dominant male genres, which were often labeled 'the woman's weepie'" (66). *A Schoolgirl's Diary* possesses a number of the traits of such "weepies." The mother, living in a small house near Pyongyang and working as a librarian in the capital, must support her two daughters and mother-in-law. The hardships the family endures are exemplified by the need to repair a chimney and by the protagonist's school friends who collectively do the repair, standing in for the absent father. When diagnosed with cancer, the mother has at her side only her daughter and mother-in-law. Once again, her husband's work precludes him from being with the family. Yet, as we noted previously, the intense *jeong* the couple shares is displaced onto *chung* for the nation.

The melodrama is a product of Western society, and its critique of social class reflects the patriarchal, capitalist world in which it was born. Kaplan (1992) stresses:

> [The Hollywood melodrama has constructed] representations whose purpose is to manipulate women in, or out of, the work-force, in accordance with capitalism's needs. The powerful ideology of the masochistic, angelic, all-sacrificing mother, produced through psychoanalytic theories as representing the healthy, "feminine" woman, has functioned (and is *still* functioning, although in ways strikingly altered via new technologies) to construct women in ways that serve forces that have nothing per se to do with women [45].

It is essential not to collapse what appears to be a North Korean film melodrama into its Western equivalent. Indeed, the DPRK may be deemed a patriarchy given the salience of the father figure, as made manifest by the three Kims. Yet North Korean society has egalitarian goals. We cannot read the mother in *A Schoolgirl's Diary* as long-suffering, even when her husband fails to be present following her cancer surgery. Her translation work for her husband is not a manifestation of masochism, but implies an essential role in scientific research. *A Schoolgirl's Diary* is thus not a "woman's weepie," but rather an ode to the sacrifice of the private for the state. The father's continued absences are not viewed as negligent, but rather as something laudable. This point is brought home near the conclusion of the film when the family, rewarded for the scientist's success, is able to move from their humble house to a high-rise apartment. It is further underscored by a photograph of Kim Jong Il visiting a factory where the father's successful computerized assembly line has been put to use. The photograph is shown to the young protagonist's university class as she begins her scientific studies.

The praiseworthy dedication of the father to his work is further textualized by the transformation of the young protagonist once she learns that her father is not a mere laborer, but rather a respected and successful scientist. She opts to attend a scientific university rather than studying the humanities. In the final sequence, her voice-over attests to how the example of her parents' dedication to their profession, which makes their relationship special, has given her the willpower to embark on her own life and, by implication, develop a similar *chung* for the nation. The final still image shows the young woman holding an umbrella while her mother is moving forward toward the departing train (off screen) that is carrying her husband away. The image suggests that the young university student will soon be following her mother's lead.

Pyongyang Nalparam

Action Films and Social Integration

Laura Mulvey draws upon the analyses of Vladimir Propp to explore the notion of the male protagonist in relation to the structure of the folk tale, and these discussions have allowed for continued assessments of narrative space in westerns and action films. For Mulvey, one of the defining functions of the narrative closure of the folk tale is marriage, which represents social integration (Mulvey, 1981, 14). Nonetheless, in North Korean cinema, we note that social integration implies an intense *chung* for the nation.

The structure of *Pyongyang Nalparam* constitutes a unique refiguring of Propp's formulation of the folk tale and Mulvey's subsequent analysis of masculinity in the cinema. When Jeongtaek plays a game of mutual deception with the Japanese imposter, there is a false sense of closure, yet one that is quickly debunked. Despite the protagonist's offering of the ring to the wrong woman, we doubt closure for two reasons: (1) the event occurs too early on in the narrative, and (2) Jeongtaek is quickly called to a new adventure—the retrieval of the volume hidden in the cave—and hence it is not yet time for him to enter the narrative space of the home. His reunion with the real

Sokyeon takes place early on in the film as well, and the lovers are soon separated as the hero goes through continued trials. For a brief moment near the end of the film, it appears that the lovers may well be united following the triumph of the Koreans in the martial arts match. In a sense they are, but in an unexpected way. When we see their figures leap into the air and hear gunshots during the massacre, their fatal wounds are implied, but never clearly depicted. As Jeongtaek hands the ring to Sokyeon, the act implies marriage. But there is no closure inasmuch as a home is never established and we fail to witness the couple's actual death. Such a narrative choice accentuates the continued development of the *jeong* under the *chung* that binds them.

A National Home

By leaving open its framing device (the story of the foreign visitor to the *taekkyeon* center), *Pyongyang Nalparam* invites the viewer to ponder the relationship between the four volumes of the *taekkyeon* manual housed in the library and the story of Jeongtaek and Sokyeon's marriage and implied death. Although we do not know how, the four volumes of the manual have safely returned to Pyongyang and found their place under glass protection in a special collection of the center's archive. Jeongtaek and Sokyeon, as their fathers had done, dedicated their lives to preventing the volumes from falling into the hands of the Japanese. One can view this task in terms of familial duty, with the books representing something dear to both sides of the family. The volumes, now stored in their proper place, can be deemed the establishment of a home of sorts, and a continuation of the legacy and dreams of the bride and groom. Their *chung* has, indeed, come to fruition. As in so many North Korean films, the importance of family is displaced onto love for the state. Although the diegetic time of *Pyongyang Nalparam* predated the founding of the DPRK by slightly less than four decades, we note that the fulfillment of the protagonists' *chung* ultimately occurs in the narrative space of the nation.

Conclusion: Other Levels of Meaning

Whereas in the foregoing chapters we have attempted to read the Korean films as much as possible from an Eastern perspective, the analyses presented here have, at times, sought linkages between East and West that may help the viewer ground the films in the key cultural concepts articulated. At other times, in the case of *Poetry* and *On the Green Carpet,* this chapter has found connections with the films of the former Soviet Union and communist Albania. The aim has been to enhance the readings of the previous chapters with additional insights that penetrate more deeply into cultural processes and reveal the importance of the cinema as a vehicle for such excavation of understanding. What we have demonstrated in this chapter is that there is no uniform way of reading these films, even when mediated by key cultural concepts. The interpretative process is a spiraling one. The closer one approaches Korean ethos, the more invocative and enticing readings can be found. Films continue to generate meaning, and both Western and Korean viewers can draw upon the knowledge they have gained to allow the texts to expand themselves and reveal new and noncontradictory levels of meaning.

Conclusion

This book has had as its main goal the illustration of key cultural concepts through the cinema as an approach to understanding Korean ethos. It has further positioned key cultural words and the cinema in such a way that they can elucidate each other. Our double lens has thus performed double duty. Granted, we acknowledge multiple positions of identification and acknowledge that there is nothing to preclude viewers from reinterpreting the works examined through their own contexts and experiences. Yet, by exploring these films through key cultural concepts, we have offered spectators well-honed parameters through which we invite them to approach their viewings. At least at one point, during at least one viewing, their spectatorship will have been filtered toward a Korean perspective. Moreover, their divergent readings are likely to be mediated by the key words.

Two Lenses on Korean Ethos

We can return here to the first part of this book's title, *Two Lenses on Korean Ethos*. While the two lenses at play primarily refer to key cultural words and cinema, they imply a plausible connection between Maslow's basic human needs and Korean key cultural words. As shown in Chapter 1, Maslow's concepts have served as a blueprint for selecting the Korean key cultural words. We were able to posit which aspects of Korean culture could be linked to Maslow's needs, and these aspects in turn helped provide a bridge between East and West. In other words, key cultural concepts are not password blocked; they can be approached from the outside in a comparative or contrastive manner.

Korean Ethos from a Cultural Perspective

Each culture establishes certain values that influence one's social, political, professional, and personal life. Yet, these values can vary across individuals within the same culture given that there are many subcultures. By the same token, the meaning of Korean ethos may diverge across individual Koreans depending on their age, gender, education, profession, lifestyle, and so forth. Nevertheless, early chapters lead us to argue that Korean ethos lies in the intersection of *han*-driven diligence, *jeong*-nurtured courage, and *deok*-mediated struggle, the last of which embraces numerous other cultural concepts.

Koreans are diligent, and this diligence is closely related to *han*. That is, *han* is the driving force for the perpetuation of hope and provides energy for meeting goals, whatever they are (e.g., getting an excellent education, working for a prestigious company, performing an outstanding task, having a great network, becoming rich); *han* makes one feel that something is deprived, denied, lost, failed, or absent in oneself, one's family, one's group, one's community, and/or one's country. This does not imply that Koreans are pessimistic and unhappy people. *Han* leads them to be viable and sustainable in a constructive way; through *han* they endure pain, reexamine past experiences, set new goals, and regenerate hope for the future (as implied in *Seopyeonje, The King and Clown,* and, in a more interwoven manner, *Pietà*). In a like manner, the characters of *On the Green Carpet* and *A Schoolgirl's Diary* demonstrate a *han* that is closely associated with the betterment of nation.

Due to *han,* protagonists are unable to give up; this characteristic persistence is a part of the fate that permeates their inner self. This does not signify that all Koreans are able to cope well with *han.* However, their daily life is associated knowingly or unknowingly with a form of *han* to which the response is *chamara*/참아라, the main cultural theme of an epic novel, titled *This Burns My Heart* (Park, Samuel 2011). *Chamara* is difficult to translate; it could marginally be described as "to stand it, to bear it, to grit one's teeth and not cry out, to hold on, to wait until the worst is over." According to a conversation posted on the author's website (Park, Samuel, 2012), the book's title and the concept of *chamara* are intertwined—one is a condition and the other is the response to it. The protagonist, who is irresistible, yet flawed, engages in *chamara* throughout the course of the novel; passions, struggles, and triumphs characterize the emotional world of the heroine. Although this novel does not use the term *han,* the demonstrative pronoun "this" is a reminiscent image of *han.* In other words, we relate *chamara* to Maslow's first basic human need (physical need) in that Koreans need inner strength to *chamda* (infinitive form of the imperative *chamara*).

Koreans are courageous from the perspective that they can be daring as well as persistent. They have the courage to do the right things when the wrong things seem to produce better results. They are willing to leave behind things they value with the hopes that those good things will return to them. They get up to ride again after a really bad fall; they stand up to their future when their past keeps knocking them down. They are willing to do something dangerous at the possible cost of their life. They are courageous in overcoming danger, fear, and injustice, while continuing to affirm inwardly that life with its all sorrow is good. In the case of North Korea, such courage is first and foremost dedicated to the nation. All these types of courage have been observed in the main characters of the films *Mother, Brotherhood of War, Joint Security Area, Oasis, Pietà, A Schoolgirl's Diary,* and *Pyongyang Nalparam.*

Similarly, what should be noted here is that this courage is generated through endurance, and this endurance can be maintained through *jeong,* as exhibited in the aforementioned films. In other words, diligent *han*-bearers are nurtured by *jeong* and encouraged to look forward. Without *jeong,* persons of *han* would feel isolated and disconnected from others. However, the special affection of family, friends, and colleagues toward the *han*-bearer strengthens the bonding of their relationship. The we-ness of *jeong* facilitates making their life meaningful, even if it looks disgraceful and pathetic to others. *Jeong,* a primordial way of relating to others, is a valuable ingredient that encourages individuals to develop, maintain, and affirm a sense of self in conjunction with others, even though *jeong*-involved people often become irrational. Its quality of interdependency helps a *han*-bearer, who needs empathic relationships for mitigating self-suffering from inner emptiness, barrenness, mistakes, or calamity. While independence and privacy are desirable for certain situations, *han*-bearers need special affection, a need for trusting and nurturing relationships to carry on a fruitful life in a constructive way. Even if they have to climb a deserted mountain, they feel that someone in their life will be on the top of the mountain, cheering them on, praying for them, pulling for them, intervening on their behalf, and waiting with open arms at the peak of the mountain. This does not imply that all Koreans have someone like that, but it suggests that their lives would be much harder without *jeong,* even if *jeong* has negative aspects that can result in one's getting sick or becoming destructive. Here, we would note that even destructiveness needs courage, which means *jeong* is needed, whether it leads to positive or negative results. From the perspective of Maslow's belongingness need, it may seem very peculiar considering that individuals in U.S. culture need to maintain a certain level of "privacy" while searching for and enjoying the state of being accepted and comfortable in a place or group. However, as the Korean self is viewed as an other-oriented person, Koreans feel that courage comes from the involvement through which they find a sense of love and belongingness. Interference, although it is not always welcome, is considered as a sign of deeply involved *jeong,* a source of courage.

Han-driven diligent and *jeong*-nurtured courageous Koreans feel open to goodness, whether they have tried to cultivate *deok* or have completely pushed it off for a while. Some Koreans may overlook or veil the *deok*-related value system in their actual life for various reasons, such as cognitive impairment, self-indulgence, or individual hidden agendas. They may not able to discern what has been traditionally valued due to the nontraditional or unfortunate environments in which they live. Alternatively, they may want to reject traditional values that they think might affect them negatively in this rapidly changing world. Nevertheless, whatever they pursue, they always seem to feel that they have not reached the level of what would be considered outstanding in the eyes of others, as well as in their own eyes. Their *han*-driven diligence, in combination with *jeong*-nurtured courage, makes them keep pushing themselves. This behavior is different from Maslow's self-actualization, but is similar to an aspect of *deok* inasmuch as the latter concept requires "mindfulness for the difficulties" that lie ahead.

Traditionally, the Korean *deok*-cultivation process exists in close proximity to the maintenance of *jungyong*/중용, a Buddhist concept roughly translated as "middle path." A path of moderation between the extremes of sensual indulgence and self-mortification is viewed as the path of wisdom in Buddhist teaching. The middle way does not indicate a midpoint in a straight line joining two extremes represented by points, but rather describes the realization of being free of the one-sided perspective that takes the extremes of any polarity as objective reality. In reality, the middle path is extremely hard to pursue, as shown in the life of the young monk depicted in *Spring, Summer, Fall, Winter ... and Spring* as well as Seungeop's life in *Chihwaseon.* Nonetheless, these characters finally begin to realize what is meaningful in life. Even though their realization occurs late, it is still significant in that it is a sign of *deok*-seeding.

While *deok* implies a middle path that embraces a wide range of self-discipline in what concerns pleasure, ambition, curiosity, frugality, contentment, and so forth, it encompasses an extensive number of subvirtues as mentioned in earlier chapters. Another interesting note concerns the *deok*-related subvirtues found in what Koreans call *insaeng deok-mok*/인생 덕목 (list of life's good work); it is a taxonomy of *deok*-related moral practices that they want themselves and others to pursue in life. A most frequently cited *deok*-

mok is that of the late Cardinal Kim Suhwan (1922–2009), which outlines the moderation of verbal behavior; the great value of books; the daily practice of a good laugh; the dumbing aspect of television; the dangerous consequence of anger; the power of prayer; the importance of neighbors; and acts that lead to love (Ohmynews, 2011). A *deok-mok* can be addressed to the general public as well as to a specific type of person, such as a political leader, a CEO of a company, a designer, a writer, a parent, and so forth. Whoever it addresses and whatever its content, it is centered on goodness, and suggests that its work is not stress-free and represents a lifelong task. That is to say, Koreans, whether famous leaders like Cardinal Kim Suhwan or ordinary people like Mija in *Poetry,* value the struggles they experience in the process of *deok*-cultivation.

To recapitulate the discussion here, Korean ethos represents a life journey characterized by *han*-driven diligence, *jeong*-nurtured courage, and *deok*-mediated struggle. The journey is like walking on a long trail that is crooked, winding, lonesome, and dangerous; it also resembles traveling along a highway that seems to extend infinitely into the distance. Intriguingly, the concepts of *han, jeong,* and *deok* provide their bearers with a powerful "mental GPS," which helps them navigate their rough and elongated trail and discover the far-reaching road that ultimately takes them to a place that is not on any map.

Korean Ethos from a Cinematic Perspective

The cinema offers avenues for truly understanding another culture. Yet this potential does not, in and of itself, promise an easy path. Particularly today, with so many codes that must be deciphered in the interpretation of a film, it is easy for viewers using the cinema as an exclusive path to an in-depth knowledge of a given ethos to get waylaid. The convergence of key cultural words and the cinema, as we have demonstrated, constitutes an optimal vehicle for this quest. Nonetheless, it stands in direct opposition to early debates on the "universal language of the cinema," upon which an entire mystique was built. We need simply recall an anecdote involving Lillian Gish, cited by Michael Cronin at the beginning of his 2009 study of translation in the cinema. The veteran actress recalls how D. W. Griffith grew angry at an actress who referred to a film as a "flicker." Gish explains:

> He told her never to use that word. She was working in the universal language that had been predicted in the Bible, which was to make all men brothers because they would understand each other. They could end wars and bring about the millennium. We were all to remember that when we faced a camera [Gish, 1973, 60].

Cronin discusses Griffith's belief that the moving image was "a way of undoing the mishap of Babel" (1). In referring to the primacy of the image, Cronin describes the position that Griffith and other like minds assumed:

> No longer would inquiries after knowledge depend on scholastic antecedent. They would not take previous generations at their word, but would confirm with their own eyes claims about the nature of the natural and material world. Believing without seeing was a culpable blindness [1].

Yet seeing alone can cause us to misappropriate the image before us and to co-opt it so that it appears to be derived from our own comfortable turf. The "for-me-ness" that Nataša Ďurovičová has described may prevent us from approaching an original cultural context more closely. In another study of translation in the cinema, Abe Mark Nornes (2007) identifies one of the drawbacks to borderlessness and globalization. He argues, "The erosion of the nation-state and the felt emergence of a homogeneous planetary space implies a threat to local cultures, or what has recently been dubbed 'McWorld' or 'Planet Hollywood'" (5). Nornes recalls Laura Marks's claim that "the further [a film] travels ... the more bits of meanings become rarefied and distanced from their material origin" (Marks, 2000, 105). Nornes explains how Marks "is most concerned with how intercultural cinema builds cultural and linguistic difference into the very fabric of the film" (Nornes, 2007, 23).

Nornes's discussions of subtitles are not unlike our use of key cultural concepts here. He contrasts early modes of translation, in which subtitles either bring "the foreign text to the spectators on their own domestic turf" (178) or "[conform] the foreign to the framework of the target language and its cultural codes" (178), with what he favorably terms "abusive translation," in which "the translator identifies strongly with the source text and the culture in which it was produced, so much that he cedes the particular powers of his own culture to accomplish a translation that invites the reader-spectator to a novel and rich experience of the foreign" (178).

In our foregoing discussions, we have purposefully not examined issues of translation and subtitling so as not to dilute our exploration of key cultural concepts as manifested in Korean cinema. Yet there is a distinct parallel. Key cultural concepts invite spectators to gain a similar "novel and rich experience of the foreign." Yet just as the culture they are penetrating is unique and different, so is the very cinema itself.

We have noted that the films we have analyzed from the New Korean Cinema display elements of genre, but cannot be neatly assigned within any such classification scheme. It is essential to remember that discussions of cinema genres tend to be Hollywood-centric. Action films, westerns, and even

horror films often rely on the resourcefulness of a hero, of individualistic challenges and feats. The melodrama notwithstanding, traditional genres are
pressed to address an other-oriented culture in which the exploits of the individual are less at stake, or at least in which heroism is distinctly defined. As in
the case of films that deal with socioeconomic concerns at the same time that
they display structural innovativeness—we need only mention Brazilian *cinema novo* or the New German Cinema of the 1960s and 1970s—the concerns
of the New Korean Cinema address the complexity of Korean culture. One
of the many faces of *han,* for instance, entails the assumption of this burden,
particularly in terms of finances and education, by a younger generation. Such
a process can also be found within the domestic space of the melodrama.
Nonetheless, *Seopyeonje* has shown us that a family drama can indeed take
place outside of the confines of a home. Likewise, *han*-venting often entails a
performance of sorts, and a filmic meditation on performance cannot necessarily be contained by a single genre, as performances assume many forms,
both public and private. The forbidden eroticism manifested in the *han*-vent-
ing of *Pietà* transcends any and all generic taxonomies.

Although on a surface level a number of manifestations of *jeong* (*jeong*
between mothers and children, *jeong* between siblings, *jeong* between lovers)
may lend themselves to the melodrama, the irrationality implied by this cultural concept transcends the norms of this genre. *Jeong* is certainly an overarching concept that can override generic boundaries. In Korean ethos, the
extremities to which mothers, brothers, friends, or lovers may go cannot be
contained by simple cinematic categories. Mother, indeed, "will stop at nothing," and she is dependent upon an unrestricted narrative space in which to
operate.

Deok is the most elusive of the cultural concepts we have explored. The
path toward it can be circuitous, and the spiritual can mix with the carnal.
Cinematographically, it lends itself to open endings and narrative fissures that
invite multiple interpretations. Its very lack of closure defies the containment
of genre. We are often left with multiple possibilities at various junctures of
the narrative. Such openness, to a greater extent than in films that explore *han*
or *jeong,* implies an active viewer. Such a viewer must negotiate the trying open
discourse of the film and continually search for and build meaning; the openness of *deok*-related films underscores that this concept is in an ever-present
state of evolution, a state of "becoming" rather than "having become."

In contrast, the socialist films of North Korea are very distinct structurally. Nonetheless, it is still very illuminating to approach them through the
lens of national ethos. The relative simplicity of the recent North Korean cin-

ema in comparison to works of the New Korean Cinema is somewhat misleading. The straightforward narratives of the films align such key cultural concepts as *han, jeong,* and *chung* with *juche* ideology, inviting the viewer to note the cultural distinction between this ideology and other socialist political structures. Our analysis of these films has been considerably different from other studies of socialist cinema, in that we have sought an intersection between the realms of politics, ideology, and national ethos. In Chapter 8, we related North Korean Cinema to the cinema of Albania. Yet, given that our study was driven by key cultural concepts, it is quite distinct from work to date on Albanian cinema, which, by and large, has been thematic in nature. If one were to approach Albanian films, both of the communist and post-communist eras, from the perspective of key cultural terms, one would come much closer to understanding Albanian ethos, regardless of the political context in which it is manifested.

What, exactly, do the New Korean Cinema and recent films from North Korea do to facilitate our approach to Korean ethos? For those who are not familiar with traditional Korean culture, drawing close to this ethos can be a daunting task. An appreciation of it, like an appreciation of the country's cinema, must mature over time. Part of what we perceive as shifting and unpredictable becomes clear as we grow in our understanding of a high-context culture. The films that we have analyzed, when considered as an ensemble, serve as a prism through which we can explore, through divergent angles and perspectives, a culture that defines the self in terms of the other, allowing defined bonds to supersede all other social protocols. These films offer a guide to how Koreans assume burdens from the past and carry them to a future in progress.

Reflections on the Uniqueness of This Book

The interdisciplinary approach used in this book has opened a new avenue to the study of key cultural concepts by treating culture-specific words in a historical context and visualizing them through the cinema. It has proved that cultural and linguistic behavior can be revealingly studied through these key concepts in a verifiable, rigorous manner, drawing upon historical records, classic stories, poems, and old sayings. Similarly, it has demonstrated that the field of cultural pragmatics (or cultural linguistics) can gain important new insights through an in-depth analysis of films in conjunction with culture-bound concepts and thoughts. Furthermore, this book has challenged traditional approaches to lexical semantics. While the traditional ways of understanding words are significant from the perspective of formal linguistics, they primarily serve to stimulate our intellectual mind. It is also important to stimulate our social mind, inasmuch as words are used in social and cultural contexts. Thus, this book, which has investigated key words in historical and cultural contexts and through cinematic communication, presents a solid impetus for sharpening our social as well as cognitive mind. In other words, it has demonstrated that culture-specific concepts serve as guides for reviewing the related history as cultural sources, and as an inquiry device for expanding the scope of our explanatory and interpretative mind-set for further exploration and understanding.

We have purposefully eschewed highly theorized discussions, yet have laid the necessary groundwork for setting the context for the viewing experience without rehashing hackneyed debates in film studies. In a like manner, our close readings are intended to engross the spectator in the viewing experience. As stated earlier, our approach goes against the grain of global trends in cinema studies, in that its primary focus is not to view how films cross borders and can be read in new, yet highly valid ways. Our book essentially reverses this trend by encouraging the *viewer* rather than the film to proceed across passport control. This return to a cultural close reading of films may be deemed "retro," as is today's renewed interest in the study of the *auteur*. Nevertheless, it is unique in its employment of key cultural words as a mediating device for the films that fosters an excavation for deeper meaning.

This book has thus reinforced the importance of multidisciplinary, applied research for further understanding of key cultural words. Even if one raises the question as to precisely which field such an approach falls under, we have demonstrated that it cuts across a variety of fields in the humanities and social sciences, among these cultural studies, cinema studies, and anthropological linguistics. Interweaving these discourses, we have created what we hope to be a welcoming template for future studies of other cultures, their language, cinema, and traditional roots.

Appendix:
Romanization of Korean
Words and Names

That the Korean writing system, invented in 1443, is not easy to Romanize is due to the variety of vowel and consonant phonemes. The two most widely used systems had traditionally been the McCure–Reischauer system, developed by George McCure and Edwin Reischauer in the 1930s, and the Yale Romanization, created at Yale University in the 1960s. More recently, the Revised Romanization of Korean—the official Korean language Romanization system in South Korea endorsed by the Ministry of Culture, Sports and Tourism—has been used widely in academia and other domains.

The Revised Romanization System was developed by the National Academy of Korean Language in late 1990s and drew upon three main principles: (1) It would be written as pronounced in Korean; (2) each Korean letter would be allocated a specific Roman letter(s) for consistent transliteration; and (3) no symbols other than the Roman alphabet would be used. One of the major distinctions of this system from the McCure–Reischauer method is the removal of special punctuation markers used to express aspirated sounds and the abolition of the half-moon sign, which shows the grammatical positions of Korean consonants. The fundamental reason for the revision is that many Koreans find it difficult to understand the meaning of the symbols. Moreover, these symbols are not easily accessible on computer keyboards. While all Korean texts have complied with the new system, English-language newspapers in South Korea initially resisted the new system. However, all of them, including *Korea Times,* a major English newspaper, have since switched to the new system.

The new system is not expected to be adopted as the official Romanization of Korean family names. Koreans have been encouraged to change given names and business names, but this is not required. While this book follows the Revised Romanization System, we have chosen to use the traditional Romanization of Korean surnames (e.g., Lee, Park, Yoon), unless the respective person uses it differently. Also, inasmuch as Koreans write their names surname first and given name last, this book will follow this pattern. In contrast, the authors of articles and books published in English will be given in the way they are cited.

With regard to Korean given names that have two syllables, these are expressed differently in the Roman alphabet depending upon individual choice. For example, they may be written (1) with a space between the syllable and both in capitals, and a hyphen (e.g., Hyun-Nam); (2) with a space and hyphen, but a lowercase letter for the second syllable (Hyun-nam); (3) without a hyphen (Hyun Nam); and (4) no space, no hyphen (e.g., Hyunnam).

In this book, we have tried to be as consistent as we can in the following ways. We write the given names of the film directors without a space or hyphen (e.g., Im Kwontaek); similarly, the fictional characters in films are written without a space and without hyphen (e.g., Yubong in *Seopyeonje*). However, we must stress that character names may be spelled in a number of ways in English subtitles and commentaries. For authors, we opt for whatever forms have been cited in English sources. For historical names, we use the most commonly used forms. Similarly, for well-known people, such as presidents and government officers, as well as city names, we choose the forms that have been employed most frequently (e.g., Kim Jong Il, Pyongyang). Nevertheless, we acknowledge that, even with the most well-known names, there are still variants in English spellings in the news media, Internet sites, and books.

While we have endeavored to be consistent in the Romanization of words and names in the aforementioned manner, inconsistency may nonetheless be perceived. This inconsistency is attributed to the differences in ways of transliterating of Korean words and names that people use in public documents.

Summary of the New Romanization System

1. Simple Vowels

ㅏ	ㅓ	ㅗ	ㅜ	―	ㅣ	ㅔ	ㅐ	ㅚ	ㅟ
a	eo	o	U	eu	I	e	ae	oe	wi

2. Diphthongs

ㅑ	ㅕ	ㅛ	ㅠ	ㅒ	ㅖ	ㅘ	ㅙ	ㅝ	ㅞ	ㅢ
ya	yeo	yo	yu	yae	ye	wa	wae	wo	we	ui

3. Consonants
    Plosive stops

ㄱ	ㄲ	ㅋ	ㄷ	ㄸ	ㅌ	ㅂ	ㅃ	ㅍ
g (k)	kk	k	d (t)	tt	t	b (p)_	pp	p

Affricates

ㅈ	ㅉ	ㅊ
j	jj	ch

Fricatives

ㅅ	ㅆ	ㅎ
s	ss	h

Nasals

ㄴ	ㅁ	ㅇ
n	m	ng

Liquid

ㄹ
r, l

Special Provisions for Romanization

Although these tables are followed for each Korean letter, there are some special provisions for Romanization. Please see the Official Site of Korea Tourism Organization for details: http://visitkorea.or.kr/ena/CU/CU_EN_8_2_3_1.jsp.

Chapter Notes

Introduction

1. For 한류 (Korean Wave), we will use the transliteration *hanryu*. The two Romanizations, however, are essentially interchangeable.

Chapter 2

1. North Korea has traditionally used "Arirang" as the basis of a major sporting event every April 15, in honor of Kim Il-Sung's birthday. Also known as a "mass games event," the "Arirang Performance" features roughly 100,000 performers and decries the separation of the peninsula, looking forward to reunification under the terms of the Great Leader's plan. The Arirang Performance textualizes the *han* that has befallen the peninsula since the separation of the two Koreas. In 2002, Pyongyang opened the event to foreigners, performed it several times each year, and began issuing visas to Americans. This policy was described as an attempt to compete with the 2002 FIFA World Cup, co-hosted by South Korea. For some nine years, the Arirang Performance has provided foreigners with one of the less problematic ways to visit North Korea.

2. One claim is that it originated from the time when Heungseon Daewongun was rebuilding the Gyeongbok palace in 1865, which had been destroyed by fire during the Japanese invasion of 1592–1598. Another version asserts that it has existed since the Silla dynasty, more than 1000 years ago, and offered praise to the virtue of Aryong, the wife of the founder of said dynasty.

3. Traditionally, Korea has been a class-oriented society in which the ruling class (the *yangban*) oppressed and abused the poor and the underclass called the *ssangnon*. Also, in traditional Confucian society, the status and role of the female are subservient to those of the male. As a result, women had to endure much hardship and injustice. The poor and powerless had no recourse to appeal this injustice. To tolerate the *status quo*, they were compelled to moderate their anger and indignation.

4. The word *han* is combined with a second word to express difference nuances of this feeling. In addition to *won-han* and *jeong-han*, two words frequently used are *hoe-han*, which means "*han* with remorse and regret," and *han-tan*, which denotes a "crying and lamenting *han*."

5. *Cheongsanbyeolgok* depicts self-compliance with reality (first stanza), loneliness and sorrow (second stanza), lingering attachment (third stanza), heartbreaking loneliness (fourth stanza), resignation to life experience (fifth stanza), a longing for a new world (sixth stanza), a feeling of impending life crisis (seventh stanza), and a dissolution of anguish (eighth stanza). See Sin (1982) and its related website: http://

www.seelotus.com/gojeon/gojeon/korea-gayo/cheong-san.htm.

6. The introduction of Taoism, Buddhism, and Confucianism did not result in the abandonment of shamanism, which has coexisted with them in a form of assimilation. That is, shamanism has remained an underlying religion of the Korean people and a vital aspect of Korean culture.

7. The process whereby *han* is released is called *han-puri* (unknotting *han*, *han*-venting). The person (usually a woman) who performs *goot* is called *mudang*. Having a life filled with *han*, she becomes a shaman following her healing through help of a shaman with a higher rank. Korean folk music, dancing, and theater are closely associated with *han*-venting of this kind.

8. In Korea, "we" often means "I bonded by *jeong* to you," whereas in English "we" just represents any multiple "I's." Non-Koreans find it strange when Koreans say "our husband" or "our wife" rather than "my husband" or "my wife." The concept of "I" seems weakened for the sake of strengthening *jeong*. One may easily interpret this as symbiosis with borderline dynamics.

9. Today, Korean mothers are known for their high involvement in their children's education, which they consider their top priority. They wake up very early to prepare breakfast and lunch boxes so that their children can maintain good health. They constantly collect information and search for better educational possibilities, forming networks through which to obtain the most up-to-date information on the best study needs. Koreans call this phenomenon "*chimabaram*" (the swish of a skirt that describes mothers running here and there). Mothers cut all other expenses so that they can send their children to well-known learning centers for academic enrichment. They live according to their offspring's schedules and will refrain from attending any social events during examination periods. All of their energy is devoted to their children's education. Although such obsessive energy has not always been regarded as favorable, Young-Ok Kwak (2005)

views that it can be channeled in a positive direction and propel Korea toward a promising future.

10. From a Confucian perspective, the virtue of a woman lies in her obedience to three men: her father, her husband, and her son. It has been said that a traditional woman has three masters during her lifetime: her father when she is young, her husband when she is married, and her son when she is old. Surprisingly enough, there are scarcely any Korean proverbs pertaining to the latter relationship.

11. As mentioned in Chapter 1, moral goodness in traditional Korean society is based on a set of principles called *samgangoryun*, meaning three bonds (sovereign–subject; parent–child; husband–wife) and five cardinal relationships (that define the three bonds jointly with two additional bonds: senior–junior and friend–friend). These five relationships constitute the Confucian paradigm. Social harmony, the great goal of Confucianism, results in part in everyone knowing his or her own place in the social order and playing his or her part well.

12. The idea of serving the king loyally and respecting and supporting one's parents—namely, *Chung-Hyo Sasang* (The Thought of Loyalty an d Filial Piety)—is the highest virtue in Confucian ethics and constitutes a valuable asset in countries influenced by Confucianism. However, one cannot expect young people today to maintain such a virtue blindly; traditionally, it was a one-way relationship that required the subject to be loyal to the king even when he was not worthy of loyalty, and children to be dutiful to their parents even if they were not worthy of respect.

13. After being imprisoned, Yu Gwan-sun continued to call for Korean independence until she died. According to a recent Internet blog post, the words in her final prayer were as follows: "My finger nails may fall off, my nose and ears may be cut off, my hands and may be legs broken. I can bear the pain. But the pain of losing my county, I cannot bear. That I only have one life to give for my country, it is my only sadness."

14. Sorensen (1990) writes, "It was thus taken to heart as a guide to proper behavior much more fully by Koreans than either the Chinese, who tended to take it for granted, or the Japanese, who never wholeheartedly accepted Confucianism as the one true Way" (4–5).

15. For more information, visit the Korean-language website, *Annals of the Joseon Dynasty*: http://sillok.history.go.kr/main/main.jsp.

16. "Sim" in Simcheong is the last name. However, she has been referred as Simcheong rather than Cheong, and her father as Simbongsa (blind man Sim).

17. In *jesa*, a special meal is placed in front of the tablets kept to represent the soul of the deceased; after the ceremony, the family consumes the meal.

Chapter 3

1. Emile Ardolino's *Sister Act* (1992), an American remake of *Dark Habits* starring Whoopie Goldberg, eliminated all references to drugs and lesbianism, which would have greatly disturbed American viewers.

2. Jeong explains that there has been mention of other films made prior to *Promises under the Moon*. Nonetheless, this film is traditionally accepted as the first Korean feature film by a Korean director with a Korean actress in a leading role.

3. *Korean Film Art* recalls a similar volume published in communist Albania in 1977 that was simply entitled *The Albanian Film*, which also provides a typology of the themes of Albanian films in relation to the needs of socialist society (Kinostudio Shqipëria e Re).

Part II

1. During the course of the writing of Chapters 5, 6, and 7, both authors concealed their work from each other until the first drafts were completed to avoid cross-pollination. These chapters present the fruit of their subsequent discussions and joint analyses. Expanded readings are presented in Chapter 8.

Chapter 4

1. The threat *to pansori* is highlighted throughout the film. In *Seopyeonje*, 1940s Korea is dominated by Japanese and Western popular culture. As the three itinerant musicians attempt to preserve an indigenously Korean genre, loudspeakers drown out their *pansori* with the international pop hit, "Bésame Mucho," whose lyrics were originally written by Consuelo Velázquez, a 15-year-old Mexican songwriter, and which was made famous internationally by singer Lucho Gatica. The song, which quickly traveled throughout the Americas and Europe and even appeared in an alternate version (with new lyrics!) performed by Josephine Baker, represents Korea's attempt to rapidly integrate itself into international culture at the expense of its own. In stark contrast to the internationalization implied by "Bésame Mucho" is the authentic Koreanness of "Arirang," which, although not a *pansori*, is meticulously taught by Yubong to his children early on in their apprenticeship. North Korea has traditionally used "Arirang" as the basis of a major sporting event every April 15, in honor of Kim Il-Sung's birthday. Also known as a "mass games event," the "Arirang Performance" features roughly 100,000 performers and decries the separation of the Korean peninsula, looking forward to reunification under the terms of the Great Leader's plan. The Arirang Performance textualizes the *han* that has befallen the peninsula since the separation of the two Koreas. In 2002, Pyongyang opened the event to foreigners and began issuing visas to Americans. This policy was perceived as an attempt to compete with the 2002 FIFA World Cup, which was co-hosted by South Korea.

2. This is an interesting contrast with what Maslow argues. Recall that the first basic need that Maslow presents is the

physical needs required for survival, which we paralleled with inner strength in the Korean context. In this film (as well as in Lady Hyegyeong's memoirs, as described in Chapter 2), the inner strength needed for survival leads individuals to reach the highest level of Maslow's hierarchy of needs, which he calls "self-actualization." In *Seopyeonje*, nonetheless, the process is not a closed one. Songhwa must move on and continue to search for further excellence.

3. The performance of *han* not only speaks to the film's spectators, but also allows the siblings to play a Freudian game of *fort/da*, at once acknowledging and disavowing their relationship.

4. In this segment of the dialogue, the word *han* is spoken several times, although in the English subtitles shown in the Taewon Entertainment DVD release, it is expressed by "grief."

5. Catholicism entered Korea by means of books written by Jesuit missionaries in China. The strong and dynamic Catholic communities were led almost entirely by lay people of the upper class, as they were the only people who could read the books written in Chinese until the arrival of the first French missionaries in 1836. There were a significant number of martyrs created during the persecutions; 103 of them were canonized in 1984.

6. In modern society, the term *gwang-dae* is used only when talking about past history. In contrast, today's term *minsok* (folk) is used as a prefix for a number of art forms: *minsok-ak* (folk music), *minsok-geuk* (folk play), *minsok-muyong* (folk dance). Also, as traditional terminology in Korean studies has become more refined and specialized, and as academic disciplines related to these cultural phenomena have been created, other affixes such as *gug* (national) and *gojeon* (classical) have come into use: *gug-ak* (national classical music), *hanguk-gojeon-muyong* (Korean classical dance), *hanguk-gojeon-geuk* (Korean classical drama), and so on.

7. Cheoseon, the court official who brought Jangsaeng and Gonggil to the court, is a good example of a person with

chung. Here, Cheoseon's loyalty vis-à-vis Yeonsan is not blind loyalty or absolute obedience no matter whether instructions by the sovereign/higher rank are right or wrong. His *chung* is to realize his ideals for Yeonsan; his action illustrates an expression of true loyalty as the willingness to be put to death rather than to do what is wrong.

8. The first literati purge was a result of opposition by the government officials who disagreed with his efforts on the basis of Seongjong's (Yeonsan's father) will. The second purge was connected to his mother's death. After Yeonsan had told details of his mother's death and was shown blood-stained pieces of clothing, which allegedly contained blood vomited by her after drinking poison, he beat to death two of his father's concubines for their responsibility for his mother's death, and executed many officials who supported the execution of his mother.

Chapter 5

1. In Korea, a mother is not called by her first name. Often she is called a "child name's mother," like "Dojun's mother." She may also be called just "mother" or *"ajume-oni,"* which is roughly translated as "lady" or "auntie."

2. People may argue that this kind of attitude and mind-set would not be beneficial to the child's future development. Yet, one often forgets that in many societies, people with disabilities are not seen as full citizens within that society. Moreover, they are underserved; society does not provide the proper special education they need.

3. This scene recalls the tale of Han Seok-bong's mother, who chops the rice cakes in the dark during his calligraphy apprenticeship (described in Chapter 2). Although the situations are very different, the scene implies that the mothers of Dojun and Seokbong are alike in that they don't think about the risk of chopping off their fingers in service of their children.

4. The trip that Mother takes appears

to be a tourist trip that is popular among women. In Korea, people, especially women, sing and even dance on tourist buses. Many women temporarily vent their *han* this way.

5. *Jeong* between siblings can be almost as irrational as *mo-jeong*, particularly in what concerns the degree of kinship. In Korea, in what concerns blood-based relationships, people often mention the degree of kinship. For instance, parents–children is one degree of kinship; siblings are two degrees; parents' siblings (uncles/aunts) are three degrees; the parents' siblings' children (i.e., cousins) are four degrees; and so on. This kinship degree implies how much one is expected to care for each other; the lower the degree of kinship, the higher the expectation. Recall the paintings "*Hyeogje tukeum*" ("Brothers' Thrown-Gold") and "*Hyeongje geubnado*" ("Painting of Imminent Danger for Brothers"). Such traditional stories privilege the constructive and touching aspect of *jeong* rather than its irrationality. They are used to reinforce the strong relationship that siblings should have. This does not mean that their relationship-related acts are all rational; on the contrary, a close examination would reveal how foolish, unreasonable, and absurd siblings can be toward each other.

6. Yeonbeon, an independent state of China located across from the northwest of North Korea, has the largest Chinese Korean population, having witnessed considerable North Korean migration following the Korean War. 7. "Elder brother knows/cares better." Traditionally speaking, an elder brother feels responsible for making sure that his younger brother is doing well. (Furthermore, he also feels obliged to care for their elderly parents when they can no longer earn a living.) In contrast, a younger brother is spoiled, either knowingly or unknowingly, and sometimes complains that his elder brother, who projects authority, seems overbearing. Nevertheless, one should note that there are many cases and situations in which the role is reversed; younger brothers can feel responsible and/or take charge.

8. The production company made it clear that the film was a work of fiction.

9. The possibility of such fraternity can be illustrated by the strong support on the part the U.S. Korean community for the North Korean team in its match against Brazil in the 2010 World Cup.

10. The symbolic meaning of the exchange of cigarettes might be a nonadversarial interaction. That is, it could represent the initiation of friendliness.

11. Again, there is a symbolic meaning in requesting a cigarette. The Swiss officer clearly wants to be friendly and show her sympathy.

12. This scene reminds us of the beginning of the film. After Sergeant Oh removes a mine from the ground and gives it to Sergeant Lee, he takes a cigarette, smokes it, whistles softly, and warns the latter to watch out for himself.

Chapter 6

1. The sex act on the rocks of the lower slope of the mountain recalls the orgiastic copulating couples in Michelangelo Antonioni's *Zabriskie Point* (1970), an ode to nature and unbridled freedom.

2. *Prajna-Paramita (-Sutra)* means the "Perfection of (Transcendent) Wisdom." It is a central concept of Buddhism, and its practice and understanding are taken to be indispensable elements for enlightenment.

3. Traditionally, some Buddhist monks do physical exercises, take a rubdown with a wet towel, and perform a rosary of 108 beads early in the morning.

4. In the Sony Pictures U.S. DVD release of *Spring, Summer, Fall, Winter, ... and Spring*, the second child is not seen tormenting the fish, the turtle, and the snake. Rather, we see him on the deck of the monastery laughing as he pounds the shell of a turtle.

Chapter 7

1. The Democratic People's Republic of Korea (DPRK) is the official name here.

It is used as much as possible in the following discussion given that the term "North Korea" is more offensive in the North than "South Korea" is in the South. Nationals of the DPRK often refer to their country as simply "Korea," suggestive of Kim Il-Sung's plan for the reunification of the two countries as a single federation with two distinct political and economic systems.

2. Moreover, we have chosen these films in part because they are available on DVD with English subtitles.

3. Known as "Arirang Performance" (one of the main themes of the performance draws upon the folksong well known throughout the Korean peninsula), the mass gymnastics show provided, until recently, the only opportunity for U.S. citizens to visit the DPRK. The art form had actually been developed in Pyongyang as early as 1946.

4. We have opted to refer to the martial art as *taekkyeon* rather than as *taekwon-do*, a Japanese form in which "do" means "way" or "discipline."

Chapter 8

1. The kiss is eliminated in the Bonzai Media DVD release of the film.

2. Panmunjon can be visited on tours originating from both South and North Korea. The second author visited it during visits to both Koreas, and has noted the difference between the sensationalism of the southern tours and the more sedate atmosphere of their northern counterparts. The briefing from the U.S. military prior to entering the DMZ from the South recalled the thrills of a theme park ride, while arrival to the "northern exposure" was devoid of excess and hoopla. He has noted that many of the visual dynamics of *Joint Security Area* reflect his moments at Panmunjon, while on the tour from the North. As the group entered the shared building from the northern entrance, the angry glares of American military soldiers upon seeing a group of Americans enter from the North were truly unforgettable.

3. Albania's foremost woman director, Xhanfise Keko, has documented the story of the first group of six future film professionals who studied at the Moscow Documentary Film Center from 1949 to 1952 in her 2008 autobiography *Ditët e jetës sime* (*The Days of My Life*). Also, in 2008, Piro and Eno Milkani's film, *The Sadness of Mrs. Schneider* ([Albanian: *Trishtimi i zonjës Shnajder*, Czech: *Smutek paní Snajdrové*]), documented the removal of Albanian film students from Prague's noted film academy FAMU and their subsequent repatriation to Albania as the country undertook its initial steps toward breaking ties with the Eastern bloc.

4. Kim Jong Il, who visited the studio 591 times, praised the Chinese street for its authenticity ("North Korean Art Film Studio Features Rich History," 2012).

5. More recently, Kim Jong Un has stressed that "more investments should be put into the industry and more films should be made that reflect people's livelihood" ("North Korean Art Film Studio Features Rich History," 2012, np).

References

Albanian Cinema Project. *The Captain/ Kapedani* Publicity Card. San Francisco, CA: 2012.

Alderfer, Clayton P. *Existence, Relatedness, and Growth*. New York: Free Press, 1972.

An, Guinam. *Yi Eungtae buin eongan* [Letter written in Korean alphabet by Lee Eungtae's wife]. 1999. http://www.hangeulmuseum.org/sub/hanLife/culture_han/lee_letter01.jsp. Accessed September 12, 2011.

An, Sang Jin. *A Study of Donghak: A Nineteenth-Century Forerunner of Local Minjung Theology in Korea*. Toronto: Emmanuel College, School of Theology; National Library of Canada, 1994.

Anderson, Benedict. *Imagined Communities*. London: Verso, 1983.

Andrew, Dudley. "Time Zones and Jet Lag: The Flows and Phases of World Cinema." In Nataša Ďurovičová and Kathleen Newman, *World Cinemas: Transnational Perspectives*, 59–89. New York: Routledge, 2010.

"Annals of the Joseon Dynasty." http://sillok.history.go.kr/main/main.jsp. Accessed May 13, 2011.

Armes, Roy. *Third World Film Making and the West*. Berkeley/Los Angeles: University of California Press, 1987.

Avramides, Anita. *Meaning and Mind: An Examination of a Gricean Account of Language*. Cambridge, MA: MIT Press, 1989.

Baker, Mona. *In Other Words: A Course Book on Translation*. London/New York: Routledge, 1992.

Bakhtin, Mikhail. *Speech Genres and Other Late Essays*. Austin: University of Texas Press, 1986.

Bakhtin. Mikhail, and Pavel Medvedev. *The Formal Method of Literary Scholarship*. Cambridge, MA: Harvard University Press, 1985.

Barthes, Roland. *Image/Music/Text*. New York: Hill and Wang, 1977.

Bassnett, Susan. *Translation Studies*, 2nd ed. London: Routledge, 1991.

Baudry, Jean-Louis. "Ideological Effects of the Basic Cinematographic Apparatus." *Film Quarterly* 28, no. 2 (1974–1975): 39–47.

Bennett, Tony, Lawrence Grossberg, and Meaghan Morris (eds.). *New Keywords: A Revised Vocabulary of Culture and Society*. London: Willey-Blackwell, 2005.

Bergstrom, Janet. "Enunciation and Sexual Difference." *Camera Obscura* 3, no. 4 (Summer 1979): 30–65.

Besemeres, Mary, and Anna Wierzbicka (eds.). *Translating Lives: Living with Two Languages and Cultures*. St. Lucia: University of Queensland Press, 2007.

Bordwell, David. *Making Meaning: Inference and Reference in the Interpretation of the Cinema*. Cambridge, MA: Harvard University Press, 1989.

Brown, Panelope, and Stephen Levinson. *Politeness: Some Universals in Language Use*. New York: Cambridge University Press, 1987.

Buckland, Warren. *The Cognitive Semiotics*

of Film. Cambridge, UK: Cambridge University Press, 2000.

Burgett, Bruce, and Glenn Hendler. *Keywords for American Cultural Studies.* New York/London: New York University Press, 2007.

Cahiers du cinéma. "Les 100 plus beaux films de l'histoire du cinéma." November 4, 2008. http://www.cahiersducinema. com/100-FILMS.html. Accessed October 18, 2011.

Campbell, Lyle. *American Indian Languages: The Historical Linguistics of Native America.* Oxford University Press, 1996.

Carroll, Lewis. *Through the Looking Glass.* Raleigh, NC: Hayes Barton, 1872.

Cavell, Stanley. *The World Viewed: Reflections on the Ontology of Film.* New York: Viking, 1971.

Central Intelligence Agency. 2013. http:// www.cia.gov/library/publications/the-world-factbook/goes/ks.html.

Chang, Hak-Geun. *Chungmugong yi sunsinui jjalbeun saengae, bitnaneun sam* [Short Life of Chugmugong Yi SunShin, Glorious Life]. Seoul, South Korea: Korean Institute for Maritime Strategy, 2002.

Chang, Hui-Ching. "Harmony as Performance: The Turbulence under Chinese Interpersonal Communication." *Discourse Studies* 3, no. 2 (2001): 155–179.

Chateau, Dominique. *Le Cinéma comme langage.* Brussels: AISS—Publications de la Sorbonne, 1987.

Chen, Xiao-Pin, and Chao C. Chen. "On the Intricacies of the Chinese *Guanxi*: A Process Model of *Guanxi* Development." *Asia Pacific Journal of Management* 21 (2004): 305–324.

Cheng, S. K. "Understanding the Culture and Behavior of East Asians: A Confucian Perspective." *Australian and New Zealand Journal of Psychiatry* 24 (1990): 510–515.

Cho, Byung-hwa. "*Beos* [A friend]." In *Meonjiwa baram sai* [Between Dust and Wind]. Seoul, Korea: Dongwha Chulpan Gongsa, 1972.

Cho, Hyung. *A Study of "Han" and "Shin-myung" Immanent in Korean Traditional Dance.* Thesis, Department of Dancing Graduate School of Hanyang University, Seoul Korea, 1986. http://theologia.kr/ zeroboard/data/koreatheo/01144393.pdf. Accessed March 1, 2011.

Cho, Young-Jin. *Sin Saimdang: pulgwa beolaereul jeulgyeo geurin hwaga* [Sin Saimdang: Painter Who Enjoyed Painting Grass and Insects]. Seoul, Korea: Namusup, 2000.

Choi, Chungmoo. "*Chihwaseon: Geundaewa melankoli* [*Chihwaseon*: Modern and Melancholy]." In *Chihwaseon,* edited by Jinhi Yoon, Nayeong Yu, and Kyeonghwa Yang, 32–47. Seoul, Korea: Institute of Media Arts at Yonsei University, Samin Publisher, 2004.

_____. "The Politics of Gender, Aestheticism, and Cultural Nationalism in *Sopyonje* and *The Genealogy.*" In *Im Kwon-Taek: The Making of a Korean National Cinema,* edited by David E. James and Kyung-Hyun Kim, 107–133. Detroit: Wayne State University Press, 2002.

Choi, Jinhee. "Preface." In *The Cinema of Japan and Korea,* edited by Justin Bowyer. London/New York: Wallflower, 2004.

_____. *The South Korean Film Renaissance: Local Hitmakers, Global Provocateurs.* Middletown, CT: Wesleyan University Press, 2010.

Choi, Sang-Chin. "The Psychology of Koreans' Experiential Mind: A Phenomenological Analysis of Koreans' *Han* and *Cheong*" [in Korean]. 1993. http:// selffind.com/zbxe/sm4_2/4653. Accessed July 1, 2011.

_____, and Gyuseong Han. "*Shimcheong* Psychology: A Case of an Emotional State for Cultural Psychology." *International Journal for Dialogical Science* 3, no. 1 (2008): 205–224.

_____, and Ki-Beom Kim. *Munwha Simlihak* [Cultural Psychology]. Seoul, Korea: Jisik Sanup Publications, 2011.

_____, and Soo Hyang Choi. "Cheong: The Socioemotional Grammar of Koreans." *International Journal of Group Tensions* 30, no. 1 (2001): 69–80.

Choi, Sangsoo. *Hanguk mingan jeonseoljip*

[Collection of Korean Folk Tales]. Seoul, Korea: Tongmunghwan, 1957.

Chomsky, Noam. "Degrees of Grammaticalness." In *The Structure of Language: Readings in the Philosophy of Language,* edited by Jerry A. Fodor and Jerrold J. Katz, 196–204. Englewood Cliffs, NJ: Prentice-Hall, 1964.

Chung, Chong-hwa (ed.). *Korean Classical Literature: An Anthology.* London/New York: Kegan Paul, 1989.

_____ (ed.). *Modern Korean Literature: An Anthology 1908–1965.* London/New York: Kegan Paul, 1995.

Colin, Michel. "Film Semiology as a Cognitive Science." In *The Film Spectator: From Sign to Mind,* edited by Warren Buckland. Amsterdam: Amsterdam University Press, 1995.

Conway, Mike. "Mining a Corpus of Biographical Texts Using Keywords." *Literary and Linguistic Computing* 25, no. 1 (2010): 23–45.

Cortazzi, Martin, and Wei Wei Shen. "Cross-Linguistic Awareness of Cultural Keywords: A Study of Chinese and English Speakers." *Language Awareness* 10, no. 2 (2001): 125–142.

Cronin, Michael. *Translation Goes to the Movies.* London: Routledge, 2009.

Cummings, Bruce. *War and Television.* London: Verso, 1992.

Dargis, Manohla. "Korean Films." *The New York Times,* December 11, 2004: 26.

Deci, Edward. *Intrinsic Motivation.* New York: Plenum, 1975.

De Mente, Boyé Lafayette. *Japan's Cultural Code Words.* Boston: Tuttle, 2004.

Diamond, Sutra. *King Sejong the Great.* Pohang, South Korea: Yong Hwa, 2008.

Doi, Takeo (1973). *The Anatomy of Dependence.* Tokyo: Kodansha, 1973.

Ďurovičová, Nataša. "Introduction." *Cinema & Cie* 4 (Spring 2004): 7–16.

_____. "Vector, Flow, Zone: Towards a History of Cinematic Translation." In Nataša Ďurovičová and Kathleen Newman, *World Cinemas: Transnational Perspectives,* 90–120. New York: Routledge, 2010.

_____, and Kathleen Newman. *World Cinemas: Transnational Perspectives.* New York: Routledge, 2010.

Ehrman, Madeline Elizabeth, and Betty Lou Leaver. "Cognitive Styles in the Service of Language Learning. *System* 31 (2003): 393–415.

Ende, Michael. *MOMO.* Toronto: Penguin Books, Canada Limited, 1985.

Erickson, Jon Dale. *Using Keywords and Computers to Assess Student Writing.* Washington State University. Chair, Gerald Maring. Dissertation Abstracts International: The Humanities and Social Sciences, 2001. Order number: DA9988955.

Fairbairn, W. R. D. *An Object Relations Theory of the Personality.* New York: Basic Books, 1952.

Forbes, Kathryn. *Mama's Bank Account.* Boston: Harvest, 1968.

Freire, Paulo. *The Pedagogy of the Oppressed.* London/New York: Continuum, 2000.

Gao, Ge, and Ting-Toomey, Stella. *Communicating Effectively with the Chinese.* Thousand Oaks, CA: Sage, 1998.

_____, and Pater MacIntyre. "An Instrumental Motivation in Language Study: Who Says It Isn't Effective?" *Studies in Second Language Acquisition* 13 (1991): 57–72.

Gardner, Robert, and Wallace Lambert. *Attitudes and Motivation in Second Language Learning.* Rowley, MA: Newbury House, 1972.

Garrett, Peter, Angie Williams, and Betsy Evans. "Assessing Social Meanings: Values of Keywords, Values in Keywords." *Acta Linguistica Hafniensia* 37 (2005): 37–54.

Gateward, Frances (ed.). *Seoul Searching: Culture and Identity in Contemporary Korean Cinema.* Albany: State University of New York Press, 2007.

Geertz, Clifford. *The Interpretation of Cultures: Selected Essays.* New York: Basic Books, 1973.

Gish, Lillian. *Dorothy and Lillian Gish.* New York: Scribner's, 1973.

Gish, Lillian, and Ann Pinchot. *The Movies, Mr. Griffith, and Me.* San Francisco: Mercury, 1988.

Goffman, Erving. *Interaction Ritual: Essays*

on Face to Face Behavior. New York: Anchor, 1967.

Goldstein, Kurt. *The Organism: A Holistic Approach to Biology Derived from Pathological Data in Man.* New York: Zone, 1934/1995.

Gombeaud, Adrien. "*Eolrukgwa hyeongtae: Yesulgawa jilryo* [Stain and Form: Artist and Substance]." In *Chihwaseon,* edited by Jinhi Yoon, Nayeong Yu, and Kyeonghwa Yang, 70–83. Seoul, Korea: Institute of Media Arts at Yonsei University, Samin Publisher, 2004.

Grice, Herbert Paul. "Presupposition and Conversational Implicature." In *Radical Pragmatics,* edited by Peter Cole, 183–198. New York: Academic Press, 1981.

_____. *Studies in the Way of Words.* Cambridge, MA: Harvard University Press, 1989.

_____. "Utterer's Meaning and Intention." *Philosophical Review* 78 (1969): 144–177.

Grodal, Torben Kragh. *Moving Pictures: A New Theory of Film Genres, Feelings, and Cognition.* Oxford, UK: Oxford University Press, 1999.

Grojean, Francois. *Life with Two Languages.* Cambridge, MA: Harvard University Press, 1982.

Guback, Thomas. "Film as International Business." *Journal of Communication* 24, no. 1 (1974): 90–101.

Gudykunst, William, and Tsukasa Nishida. *Bridging Japanese/North American Differences.* Thousand Oaks, CA: Sage, 1994.

Haboush, Jahyun Kim (trans.). *The Memoirs of Lady Hyegyong: The Autobiographical Writings of a Crown Princess of Eighteenth-Century Koreans.* University of California Press, 1996.

Hall, Edward T. *Beyond Culture.* Garden City, NY: Doubleday/Anchor, 1976.

Ham, Sok Hon. "Five Poems by Ham, Sok Hon: Resource Site." http://www2.gol.com/users/quakers/Five%20Poems%20by%20Ham%20Sok%20Hon.htm. Accessed June 13, 2011.

_____. *Ham Sok Hon Jeon Jip* [Complete Works of Ham Sok Hon]. Seoul, Korea: Hangilsa, 1988.

_____. *Tteuseuro bon hanguk yeoksa* [Korean History from the Perspective of Its Meaning]. Seoul, Korea: Hangilsa, 2003.

Han, Bok Jin, et al. *An Illustrated Guide to Korean Cultures.* National Academy of the Korean Language. Seoul, Korea: Hakgojae, 2002.

Harris, Roy. *Language, Saussure and Wittgenstein: How to Play Games with Words.* London/New York: Routledge, 1998.

Hartzell, Adam. "*Soponje.*" *Ohmynews,* March 24, 2006. http://english.ohmynews.com/articleview/article_view.asp?at_code=318917. Accessed August 4, 2011.

Hayes, Steven C., Kirk Strosahl, and Kelly G. Willison. *Acceptance and Commitment Therapy: An Experimental Approach to Behavior Change.* New York: Guildford, 1999.

Heath, Stephen. *Questions of Cinema.* Bloomington: Indiana University Press, 1981.

Hjort, Mette. "On the Plurality of Cinematic Transnationalism." In *World Cinemas, Transnational Perspectives,* edited by Nataša Ďurovičová and Kathleen Newman. New York/London: Routledge, 2010.

Hofstede, Geert, and Michael Harris Bond. "Hofstede's Culture Dimensions." *Journal of Cross-Cultural Psychology* 15 (1984): 417–433.

Hogan, Patrick Colm. *Understanding Indian Movies: Culture, Cognition, and Cinematic Imagination.* Austin: University of Texas Press, 2009.

Huang, Chichung. *The Analects of Confucius (Lun Lu).* Oxford, UK: Oxford University Press, 1997.

Il Yeon (1277–1281). *Samgukyusa* [Legends and History of the Three Kingdoms of Ancient Korea]. Written in Chinese; translated into Korean by Lee Ka-won and Hur Kyoung-jin. Seoul, Korea, Hangilsa, 2006.

Institute for Education of Overseas Koreans, Seoul National University, *Tteostteoshan hangukin* [Honorable Koreans]. Seoul, Korea: DaeHan Gyogwaseo Jusikhoesa, 1986.

James, David E. *Yesul, yeonghwa, yesu-*

lyeonghwa: Chihwaseongwa geu dongryu yeonghwadeul [Arts, Cinema, Artistic Cinema: *Chihwaseon* and Films of the Same Type]. In *Chihwaseon,* edited by Jinhi Yoon, Nayeong Yu, and Kyeonghwa Yang, 84–109. Seoul, Korea: Institute of Media Arts at Yonsei University, Samin Publisher, 2004.

_____, and Kyung-Hyun Kim (eds.). *Im Kwon-Taek: The Making of a Korean National Cinema.* Detroit: Wayne State University Press, 2002.

Jameson, Fredric. "Globalization and Hybridization." In *World Cinemas: Transnational Perspectives,* edited by Nataša Ďurovičová and Kathleen Newman, 315–319. New York: Routledge, 2010.

Jangseoga Royal Digital Archives. *Silhakja Yi IK* [Practical Learning Scholar, Yi Ik]. http://yoksa.aks.ac.kr. Accessed June 12, 2011.

Jay, Martin. *Cultural Semantics: Keywords of Our Time.* Amherst: University of Massachusetts Press, 1998.

Jeong, Jong Hwa. *Hanguk Yeonghwa Sa* [History of Korean Films]. Seoul, Korea: Korean Film Archive, 2008.

Jeong, Jong-Mok. *Hong Gildong-Jeon* [Tale of Hong Gildong]. Seoul, Korea: Changbi, 2003.

Joang, Cho Hae. "Sopyonje: Its Cultural and Historical Meaning." In *Im Kwon-Taek: The Making of a Korean National Cinema,* edited by David E. James and Kyung-Hyun Kim, 134–156. Detroit: Wayne State University Press, 2002.

Jong, Un Hyun. *Jeongiran mueosinga* [What Is *Jeong*?]. Seoul, Korea: Chaekbose, 2011.

Kahane, Henry, and Renee Kahane. "Linguistic Aspects of Sociopolitical Keywords." *Language Problems and Language Planning* 8, no. 2 (1984): 143–160.

Kang, Jae-Eun. *The Land of Scholars: Two Thousand Years of Korean Confucianism,* translated by Suzanne Lee. Paramus, NJ: Homa & Sekey Books, 2006. Published in Korean by Hangilsa Publishing in Korea, 2003.

Kang, Tae-Hyeong. *Sin Saimdang* [In Korean]. Seoul, Korea: Unggin Chulpansa, 1987.

Kaplan, E. Ann. *Motherhood and Representation: The Mother in Popular Culture and Melodrama.* New York: Routledge, 1992.

Keko, Xhanfise. *Ditët e jetës sime.* Tirana: Adrian Laperi, 2008.

Kemppainen, Hannu. "Keywords and Ideology in Translated History Texts: A Corpus-Based Analysis." *Across Languages and Cultures* 5, no. 1 (2004): 89–106.

Këshilli Ministerial nr. 163. Tirana: 10 prill, 1947.

Kim, Dong Kuk. "*Uiwondeul 45charyeo baksu … MB yeonseol 15bun gileojyeo* [45 Standing Ovations … Extended MB Speech by 15 Minutes]," *The Korea Times,* October 15, 2011.

Kim, Hyeong-Ju, and Chan-Yeong Park (compilers). *Godeung Gojeon Soseo 30* [30 Classic Stories for a Higher Level]. Seoul, Korea: Ribereu sukul, 2011.

Kim, Il Sung. "Yŏngha-nŭn hososŏng-i nopaya hamyŏ hyŏnshil-boda apsŏ nagaya handa" [Film Should Strongly Appeal to the Masses and Advance Them More Than Reality]. *Kim Il Sung Chŏjak Sŏnjip* 12 (1958). Pyongyang: Korean Workers' Party Publishing House, 1981: 9.

Kim, Ji Ha. "Adopted Stylistic Features of *Pansori.*" 1941. http://afe.easia.columbia.edu/ps/korea/critique_of_development.pdf. Accessed May 30, 2011.

Kim, Jong Il. *On the Art of the Cinema.* Pyongyang: Foreign Languages Publishing House, 1973 (English translation, 1989).

Kim, Kyeong-Bok, Hyeong-Dae Myeong, and Jong-Hyeon Byeon. *Hanguk munhakui ihaewa gamsang* [Understanding and Appreciation of Korean Literature]. Pusan, Korea: Kyeongnam University Press, 2010.

Kim, Kyung Hyun. "The Fractured Cinema of North Korea: The Discourse of the Nation in *Sea of Blood.*" In *In Pursuit of Contemporary East Asian Culture,* edited by Xiaobing Tang and Stephen Snyder, 86–106. New York: Westview, 1996.

_____. *The Remasculinization of a Korean National Cinema.* Durham, NC: Duke University Press, 2004.

Kim, Luke. "Korean Ethos." *Journal of Ko-*

rean American Medical Association 2, no. 1 (1996): 13–22.

_____. "Korean Ethos." 2010. http://www.lukeandgracekim.com/10.htm. Accessed May 7, 2011.

Kim, Paul Tchang Ryoel. "Korean Han and Evangelization: An essay by Bishop Kim of Jeju Diocese, South Korea." *Mary's Touch by Mail,* 1986. http://www.marys-touch.com/truth/han.htm. Accessed April 4, 2011.

Kim, So-wol. "*Nimgwa beos* [Lover and Friend]." In *Kim So-wol Si-jib Collection of Kim So-wol's Poems* [In Korean]. Seoul, Korea: Haseo, 1999. http://blog.daum.net/dw0179/1167.

Kim, Soyeong. "*Chihwaseongwa hanguk yeonghwasa* [Chiwhaseon and Korean Cinema History]." In *Chihwaseon,* edited by Jinhi Yoon, Nayeong Yu, and Kyeonghwa Yang, 12–31. Seoul, Korea: Institute of Media Arts at Yonsei University, Samin Publisher, 2004.

Kim, Tae-ung. *Yi, Kim Tae-ung higokjip* [Yi, Collection of Plays by Kim Tae-ung]. Seoul, Korea: Pyeongminsa, 2005.

Kim, Young. *The Future: A Road to Unification of the Korean Peninsula.* Bloomington, IN: AuthorHouse, 2010.

Kim-Renaud, Young-Key (ed.). *King Sejong the Great: The Light of Fifteenth Century Korea.* Washington, DC: International Circle of Korean Linguistics, 1997.

Kinder, Marsha. *Blood Cinema: The Reconstruction of Cultural Identity in Spain.* Berkeley/Los Angeles: University of California Press, 1993.

Kinostudio Shqipëria e Re. *The Albanian Film.* Tirana: 8 Nëntori, 1977.

Ko, Chang-soo. *Best Loved Poems of Korea.* Elizabeth, NJ: Hollym, 1984.

Ko, Un. "*I ttangeso haneun mueosinga?* [What Is *Han* in This Land?]." *Gyeogan Sasang* 5 (1990): 36–89.

Kohls, L. Robert. *Learning to Think Korean.* Yarmouth, ME: Intercultural Press, 2001.

Koo, John H., and Andrew C. Nam (eds.). *An Introduction to Korean Culture.* Elizabeth, NJ/Seoul: Hollym, 1997.

Korean Film Art. Pyongyang: Korean Film Export and Import Corporation, 1985.

Korean Friendship Association. "*Juche* Ideology." Democratic People's Republic of Korea, 2001. http://www.korea-dpr.com/index.html. Accessed August 1, 2013.

Kornblum, Janet. Study: 25% of Americans Have No One to Confide in. *USA Today,* June 22, 2006. http://www.usatoday.com/news/nation/2006-06-22-friendship_x.htm. Accessed May 21, 2011.

Kristeva, Julia. *Semeiotike: Recherches pour une semanalyse.* Paris: Seuil, 1969.

Kwak, Young-Ok. *Chima baram ttaeroneun pilryohada* [The Swish of a Skirt Is Sometimes Needed]. South, Korea: Leader Books, 2005.

Lee, Cheong Jun. "Seopyeonje." In *Seopyeonje* [In Korean], 7–30. Seoul, Korea: Yeolimwon, 1993.

Lee, Eo-ryeong. *Tteuseuro ilkneun hangukeo sajeon* [Korean Dictionary of Meaning-Based Readings]. Seoul, Korea: Munhaksasangsa, 2002.

Lee, Grace. "The Political Philosophy of Juche." *Stanford Journal of East Asian Affairs* 3, no. 1 (Spring 2003): 105–112.

Lee, Hae-in. "*Beosege*" [To a Friend]. In Hae-in Lee, *Oettan maeule binjipi doigosipda* [I Want to Be an Empty House in a Remote Village]. Seoul, Korea: Yeolimwon, 1999.

Lee, Hyangjin. *Contemporary Korean Cinema: Identity, Culture Politics.* Manchester: Manchester University Press, 2000.

_____. "*Minjung complexwa sinseon iyagi: Hanguk yeonghwa, jeongcheseongui jeongchihak*" [People's Complex and Fairy Tale: Korean Cinema, Politics of Identity-Nature]. In *Chihwaseon,* edited by Jinhi Yoon, Nayeong Yu, and Kyeonghwa Yang, 110–135. Seoul, Korea: Institute of Media Arts at Yonsei University, Samin Publisher, 2004.

Lee, Hyo-Won. "How Korean Sleeper Hits Are Finding Their Niche." *The Hollywood Reporter,* 2011. http://www.hollywoodreporter.com/news/how-korean-sleeper-hits-are-188261?page=2. Accessed June 4, 2011.

Lee, Hyun-Su. *Iyagi hanguksa* [Stories: Korean History]. Seoul, Korea: Cheonga, 1987.

Lee, Ka-won, and Hur, Kyoung-jin (trans.). *Samgukyusa* [Legends and History of the Three Kingdoms of Ancient Korea]. [Originally written by Il Yeon (1277–1281) in Chinese.] Seoul, Korea: Hangilsa, 2006.

Lee, Peter H., and William Theodore de Bary (eds.). *Sources of Korean Tradition: From Early Times through the Sixteenth Century.* New York: Columbia University Press, 1997.

Leitch, Shirley, and Sally Davenport. "Strategic Ambiguity as a Discourse Practice: The Role of Keywords in the Discourse on 'Sustainable' Biotechnology." *Discourse Studies* 9, no. 1 (2007): 43–61.

Li, Wei, Hua Zhu, and Yue Li. "Interpersonal Harmony and Textual Coherence in Chinese Business Interaction." *Multilingual* 20, no. 3 (2001): 285–310.

Lotman, Juri, and Boris Uspensky. "On the Semiotic Mechanism of Culture." *New Literary History* 9, no. 2 (1978): 211–232.

Marks, Laura. *The Skin of the Film.* Durham, NC: Duke University Press, 2000.

Maslow, Abraham. "A Theory of Human Motivation." *Psychological Review* 50 (1943): 370–396.

Maslow, Abraham. *Motivation and Personality.* New York: Harper, 1954.

_____, and Richard Lowry. *Toward a Personality of Being.* New York: John Wiley, 1998.

Mathes, Eugene. "Maslow's Hierarchy of Needs as a Guide for Living." *Journal of Humanistic Psychology* 21 (1981): 69–72.

Max-Neef, Manfred. *Human Scale Development.* New York/London: Apex, 1991.

Max-Neef, Manfred, et al. "Human Scale Development: An Option for the Future. Development." *Dialogue: A Journal of International Development Cooperation* 1 (1989): 7–80.

McPherson, Miller, Lynn Smith-Loving, and Matthew E. Brashears. "Social Isolation in American: Changes in Core Discussion Networks over Two Decades." *American Sociological Review* 71 (2006): 353–375.

Metz, Christian. *Film Language: A Semiotics of the Cinema.* Oxford, UK: Oxford University Press, 1974a.

_____. *Language and Cinema.* The Hague: Mouton, 1974b.

Min, Eungjun, Jinsook Joo, and Han Ju Kwak. *Korean Film: History Resistance, and Democratic Imagination.* Westport, CT: Praeger, 2003.

Mulvey, Laura. "Afterthoughts on 'Visual Pleasure and Narrative Cinema' Inspired by *Duel in the Sun.*" *Framework* 15–17 (1981): 12–15.

_____. "Notes on Sirk and Melodrama." *Movie* 25 (1977–1978): 54.

_____. *Visual and Other Pleasures.* Bloomington: Indiana University Press, 2009.

_____. "Visual Pleasure and Narrative Cinema." *Screen* 16, no. 3 (1973): 6–18.

Murdock, Graham. "Large Corporations and the Control of Communication Industries." In *Large Corporations and the Control of Communication Industries,* edited by Michael Gurevitch. New York: Methuen, 1982.

Myers, Isabel Briggs. *The Myers-Briggs Type Indicator.* Palo Alto, CA: Consulting Psychologists, 1962.

Nabokov, Vladimir. *Eugene Onegin: A Novel in Verse. Volume II: Commentary and Index.* Princeton, NJ: Princeton University Press, 1991.

Nahm, Andrew C. (ed.). *Korea under Japanese Colonial Rule.* (Proceedings of the Conference on Korea, November 12–14, 1970). Center for Korean Studies, Western Michigan University, 1973.

Newman, Kenneth M., and Howard A. Bacal. *Theories of Object Relations: Bridge to Self-Psychology.* New York: Columbia University Press, 1989.

Newmark, Peter. *A Textbook of Translation.* London: Prentice Hall, 1988.

"N. Korea Film Hunts Buyers at Cannes." *Korea Herald,* May 23, 2007. https://www.google.com/#q=%5E+%22North+Korea+film+hunts+buyers+at+Cannes.

Nongae Cyber Museum. http://www.jinjunongae.com/main/. Accessed May 13, 2011.

"North Korean Art Film Studio Features Rich History." *Newslook,* 2012. http://

www.newslook.com/videos/487130-north-korea-art-film-studio-features-rich-history. Accessed July 27, 2013.

O, Si-rim. *Sin Saimdang: Hanguk yeoseongui daepyojeok jiseong ingyeokjeok model, Sin Saimdang ui sam* [The Life of Sin Saimdang, the Most Representative Intellectual and Humanist Model]. Seoul, Korea: Minsongsa, 1992.

Oak, Susan, and Virginia Martin. *American/Korean Contrasts*. Elizabeth, NJ: Hollym, 2000.

Ohmynews blog. *Park Kyeong Ni: Goeihan hanui jeondosa* [Park Kyung-Ni: Peculiar Preacher *of Han*]. Interview with Park in 1981. 2006. http://blog.ohmynews.com/syung/127347. Accessed October 31, 2011.

Olsen, Mark. "Contrasting Keywords: Cognates in the Political Discourses of the Society de 1789 and the American Revolution." *Contrastes* 18–19 (1989): 109–129.

Park, Ji-Won (1737–1805). *Heosaeng-jeon* and *Yangban-jeon* [Tale of Heosang and Tale of Yangban], In *Godeung Gojeon Soseo 30l* [30 Classic Stories for a Higher Level], compiled by Hyeong-Ju Kim and Chan-Yeong Park. Seoul, Korea: Ribereu sukul, 2011.

Park, Kyung-Ni. "The Feelings and Thoughts of the Korean People in Literature." Keynote speech at a special colloquium organized by the University of Paris 7 and the Korean Arts and Foundation, Paris, November 26, 1994. http://www.koreantranslation.com/RETHINGS KOREAN/ArticlesInfo/HanTheSoulof KoreanLiterature/tabid/1557/Default.aspx. Accessed July 10, 2011.

_____. "Grafted Apple Trees." In *The Story That Brought Me Here: To Alberta from Everywhere,* edited by Linda Goyette. Victoria, BC: Brindle & Glass, 2008.

_____. *Toji* (Land). 21 volumes. Seoul, Korea: Nanam, 2003.

Park, Samuel. "A Conversation with Samuel Park." 2012. http://samuelpark.com/bio/q-a/. Accessed January 31, 2012.

_____. *This Burns My Heart*. New York: Simon & Schuster, 2011.

Park, Sangyil. *Korean Preaching, Han, and Narrative*. New York: Peter Lang, 2008.

Park, Sangyeon. *DMZ*. Seoul, Korea: Mineumsa, 1997.

Pasternak, Boris. *Doctor Zhivago*. New York: Pantheon, 1958.

Peirce, Charles Stanley. *Collected Papers*, Vols. I–VIII Cambridge, MA: Harvard University Press, 1985.

Propp, Vladimir. *Morphology of the Folk Tale*. Austin: University of Texas Press, 1968.

Rayna, Tony. *Seoul Stirring: Five Korean Directors*. London: Institute of Contemporary Arts, 1994.

Robinson, Douglas. *Translation and Empire: Postcolonial Theories Explained*. Manchester, UK: St. Jerome, 1997.

Robinson, Michael Edson. *Cultural Nationalism in Colonial Korea, 1920–1925*. University of Washington Press, 1988.

Sanders, Terry. *Lillian Gish: The Actor's Life for Me* [Television documentary]. American Film Foundation, 1988.

Sapir, Edward. *Selected Writings of Edward Sapir in Language, Culture and Personality,* edited by David G. Mandelbaum. Berkeley: University of California Press, 1949.

Schaffner, Christina, and Uwe Wiesemann. *Annotated Texts for Translation: English–German: Functionalist Approaches*. Clevedon, UK: Multilingual Matters, 2001.

Schönherr, Johannes. *North Korean Cinema: A History*. Jefferson, NC: McFarland, 2012.

Scott, A. O. "*Chi-hwa-seon*: New York Film Festival Reviews: Living the Artistic Life in 19th-Century Korea." *The New York Times,* December 13, 2002. http://movies.nytimes.com/movie/review?res=950CE7DF1638F93BA1575AC0A9649C8B63. Accessed April 21, 2011.

Seo, Daeseok, and Peter H. Lee, compilers and eds. *Oral Literature of Korea*. Seoul, Korea: Jimoomdang, 2005.

Shin Chi-Yun, and Julian Stringer. *New Korean Cinema*. Edinburgh: Edinburgh University Press, 2005.Shohat, Ella, and Robert Stam. "The Cinema after Babel: Language, Difference, Power." *Screen* 26, nos. 3–4 (1985): 35–58.

Shohat, Ella, and Robert Stam. *Unthinking*

Eurocentrism. New York: Routledge, 1994.

Sin, Dong Uk. "*Cheongsan byeolgok ui pyeongminjeok sam uisik* [Plebeian Life Consciousness in Cheongsan Byeolgok]. In *Popular Literature of the Goryeo Dynasty* [In Korean]. Seoul, Korea: Saemunsa, 1982.

Sobchack, Vivian. *The Address of the Eye: A Phenomenology of Film Experience.* Princeton, NJ: Princeton University Press, 1992.

Son, Chang Hee. *Haan of Minjung Theology and Han of Han Philosophy: In the Paradigm of Process Philosophy and Metaphysics of Relatedness.* Lanham, MD: University Press of America, 2000.

Sorensen, Clark W. "Modernization and Filial Piety in Contemporary Korea." *The World and I (Online Journal),* January 1990. http://faculty.washington.edu/sangok. Accessed June 12, 2011.

Stam, Robert. *Subversive Pleasure: Bakhtin, Cultural Criticism and Film.* Baltimore: Johns Hopkins University Press, 1989.

_____, Robert Burgoyne, and Sandy Flitterman-Lewis. *New Vocabularies in Film Semiotics: Structuralism, Post-Structuralism and Beyond.* New York: Routledge, 1992.

Stern, Lesley. "How Movies Move: Between Hong Kong and Bulawayo, between Stage and Film...." In *World Cinemas: Transnational Perspectives,* edited by Nataša Ďurovičová and Kathleen Newman, 186–216. New York: Routledge, 2010.

Stringer, Julian. "*Sopyonje* and the Inner Domain of National Culture." In *Im Kwon-Taek: The Making of a Korean National Cinema,* edited by David E. James and Kyung-Hyun Kim, 157–181. Detroit: Wayne State University Press, 2001.

Stuart-Leach, Hannah. "Discovering Korea through Film." *The Korea Herald,* July 11, 2011.

Tadelis, Steven. "What's in a Name? Reputation as a Tradeable Asset." *American Economic Review* 89, no. 3 (1999): 548–563.

Tan, Amy. "The Language of Discretion." In *Exploring Language,* edited by Gary Goshgarian, 265–273. HarperCollins College Publishers, 1990.

Tannen, Deborah. *That's Not What I Meant.* New York: Ballantine, 1986.

Tannen, Deborah. *You Just Don't Understand.* New York/London: Harper, 1990.

Todorov, Tzvetan. "Three Conceptions of Poetic Language." In *Russian Formalism: A Retrospective Glance,* edited by Robert L. Jackson and Stephen Rudy, 130–147. New Haven, CT: Yale Center for International and Area Studies, 1985.

Torrance, Ellis Paul. *Your Style of Leaning and Thinking: Forms B and C.* Athens: University of Georgia Press, 1980.

Tripp, Rhoda Thomas. *The International Thesaurus of Quotations.* New York: Crowell, 1970.

Tyson, Rodney. "Toward Defining the Korean Emotion Word *Ceng*: A Cultural Models Approach." *Daejin Theses Collection,* 5: 7–18. Pocheon, Korea: Daejin University, 1997.

Underwood, Horace, and Nancy Underwood (eds.). *An Illustrated Guide to Korean Culture.* Seoul, Korea: Hakojae, 2002.

Vick, Tom. *Asian Cinema.* New York: HarperCollins, 2007.

Wardhaugh, Ronald. *Sociolinguistics,* 4th ed. Oxford, UK: Blackwell, 2002.

Watson, John B. *Behaviorism,* rev ed. Chicago: University of Chicago Press, 1930.

Weber, Jean-Jacques, and Kristine Horner. "Orwellian Doublethink: Keywords in Luxembourgish and European Language-in-Education Policy Discourses." *Language Policy* 9, no. 3 (2010): 241–256.

Webster, Sandra K., and Y. G. Ko. "Generational and Gender Effects on Korean Perceptions of *Han*." Poster presented at the Annual Convention of the American Psychological Association, Chicago, August 2002.

_____. "South Korean and American Negative Emotion Attribution: Gender and Age." Poster presented at the Annual Convention of the American Psychological Association, Toronto, Canada, August 2003.

Whorf, Benjamin Lee. *Language, Thought*

and Reality: Selected Writings of Benjamin Lee Whorf. Cambridge, MA: MIT Press, 1956.

Wierzbicka, Anna. *Understanding Cultures through Their Key Words*. New York: Oxford University Press, 1997.

Wierzbicka, Anna. "Cross-Cultural Communication and Miscommunication: The Role of Cultural Keywords." *Intercultural Pragmatics* 7, no. 1 (2010): 1–23.

Wilkie, Christina. "At Obama's Korea State Dinner, Real Star Is Free Trade Deal." *The Huffington Post*, October 14, 2011. http://www.huffingtonpost.com/2011/10/13/obama-korea-state-dinner_n_1010057.html. Accessed October 15, 2011.

Williams, Bruce. "The Bridges of Los Angeles County: Marketing Language in the Chicano Cinema of Gregory Nava." *Canadian Journal of Film Studies* 14, no. 2 (2005): 57–73.

_____. "A Cinema in Search of Itself: Metafilmic Trends in *Cinema Novo*." *Encruzilhadas/Crossroads* 4 (1995): 49–51.

_____. "Frysky Business: Micro-regionalism in the Era of Post-nationalism." *Film History* 14, no. 1 (2002): 100–112.

_____. "Julie Christie down Argentine Way: Reading Repression Cross-nationally in Bemberg's *Miss Mary*." *Journal of Film and Video* 55, no. 4 (Winter 2003): 15–29.

_____. "Straight from Brazil? National and Sexual Disavowal in Mário Peixoto's *Limite*." *Luso-Brazilian Review* 38, no. 1 (Summer 2001): 31–40.

_____. "Two Degrees of Separation: Xhanfise Keko and the Albanian Children's Film." *Framework* 54, no. 1 (Spring 2013): 49–58.

Williams, Raymond. *Keywords: A Vocabulary of Culture and Society*. New York: Oxford University Press, 1983.

Wittgenstein, Ludwig. *Tractus Logico-philosophicus*. London/New York: Routledge & Kegan Paul, 1988.

"*Wolgan changseok hyeongje geumnando*" [Wolgan Changseok, Painting of Brothers Facing Danger]. *Cultural Assets of Gyeongbuk*. http://www.chis.go.kr/daekwan/WebContent/popsrc/07/217.html. Accessed April 13, 2011.

Wollen, Peter. *Signs and Meaning in the Cinema*. Bloomington: Indiana University Press, 1972.

Yabuuchi, Akio. "Face in Chinese, Japanese and U.S. American Cultures." *Journal of Asian Pacific Communication* 14, no. 2 (2004): 261–297.

Yecies, Brian. "Parleying Culture against Trade: Hollywood's Affairs with Korea's Creen Quotas." *Korea Observer* 38, no. 1 (Spring 2007): 1–32.

Yeo, Sang-deok (2013). "Collection of Five Poems by Hwang, Jini." Nabizone.net. http://nabizone.net/nara/sub2_5/19786. Accessed 5 October 2014.

Yi, Ik. "*Silhakja Yi Ik*" [Silhak Scholar Yi Ik]. Jangseoga Royal Digital Archives. http://yoksa.aks.ac.kr. Accessed December 13, 2011.

Yi, Sang (1910–1937). "*Nalgae*" [Wings]. In *Modern Korean Literature: An Anthology 1908–1996*, edited by Chong-wha Chung, translated by Moon Hi-kyung, 104–123. London/New York: Kegan Paul, 1995.

Yoon, Jinhi, Nayeong Yu, and Kyeonghwa Yang. *Chihwaseon*. Seoul, Korea: Institute of Media Arts, Yonsei University, Samin Publisher, 2004.

Yu, Jungha. "Yanghwa: Muneihaeui iyagi" [Western Painting: A Talk by an Outsider]. In Chihwaseon, edited by Jinhi Yoon, Nayeong Yu, and Kyeonghwa Yang, 48–69. Seoul, Korea: Institute of Media Arts at Yonsei University, Samin Publisher, 2004.

Index